1993-94

WORLDS BEYOND

Grateful acknowledgment is made to the following publishers, authors, and agents for their permission to reprint copyrighted material. Any adaptations are noted in the individual acknowledgments and are made with the full knowledge and approval of the authors or their representatives. Every effort has been made to locate all copyright proprietors; any errors or omissions in copyright notice are inadvertent and will be corrected in future printings as they are discovered.

"Aerin's Dragon" from *The Hero and the Crown* by Robin McKinley. Text copyright © 1984 by Robin McKinley. Published in Great Britain by Julia MacRae Books. By permission of Greenwillow Books (A Division of William Morrow), and of the author's agents, Writer's House Inc. Illustrations copyright © 1989 by Leo and Diane Dillon.

"Bigger than Life" excerpt adapted from *Great Animals of the Movies* by Edward Edelson. Copyright © 1980 by Edward Edelson. Reprinted by permission of Doubleday, a division of Bantam, Doubleday, Dell Publishing Group, Inc.

"The Boy and the Piano Tuner" by Saavedra Fontes, translated from the Portuguese by Barbara Meza. Copyright © by Saavedra Fontes. Reprinted from *Américas,* bimonthly magazine published by the Organization of American States in English and Spanish. By permission of the Organization of American States.

"Buffalo Dusk" from *Smoke and Steel* by Carl Sandburg, copyright 1920 by Harcourt Brace Jovanovich, Inc. and renewed 1948 by Carl Sandburg, reprinted by permission of the publisher.

"Chasing a Dream" from *The Silent Voice* by Julia Cunningham. Copyright © 1981 by Julia Cunningham. Adapted and reprinted by permission of E.P. Dutton, a division of NAL Penguin Inc., and of the author's agents, Bill Berger Associates.

Acknowledgments continue on pages 638–639, which constitute an extension of this copyright page.


ISBN 0-663-52353-2

World of Reading

# Worlds Beyond


P. David Pearson Dale D. Johnson

Theodore Clymer Roselmina Indrisano Richard L. Venezky

James F. Baumann Elfrieda Hiebert Marian Toth

*Consulting Authors*

Carl Grant Jeanne Paratore



**SILVER BURDETT & GINN**

**NEEDHAM, MA · MORRISTOWN, NJ**

ATLANTA, GA · CINCINNATI, OH · DALLAS, TX

MENLO PARK, CA · DEERFIELD, IL

*UNIT ONE*

# DREAM WEAVERS

*UNIT TWO*

# WHEN BUFFALO ROAMED

UNIT THREE

# FLIGHTS OF FANCY

*UNIT FOUR*

# FREE TO CHOOSE

UNIT ONE

# DREAM WEAVERS

*Writers are often dream weavers.*

*What dreams do you think are worth a good story?*

LA VUE, *French tapestry*

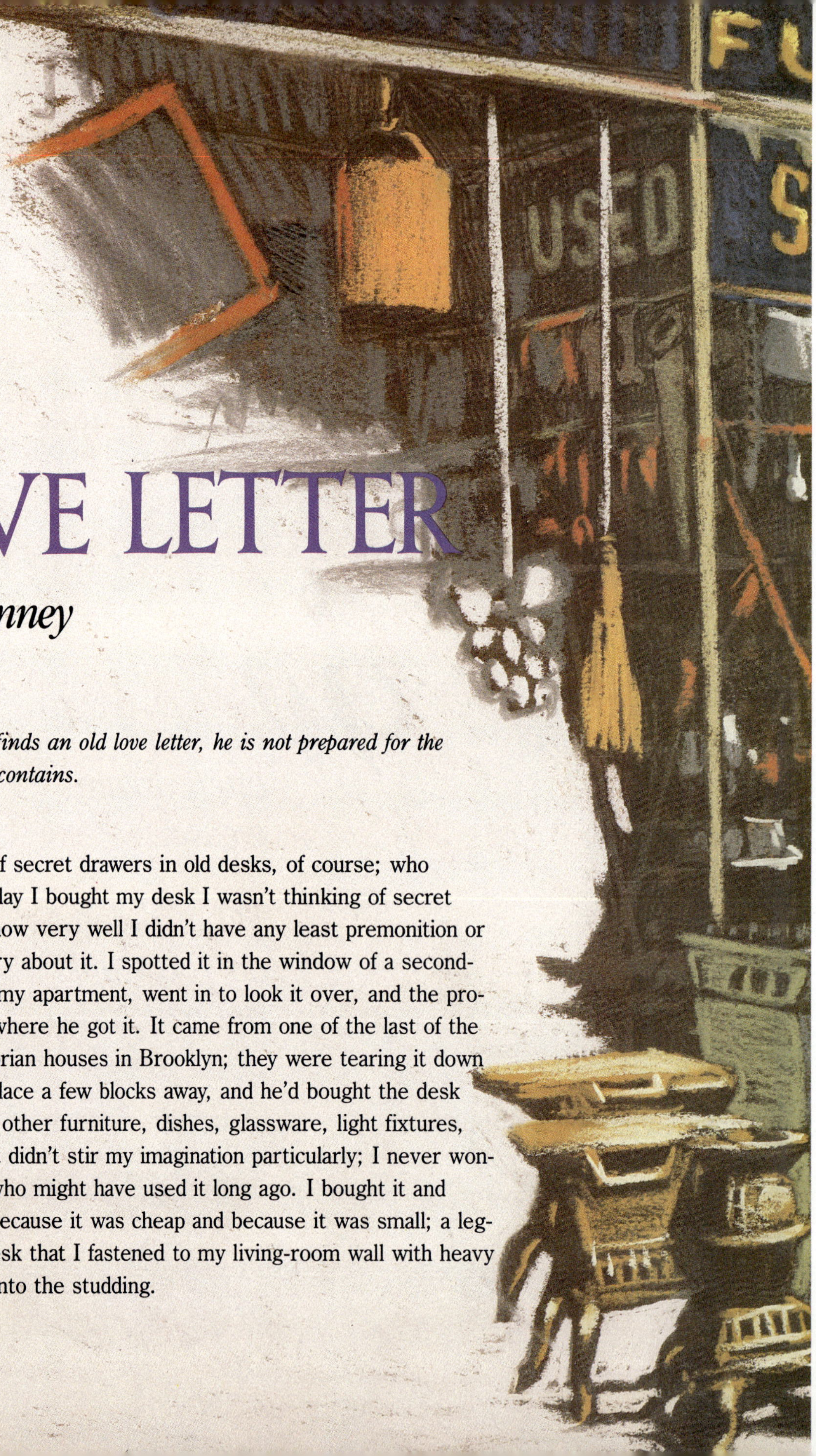


# The LOVE LETTER

## *by Jack Finney*

*When Jake finds an old love letter, he is not prepared for the startling story it contains.*

I've heard of secret drawers in old desks, of course; who hasn't? But the day I bought my desk I wasn't thinking of secret drawers and I know very well I didn't have any least premonition or feeling of mystery about it. I spotted it in the window of a second-hand store near my apartment, went in to look it over, and the proprietor told me where he got it. It came from one of the last of the big old mid-Victorian houses in Brooklyn; they were tearing it down over on Brock Place a few blocks away, and he'd bought the desk along with some other furniture, dishes, glassware, light fixtures, and so on. But it didn't stir my imagination particularly; I never wondered or cared who might have used it long ago. I bought it and lugged it home because it was cheap and because it was small; a legless little wall desk that I fastened to my living-room wall with heavy screws directly into the studding.

I'm twenty-four years old, tall and thin, and I live in Brooklyn to save money and work in Manhattan to make it. When you're twenty-four and a bachelor, you usually figure you'll be married before much longer and since they tell me that takes money I'm reasonably ambitious and bring work home from the office every once in a while. And maybe every couple weeks or so I write a letter to my folks in Florida. So I'd been needing a desk; there's no table in my phone-booth kitchenette, and I'd been trying to work at a wobbly end table I couldn't get my knees under.

I bought the desk one Saturday afternoon and spent an hour or more fastening it to the wall. It was after six when I finished. I had a date that night, so I had time to stand and admire it for only a minute or so. It was made of heavy wood with a slant top like a kid's school desk and with the same sort of space underneath to put things into. But the back of it rose a good two feet above the desk top and was full of pigeonholes like an old-style roll-top desk. Underneath the pigeonholes was a row of three brass-knobbed little drawers. It was all pretty ornate; the drawer ends carved, some fancy scrollwork extending up over the back and out from the sides to help brace it against the wall. I dragged a chair up, sat down at the desk to try it for height, then got showered, shaved, and dressed, and went over to Manhattan to pick up my date.

I'm trying to be honest about what happened and I'm convinced that includes the way I felt when I got home around two or two-thirty that morning; I'm certain that what happened wouldn't have happened at all if I'd felt any other way. I'd had a good enough time that evening; we'd gone to an early movie that wasn't too bad, then had dinner, and some dancing afterward. And the girl, Roberta Haig, is pretty nice—bright, pleasant, good-looking. But walking home from the subway, the Brooklyn streets quiet and deserted, it occurred to me that while I'd probably see her again I really didn't care whether I did or not. And I wondered, as I often had lately, whether there was something wrong with me, whether I'd ever meet a girl I desperately wanted to be with—the only way a man can get married, it seems to me.

So when I stepped into my apartment I knew I wasn't going to feel like sleep for a while. I was restless, half-irritated for no good reason, and I took off my coat and yanked down my tie, wondering whether I wanted some coffee. Then—I'd half forgotten about it—I saw the desk I'd bought that afternoon and I walked over and sat down at it, thoroughly examining it for the first time.

I lifted the top and stared down into the empty space underneath it. Lowering the top, I reached into one of the pigeonholes and my hand and shirt cuff came out streaked with old dust; the holes were a good foot deep. I pulled open one of the little brass-knobbed drawers and there was a shred of paper in one of its corners, nothing else. I pulled the drawer all the way out and studied its construction, turning it in my hands; it was a solidly made, beautifully mortised little thing. Then I pushed my hand into the drawer opening; it went in to about the middle of my hand before my fingertips touched the back; there was nothing in there.

For a few moments I just sat at the desk, thinking vaguely that I could write a letter to my folks. Then it suddenly occurred to me that the little drawer in my hand was only half a foot long while the pigeonholes just above the drawer extended a good foot back.

Shoving my hand into the opening again, exploring with my fingertips, I found a tiny grooved indentation and pulled out the secret drawer which lay in back of the first. For an instant I was excited at the glimpse of papers inside it. Then I felt a stab of disappointment as I saw what they were. There was a little sheaf of folded writing paper, plain white but yellowed with age at the edges, and the sheets were all blank. There were three or four blank envelopes to match, and underneath them a small, round, glass bottle of ink; and because it had been upside down, the cork remaining moist and tight in the bottle mouth, a good third of the ink had remained unevaporated still. Beside the bottle lay a plain, black wooden pen holder, the pen point reddish-black with old ink. There was nothing else in the drawer.

And then, putting the things back into the drawer, I felt the slight extra thickness of one blank envelope, saw that it was sealed, and I ripped it open to find the letter inside. The folded paper opened stiffly, the crease permanent with age, and even before I saw the date I knew this letter was old. The handwriting was obviously feminine, and beautifully clear—it's called Spencerian, isn't it?—the letters perfectly formed and very ornate, the capitals especially being a whirl of dainty curlicues. The ink was rust-black, the date at the top of the page was May 14, 1882, and reading it I saw that it was a love letter. It began:

> *Dearest! Papa, Mamma, Willy and Cook are long retired and to sleep. Now the night far advanced, the house silent, I alone remain awake, at last free to speak to you as I choose. Yes, I am willing to say it! Heart of mine, I crave your bold glance, I long for the tender warmth of your look; I welcome your ardency, and prize it; for what else should these be taken but sweet tribute to me?*

I smiled a little; it was hard to believe that people had once expressed themselves in elaborate phrasings of this kind, but they had. The letter continued, and I wondered why it had never been sent:

*Dear one, do not ever change your ways. Never address me other than with what consideration my utterances should deserve. If I be foolish and whimsical, deride me sweetly if you will. But if I speak with seriousness, respond always with what care you deem my thoughts worthy. For, oh my beloved, I am sick to death of the indulgent smile and tolerant glance with which a woman's fancies are met. As I am repelled by the false gentleness and nicety of manner which too often ill conceal the wantonness they attempt to mask. I speak of the man I am to marry; if you could but save me from that!*

*But you cannot. You are everything I prize; warmly and honestly ardent, respectful in heart as well as in manner, true and loving. You are as I wish you to be—for you exist only in my mind. But figment though you are, and though I shall never see your like, you are more dear to me than he to whom I am betrothed.*

*I think of you constantly. I dream of you. I speak with you in my mind and heart; would you existed outside them! Sweetheart, good night; dream of me, too.*

*With all my love, I am,*
*your Helen*

At the bottom of the page, as I'm sure she'd been taught in school, was written, "Miss Helen Elizabeth Worley, Brooklyn, New York," and as I stared down at it now I was no longer smiling at this cry from the heart in the middle of a long-ago night.

The night is a strange time when you're alone in it, the rest of your world asleep. If I'd found that letter in the daytime I'd have smiled and shown it to a few friends, then forgotten it. But alone here now, a window partly open, a cool late-at-night freshness stirring the quiet air, it was impossible to think of the girl who had written this letter as a very old lady or maybe long since dead. As I read her words, she seemed real and alive to me, sitting, or so I pictured

her, pen in hand at this desk in a long, white, old-fashioned dress, her young hair piled on top of her head, in the dead of a night like this, here in Brooklyn almost in sight of where I now sat. And my heart went out to her as I stared down at her secret hopeless appeal against the world and time she lived in.

I am trying to explain why I answered that letter. There in the silence of a timeless spring night it seemed natural enough to uncork that old bottle, pick up the pen beside it, and then spreading a sheet of yellowing old notepaper on the desk top, to begin to write. I felt that I was communicating with a still-living young woman when I wrote:

*Helen: I have just read the letter in the secret drawer of your desk and I wish I knew how I could possibly help you. I can't tell what you might think of me if there were a way I could reach you. But you are someone I am certain I would like to know. I hope you are beautiful but you needn't be; you're a girl I could like, and maybe ardently, and if I did, I promise you I'd be true and loving. Do the best you can, Helen Elizabeth Worley, in the time and place you are; I can't reach you or help you. But I'll think of you. And maybe I'll dream of you, too.*

*Yours,*
*Jake Belknap*

I was grinning a little sheepishly as I signed my name, knowing I'd read through what I'd written, then crumple the old sheet and throw it away. But I was glad I'd written it and I didn't throw it away. Still caught in the feeling of the warm, silent night, it suddenly seemed to me that throwing my letter away would turn the writing of it into a meaningless and foolish thing, though maybe what I did seems more foolish still. I folded the paper, put it into one of the envelopes and sealed it. Then I dipped the pen into the old ink, and wrote "Miss Helen Worley" on the face of the envelope.

I suppose this can't be explained. You'd have to have been where I was and felt as I did to understand it, but I wanted to mail that letter. I simply quit examining my feelings and quit trying to be rational; I was suddenly determined to complete what I'd begun, just as far as I was able to go.

My parents sold their old home in New Jersey when my father retired two years ago, and now they live in Florida and enjoy it. And when my mother cleared out the old house I grew up in, she packed up and mailed me a huge package of useless things I was glad to have. There were class photographs dating from grammar school through college, old books I'd read as a kid, Boy Scout pins—a mass of junk of that sort, including a stamp collection I'd had in grade school. Now I found these things on my hall-closet shelf in the box they'd come in, and I found my old stamp album.

It's funny how things can stick in your mind over the years;

standing at the open closet door I turned the pages of that beat-up old album directly to the stamps I remembered buying from another kid with seventy-five cents I'd earned cutting grass. There they lay, lightly fastened to the page with a little gummed-paper hinge—a pair of two, mint condition two-cent United States stamps, issued in 1869. Standing in the hallway looking down at them I once again got something of the thrill I'd had as a kid when I acquired them. It's a handsome stamp, square in shape, with an ornate border and a tiny engraving in the center, a rider on a galloping post horse. For all I knew they might have been worth a fair amount of money by now, especially an unseparated pair of two stamps. But back at the desk I pulled one of them loose, tearing carefully through the perforation, licked the back and fastened it to the faintly yellowing old envelope.

I'd thought no further than that; by now, I suppose, I was in a kind of trance. I shoved the old ink bottle and pen into a hip pocket, picked up my letter, and walked out of my apartment.

Brock Place, three blocks away, was deserted when I reached it; the parked cars motionless at the curbs, the high, late moonlight softening the lines of the big concrete supermarket at the corner. Then, as I walked on, my letter in my hand, there stood the old house just past a little shoe-repair shop. It stood far back from the broken cast-iron fence in the center of its weed-grown lot, black-etched in the moonlight, and I stopped on the walk and stood staring up at it.

The high-windowed old roof was gone, the interior nearly gutted, the yard strewn with splintered boards and great chunks of torn plaster. The windows and doors were all removed, the openings hollow in the clear wash of light. But the high old walls, last of all to go, still stood tall and dignified in their old-fashioned strength and outmoded charm.

I walked through the opening where a gate had once hung, up the cracked and weed-grown brick pavement toward the wide old porch. And there on one of the ornate fluted posts I saw the house number deeply and elaborately carved into the old wood. At the wide flat porch rail leading down to the walk I brought out my envelope; 972 I printed under the name of the girl who had once lived here, Brock Place, Brooklyn, New York. Then I turned toward the street again, my envelope in my hand.

There was a mailbox at the next corner and I stopped beside it. But to drop this letter into that box, knowing in advance that it could go only to the dead-letter office, would again, I couldn't help feeling, turn the writing of it into an empty meaningless act; and after a moment I walked on past the box, crossed the street and turned right, knowing exactly where I was going.

I walked four blocks through the night passing a hack stand with a single cab, its driver asleep with his arms and head cradled on the wheel, passing a night watchman sitting on a standpipe protruding from the building wall smoking a pipe—he nodded as I passed and I nodded in response. I turned left at the next corner, walked half a block more, then turned up onto the worn stone steps of the Wister postal substation.

It must easily be one of the oldest postal substations in the borough, built, I suppose, not much later than during the decade following the Civil War. And I can't imagine that the inside has changed much. The floor is marble, the ceiling high, the woodwork dark and carved. The outer lobby is open at all times as are post office lobbies everywhere, and as I pushed through the old swinging doors I saw that it was deserted. Somewhere behind the opaque windows a light burned dimly far in the rear of the post office and I had an impression of subdued activity back there. But the lobby was dim and silent and, as I walked across the worn stone of its floor, I knew I was seeing all around me precisely what Brooklynites had seen for no telling how many generations long dead.

The post office has always seemed an institution of mystery to me, an ancient, worn, but still functioning mechanism that is not operated but only tended by each succeeding generation of men to come along. It is a place where occasionally plainly addressed letters with clearly written return addresses go astray and are lost, to end up no one knows where and for reasons impossible to discover, as the postal employee from whom you inquire will tell you. Its air of mystery, for me, is made up of stories—well, you've read them, too, from time to time, the odd little stories in your newspaper. A letter bearing a postmark of 1906, written over half a century ago, is delivered today—simply because inexplicably it arrived at some post office along with the other mail with no explanation from anyone now alive. Sometimes it's a postcard of greeting—from the Chicago World's Fair of 1893, maybe. And once, tragically, as I remember reading, it was an acceptance of a proposal of marriage offered in 1901 and received today, a lifetime too late, by the man who made it and who married someone else and is now a grandfather.

I pushed the worn brass plate open, dropped my letter into the silent blackness of the slot, and it disappeared forever with no sound. Then I turned and left to walk home with a feeling of fulfillment, of having done, at least, everything I possibly could in response to the silent cry for help I'd found in the secrecy of the old desk.

Next morning I felt the way almost anyone might. Standing at the bathroom mirror shaving, remembering what I'd done the night before, I grinned, feeling foolish but at the same time secretly pleased with myself. I was glad I'd written and solemnly mailed that letter and now I realized why I'd put no return address on the envelope. I didn't want it to come forlornly back to me with "no such person," or whatever the phrase is, stamped on the envelope. There'd once been such a girl and last night she still existed for me. And I didn't want to see my letter to her—rubber-stamped, scribbled on, and unopened—to prove that there no longer was.

I was busy all the next week. I work for a wholesale-grocery company; we got a big new account, a chain of supermarkets, and that meant extra work for everyone. More often than not I had my lunch at my desk in the office and worked several evenings besides. I had dates the two evenings I was free. On Friday afternoon I was at the main public library in Manhattan at Fifth Avenue and Forty-second copying statistics from half a dozen trade publications for a memorandum I'd been assigned to write over the weekend on the new account.

Late in the afternoon the man sitting beside me at the big reading-room table closed his book, stowed away his glasses, picked up his hat from the table and left. I sat back in my chair

glancing at my watch. Then I looked over at the book he'd left on the table. It was a big one-volume pictorial history of New York put out by Columbia University, and I dragged it over, and began leafing through it.

I skimmed over the first sections of colonial and precolonial New York pretty quickly, but, when the old sketches and drawings began giving way to actual photographs, I turned the pages more slowly. I leafed past the first photos, taken around the midcentury, and then past those of the Civil War period. But when I reached the first photograph of the 1870s—it was a view of Fifth Avenue in 1871—I began reading the captions under each one.

I knew it would be too much to hope to find a photograph of Brock Place, in Helen Worley's time especially, and of course I didn't. But I knew there'd surely be photographs taken in Brooklyn during the 1880s, and a few pages farther on I found what I'd hoped I might. In clear, sharp detail and beautifully reproduced lay a big

half-page photograph of a street less than a quarter mile from Brock Place; and staring down at it, there in the library, I knew that Helen Worley must often have walked along this very sidewalk. VARNEY STREET, 1881, the caption said. A TYPICAL BROOKLYN RESIDENTIAL STREET OF THE PERIOD.

Varney Street today—I walk two blocks of it every night coming home from work—is a wasteland. I pass four cinder-packed used-car lots; a shabby concrete garage, the dead earth in front of it littered with rusting car parts and old tires; and a half dozen or so nearly paintless boardinghouses, one with a soiled card in its window reading MASSAGE. It's a nondescript joyless street and it's impossible to believe that there has ever been a tree on its entire length.

But there has been. There in sharp black and white in the book on the table before me lay Varney Street, 1881, and from the wide grass-covered parkways between the cut-stone curb and sidewalks, the thick old long-gone trees rose high on both sides to meet, intertwine and roof the wide street with green. The photograph had been taken, apparently, from the street—it had been possible to do

that in a day of occasional slow-trotting horses and buggies—and the camera was aimed at an angle to one side toward the sidewalk and the big houses beyond it, looking down the walk for several hundred feet.

The old walk, there in the foreground under the great trees, appeared to be at least six feet wide—spacious enough easily for a family to walk down it four or five abreast, as families did in those times walk together down the sidewalks under the trees. Beyond the walk, widely separated and set far back across the fine old lawns, rose the great houses, the ten-, twelve-, and fourteen-room family houses two or more stories high and with attics above them for the children to play in and discover the relics of childhoods before theirs. Their windows were tall and they were framed on the outside with ornamented wood. And in the solid construction of every one of those lost houses in that ancient photograph there had been left over the time, skill, money, and inclination to decorate their eaves with scrollwork; to finish a job with craftsmanship and pride. And time, too, to build huge wide porches on which families sat on summer evenings with palm-leaf fans.

Far down that lovely tree-sheltered street—out of focus and indistinct—walked the retreating figure of a long-skirted puff-sleeved woman, her summer parasol open at her back. Of the thousands of long-dead girls it might have been I knew this could not be Helen Worley. Yet it wasn't completely impossible, I told myself; this was a street, precisely as I saw it now down which she must often have walked; and I let myself think that, yes, this was she. Maybe I live in what is for me the wrong time and I was filled now with the most desperate yearning to be there on that peaceful street—to walk off past the edges of the scene on the printed page before me into the old and beautiful Brooklyn of long ago. And to draw near and overtake that bobbing parasol in the distance, and then turn and look into the face of the girl who held it.

I worked that evening at home, sitting at my desk and once more Helen Elizabeth Worley was in my mind. I worked steadily all evening and it was around twelve-thirty when I finished—eleven handwritten pages which I'd get typed at the office on Monday. Then I opened the little center desk drawer, into which I'd put a supply of rubber bands and paper clips, took out a clip and fastened the pages together, and sat back in my chair. The little center desk drawer stood half open as I'd left it and as my eye fell on it I realized that of course it, too, must have another secret drawer behind it.

I hadn't thought of that. It simply hadn't occurred to me the week before, in my interest and excitement over the letter I'd found behind the first drawer of the row; and I'd been too busy all week to think of it since. But now I pulled the center drawer all the way out, reached behind it, and found the little groove in the smooth wood I touched. Then I brought out the second secret little drawer.

I'll tell you what I think, what I'm certain of, though I don't claim to be speaking scientifically; I don't think science has a thing to do with it. The night *is* a strange time; things *are* different then, as every human being knows. And I think this: Brooklyn has changed over seven decades; it is no longer the same place at all. But here and there, still, are little islands—isolated remnants of the way things once were. And the Wister postal substation is one of them; it hasn't really changed at all. And I think that at night—late at night, the world asleep, when the sounds of things as they are now are nearly silent and the sight of things as they are now is vague in the darkness—the boundary between here and then wavers. At certain moments and places it fades. I think that in the dimness of the old Wister post office in the dead of night, lifting my letter to Helen Worley toward the old brass door of the letter drop—I think that I stood on one side of that slot in the year 1962 and that I dropped my letter, properly stamped, written and addressed in the ink and on the very paper of Helen Worley's youth, into the Brooklyn of 1882 on the other side of that worn old slot.

I believe that—I'm not even interested in proving it—but I believe it. Because now from that second secret little drawer I brought out the paper I found in it, opened it, and in rust-black ink on yellowing old paper I read:

*Please, oh, please—who are you? Where can I reach you? Your letter arrived today in the second morning post, and I have wandered the house and garden ever since in an agony of excitement. I cannot conceive how you saw my letter in its secret place, but since you did, perhaps you will see this one too. Oh, tell me your letter is no hoax or cruel joke! Willy, if it is you; if you have discovered my letter and think to deceive your sister with a prank, I pray you to tell me! But if it is not—if I now address someone who has truly responded to my most secret hopes—do not longer keep me ignorant of who and where you are. For I, too—and I confess it willingly—long to see you! And I, too, feel and am most certain of it, that if I could know you I would love you. It is impossible for me to think otherwise.*

*I must hear from you again; I shall not rest until I do.*

*I remain, most sincerely,*
*Helen Elizabeth Worley*

After a long time I opened the first little drawer of the old desk and took out the pen and ink I'd found there, and a sheet of the note paper.

For minutes then, the pen in my hand, I sat there in the night staring down at the empty paper on the desk top; finally I dipped the pen into the old ink and wrote:

*Helen, my dear: I don't know how to say this so it will seem even comprehensible to you. But I do exist, here in Brooklyn, less than three blocks from where you now read this—in the year 1962. We are separated not by space but by the years which lie between us. Now I own the desk which you once had and at which you wrote the note I found in it. Helen, all I can tell you is that I answered that note, mailed it late at night at the old Wister station, and that somehow it reached you as I hope this will too. This is no hoax! Can you imagine anyone playing a joke that cruel? I live in a Brooklyn within sight of your house that you cannot imagine. It is a city whose streets are now crowded with wheeled vehicles propelled by engines. And it is a city extending far beyond the limits you know, with a population of millions, so crowded there is hardly room any longer for trees. From my window as I write I can see—across Brooklyn Bridge, which is hardly changed from the way you, too, can see it now—Manhattan Island, and rising from it are the lighted silhouettes of stone-and-steel buildings more than one thousand feet high.*

*You must believe me. I live, I exist eighty years after you read this, and with the feeling that I have fallen in love with you.*

I sat for some moments staring at the wall, trying to figure out how to explain something I was certain was true. Then I wrote:

*Helen, there are three secret drawers in our desk. Into the first you put only the letter I found. You cannot now add something to that drawer and hope that it will reach me. For I have already opened that drawer and found only the letter you put there. Nothing else can now come down through the years to me in that drawer for you cannot alter what you have already done.*

*Into the second drawer you put the note which lies before me, which I found when I opened that drawer a few minutes ago. You put nothing else into it, and now that, too, cannot be changed.*

*But I haven't opened the third drawer, Helen. Not yet! It is the last way you can still reach me and the last time. I will mail this as I did before, then wait. In a week I will open the last drawer.*

*Jake Belknap*

It was a long week. I worked, I kept busy daytimes, but at night I thought of hardly anything but the third secret drawer in my desk. I was terribly tempted to open it earlier, telling myself that whatever might lie in it had been put there decades before and must be there now, but I wasn't sure and I waited.

Then, late at night, a week to the hour after I'd mailed my second letter at the old Wister post office, I pulled out the third drawer, reached in and brought out the last little secret drawer which lay behind it. My hand was actually shaking and for a moment I couldn't bear to look directly—something lay in the drawer—and I turned my head away. Then I looked.

I'd expected a long letter, very long, of many pages, her last communication with me, and full of everything she wanted to say. But there was no letter at all. It was a photograph, about three inches square, a faded sepia in color, mounted on heavy stiff cardboard, and with the photographer's name in tiny gold script down in the corner: *Brunner & Holland, Parisian Photography, Brooklyn, N.Y.*

The photograph showed the head and shoulders of a girl in a high-necked dark dress with a cameo brooch at the collar. Her dark hair was swept tightly back, covering the ears, in a style which no longer suits our ideas of beauty. But the stark severity of that dress

and hair style couldn't spoil the beauty of the face that smiled out at me from that old photograph. It wasn't beautiful in any classic sense, I suppose. The brows were unplucked and somewhat heavier than we are used to. But it is the soft warm smile of her lips and her eyes—large and serene as she looks out at me over the years—that made Helen Elizabeth Worley a beautiful woman. Across the bottom of her photograph she had written, "I will never forget." And as I sat there at the old desk staring at what she had written, I understood that of course that was all there was to say—what else?—on this, the last time, as she knew, that she'd ever be able to reach me.

It wasn't the last time, though. There was one final way for Helen Worley to communicate with me over the years and it took me a long time, as it must have taken her, to realize it. Only a week ago, on my fourth day of searching, I finally found it. It was late in the evening and the sun was almost gone, when I found the old headstone among all the others stretching off in rows under the quiet trees. Then I read the inscription etched in the weathered old stone: HELEN ELIZABETH WORLEY—1861–1934. Under this were the words, I NEVER FORGOT.

And neither will I.

### ♦ Library Link ♦

*If you enjoyed this story, you might like to read other time-travel stories in* Tales Out of Time, *selected by Barbara Ireson.*

## *Reader's Response*

As you read this story, which event surprised you and lingered in your memory? Try to explain why this happened.

## Thinking It Over

1. Describe the desk that Jake bought.
2. Summarize the contents of the first letter that Jake found in the drawer.
3. Why do you think Jake answered the first letter to Helen?
4. What might the Wister post office symbolize in the story? How did you figure out your answer to this?
5. Describe Jake's feelings the morning after he mailed his first letter to Helen.
6. Contrast Varney Street of the 1870s with the Varney Street of Jake's time.
7. What final way, other than the inscription, might Helen have found to communicate with Jake?

## Appreciating Literature

To be successful, a time-travel story must be realistic enough so the reader can think it *could* happen. Think about the character of Jake, the narrator of this story. How do Jake's character traits contribute to the believability of the story?

## Writing to Learn

**Think and Infer** "The Love Letter" uses the opening of the three secret compartments and Jake's response to each letter to advance the story. Copy the drawings of the three drawers. List on each drawer words to tell how you think Jake felt when he saw the contents of each drawer.

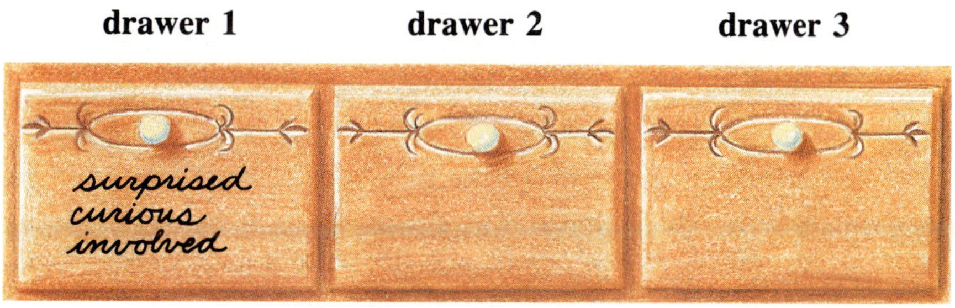


**Write** How would you have felt if the desk had been yours? Reread one of Helen's letters. Then write your own letter to Helen.

Thinking ◆ Reading ◆ Writing

# Analyzing Structure in Writing

People often give this advice about making speeches: First, tell your audience what you are going to tell them. Second, tell them. Third, tell them what you told them. It is a funny way to organize a speech, but it works. It works because you prepare the audience for your message, you deliver the message, and you review it so that you are sure you have gotten the message across.

Writers use a similar structure when they write nonfiction. Every good piece of writing will have a beginning, a middle, and an end. Within the middle, there is often additional structure. A good writer will let you know how his or her writing is organized by giving hints about the structure, usually in the beginning of the article. If you can follow the structure, you will have a better understanding of how all the information fits together, and the author's message will be clearer.

## *Learning the Strategy*

Read the following paragraph, which reviews the story "The Love Letter." As you read, notice how the paragraph is organized.

> "The Love Letter" is a short story that deals with time, love, and hope. In the story, a chance discovery of a hidden letter connects a man in 1962 with the woman who wrote and hid the letter in 1882. Through their writing, the man and woman share the secrets of their hearts; one can sense a love between them, although their lives are separated by eighty years. By the end of the story, when Jake reads the words on Helen's tombstone—"I

never forgot"—the hope she held becomes clear. The author uses these three threads—time, love, and hope—to show us one of the basic tragedies of human existence, that our emotions and dreams are inevitably caught in the ceaseless flow of time.

Now look at the structure of the paragraph.

| | |
|---|---|
| Beginning → | The first sentence tells you that the story is about time, love, and hope. |
| Middle → | The second sentence is about time.<br>The third sentence is about love.<br>The fourth sentence is about hope. |
| End → | The final sentence draws time, love, and hope back together again. |

Do you see how the author used the first sentence to establish the structure for the middle sentences? The same strategy can be used for longer selections as well, by looking for clues to an article's organization in the introduction.

## *Using the Strategy*

Write a paragraph of your own. *Beginning:* Use the sentence below as the first sentence. *Middle:* Follow the structure established by the beginning sentence. *End:* Write a final sentence that draws all of the topics back together.

> I'll never forget my grandmother's letter that described what my dad liked, what he didn't like, and what he dreamed of doing when he was my age.

## *Applying the Strategy to the Next Selection*

In the next selection, "You, Too, Can Be a Storyteller," look for clues to the selection's organization. Then summarize the beginning, middle, and end of the article.

The writing connection can be found on page 91.

## You, Too, Can Be A

# STORYTELLER

by David Holt

*Today there is renewed interest in the ancient art of storytelling, and the best aspect of it is that anyone can learn it.*

Telling stories is an exciting act of creation, both for the teller who spins out a chronicle and for the listener who re-creates the tale in his or her mind. It involves a special kind of sharing and enjoyment . . . one that people have loved ever since our ancestors first huddled around a fire.

What's more, a *national* resurgence of interest in storytelling is underway today in homes, schools, colleges, community centers, and libraries. Spearheading this renaissance are an increasing number of accomplished tale-spinners who—by expanding, refining, and experimenting with different styles and techniques—are making more and more people aware of storytelling as an art form (and often earning a good living, as well). There's even a full-blown society—The National Association for the Preservation and Perpetuation of Storytelling—that sponsors the National Storytelling Festival every October.

And just *why* is there an upswing of enthusiasm for the age-old form of entertainment? Well, perhaps one reason is that storytelling is both fun *and* meaningful. Narratives can cover the full range of human experience . . . inciuding adventure, terror, romance, sorrow, joy, and humor. In addition, storytelling is no longer considered "just" a diversion for children, but is enjoyed by people of all ages. Relating a good narrative is also seen as *real*—person-to-person and mind-to-mind—entertainment. But the single most important factor in the current storytelling renaissance (and one of the most wonderful things about the art itself) may well be the fact that *anyone* can be a storyteller.

After all, you need only to be able to talk. No, I can't place even *that* limitation upon you . . . because some of the best storytelling I've ever witnessed was done by a young deaf man who didn't speak at all! Actually, all you really need to become a storyteller is the desire to *do it*.

This article will—I hope—help you focus on that interest . . . by giving you some tips on choosing, learning, and relating stories.

*Beginning:* What three aspects of storytelling will be discussed in the rest of the article?

## SELECTING A TALE

The first rule of choosing a story to share is to find one you really like. Only if a narrative is meaningful and entertaining to you will you be able to transmit its magic to others. And indeed, not *everyone* can tell the same kind of story successfully. I think most people have built-in affinities for the types of tales they tell best. I have a friend, for instance, who has to work to make a humorous story funny . . . but can—seemingly without effort—spin a ghost tale that'll make your hair stand on end!

So your first task as a prospective oral chronicler is to find a story you can relate to. But *where*—you may want to know—can a person find such stories? Well, it's *easy* . . . because they're everywhere. Great tales can be shaped from the reminiscences of old people, conversations with friends, or stories remembered from childhood. In fact, I'll often take a brief anecdote that I've heard and expand on it to make a full-fledged story.

Your local library is also a fine source of folktale, history, and science fiction books that can provide you with an abundance of good story material. My own favorite technique for finding worthwhile tales in the library is to head straight for the folklore section (look for Dewey Decimal number 398) and then follow "Holt's Magnetic Method of Story Selection" . . . that is, I stand before the shelves and wait to be magically drawn to a book. I glance a bit through every book that draws me and, if it still looks good after a brief perusal, I take it home. (Mind you, really *great* stories are few and far between. I feel lucky if I find one in an entire collection!)

When you're just beginning, it's best to pick a narrative that has an easy-to-follow sequence, and save the more complicated recitations for later. One such basic story—"The Tailor"—accompanies this article. You can, of course, start off with any account you like, but I'll use this one to demonstrate ways to learn and tell a story.

*Middle:* Look back at the section you just read. What was the first topic the author discussed?

# The Tailor

In a village once lived a poor tailor. He had made overcoats for many people, but he had never made one for himself, though an overcoat was the one thing he wanted. He never had enough money to buy material and set it aside for himself, without making something to sell. But he saved and saved, bit by bit, and at last he had saved enough.

He bought the cloth and cut it carefully, so as not to waste any. He sewed up the coat, and it fit him perfectly. He was proud of that coat. He wore it even when it was the least bit cold. He wore it until it was all worn out.

At least he thought it was all worn out, but then he looked closely and he could see that there was just enough good material left to make a jacket. So he cut up the coat and made a jacket. It fit just as well as the coat, and he could wear it even more often. He wore it until it was all worn out.

At least it seemed to be all worn out, but he looked again, and he could see that there was still enough good material to make a vest. So he cut up the jacket and sewed up a vest. He tried it on, and he looked most distinguished. He wore that vest every single day. He wore it until it was all worn out.

At least he thought it was all worn out, but when he looked it over carefully, he saw some places here and there that were not worn. So he cut them out, sewed them together, and made a cap. He tried it on, and it looked just right. He wore it outdoors and in, until it was all worn out.

At least it seemed to be all worn out, but when he looked, he could see that there was just enough left to make a button. So he cut up the cap and made a button. It was a good button. He wore it every day, until it was all worn out.

At least he thought it was all worn out, but when he looked closely, he could see that there was just enough left of that button to make this story.

## READ THE STORY OVER (AND OVER)

To learn a tale yourself, read it over a few times . . . until you can visualize all the events in your mind when you think it through. I like to peruse a new narrative two or three times and then put the book down and start telling the tale. After the trial run, if I don't feel clear about a certain section, I'll go back to the book.

I know some people who read a story as many as 60 times, to implant it, *word for word*, in their minds . . . but I don't enjoy memorization myself. Besides, I consider ad-libbing part of the fun, so I don't worry about repeating the story exactly. Literary language doesn't always translate well into speech anyway. (Of course, some pieces—such as poetry and prose poems—*demand* to be performed verbatim.)

Another technique that can be helpful when learning a tale is to make a tape of yourself reading it aloud. Then you can listen to it whenever you have a minute. Or—this old standby always seems to work for me—you can read the saga right before going to bed and then go over it again in the morning. (It's amazing how fast some folks can absorb a story by doing that!) Try them all . . . then settle on whatever method or methods best help you get the basic outline of the tale in mind. After that, concentrate on the parts that *will* need to be memorized: the beginning, ending, and any key lines.

*The beginning*. If you have the first few sentences of a story committed to memory, you can get up before a group with confidence, because you'll know exactly how you're going to start. A strong opening will also give the audience confidence in you and let them relax. From there, you can just relate the story as it comes. In time, after repeated tellings, any narrator's version of a story tends to crystallize into a certain form. But the first few times of sharing a new narrative are like walking through an enchanted forest . . . you never know what to expect. So go ahead and say what occurs to you. Some of your best ideas will evolve that way.

*The ending*. The end of a story is like the punch line of a joke. You need to know it *and* know how to deliver it. A weak conclusion will hurt the whole tale, but a strong closing will leave people with the feeling that the story had power. (Sometimes you'll have to play with the written phrasing to make it work effectively when spoken.)

As an example, take a look at "The Tailor." I'd memorize this much of the beginning: "In a village once lived a poor tailor. He had made overcoats for many people, but he had never made one for himself, though an overcoat was the one thing he wanted." From there, I'd pretty much rely on my vision of the story to carry me through . . . until I got to the end, when I would say exactly this: ". . . there was just enough left of that button to make this story."

It's important, too, to concentrate on *how* to deliver that last line. If you race through the words, the whole conclusion will fall flat. But if you make a short pause (of three seconds or so) before you finally say, "to make this story," you will be almost guaranteed a good reaction from the audience.

*Key lines*. Many old stories contain passages or rhymes that are particularly powerful. Such lines add substance to the narrative and are often worth committing to memory. In "The Tailor," for instance, the catch phrase is "He wore it until it was all worn out. At least he *thought* it was all worn out, but . . ." These lines—repeated, with only slight variation, several times throughout the story—are, in large part, why the tale works so well when told out loud. Indeed, the audience will usually begin to chuckle when they hear the words for the third time.

***Middle:*** **Look back at the section you just read. What was the second topic the author discussed?**

## PRACTICE

Once you've memorized the necessary parts and feel comfortable with the flow of your narrative, it's time to practice actually *telling* it. My favorite time for working on a story is while I'm driving my car . . . I just roll up the windows and have at it. I've also found that small children make wonderfully forgiving practice audiences. I even have a friend who rehearses in front of her German Shepherd!

## TELLING THE TALE

After you've practiced long enough to build your confidence, you'll be prepared for a more *critical* audience: an entire *classroom* full of children, a group of friends, or perhaps only a passenger in your car. It doesn't matter who it is . . . but until you've told the story to someone else, you won't really *know* it. Sharing makes a tale become part of you and makes it live for others. The actual relating and the joy that it brings are the heart and soul of story-telling.

Don't worry about being nervous. Just plunge in and start telling! Most of your anxiety will subside after you've presented the tale often enough to really know it. Besides, I find that a *little* nervousness is essential, because it gives a story a special effervescence.

Naturally, the more *you're* absorbed in the narrative—feeling it, seeing it, experiencing it—the more you'll be able to pull others into it. But you shouldn't have any trouble grabbing the audience's interest. Remember, the listeners *want* to be invited into the imaginary land that a good story creates . . . and they *won't* want to be pulled back to reality until the story is over. You know the feeling of being interrupted while reading a good book: it's almost painful to wrench your imagination out of that other world. A storyteller's listeners should be under the same spell.

Here are a few suggestions to help you put—and keep—them there.

*Don't make excuses . . . forge ahead.* If you start off by apologizing about not really knowing the narrative or being very nervous, your remarks will put the listeners on edge. The audience will start concentrating on your lack of confidence rather than on the story.

If you do make a mistake, work around the error. (Fake it!) The audience will tolerate little slip-ups. If, on the other hand, you say, "Oh, I made a mistake," you'll have broken the chain of images that holds the story together. Most small errors won't make any real difference to the narrative anyway. And if you leave out something *important*, you can always insert it the way folklorist Richard Chase does. He'll simply say, "And you must remember . . ." and *then* relate the critical information that he forgot.

*Pause if you get lost*. If you lose your place in a story, don't say anything . . . just pause long enough to determine what should happen next in the tale. Stopping the narrative momentarily doesn't upset the flow of the story for the listeners. They can stand a period of silence better than they can deal with stammering around or excuses that may make them uncomfortable and break their concentration.

*Gestures*. Movements of the hands and body enliven some tales . . . particularly those stories with a lot of excitement. It's a safe bet that if your actions grow out of your concentration on the narrative, they'll enhance your performance. I can't *stop* using my hands when I'm sharing a tale. It's become part of my storytelling style.

The only gestures you'll want to avoid are those that call attention to *you*. Biting your fingernails, pulling at your hair, or nervously kicking your leg will distract the listeners and tell them you're not really caught up in the tale. So have a friend watch and point out any unconscious anxious gestures. You may have such nervous habits when you start out, but don't worry . . . they'll probably fade as you gain experience and are able to focus all your energy on the story.

*Make your voice dynamic*. Nothing will extinguish an audience's interest more quickly than will a monotonous delivery. Did you ever notice how disk jockeys and television announcers use their voices?

If you try imitating sentences you hear on the air, you'll observe that the speech varies from extreme high to extreme low pitch in a single phrase. They do it to keep us listening, yet most times we're not consciously aware of this tonal movement. So take a tip from the professionals and put variety in your voice.

*Speak slowly enough.* Like most people, you probably tend to talk fast when you get nervous. If this starts to happen, take a breath or two . . . relax . . . picture your story . . . and *then* relate it. Remember, there's no need to spill forth a continuous flow of words. Pauses in a narrative can actually heighten its effect.

*Speak loudly enough.* A good storyteller sends his or her voice *out*, into the audience, rather than letting it fall on the floor. Tell your story to the people at the *back* of the group. You'll still be able to relate the saga in a quiet manner if desired . . . just be sure to deliberately *project* your voice.

*Make eye contact.* Eye contact helps you communicate well. There will always be some encouraging faces in the audience. (Those folks *want* you to do well, remember?) So direct your story to responsive individuals, and let them know you're talking to them. (Eye contact will also keep *you* involved in your story, help you project your voice, and let you stay in touch with the audience's reactions.)

***Middle:*** **Look back at the section you just read. What was the third topic the author discussed?**

## ENJOY THE MAGIC OF STORYTELLING

When it's your turn to tell a story, take over the time and space with confidence, and then *do it*. Those last two words—*do it*—are the key phrase in this whole article. After all, the more you tell stories, the better you'll get, the more fun you'll have, and the more enjoyment you'll give.

***End:*** **In the first sentence of this paragraph, how does the author bring the topics back together? Write a brief summary of the beginning, middle, and end of the article.**

For me, every aspect of storytelling is a pleasure . . . including the entertainment I give and receive from telling, the people I meet, and the stories I discover. But—on top of all that—there's something more. I can't imagine many activities more satisfying than holding an audience in my spell while I weave a tapestry of pictures in their imagination. Try it. You'll experience a feeling of breathing new life into the most ancient of art forms and, in turn, having *it* breathe new life into *you*.

### ♦ Library Link ♦

*If you enjoyed Holt's article on the techniques of storytelling and would like to know more about this art form, take a look at master storyteller Ruth Sawyer's* The Way of the Storyteller.

### *Reader's Response*

What would you enjoy about being a storyteller, as the author described the role? Do you think you would be a good one?

## Thinking It Over

1. Why is there a renewed interest in storytelling?
2. According to the author, where can people find ideas for stories?
3. List four techniques storytellers can use to help them learn a story. How did you decide on your answers?
4. Why do you think the author said that small children make wonderfully forgiving practice audiences?
5. What was the author's purpose in writing this selection?
6. Change the ending of "The Tailor" by writing a different last sentence from the one that is there now. Begin your sentence with "At least he thought it was all worn out, but . . ."

## Appreciating Literature

The author of this "how-to" article uses a casual, informal style—almost as if he's talking with you. Find some examples of this style and explain why it's appropriate for the subject matter. How does the author make you feel that you really *can* be a storyteller?

## Writing to Learn

**THINK AND CREATE** One device for remembering details is a tree graph. Note the tree graph below showing details from the story "The Love Letter."

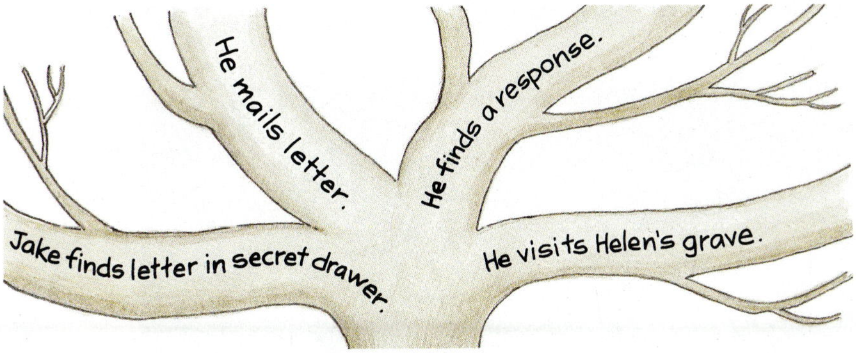


**WRITE** Find or recall a story you think would be interesting to tell aloud. Make a tree graph of the important details you would want to remember in telling the story. Then use the tree graph to help you write a brief summary of the story.

A W A R D
W I N N I N G
Author

# This Is Just to Say

I have eaten
the plums
that were in
the icebox

and which
you were probably
saving
for breakfast

Forgive me
they were delicious
so sweet
and so cold

WILLIAM CARLOS WILLIAMS

PURPLE PLUMS, *oil on canvas by Carducius Plantagenet Ream, 1865.*

# Those Winter Sundays

Sundays too my father got up early
and put his clothes on in the blueblack cold,
then with cracked hands that ached
from labor in the weekday weather made
banked fires blaze. No one ever thanked him.

I'd wake and hear the cold splintering, breaking.
When the rooms were warm, he'd call,
and slowly I would rise and dress,
fearing the chronic angers of that house,

Speaking indifferently to him,
who had driven out the cold
and polished my good shoes as well.
What did I know, what did I know
of love's austere and lonely offices?

ROBERT HAYDEN

MAN IN A VEST, *oil on canvas*
*by William H. Johnson.*

# THE BOY AND THE PIANO TUNER

by Saavedra Fontes

*Have you ever talked to someone who has a natural gift for story-telling? As the young boy in this story discovers, such people can make ideas come alive.*

His long legs moved in measured strides, in constant harmony with his serene temperament and the careworn dignity of his thin features. He walked down the steeply sloping street as always, without a trace of weariness. His wife watched from the upstairs window until he disappeared around the corner.

He was a man who stood tall, mentally and physically. People who spoke with him were impressed by the lustrous sweetness of his eyes and the kindliness of his voice. Peace reigned in his uncomplicated soul, an eternal symphony in his humble heart. A band leader out of sheer love for music, he supported his family by tuning pianos. The heavy, square, painted-tin tool chest that he carried throughout the city somehow seemed to suit his lanky figure and preoccupied manner. A constant stream of thoughts filtered through his mind as he walked along, musing about the wrongs of this world. A noble idealist, the maestro conducted an unending succession of fugues, sonatas, preludes and fantasies.

The sensitive, intelligent, observant man was no slave to the clock. Quite the contrary—he could make time stand still in the ecstasy

of a sunset or the rare beauty of filigreed butterfly wings. Alert to—and curious about—the demands of the human soul, he was easily moved and never missed an opportunity to say a friendly word or engage in a bit of constructive conversation.

The sun had begun to take refuge behind the hill-tops, and shadows traced their silhouettes on the pavement. Geraldo Rodrigues was marching down the middle of the street, a Quixote-like figure ready to do battle with the world, when his spirits lifted at the sight of a child who smiled at him while sitting on the curb, tossing pebbles.

"Are you a plumber, Sir?" the boy asked, peering up at the old man's face.

Only half surprised, Geraldo stopped short and responded warmly to the youngster's curiosity. He explained patiently that he was a piano tuner, a member of a different kind of profession, and that although his tool chest resembled those carried by plumbers, its contents were not at all the same. He sat down beside the boy and answered every question in great detail. The two figures presented an unusual picture of shared happiness.

Plumbers, he explained, fix plumbing, while piano tuners fix pianos, which means that they must have a good ear and a knowledge of music.

He described the workings of the piano, with its little hammers striking the strings to produce sounds, and the difference between a piano and a harpsichord. He related anecdotes about famous pianists, hummed well-known bits of classical music, tapped out different rhythms and tried to teach the boy the notes of the scale, which he drew on the sidewalk with some pieces of broken tile he found there. The elaborate detail and antic gestures he used to describe the theory of the tuning fork were so hilarious that the boy burst out laughing.

They sat side by side on the curb, enjoying each other's company, the man with his long legs drawn up to his chin, the small boy with an enraptured look and a runny nose. Anyone seeing them thus might have thought they were figures from a fairy tale, such were the adult's patience and the child's merriment.

The maestro opened the chest and took out a small metal fife. Gesturing elegantly with both hands, he lifted it to his mouth. With his eyes trained on a bird perched on a post, he played a short, soft tune to which the frisky little creature trilled an enthusiastic response. Then he handed the instrument to his companion, who tried to imitate his playing. Despite a series of sour notes, the boy began to think of himself as a musician and was told he could keep the little flute as a present. The minutes slipped by unnoticed, and then, inevitably, it was time to come back to reality. To say goodbye. The happy and enraptured youngster spoke up boldly:

"When I grow up, I'm going to be like you!"

The maestro was moved and placed his long, slender fingers on the perspiring little head. Proud and satisfied that he had conveyed such a favorable impression of his profession, he asked, "Then you're going to be a piano tuner?"

"No," said the little boy confidently. "I'm going to talk with children."

## Reader's Response

Is the piano tuner someone with whom you would like to talk? Explain why.

## Thinking It Over

1. Describe the kind of man the piano tuner was.
2. What confused the boy about the piano tuner's profession?
3. Why might the piano tuner have stopped to talk to the boy?
4. Which details show that the piano tuner knew a great deal about music?
5. What made the ending of the story both serious and humorous?
6. Do you think the piano tuner's attitude toward children is typical of that of most adults? What makes you think it is or isn't?

## Appreciating Literature

*Irony of situation* is when an event occurs that contradicts the expectations of the characters or the readers. Explain the irony of the boy's last words, "I'm going to talk to children."

## Writing to Learn

**THINK AND PREDICT** Geraldo is never at a loss for words. Read the young boy's unexpected comment in the cartoon below. Copy the cartoon and fill in the response you think Geraldo would have made.

**WRITE** Write a conversation. Begin with the boy's comment "I'm going to talk with children." Continue the dialogue with Geraldo's response and the rest of the conversation.

*A favorite book . . . a holiday custom . . . something a person you care about always says or does. . . . When you are an adult, what do you think you will remember about your life today? Here, Gwendolyn Brooks shares her memories.*

# GWENDOLYN BROOKS, *a Memoir*

BY GWENDOLYN BROOKS

**AWARD WINNING AUTHOR**

Home always warmly awaited me. Welcoming, enveloping. Home meant a quick-walking, careful, Duty-Loving mother, who played the piano, made fudge, made cocoa and prune whip and apricot pie, drew tidy cows and trees and expert houses with chimneys and chimney smoke, who helped her children with arithmetic homework, and who sang in a high soprano voice.

Home meant my father, with kind eyes, songs, and tense recitations for my brother and myself. A favorite of his, a wonderful poem about a pie-making lady. Along had come a man, weary, worn, to beg of the lady a pie. Those already baked, she informed him, were too large for the likes of him. She said she would bake another. It, too, was "large." And the next was large. And the next, and the next. Finally the traveler, completely out of patience, berated her and exclaimed that henceforth she should draw her own sustenance from the bark of trees. And she became, *mirabile dictu,*[1] a woodpecker and flew off. We never tired of that. My father seemed to me and my brother, Raymond, a figure of power. He had those rich Artistic Abilities, but he had more. He could fix anything that broke or stopped. He could build long-lasting fires in the ancient furnace below. He could paint the house, inside and out, and could whitewash the basement. He could spread the American Flag in wide, loud magic across the front of our house on the Fourth of July and Decoration Day. He could chuckle. No one has ever had, no one will ever have, a chuckle exactly like my father's. It was gentle, it was warmly happy, it was heavyish but not hard. It was secure, and seemed to us an assistant to the Power that registered with his children. My father, too, was almost our family doctor. We had Dr. Carter, of course, precise and semi-twinkly and effective—but it was not always necessary to call him. My father had wanted to be a doctor. Thwarted, he read every "doctor book" (and he remembered much from a black tradition) he could reach, learning fine secrets and curing us with steams, and fruit compotes, and dexterous rubs, and, above all, with bedside compassion. "Well, there, young lady! How's that throat now?" "Well, let's see now. This salve will take care of that bruise! Now, we're going to be all right." In illness there was an advantage: the invalid was royalty for the run of the seizure.

[1]mirabile dictu (mə rä′ bəlē dik′ to͞o): strange to say

And of course my father furnished All the Money. The "all" was inadequate, felt Keziah Wims Brooks: could he not leave the McKinley Music Publishing Company, which was paying him about twenty-five dollars a week (from thirty to thirty-five when he worked overtime)? Uncle Paul, husband of my mother's sister Gertrude, worked at City Hall—had a "snap" job—made *fifty dollars* a week. . . . True, during the bad times, during the Depression, when McKinley, itself stricken, could pay my father only in part—sometimes eighteen dollars, sometimes ten dollars—our family ate beans. But children dread, often above all else, dissension in the house, and we would have been quite content to entertain a beany diet every day, if necessary, and *not* live in Lilydale as did bungalow-owning Aunt Gertrude and Uncle Paul, if only there could be, continuously, the almost musical Peace that we had most of the time.

Home. Checker games. Dominoes. Radio (Jack Benny, Ben Bernie, and Kate Smith; "Amos and Andy"; Major Bowes' "Amateur Hour"; Wayne King, the Waltz King; and "Ladies and Gentlemen: Ea-sy Aces"). Christmases. I shall stop right here to tell about those. They were important.

The world of Christmas was firm. Certain things were done. Certain things were not done.

We did not put Christmas trees outdoors.

We did not open Christmas presents on Christmas Eve.

And we had *not* made fruitcakes two or three months ahead of time.

A Christmas tree, we felt—my mother, my father, my brother, and I—belonged in the living room. Green, never silver or gold or pink. Full-branched and aspiring to the ceiling.

Christmas presents were wrapped and hidden on Christmas Eve. Oh, the sly winks and grins. The furtive rustle of tissue, the whip of ribbon off the spool, semiheard. The trippings here and there in search of secure hiding places. Our house had nooks and crannies, a closet, a pantry, alcoves, "the little room," an extensive basement: There were hiding places aplenty.

Fruitcakes were made about a week before Christmas. We didn't care what the recipe books said. We liked having all the Christmas joy as close together as possible. Mama went downtown, as a rule, for the very freshest supplies. Candied cherries and pineapple but no citron. Mama didn't like citron (*I* did and do), so that was out. Candied orange and lemon, however. Figs galore. Dates galore. Raisins, raisins, raisins.

It was the baking of the fruitcakes that opened our Christmas season. After that, there was the merriest playing of Christmas carols on the piano by my mother and me, with everybody singing: mysterious shopping jaunts; the lingering, careful purchase of Christmas cards: the visit to Santa Claus: the desperately scrupulous housecleaning: for my mother and myself, the calls at the beauty shop for Christmas hairdos (you had to look your very best on Christmas Day): the Christmas hunt, undertaken by all, with the marvelous pungent symbol *found* and borne back triumphantly through the dusk of the third or fourth day before Christmas.

All this. So much more that fades, and fades. I almost forgot the high, high angel-food cake, made a day or two before Christmas. We were, somehow, not great Christmas-cookie advocates, but there would be a few frosted cookies about. We had Christmas candy. And filled candies and Christmas mints. Some of those dates, too, were stuffed with nuts and sugared over, to make another sort of confection.

On Christmas Eve we decorated the Christmas tree. So much silver tinsel. And ropes of fringed gold, and red, silver, blue, and gold balls, and a star on top. We children hung our stockings on the mantel—in the morning they would ache with apples, oranges, nuts, and tiny toys—over our, yes, *real* fireplace! That night we were allowed to "sample the sample"—that is, "test" fruitcake that my mother always made in a shallow pan, along with the proper proud giants—and with it we had eggnog with nutmeg on top.

Next day it was so hard to wait for the sky to turn on its light. As soon as it did, out of bed we children threw ourselves and rushed into the living room. There we found, always, that Papa had turned on the Christmas-tree lights, and under the tree shone *just about* everything we had asked of Santa Claus. (Of course, Mama *always* "helped" us with our letters to Santa Claus.) My brother remembers trains and tracks, baseball equipment, wagons, skates, games. Various Christmases brought me dishes, a rocking chair, a doll house, paper dolls which I liked better than hard dolls because so much more could

be done with the paper ones. My most delicate and exquisite Christmas-gift memory is of a little glass deer, dainty-antlered, slender-legged, and filled with perfume.

Of course, there were clothes—"secondary" gifts.

And BOOKS.

About books. My "book Christmas" had already begun, on Christmas Eve, soon after the Christmas tree was strung with lights. It was for long my own personal tradition to sit behind the tree and read a paper book I still own: *The Cherry Orchard,* by Marie Battelle Schilling, and published by the David C. Cook Publishing Company. It had been given me by Kayola Moore, my Sunday school teacher. I don't know why I enjoyed reading that book, Christmas Eve after Christmas Eve, to the tune of black-walnut candy crunching.

And back I went—to the back of the Christmas tree—with my new books. Late, late. After the relatives, after the Christmas turkey, after the cranberries—fresh!—none of your canned cranberries for us—and the mashed potatoes and gravy and baked macaroni and celery and candied sweet potatoes and peas-and-carrots, and the fruitcake and angel cake and eggnog. Back, while the rest of the family forgot it all in bed, to the else-dark room. The silence. The black-walnut candy. And the books that began the giving again. . . .

I ask my mother to write for me some of her own memories of early Gwendolynian life. And presently she offers, with pride, a

Document. In it she presents *herself,* though she pretends that I am speaking. . . .

"When Mother discovered my ability to write, she did most of the housework, with the assistance of my brother and my father. At an early age I knew I was expected to relieve her of the dishwashing, so I did not need to be reminded of that chore. One day she mentioned the fact that she preferred washing dishes to doing anything else in the house. When I finally finished laughing, I asked her why she didn't do it, then, since she liked it so well. She said she would be a poor mother to demand nothing of me. When I was old enough, dusting, some sweeping, and laundry were added to my dishwashing chore. . . .

"When I was busy writing, I preferred not to be disturbed, regardless of the magnitude of any happenings. One day there was a major fire in the block. Since I did not join the spectators, who included every person able to walk, my mother came to tell me that there was 'a big fire down the street.' My answer was 'Yes.' But I continued to write; I did not leave my room. She thought this was strange." . . .

Dreamed a lot. As a little girl I dreamed freely, often on the top step of the back porch—morning, noon, sunset, deep twilight. I loved clouds, I loved red streaks in the sky. I loved the gold worlds I saw in the sky. Gods and little girls, angels and heroes and future loves labored there, in misty glory or sharp grandeur.

I was writing all the time. My mother says I began rhyming at seven—but my notebooks date back to my eleventh year only. Careful rhymes. Lofty meditations.

When I was thirteen I met, somehow, *Writer's Digest.* A milestone. Why, there were *oodles* of *other* writers! They, too, suffered, and had suffered. They, too, ached for the want of the right word—reckoned with mean nouns, virtueless adjectives. They, too, sent Things out, got Things back. They, too, knew the coldness of editors, spent much money on stamps, waited, loud-hearted, for the postman.

My father provided me with a desk, an old desk given him "at McKinley's," a desk with many little compartments, with long drawers at the bottom, and a removable glass-protected shelf at the top, for books. Certainly up there, holding special delights for a writing-girl, were the Emily books, L.M. Montgomery's books about a Canadian girl who wrote, kept notebooks even as I kept notebooks, dreamed, reached. I loved the little adventures—yearning to meet their splendid creator. But who ever met an Author? Certainly there, also, to look down at me whenever I sat at the desk, was Paul Laurence Dunbar. "*You,*" my mother had early announced, "are going to be the *lady* Paul Laurence Dunbar." I still own the Emily books and the "Complete Paul Laurence Dunbar."

*Of course* I would be a poet! *Was* a poet! Didn't I write a poem every day? Sometimes *two* poems?

### ♦ Library Link ♦

*Now that you've read some reminiscences of Gwendolyn Brooks's early life, you might like to read some of her poetry from her collection entitled* Selected Poems.

## Reader's Response

Did any of Gwendolyn's memories lead you to think of memories of your own? What were those memories?

## Thinking It Over

1. Which of her father's qualities do you think Gwendolyn Brooks most admired?
2. What were some of the things the Brooks family did together, and how did these things affect Gwendolyn?
3. Why do you think Gwendolyn describes the books as the gift "that began the giving again"?
4. How did Gwendolyn's mother encourage her and help her to write? What evidence led you to your answer?
5. Why do you think Gwendolyn was so happy to discover that there were many other writers?
6. Writers are often advised to write about things that mean a lot to them. How did Gwendolyn Brooks follow this advice?

## Appreciating Literature

In the last paragraph, Gwendolyn Brooks is making gentle fun of her own childhood dreams. Describe the tone of the last paragraph and explain how the adult Gwendolyn might feel about looking back on herself as a child.

## Writing to Learn

**Think and Recall** Gwendolyn Brooks's memories of early childhood introduce us to her family, her home, holiday traditions, and her first steps toward her career. Below is a cluster of topics that she develops as she writes about her father. Select a person who influenced your early childhood. Cluster topic ideas around the person's name.

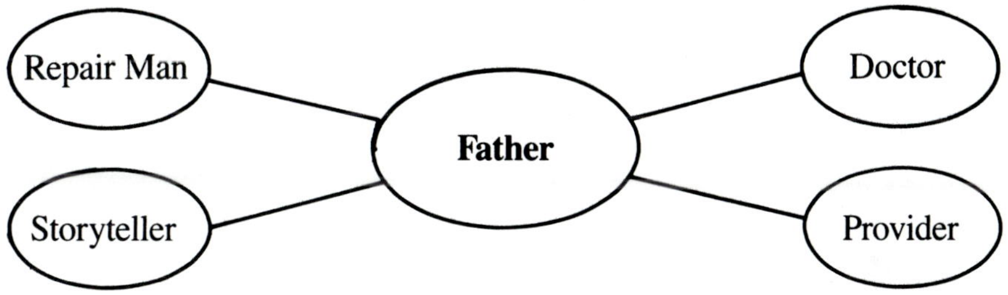


**Write** Use your cluster and write a brief personality sketch of the person who influenced your life when you were younger.

AWARD WINNING *Author*

## *IN HONOR OF DAVID ANDERSON BROOKS,*
## *My Father*

July 30, 1883–November 21, 1959

A dryness is upon the house
My father loved and tended.
Beyond his firm and sculptured door
His light and lease have ended.

He walks the valleys, now—replies
To sun and wind forever.
No more the cramping chamber's chill,
No more the hindering fever.

Now out upon the wide clean air
My father's soul revives,
All innocent of self-interest
And the fear that strikes and strives.

He who was Goodness, Gentleness,
And Dignity is free,
Translates to public Love
Old private charity.

GWENDOLYN BROOKS

# *REMEMBERED*

She sang, and I listened the whole song thro'.
    (It was sweet, so sweet, the singing.)
The stars were out and the moon it grew
From a wee soft glimmer way out in the blue
    To a bird thro' the heavens winging.

She sang, and the song trembled down to my breast, —
    (It was sweet, so sweet the singing.)
As a dove just out of its fledgling nest,
And, putting its wings to the first sweet test,
    Flutters homeward so wearily winging.

She sang and I said to my heart "That song,
    That was sweet, so sweet i' the singing,
Shall live with us and inspire us long,
And thou, my heart, shalt be brave and strong
    For the sake of those words a-winging.

The woman died and the song was still.
    (It was sweet, so sweet, the singing.)
But ever I hear the same low trill,
Of the song that shakes my heart with a thrill,
    And goes forever winging.

PAUL LAURENCE DUNBAR

# Literature Link

## *What makes a story a short story?*

**H**ave you ever heard an orchestra play a symphony? If so, you know that it took a long time, perhaps forty or fifty minutes. A symphony is made up of different parts, or movements, in which the composer may explore a range of moods. A pop song, on the other hand, is a short composition—only three or four minutes in length. Because the song is relatively brief, the pop song writer prefers to focus on one dominant mood.

### *One Theme—Simple Structure*

Just as the pop song is simpler in form than the symphony, so in literature, the short story is a simpler form than the novel. A novel presents a variety of changing experiences over a long period of time, sometimes many years. A short story, on the other hand, usually focuses on a single episode. It aims at communicating one dominant theme, or message, about life or human nature.

The brevity of a short story demands that a writer not delay in introducing the setting and characters. The plot must be kept simple and the story must be developed quickly. Traditionally, the short story has a narrative structure made up of three parts—beginning, middle, and end.

In the beginning of a short story, the author introduces the setting, mood, and main character. Consider this opening passage from the short story "The Love Letter."

> I've heard of secret drawers in old desks, of course; who hasn't. But the day I bought my desk I wasn't thinking of secret drawers and I know very well I didn't have any least premonition or feeling of mystery about it. I spotted it in the

window of a second-hand store near my apartment, went in to look it over, and the proprietor told me where he got it. It came from one of the last of the big old mid-Victorian houses in Brooklyn... .

Notice how the author, Jack Finney, creates a mood of suspense by referring to *secret drawers, premonition,* and *mystery.* His use of first-person narration establishes a personal tone and immediately draws you into the mind and actions of the main character, Jake Belknap.

In the next paragraphs, you learn more about Jake.

When you're twenty-four and a bachelor, you usually figure you'll be married before much longer. I'm reasonably ambitious and bring work home from the office every once in a while... every couple weeks or so I write a letter to my folks. ...

I'm trying to be honest about what happened. ... And I wondered, as I often had lately, whether there was something wrong with me, whether I'd ever meet a girl I desperately wanted to be with—the only way a man can get married, it seems to me.

These details tell you about Jake's character traits and establish him as a reliable person. Jake's concern about finding the right person to marry hints at the main problem, or conflict, of the story.

In the middle part of a story, an author develops the characters and describes their attempts to resolve a conflict that has arisen. In "The Love Letter," for example, the author introduces Helen Worley, reveals her character traits, and establishes the relationship between her and Jake. The strange conflict they face—being separated by time—is explored through the letters they write and receive from each other. Jake's first letter is an example.

*Helen: I have just read the letter in the secret drawer of your desk and I wish I knew how I could possibly help you. I can't tell what you might think of me if there were a way I could reach you. But you are someone I am certain I would like to know. I hope you are beautiful but you needn't be; you're a girl I could like, and maybe ardently, and if I did, I promise you I'd be true and loving. Do the best you can, Helen Elizabeth Worley, in the time and place you are; I can't reach you or help you. But I'll think of you. And maybe I'll dream of you, too.*

*Yours,*
*Jake Belknap*

This middle part of the story usually leads to a crucial event called a turning point. The nighttime scenes in "The Love Letter" contribute to the growing suspense until this point when the tension is at its peak.

It was a long week. I worked, I kept busy daytimes, but at night I thought of hardly anything but the third secret drawer in my desk. I was terribly tempted to open it earlier, telling myself that whatever might lie in it had been put there decades before and must be there now, but I wasn't sure and I waited.

Then, late at night, a week to the hour after I'd mailed my second letter at the old Wister post office, I pulled out the third drawer, reached in and brought out the last little secret drawer which lay behind it. My hand was actually shaking and for a moment I couldn't bear to look directly—something lay in the drawer—and I turned my head away. Then I looked.

Do you agree that this is the turning point of the story? After this, the author lets the tension subside as he describes Helen's gentle features and the pledge she made, never to forget.

## *How Is the Conflict Resolved?*

In the end, or resolution, of a story, an author may solve conflicts or sum up the main theme. In the end of "The Love Letter," the author ties up loose ends with some information about what had happened to Helen. How would you describe her fate? How does Helen's final communication suggest that she had remained true to Jake? Can you think of a single sentence to sum up the message of the story?

Your reading enjoyment will be greatly enhanced if you can think about each short story you read in the same way you have thought about "The Love Letter" in this lesson. Then you will understand the way each author explores a theme, using a variety of techniques within the three-part structure. When reading, notice how a setting is established and how characters are introduced. For example, how does the author's choice of first- or third-person narration contribute to the effectiveness of the story? Does the author use specific devices, such as flashback or dialogue, to develop the plot? See if you are able to identify a major problem or conflict in the story. If so, does the plot develop towards a crucial turning point, or does the main character simply progress to a new discovery or awareness? Finally, you might try to state the theme of the story in a single sentence.

**A**s you read "The Story-Teller," you will notice that this is a story within a story. Look for the theme, the message that the author wishes to communicate. Try to identify the three parts of the story structure as you come to them. Keep an eye out for any unusual techniques, as well as the author's use of humor.

*On a long train journey, three restless children drive their aunt nearly to distraction—until a stranger begins to tell a most unusual story.*

# The Story-Teller

## by Saki

READERS' CHOICE AWARD

It was a hot afternoon, and the railway carriage was correspondingly sultry, and the next stop was at Templecombe, nearly an hour ahead. The occupants of the carriage were a small girl, and a smaller girl, and a small boy. An aunt belonging to the children occupied one corner seat, and the further corner seat on the opposite side was occupied by a bachelor who was a stranger to their party, but the small girls and the small boy emphatically occupied the compartment. Both the aunt and the children were conversational in a limited, persistent way, reminding one of the attentions of a housefly that refused to be discouraged. Most of the aunt's remarks seemed to begin with "Don't," and nearly all of the children's remarks began with "Why?" The bachelor said nothing out loud.

"Don't, Cyril, don't," exclaimed the aunt, as the small boy began smacking the cushions of the seat, producing a cloud of dust at each blow.

"Come and look out of the window," she added.

The child moved reluctantly to the window. "Why are those sheep being driven out of that field?" he asked.

"I expect they are being driven to another field where there is more grass," said the aunt weakly.

"But there is lots of grass in that field," protested the boy; "there is nothing else but grass there. Aunt, there's lots of grass in that field."

"Perhaps the grass in the other field is better," suggested the aunt fatuously.

"Why is it better?" came the swift, inevitable question.

"Oh, look at those cows!" exclaimed the aunt. Nearly every field along the line had contained cows or bullocks, but she spoke as though she were drawing attention to a rarity.

"Why is the grass in the other field better?" persisted Cyril.

The frown on the bachelor's face was deepening to a scowl. He was a hard, unsympathetic man, the aunt decided in her mind. She was utterly unable to come to any satisfactory decision about the grass in the other field.

The smaller girl created a diversion by beginning to recite

"On the Road to Mandalay." She only knew the first line, but she put her limited knowledge to the fullest possible use. She repeated the line over and over again in a dreamy but resolute and very audible voice; it seemed to the bachelor as though someone had had a bet with her that she could not repeat the line aloud two thousands times without stopping. Whoever it was who had made the wager was likely to lose his bet.

"Come over here and listen to a story," said the aunt, when the bachelor had looked twice at her and once at the communication cord.

The children moved listlessly towards the aunt's end of the carriage. Evidently her reputation as a story-teller did not rank high in their estimation.

In a low, confidential voice, interrupted at frequent intervals by loud, petulant questions from her listeners, she began an unenterprising and deplorably uninteresting story about a little girl who was good, and made friends with everyone on account of her goodness, and was finally saved from a mad bull by a number of rescuers who admired her moral character.

"Wouldn't they have saved her if she hadn't been good?" demanded the bigger of the small girls. It was exactly the question that the bachelor had wanted to ask.

"Well, yes," admitted the aunt lamely, "but I don't think they would have run quite so fast to her help if they had not liked her so much."

"It's the stupidest story I've ever heard," said the bigger of the small girls, with immense conviction.

"I didn't listen after the first bit, it was so stupid," said Cyril.

The smaller girl made no actual comment on the story, but she had long ago recommenced a murmured repetition of her favorite line.

"You don't seem to be a success as a story-teller," said the bachelor suddenly from his corner.

The aunt bristled in instant defence[1] at this unexpected attack.

[1]Some words in this selection are spelled in the British style.

"It's a very difficult thing to tell stories that children can both understand and appreciate," she said stiffly.

"I don't agree with you," said the bachelor.

"Perhaps *you* would like to tell them a story," was the aunt's retort.

"Tell us a story," demanded the bigger of the small girls.

"Once upon a time," began the bachelor, "there was a little girl called Bertha, who was extraordinarily good."

The children's momentarily-aroused interest began at once to flicker; all stories seemed dreadfully alike, no matter who told them.

"She did all that she was told, she was always truthful, she kept her clothes clean, ate milk puddings as though they were jam tarts, learned her lessons perfectly, and was polite in her manners."

"Was she pretty?" asked the bigger of the small girls.

"Not as pretty as any of you," said the bachelor, "but she was horribly good."

There was a wave of reaction in favour of the story; the word horrible in connection with goodness was a novelty that commended itself. It seemed to introduce a ring of truth that was absent from the aunt's tales of infant life.

"She was so good," continued the bachelor, "that she won several medals for goodness, which she always wore, pinned on to her dress. There was a medal for obedience, another medal for punctuality, and a third for good behaviour. They were large medals and they clinked against one another as she walked. No other child in the town where she lived had as many as three medals, so everybody knew that she must be an extra good child."

"Horribly good," quoted Cyril.

"Everybody talked about her goodness, and the Prince of the country got to hear about it, and he said that as she was so very good she might be allowed once a week to walk in his park, which was just outside the town. It was a beautiful park, and no children were ever allowed in it, so it was a great honour for Bertha to be allowed to go there."

"Were there any sheep in the park?" demanded Cyril.

"No," said the bachelor, "there were no sheep."

"Why weren't there any sheep?" came the inevitable question arising out of that answer.

The aunt permitted herself a smile, which might almost have been described as a grin.

"There were no sheep in the park," said the bachelor, "because the Prince's mother had once had a dream that her son would either be killed by a sheep or else by a clock falling on him. For that reason the Prince never kept a sheep in his park or a clock in his palace."

The aunt suppressed a gasp of admiration.

"Was the Prince killed by a sheep or by a clock?" asked Cyril.

"He is still alive, so we can't tell whether the dream will come true," said the bachelor unconcernedly; "anyway, there were no sheep in the park, but there were lots of little pigs running all over the place."

"What colour were they?"

"Black with white faces, white with black spots, black all over, grey with white patches, and some were white all over."

The story-teller paused to let a full idea of the park's treasures sink into the children's imaginations; then he resumed:

"Bertha was rather sorry to find that there were no flowers in the park. She had promised her aunts, with tears in her eyes, that she would not pick any of the kind Prince's flowers, and she had meant to keep her promise, so of course it made her feel silly to find that there were no flowers to pick."

"Why weren't there any flowers?"

"Because the pigs had eaten them all," said the bachelor promptly. "The gardeners had told the Prince that you couldn't have pigs and flowers, so he decided to have pigs and not flowers."

There was a murmur of approval at the excellence of the Prince's decision; so many people would have decided the other way.

"There were lots of other delightful things in the park. There were ponds with gold and blue and green fish in them, and trees with beautiful parrots that said clever things at a moment's notice, and humming birds that hummed all the popular tunes of the day. Bertha walked up and down and enjoyed herself immensely, and thought to herself: 'If I were not so extraordinarily good I should not have been allowed to come into this beautiful park and enjoy all that there is to be seen in it,' and her three medals clinked against one another as she walked and helped to remind her how very good she really was. Just then an enormous wolf came prowling into the park to see if it could catch a fat little pig for its supper."

"What colour was it?" asked the children, amid an immediate quickening of interest.

"Mud-colour all over, with a black tongue and pale grey eyes that gleamed with unspeakable ferocity. The first thing that it saw in the park was Bertha; her pinafore was so spotlessly white and clean that it could be seen from a great distance. Bertha saw the wolf and saw that it was stealing towards her, and she began to wish that she had never been allowed to come into the park. She ran as hard as she could, and the wolf came after her with huge leaps and bounds. She managed to reach a shrubbery of myrtle bushes and she hid herself in one of the thickest of the bushes. The wolf came sniffing among the branches, its black tongue lolling out of its mouth and its pale grey eyes glaring with rage. Bertha was terribly frightened, and thought to herself: 'If I had not been so extraordinarily good I should have been safe in the town at this moment.' However, the scent of the myrtle was so strong that the wolf could not sniff out where Bertha was hiding, and the bushes were so thick that he might have hunted about in them for a long time without catching sight of her, so he thought he might as well go off and catch a little pig instead. Bertha was trembling very much at having the wolf prowling and sniffing so near her, and as she trembled the medal for obedience clinked against the medals for good conduct and punctuality. The wolf was just moving away when he heard the sound of the medals clinking and stopped to listen; they clinked again in a bush quite near him. He dashed into the bush, his pale grey eyes gleaming with ferocity and triumph, and dragged Bertha out and devoured her to the last morsel. All that was left of her were her shoes, bits of clothing, and the three medals for goodness."

"Were any of the little pigs killed?"

"No, they all escaped."

"The story began badly," said the smaller of the small girls, "but it had a beautiful ending."

"It is the most beautiful story that I ever heard," said the bigger of the small girls, with immense decision.

"It is the *only* beautiful story I have ever heard," said Cyril.

A dissentient opinion came from her aunt.

"A most improper story to tell to young children! You have undermined the effect of years of careful teaching."

"At any rate," said the bachelor, collecting his belongings preparatory to leaving the carriage, "I kept them quiet for ten minutes, which was more than you were able to do."

"Unhappy woman!" he observed to himself as he walked down the platform of Templecombe station; "for the next six months or so those children will assail her in public with demands for an improper story!"

♦ LIBRARY LINK ♦

*You might enjoy reading "Naftali the Storyteller and His Horse, Sus" from Isaac Bashevis Singer's collection,* Stories for Children.

## Reader's Response

If you could walk in and out of this story, when would you enter and when would you leave? Why did you enjoy this part of the story?

## Thinking It Over

1. Why were the children bored? What clues led you to this conclusion?
2. What made the bachelor decide to tell the children a story?
3. Identify the phrase in the bachelor's story that immediately aroused the children's interest. Why did the children react favorably to those words?
4. Why do you think the children enjoyed the bachelor's story more than the aunt's story?
5. Predict what the aunt might say to the children the next time they ask her to tell them a story as interesting as the one told by the bachelor.

## Appreciating Literature

The children think the bachelor's story is "beautiful," and readers enjoy it, too. The story isn't like the usual, conventional stories they have heard all too often. Think about how the bachelor's story departs from some of the conventions. How does this make his story appealing?

## Writing to Learn

**THINK AND INVENT** Saki delights his readers by presenting the reverse of what they expect. Look at the flowchart below. On your paper, note an idea for a new ending to go in the last box.

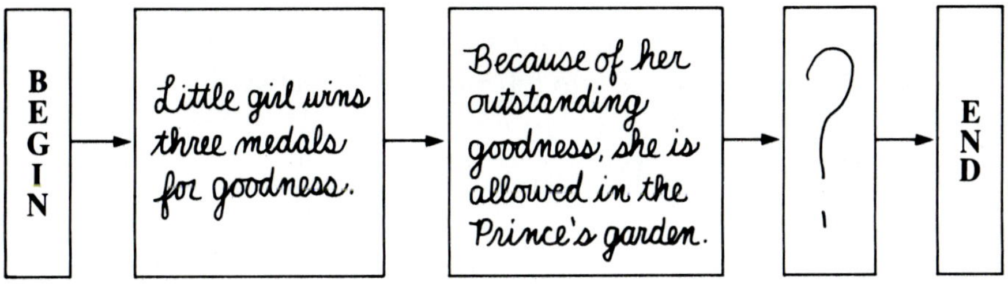


**WRITE** Use the idea you developed for the flowchart and compose a new ending for this story. Try to surprise your classmates in the same manner that Saki's storyteller surprised his audience.

# LITERATURE LINK

## *How can expressing ideas in your own words unlock their meaning?*

**H**ave you ever heard a really *great* story—one you wanted to share with everyone? Did you retell the story in *exactly* the same words? Most likely you didn't, because it's difficult to remember someone's exact words, and you have your own special way of expressing yourself.

In an article you read earlier in this unit, "You, Too, Can Be a Storyteller," David Holt writes that he enjoys being able to tell stories in his own words. This is the way *he* expresses it: "… I consider ad-libbing part of the fun, so I don't worry about repeating the story exactly." He also believes that "*anyone* can be a storyteller," and he encourages you to tell stories in your own words.

### *In Your Own Words*

Putting someone else's ideas into your own words is called paraphrasing. Paraphrasing is not just for storytelling. The ability to restate ideas that you hear or read is useful for other activities as well. It's a vital strategy for checking your own reading. If you can take an author's words and express them in your own way, you will know that you understand the ideas you are reading. You'll be taking charge of your own learning and gaining independence as a student.

For practice, see if you can paraphrase this passage from "You, Too, Can Be a Storyteller." Ignore the numbers for now.

> So your first task as a prospective oral chronicler is to find a story you can relate to. But *where*—you may want to know—can a person find such stories? Well, it's *easy* … because they're everywhere.

Do you usually use words like *task, prospective,* or *chronicler*? If you're not sure of their meanings, you might have trouble putting them into your own words. Once you find out the meaning of any unfamiliar words, your paraphrase might read like this:

> If you're going to be a storyteller, your first job is to find a story you like and would enjoy telling. Don't worry about finding good stories. They're all around you.

The numbers in the passage show you the key words and phrases that make up the author's complete message. By matching the numbers in the paraphrase with the numbers in the passage, you can see that all the details are covered. That's because paraphrasing is not just summarizing main ideas. You need to be sure that you express all of an idea with all of its details. Then you can be sure that you truly understand the author's message. Here's how to use paraphrasing when you read:

- Ask yourself what the author's basic ideas are.
- Note the key words. Be sure you understand them.
- Express each idea in your own words. Be sure to include necessary details so the author's message is complete.

There are many interesting details in "The Inside Story." Read the article carefully, pausing often to check your understanding. See if paraphrasing helps.

# The INSIDE

*Do you remember the last newspaper article you read? What if you were told it was written by someone your own age? Impossible, right? Not at Children's Express!*

# Children's Express

"Watch out—" reads a handwritten sign over the clock on the wall, "this clock is now set to *real time*!" There is no lack of activity in the crowded offices of this New York City newsroom. Telephones are ringing. Two reporters are going over some last-minute notes and questions before they start out on an interview. An editor is on the phone, assigning a team of reporters to cover a new story. The hustle and bustle is typical of any newspaper staff. But something is different. The two reporters are eleven and thirteen years old. The editor is sixteen.

This is the headquarters of Children's Express, a news service run primarily by children. Here, reporters thirteen years old and under conduct interviews and write newspaper articles under the guidance of assistant editors fourteen to eighteen years of age. Their articles appear in many newspapers here and abroad—newspapers such as the *San Francisco Chronicle*, the *New York Times*, the *Atlanta Constitution*, the *Toronto Star*, and even the Japanese *Yomiuri Shimbun*, which has a circulation of over nine million copies.

Founded in 1975 by lawyer and businessman Robert Clampitt, Children's Express has news bureaus in places as wide-ranging as Northeast Massachusetts; San Francisco; New York City; Wellington, New Zealand; Newark, N.J.; Melbourne, Australia and Tokyo. In addition, children from many other places write or call to share news, ideas and opinions with the Children's Express staff.

In a world of many journalists and newspapers, what does Children's Express contribute that is so special? In a 1985 statement commemorating Children's Express's tenth anniversary, Robert Clampitt summed up the organization's purposes: ". . . to speak for children everywhere; to advocate; to report on the issues that affect children's lives; and to explore the experiences, feelings and needs of children."

As a news service, Children's Express is unique because, no matter what the topic, its main focus is on children. It makes sense, then, that children make

# STORY

by Jeanette Leardi

**The international office of Children's Express, New York City, buzzes with activity.**

up most of the staff at each Children's Express bureau. Managing Editor Melanie Wright, twenty-five, is one of the few adults in charge at the New York headquarters. She explains that several adults are needed for legal and business reasons, but that all of the reporting is done by the children themselves. She believes that children are capable of understanding and writing about the issues that affect their lives.

Issues have been important to the success of Children's Express. The organization first called major attention to itself during the 1976 Democratic National Convention. A team of Children's Express reporters was there to cover the event. Melanie Wright recalls that at first the team was expected to interview people on the sidelines, such as political-button sellers, television-camera operators, perhaps even convention delegates. But the young people soon decided on their own to go after the political newsmakers.

**Children's Express reporter on assignment in Africa chats with young people.**

**Reporter Albert Lin travelled to London for Children's Express to meet with Great Britain's prime minister Margaret Thatcher.**

At the convention, professional journalists wondered whom presidential candidate Jimmy Carter would choose as his vice-presidential running mate. Children's Express reporter Gilbert Giles, then twelve years old, followed a hunch based on his own investigation. The Children's Express headline, "IT'S OFFICIAL: MONDALE/CARTER!" came out twenty-four hours before any other journalists got the word. Children's Express had "scooped" every other professional news service. The young organization was on its way. It would cover serious issues from then on: from the problems of runaways, dropouts, and poor and homeless children, to politics and nuclear war. Already Children's Express teams have travelled to many places, including Italy, Japan, Thailand, Cambodia, and the U.S.S.R.

# Working as a Children's Express Reporter

**Senior editor Glenn Golz follows up lead from his New York office.**

Who can become a Children's Express reporter? And how do Children's Express reporters and editors learn their trade? Glenn Golz, sixteen, has been with Children's Express for several years. He is now a senior editor, but he has also done his share of reporting. According to Glenn, any child can be a Children's Express reporter: "Some people think that to be a Children's Express reporter you have to be very brilliant, but that's not true. All you have to be is very interested."

Glenn has covered some very exciting stories. He has even been to the U.S.S.R., where he met with Soviet children and discussed world peace. Now, as a senior editor, his job is to guide other reporters and editors in their tasks.

Samantha Mandor, eleven, is a reporter who joined Children's Express a short time ago. She has already worked on several stories, including an interview with tennis star Martina Navratilova. She is learning much about herself, including, as she puts it, ". . . how to ask questions. I know that I am not afraid to ask people questions."

Children's Express reporters work in teams together with an assistant editor. They learn how to cover a story in a clear and interesting way. Each team is made up of some experienced reporters and some inexperienced reporters/trainees. The children train by doing; the experience makes a difference. Some children even discover that they like journalism enough to want to make a career of it. But inspiring future journalists is not what Children's Express is really about. "We're not a preparatory school for journalists," says Melanie Wright. "We are advocates for children's issues and rights. We try to call the attention of the media to the needs and concerns of children." Glenn Golz agrees: "At first I joined Children's Express because I heard that I would get to interview famous people. I didn't really know what it was all about. But as I got to be an editor, I realized that I was being a voice for other children."

Glenn, Samantha, and others like them, take their jobs seriously. They know that the stories they tell are often the stories of children who have little say in how their lives are to be lived. That is why Children's Express teams practice "oral journalism." That is, they rely on tape recording all of their information so that the many ways children and adults express their views can be presented in their own words.

Children's Express articles are not written mainly for children. In fact, adult readers are the ones people like Glenn and Samantha hope to reach. "When I edit a story," explains Glenn, "I don't think about whether children or adults will read it. We just write the best story that we can." For these amateurs, writing the best story means learning to be as professional as possible. They suggest and research ideas for stories and interview adults as well as children.

What are the reactions of adult interviewees to the Children's Express reporters? According to Melanie Wright, the adults "are either caught off guard by the children's questions or they are forgiving" when they think they have been asked an embarrassing or awkward question by a young reporter. Usually, though, adults are very pleased and enthusiastic about being interviewed by Children's Express. "People are usually very impressed with us," Glenn Golz remarks. Samantha Mandor adds: "Sometimes we're more prepared than the other [professional] reporters."

Even many journalists treat Children's Express reporters as colleagues. Glenn Golz recalls that during his 1986 trip to the U.S.S.R., he and another journalist exchanged ideas and observations in the spirit of mutual support. A mark of Children's Express' success is the fact that professional journalists have begun to see nothing unusual about the presence of Children's Express teams at the same newsmaking event.

Nevertheless, Children's Express is making news of its own. Members of the organization have made television appearances on "60 Minutes," "The Donahue Show," and "Today." Children's Express has written reports for *Family Circle*, *Elle*, and *Rolling Stone* magazines.

A 1980 *Rolling Stone* assignment was particularly important. A New York bureau team travelled to Thailand and Cambodia to interview children in refugee camps who were orphans or had been separated from their parents. Their hard work and careful reporting of the situation helped Children's Express in 1981 to receive a Pulitzer Prize nomination for commentary.

**Reporters Michael Ford and Caroline Meckler research news assignment before briefing session.**

# How a News Story Develops

If the stories Children's Express teams cover are "grown-up" in their subject matter, the way a Children's Express article develops from idea to printed page is just as mature. Once an interesting story idea has been approved and an assignment editor chooses a Children's Express team to cover it, the team goes into action. A Children's Express story goes through four stages of development: 1) research and preparation, 2) the briefing, 3) the interview, and 4) the debriefing. The second through fourth stages are tape-recorded. In this way every word of the final article comes from the reporting team and the people it has interviewed.

## *Research and Preparation*

Before the Children's Express team begins its investigation, the assistant editor and the reporters gather information on the topic and on the people they are about to interview. They learn what they can from books, magazines, newspaper articles and organizations. Then they prepare questions that they would like to have answered about the topic and bring these to the briefing.

## *The Briefing*

Just like professional newspaper staffs, Children's Express teams hold a briefing session before going out to cover a story. The assistant editor and the reporters discuss the information they have gathered and the questions that the reporters have prepared. They decide how they will cover the story, which issues are most important, and which facts are missing and need to be found. After the discussion, each reporter writes a new list of about twenty questions to ask during the interview. This is the time when a reporter relies on his or her own judgment, curiosity and organizing skills. The reporters then read their questions aloud. The assistant editor helps the team narrow down or expand the question list and makes sure that the questions are clear and precise. When the team has decided on the order of the questions to be asked and which questions should be asked by each reporter, the group is ready to hold the interview.

## *The Interview*

The Children's Express team may interview several different people to get all the facts and opinions they need to complete their investigation. One of the most important things each Children's Express reporter and editor learns is to remain objective when covering a story. Each team makes sure it interviews people and gathers information from sources that hold differing opinions on the topic. As soon as possible after the interview process, the debriefing takes place.

## *The Debriefing*

Surprisingly, the debriefing, not the interview, is the most important stage in the development of a Children's Express article. During the debriefing, the team members "write" the story by sharing their feelings, reactions, and conclusions about the topic and the people they interviewed. Once again, the assistant editor plays an important role by guiding the discussion so that as much information as possible is tape recorded.

With the help of teen and adult typists, the briefing, interview and debriefing tapes are transcribed, that is, transferred onto paper. Once this is done, a staff editor chooses and combines taped excerpts and creates a clear presentation of the story. The article is finished and ready to be sent to newspapers that carry the Children's Express column.

**A team briefing brings together several C.E. staff. Shown clockwise are senior editors Glenn Golz and Rebecca Walkowitz, reporter Samantha Mandor, editor Adam Horowitz, reporters Caroline Meckler and Michael Ford.**

# In-depth Reporting

Sometimes Children's Express decides to cover a topic in greater depth. Two types of its in-depth coverage are the *round table* and the *hearing*. In a round table discussion, the team poses questions to a group of four to six children, all of whom are thirteen years old and younger. In these sessions, children get the chance to speak out about their problems, fears, hopes and experiences concerning the topic at hand. Children's Express has conducted roundtables on topics such as friendship, sex education, the influence of television, good and bad parenting, and war.

In a round table discussion, children are the only interviewees. However, a hearing usually includes interviews with adult experts in the field of the topic being investigated. When, for example, Children's Express held hearings on the topic "The Media and Children's Issues," the adults questioned included a newspaper editor, a university professor, a rock musician, a government health administrator, and a juvenile-court judge, as well as numerous parents. Of course, children were interviewed, too. The findings from these hearings were published in booklet form and sent to news agencies all over the country. Children's Express hopes that the media will begin to make children's opinions an important part of their coverage.

# Experiencing an Interview

**Telephone interviews allow teams to cover long distance assignments without leaving the office.**

A recent investigation of the problems of school dropouts has taken teams to different parts of the country. In the basement of the New York headquarters, an interview is about to take place. Samantha Mandor's team will be interviewing Irving Harris, the founder of Project Beethoven, a unique school-dropout prevention program. Mr. Harris is in Chicago. Connecting the phone to the tape recorder is sixteen-year-old assistant editor Linda Holmes. She will introduce to Mr. Harris, herself, Samantha, and the other reporters on the team: Elisabeth Coffey, 13; Michael Ford, 10; and Max Cherpitel, 13.

Before Linda picks up the phone to call Mr. Harris, she and the reporters double-check the order of the questions that will be asked and go over any last-minute problems. As the team editor on this story, Linda will not ask Mr. Harris any questions herself. She will only take notes for the debriefing session that will follow. She asks if everyone is ready. The reporters nod and become silent as Linda starts the tape recorder, contacts Mr. Harris, introduces the team and asks the reporters to begin presenting their questions.

The questions they ask Irving Harris are precise: How did the program get its name? Why is this program important? How serious is the dropout situation in Chicago? As Mr. Harris answers these and other questions, it is clear that the news team has done its homework. They are well prepared and alert. Occasionally Mr. Harris's answers spark new questions in their minds. They jot down these "follow-up" questions as he speaks, then ask them, always remembering to return to the list of questions they planned to ask. The reporters are polite, but not shy. Their questions are as probing as those of any professional journalist and from Mr. Harris's serious tone and detailed answers, it's obvious that he agrees.

The news team listens with concentration. They do not hear the hectic activity going on one floor above. There, a copying machine is churning out forms. Phones are ringing, and a teen typist is transcribing a tape. The sixteen-year-old editor is still working out the details of the latest team assignment while younger reporters come and go through the busy office. This is what it's all about.

# Speaking Out About Children's Express

**Rebecca Walkowitz jots notes before going out on assignment.**

In the tenth anniversary journal, several children then in the organization had this to say about Children's Express:

AARON RETICA, 18: "One of the things I learned was that everywhere you look, every person you come up against or meet has a voice that you can tap. CE opened a whole range of voices that I probably never would have heard."

ELAINE SCHEINDLING, 15: "CE doesn't take away from your childness so much as it adds an outlet for a natural desire to be useful, to do real things, and to take responsibility."

CAITLIN GUTHEIL, 17: "CE has the philosophy of children can, children should and children will. It's the one place where children are their own advocates."

ROBIN MOULDS, 11: "I never dreamed that I would be a reporter. I was only a kid, you know, and now I feel I can do it and I am capable. And you know, I think I'm more sure of myself, not only as a reporter but as a person."

REBECCA WALKOWITZ, 15: "I feel responsibility to those kids out there in the world who are in some ways depending on me to speak for them and be their advocate. Nobody else is going to do it."

JULIE WALLACE, 17: "CE helps make children heard, not only because they are the future, but just because they are."

BOB BLUMENFIELD, 17: "I can tell you what CE is, but you're not going to know what it is until you've done it. The best I can say is that it's unique, it's powerful, empowering, essential, vibrant. It gives life, it brings life to the mind, to people who read it. It gave me a type of life, another sense of life."

Melanie Wright sums it up: "Nothing is more satisfying than to see a kid learn that what he or she thinks and does can make a difference in others' lives."

Like that "real time" clock on the wall, Children's Express reporters and editors are into "real" issues. Watch out, world. They are making a difference.

## *Reader's Response*

You need some skill and wholehearted dedication to become a Children's Express reporter. Would you like to become one? Why or why not?

## Thinking It Over

1. What is the main purpose of Children's Express?
2. What are some advantages and disadvantages of staffing Children's Express with children?
3. List, in order, what takes place during the briefing stage of a story's development.
4. Compare a round table discussion with a hearing. What did you think about as you made the comparison?
5. In your opinion, what is the most valuable contribution of Children's Express?
6. Paraphrase what several children said about Children's Express in its tenth anniversary journal.

## Appreciating Literature

Reading informational articles about things other people have done can inspire us to try new things ourselves. Did this article make you want to be a reporter for Children's Express? Think of other articles you have read that have given you ideas for things you want to do.

## Writing to Learn

**THINK AND PREDICT** The sentence below creates the organization for a discussion about "The Children's Express." List three ideas that you would expect to find following this statement.

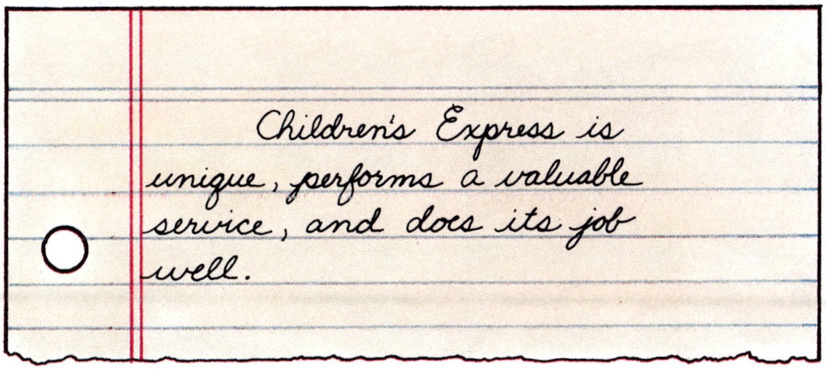


**WRITE** Write the rest of a paragraph that begins with the sentence above. Be sure the ideas you listed are all included in the paragraph and that the last sentence ties the ideas back together.

# Literature Link

## *What can you do when you get lost in the details of narrative nonfiction?*

When you're reading, do you ever feel as though you have wandered into a maze? One minute the text seems perfectly clear. The next minute, you're lost. All readers feel that way at times. Fortunately, you can find your way again with these strategies:

- **Stop, Think, and Read Ahead**—Stop and think about what puzzles you. Then read ahead for clarifying information.
- **Find the Problem**—Is it difficult vocabulary? A complicated sentence? An unfamiliar character? Conflicting concepts?
- **Reread**—Often you can figure out the meaning just by identifying the problem and rereading the confusing part.

- **Use Context for Difficult Vocabulary**—Use context clues to search for meaning. Use the dictionary for really tough words.
- **Write Down Your Questions**—If you're still confused, jot down your remaining questions. As you read ahead and reread, take notes that might help answer your questions.

With these strategies, you will find your way out of any reading maze. Try using them as you read part of an essay from *The Second Tree from the Corner* by E. B. White.

> We have never regarded the decibel as a particularly trustworthy index of sound. Sound is not easily measured. Some of the loudest sounds wouldn't give a decibel machine the faintest tremor: a hushed voice in a house where someone has died; or a child's finger on the latch of a door where a man is trying to work, timorously testing the lock to see if the man won't come out and play. The quality of sound is much more telling than the volume, and this is true in the city, where noise is inevitable. A country sawmill is rich in decibels, yet the ear adjusts easily to it, and it soon becomes as undisturbing as a cicada on a suburban afternoon. New York's noise, even in its low decibel range, has an irritating quality, full of sharp distemper.

Did you lose your footing in the middle of the third sentence? You could have paused and asked yourself: In what way is a hushed voice or the clicking of a door latch the loudest of sounds? You know that E. B. White could not be writing about the actual level of noise in the quiet situations he describes. Think it through by imagining yourself in each of the situations. Perhaps White means that even the tiniest sounds become the loudest in these silent settings. In contrast, each sound loudly disturbs the empty stillness of sorrow or the deep silence of solitary thought. What strategies did you use to make sense of this passage?

Next you will read "Standing in the Wings," a personal essay. If anything confuses you, use the strategies you've learned to get yourself back on track.

*How does an author create characters? For Julia Cunningham, it's all a matter of thinking, watching . . . and then standing in the wings.*

# Standing in the Wings

## *by Julia Cunningham*

When I was recently asked, "What is the creative process?" an image immediately rose in my mind. It was a stage, empty and waiting, at that moment, for me. I was standing in the wings, watching for the first entrance of the first character (as I had for so many years as a writer), both welcoming and dreading the first cue that would begin the book, the commitment, the overwhelming responsibility to be honest. I was once more involved in what I like to call the second reality.

There are, in my thinking, two realities: The first need not be described. It is where we all live, where the oatmeal cools on the

kitchen table, where night sometimes descends at noon, where buttered popcorn is to some a vintage food, where the roof shelters space and serenity or dust, hunger and desperation. It is where we wake and sleep, however and wherever.

But the second reality is another landscape altogether. It shares in the first and is furnished by its observations, feelings and learning. But one passes through a kind of gate into a country where the imagination is completely alive, where the attic of the unconscious is released into words. All the stored trunks and boxes fly open. The old letters scatter in the air and find their voices. The remembering of an ancient terror may form the villainy of a devil in human clothing, or a moment of grace, of loving someone, may become the base for a story of passion and compassion. All is ready, free to move, to run, to love, to strike. And this second world is always present. One needs only to wait in a kind of concentrated quiet to enter it.

Upon my imaginary stage come the people we call characters. The tree house, the castle, the fetid cellar, the hut, the cave have no meaning without them. They are all of us, but newly translated, transformed, given their own lives by the writer's invitation to them to come into being. They lead you, follow you, haunt you, occasionally club you to death, keep you a hundred years in a dungeon. They love, hate, torment, and amuse. Most important of all, I belong to them first and before all else and all others. And, great friends that they are, they belong to me.

There exists a mutual seesaw of trust and friendship between them and me. And the keystone is sincerity. We must as writers be as clear and honest as possible. Falsify the accent of a French mouse, carelessly describe the light-footedness of a heavyweight, forget that Emily Batsford gets indigestion from eating raw onions, and the characters will turn their backs on you, leave you very lonely indeed in front of a silent typewriter. We need not love the evil characters, but we must understand them; we are there to record, not to judge. All the time there will be a deep, almost subterranean bond between writer and characters. They will be loyal, but only if I am. They will act with conviction and style and proceed convincingly to their natural or unnatural ending.

## *Writers' habits*

I suppose there are as many definitions of what a writer is as there are writers, but, aside from the instinctive drive, unconsciously present, to me a writer is a person of certain habits, and the first of these is the ability to listen. It's as though we had three ears instead of two. We may be crouched in grief or aching in the ribs with laughter, but that third ear is recording the moment. And at the same time, the mind is storing each detail in a vast attic where nothing is ever lost or forgotten, but perhaps unused. The simplest place to see this habit in action is at a party of more than three people. It is impossible to resist the role of eavesdropper. I have an actress friend, a master eavesdropper, who can hear and remember three conversations going on simultaneously. I hear only my own and one other.

Another useful habit is looking. All of this sounds so obvious—listening and looking—but perhaps the difference between the ordinary participation of all people and the writer is a matter of intensity. You see and hear not only for yourself, but for your writer self. In some ways, this sounds like intrusive rag-picking, and maybe it is, but it remains irresistible.

Still another good habit is daydreaming. This may seem to some to be an alibi for laziness, but it isn't. It is creating without recording. If you are or want to be a writer, don't allow any criticism of this occupation to diminish its place in your life. Take to the hills (or to another room) where you won't be observed, or go wandering anywhere, at any time, with anyone.

Awareness of smell and taste is also on my list of worthwhile habits. I think that sometimes these two senses are neglected in books, especially for children in middle grades. Yet, these two senses are often the most evocative of mood and feeling. And a smell does not always have to evoke a rose. A stable, a cow pasture, acrid smoke from burning cloth, sweat—there are thousands of smells—can express what nothing else can. Someone once asked me what France smelled like. I happily rummaged in my memories of streets and alleys and churches and crowds and came up with three major sources: animal, architectural, and human, meaning drains, damp stones, and wine.

All these habits contribute to that fateful moment when the first sentence is put down on paper, and maybe they can be headed by the word *attention*—attention to everything that passes, that happens, that makes for terror, joy, sorrow, humor—that same kind of intense attention that a very young child gives to whatever is suddenly new.

I had intended here not to mention the habit of imagination because it must be active inside the writer all the time. But then it occurred to me that this imagination can also be expanded. It can become freer and freer, if unrepressed, until there is nothing that doesn't stimulate it and no distance it cannot travel. For the purpose of a story, imagination has to be grounded in reality (even a dragon must be made plausible), but the habit of giving the imagination wings can be achieved by encouraging short flights to become longer ones.

The last habit is discipline—sitting down and doing—which can make a very minor talent show results that an undisciplined near-genius will never know. Just plain grubbing has inchwormed many writers to success.

## *Afterthoughts, after-memories*

The setting of a story should at least be mentioned here, though I am guilty, sometimes under disguises, of returning my characters to the landscape I love best—France. These fictional creations of mine seem to prefer acting out their adventures there—a place that has a magic that just makes me happy. But I believe that settings in general are more than the boundaries of a country and are truly inhabited by the writer. In my book *Onion Journey*, where the indoor scene was a very poor room with not much more than two beds, a table, a chair for Gilly and another for his grandmother, that setting became so real to me, I could taste the half-filled crock of apple butter in the almost empty cupboard, though it never appeared in the story. And the not quite tight window frames that allowed little slivers of wind to enter the room cut across my own cheeks as I was writing.

I don't know where the props come from—memory, probably. Long after I had written *Dorp Dead*, I recognized the tower where Gilly retreated to be with himself as a ruined tower I had found long ago when I was walking up a grassy hill in France. I was seeking shelter from the cold (it was autumn) and a place to eat my enormous French sandwich; more than that, I needed to shut out my own loneliness. Again, the terraced orchard I used in *The Treasure Is the Rose* was the rear, walled garden of a chateau.[1] But these are afterthoughts, "after-memories." I am very grateful that they rise up out of the half-forgotten at the very instant their appearance is vital to the story I am writing.

Now for plots. I make a very complete outline of each chapter before I begin to write a book. There are certain ingredients I believe necessary. There has to be conflict, a building to a climax, excitement of one kind or another, and that most difficult of all elements, a satisfying conclusion. Also, to me there has to be contrast in the scenes

[1]chateau (sha tō'): house

as they happen. After violence or high tragedy, I am aware of the need, however brief, of a kind of quiet, a release from the preceding tension. It strengthens the next blow of the hammer. Humor can accomplish this, if you can pull it off. I also try to let the characters play their parts in relative importance to their roles, to give each one a fair share, while I attempt always to control their tendency to lead the writer down deserted roads that never lead back to the main direction of the story. But so much arrives unexpectedly. While writing *Dorp Dead* in a small garage room that was filled with leaf shadows and silence, I came to the part where Gilly is looking for the dog and, instead, sees a trail of blood across the kitchen floor. This was an utter surprise to me, and it frightened me so that I had to stop right there and rush out.

Style, it seems to me, is the outcome of work. It grows as the writer grows and quite without urging or instruction. I have been told that my style varies a little with each book, but I am not aware of this. In *Dorp Dead*, I admit to having purposely had Gilly tell his story his way, and, in another book, to having the naïve American rat in France use his own rather slang-filled language. But after that, they chose their own rhythms of speech, of telling, and I simply tried to keep my ear true to their individual pitch.

A writer friend once said that to her a really fine story was like a balloon, suspended lightly in air by its own inner breath, holding perfect shape. This has meant a great deal to me through the years. I can feel its rightness even when my own balloon sometimes leaks into lopsidedness.

I've been standing in the wings for quite a while. A moment ago, the stage was empty because I was thinking of letting impressions and shadows and moods of new characters arrive to fill it. But now, to end, let me step down and offer what to me is a superb gift—something that the great artist Georges Rouault wrote in a letter, expressing his experience with the whole wonderful mystery at the base of any art—inspiration:

*I saw what I had seen before, but the form of it and the harmony were new. . . . A gypsy caravan halted at the side of the road, a weary*

Burnish Me Bright
by Julia Cunningham
Drawings by Don Freem
COME TO THE EDGE
by
Julia Cunningham
Flight of the Sparrow
JULIA CUNNINGHAM
JULIA CUNNINGHAM
The Treasure is the Rose
ILLUSTRATED BY JUDY GRAESE
THE SILENT VOICE
by Julia Cunningham

*old horse nibbling stunted grasses, an old clown patching his costume—the contrast, in fact, between the brilliance and scintillation of laughter and the intense sadness of life itself, that was how it began. Then I enlarged it all. I saw quite clearly that the clown was myself, us, all of us, almost. The gaudy, spangled dress was what life gives us. We all wear spangled dress of some sort, but if someone catches us with the spangles off, as I caught that old clown, oh! the infinite pity of it. I have made the mistake (if it is a mistake; certainly it causes me suffering beyond description) of never allowing people to keep their spangles on. King or Emperor, it's all the same. I want to see through to his soul, and the more the world thinks of him, the more I fear for that soul.*

There is one last element that perhaps should be left to speak from between the lines, silently, but without which all the words, all the work, all the talent are as nothing, and that element is love.

### ♦ Library Link ♦

*This article taken from* The Writer *magazine gives the reader some insight into the art of fiction writing. For additional reading on the techniques of writing, look at Sylvia Cassedy's* In Your Own Words: A Beginner's Guide to Writing *or Bentz Plagemann's* How to Write a Story.

## *Reader's Response*

Based on Julia Cunningham's description of what it is like to create fiction, do you think you would like to be a fiction writer? Why or why not?

## Thinking It Over

1. Compare the two realities the author describes.
2. List six routines that writers have, as discussed in this selection.
3. Of all the writers' routines, which do you think is most important? What thought process did you go through to decide on the most important?
4. According to Cunningham, what are the essential ingredients of a good plot?

## Appreciating Literature

In this essay, Julia Cunningham uses figurative language to describe what it's like to be a writer. The characters she creates for her novels seem to perform for her on an imaginary stage, and she compares the creative process to stored trunks and boxes in an attic that fly open and scatter their contents in the air. How do these descriptions convey a sense of the excitement and the magic of creating a story?

## Writing to Learn

**THINK AND DISCOVER** When she describes the creative process, Ms. Cunningham sees "a stage empty and waiting." Writers sometimes learn more about how they write by trying to describe their own writing experiences. The notes below may give you a hint about how *you* write.

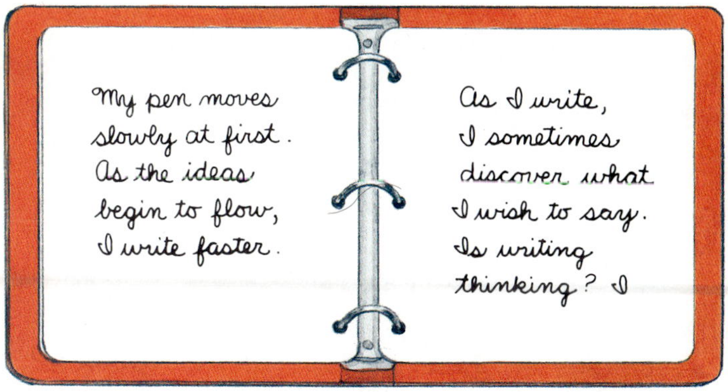


**WRITE** Try to tell what happens as you write. Explain what you do as you place words on paper.

AMERICAN
LIBRARY
ASSOCIATION
*1981*

*There is a special kind of storytelling in which gestures and movement do all the talking. The particular artist who tells stories this way is the mime.*

# CHASING a Dream

**by Julia Cunningham from <u>The Silent Voice</u>**

*For Auguste, who cannot speak, mime is more than a form of entertainment—it is the method he uses to communicate with others. Auguste is an orphan who has been befriended by a young woman, Astair, and her companions. Together they support themselves by performing music, dance, and mime in Paris. As the story opens, Astair is describing to Auguste a theater she has seen.*

Astair told Auguste about the first time she went into a theatre. Her eyes were glowing and her voice dropped to a near whisper.

"It was a big house full of hundreds of seats and in front was a kind of enormous room all lighted around the edges, and in this room were fake trees and a painted mountain in the back and then people in funny clothes talking at each other like real life, only it wasn't. And they came in and out and sometimes a man standing below stopped them and told them what to do."

She fell silent and seemed to forget her listener, lost in what she was remembering.

Then she saw that Auguste was standing before her. He gestured toward the door, drew on an imaginary coat, and began to walk in place as though down a street. With a wide motion of his arms, he stopped. His face was lighted with wonder at something he pretended to see.

"You want me to take you there, is that what you are saying?" she asked.

Auguste nodded violently.

"Then I will. Tomorrow. I promise. But now I need to sleep. You, too. Good night, Auguste, and thank you."

Astair didn't know why she thanked this odd boy, but she was too tired to think about it.

It was late afternoon the next day before Astair could keep her promise. Thomas had been forced to stay off the streets by a severe chill, so the girl became the group's musician. Her instrument was simply a cracked recorder but it was better than nothing. Auguste had joined the others and contributed a brief pantomime of a bear chasing an elephant that brought in enough coins to buy Thomas some hot soup to cheer his supper.

Finally Astair, holding Auguste by the hand as though he were a child, led him to the back of the theatre.

"This is where I went in." She turned the doorknob very slowly to avoid any squeaking and peered in, then closed the door as cautiously. "The guard is there tonight. We can't get in." She guided Auguste around the block to the front entrance. "Now you've seen the whole building. All except the best," she added. "Maybe some other time we'll have better luck. Come on. My toes are frozen—they may drop off when I remove my shoes."

She laughed and skipped to the corner, but when she looked back she saw that Auguste was standing, seemingly enchanted, gazing up at the billboards announcing something she couldn't read.

She whistled twice but he only glanced at her and then returned to studying the large, printed letters. She shrugged and left him to himself.

She could never know why the name, Le Théâtre Maritain,[1] had sent the boy's mind shuttling backwards to a far ago memory. The same name was printed on a yellowed, forgotten theatre program, shown to him by the only person he had ever been given the chance to love. Nor could she know that this was the end of his quest. Auguste focused on one, sole desire. He must enter this place. Now. The memories could come later.

He raced to the back entry and without caution or caring let himself in, forgetting the threat of the guard. He stood watching the workers, who were intent on setting up the scenery. He had forgotten the cold of the world outside as he became absorbed in the crisscrossing of the people in front of him, each one moving purposefully, stirring the musty air as they passed him. He might have been a shadow pressed against the scarred wall.

Ahead of him on the lighted stage three boys who seemed about his age were grouped around a tall, gray-bearded man who was demonstrating to them a series of movements, aggressive advances and retreats.

"But Monsieur[2] Bernard," said the one with the widest shoulders and curling, yellow hair, "that's just what I was doing."

"No, Philippe, you were not. You were dancing the action, not acting," the teacher replied. "Let's try it again, more forcefully."

Unaware that he had left the protection of the wall, Auguste moved up to the inner edge of the open curtain, half concealed by its thick folds. As he watched the mime, he felt the fatigue leave his body and he memorized the boy's movements.

"No," sighed Monsieur Bernard. "It's still not what I want. Take it from where your squires arrive. Jean-Louis, Raymond, you are in distress. Show it."

Something—the long line of the director's jaw, the delicate hollows at his temples, or was it the faint lines of sorrow around his mouth? —something thrust Auguste back to another time and an aching sadness.

He saw himself, Auguste, unwanted, orphaned, in the presence of the old man who had once been the greatest mime in France. He saw Hercule Hilaire,[3] who had loved him, taught

[1]Le Théâtre Maritain (lə tā ä′ trə mä rē tang′)
[2]Monsieur (moo sēər)
[3]Hercule Hilaire (ār kyool′ ē lār)

him, then left him in death. He recognized that this new teacher and Monsieur Hilaire shared the same gift. Auguste wished urgently to touch the transposed image of his dead master, to know the man was real. He took two steps forward.

Sudden pain gripped him. Someone loomed before him. He tried to twist free of the fingers that squeezed his shoulder muscles. Then a hoarse voice filled his ears.

"How did you get in here, you dirty little street rat? Came to steal, did you? Well, I'll soon rid the place of you!"

He took Auguste and pushed him to the floor.

The man had raised one foot as if to kick him when the other one called out, "Stop that, Bragge! Enough!"

Glancing up at Monsieur Bernard, Auguste impulsively reached out his hand and laid his forefinger on the felt toe of the man's shoe. Then he got to his feet. He waited.

"Want me to throw him out?" said the boy he now recognized as the one named Philippe. Two others were grinning behind him.

"Let him speak for himself," Monsieur Bernard said. "He may have business here in the theatre."

Philippe started to guffaw but was immediately silenced by the severity of his teacher's glance. "Not likely," the boy muttered.

The man who had found him joined in. "My goodness, Bernard, you'd have every stray in Paris adopted and dressed like a lord if you had your way. That's your trouble. You're soft."

"That is as may be," said the master mime, his gaze steady on the boy in front of him. "You give the child no chance to answer. Come, don't be afraid. Tell us who you are and what you are doing here."

Auguste felt wonder at the closeness as he and Monsieur Bernard stood together in a kind of private silence. Philippe jeered, "Maybe his brains are missing," but it did not jar the communication between them.

Then Monsieur Bernard turned to Bragge and the three boys. He said, very slowly, as though he were himself surprised to know it, "The boy can't talk. He is a mute."

"So what?" said Bragge. "I'm the manager of a theatre, not a philanthropist, and he's cluttered up my stage." He pushed Auguste towards the door. "You know where you came in. Now take the same way out!"

"No, wait." It was Monsieur Bernard. "I want to talk to the boy after rehearsal. Then he can go."

Bragge shrugged. "As you please. Just so he doesn't get into the dressing rooms or the offices. I'll hold you responsible."

Behind Monsieur Bernard's back Jean-Louis, stout, and blunt-featured in contrast to Raymond, who was slender, waggled his protruding tongue at Auguste. Raymond imitated his companion. Philippe showed his dislike for the intruder by a grimace of scorn.

Monsieur Bernard clapped his hands together and called out, "Places, please. We've work to do."

Auguste seated himself on the floor, once more in the shelter of the curtain. This had been the world of his beloved master. Hercule Hilaire had known this very stage. He shut his eyes for a moment and behind his lids formed the arch above him. The deep red curtain was closed now, the footlights restoring a rich luster to the folds of worn velvet. Alone before the curtain, facing the filled theatre, the gilt-edged boxes, the balcony that almost nudged the ceiling where painted cherubim circled the great crystal chandelier, stood his dead master, bowing his acknowledgment of unending applause.

Auguste was so locked into his vision he got up and moved backwards into the left wing, ready to embrace the reality of this beloved ghost. He collided with someone.

"That's enough!" growled the voice of Monsieur Bragge, the manager. "Out you go!"

He pushed the boy ahead until he reached the backstage door and flung him down the short flight of steps that touched the street. "And that's just a warning! Come back and I'll have your hide!" The door slammed on the light and the warmth within.

As Auguste walked slowly home, unaware of the night wind that stalked him, the threats were forgotten. Only the theatre lived in his mind, and the image of the teacher.

The next morning he woke early and went to see Astair. For the first time since coming to Paris, he began the routine of exercises given him long ago by the master mime, who had shown him how his body could speak for him, be his voice.

Astair's dingy room was filled with motion so graceful even the grayed light from the window seemed bright.

She waited until Auguste had finished, then got up and went to her cupboard. "That deserves a can of spaghetti," she said. "Been saving it for something special." She looked at her guest intently. "There was a moment just now when I wondered if you were real or if I had made you up. But I don't have enough imagination for that, not nearly."

Auguste stood smiling at her as she punctured the top of the can, poured the contents into a saucepan, and set it over the Sterno. When it was bubbling she scooped it all out onto a single dish. "We'll have to share. My butler smashed the others just last week and I had to fire him." She handed the boy a battered spoon and the two of them soon scraped the plate clean.

Astair licked the smudges of tomato from the corners of her mouth and put on her jacket that was so much too big for her it looked like sacking. "Told the boys we'd meet them at the bird market. Come on."

She went out and Auguste hurried after her.

"Funny thing about that market," she chatted as they strode through a network of streets toward the river. "The people who stop to watch the birds seem gentler than most, maybe because they want something to love, something small and soft. You'll see."

The market announced itself before it came in sight. A cloud of chittering and cheeping and warbling hung over the block of cages and crates, and when Astair led him into the center of it, Auguste opened his own mouth as if he were compelled to sing with them, even silently.

At that instant they were surrounded.

"*Bonjour, Comtesse,*[4]" said Jerome.

"How goes it?" asked Francois. "Ready to serenade the money spenders?"

"Hope you don't mean the birds," said Thomas, hopping like a canary to keep warm.

[4]Bonjour, Comtesse (bōng zhōōr' cōng tes')

"Not unless birdseed has suddenly turned into gold," countered Francois.

"What shall we give them?" asked Astair.

For reply Thomas drew out his harmonica and began a flurry of staccato notes that seemed to mock the birds. Francois picked up the cue and, bowing to the one person near them, leaped into a tap dance to match the rhythm of Thomas's notes. Six onlookers paused on their way to work, then eight more. When the act was over the group had collected enough coins to buy breakfast at a cheap cafe. The coffee was left over from the night before, but it was hot.

Jerome sat back in his chair, his eyes grave. "Listen, friends, I've something to say. It's about him," and he nodded at Auguste.

"It's all very well to be charitable, to help others, all that Sunday stuff they tell you about over there." He jerked his thumb toward the cathedral on the south side of the square. "But I don't believe in getting thin while another gets fat."

Immediately interpreting his meaning, everyone looked at Auguste.

"Just a minute!" Astair's protest was vehement. "He did all right yesterday with the jig!"

"That's true," said Jerome, "but he couldn't finish. Nobody wants to see someone faint before their eyes. Too depressing. Keeps their hands out of their wallets."

Astair seemed to recognize the truth of what Jerome was saying, and she took a moment to search for a solution. Auguste mustn't be thrown out into the streets again. He wouldn't survive. But of what use was he to anyone? Unless—

"Give him a second chance. Come on—be fair. Francois?"

Francois nodded. "Just one more."

"Thomas?"

He also consented.

"Jerome?"

Jerome stared directly at Auguste. "You think you can make it?"

In answer Auguste got up and stood in the doorway. He waited.

"All right," said Jerome. "Let's see you prove it."

At Astair's suggestion they took the corner to the right of the cathedral. From long experience they knew that there would soon be an exodus from the morning mass.

"Need some music?" asked Thomas, wanting to help. He knew how he would feel if he were thrust out of the group.

Auguste shook his head.

"Just making it harder for yourself," advised Francois. "They like tunes."

Auguste did not respond. He gestured them back and then, as if inscribing a circle around himself with one turn, his arms outstretched, he performed what he had seen in the theatre, what the boy Philippe had failed to do. He mimed exactly what Monsieur Bernard had asked for. From a crouch close to the ground, defeat demonstrated in every line of his body, he gradually, inch by inch, began to rise from the cobblestones, and as

he rose his movements quickened, his arms seemed to become wings, his head lifted as if to search the sky for passage. And then he leaped, once, twice, and a third time. Those who watched held their breaths. He was going to fly!

Auguste vanished into the crowd that had gathered.

There was silence, then applause. A man called out, "Come back!"

"Where did he go?"

"Who is he?"

Thomas had already taken off his cap to circulate it among the clapping people. The contributions were so heavy he had to hold on to the cap with both hands.

Astair hugged Jerome, who hugged Francois, who was shouting "Bravo!"

But Auguste was gone.

At last the audience gave up and went about their own affairs.

Jerome was about to start a search when they were approached by a very tall, aristocratic man in a cape. "Tell your friend that I must speak to him," he said.

Astair gasped. "But I know you. You're Monsieur Bernard and your housekeeper is Madame Louva and I work for her sometimes and you run that school and last night I took Auguste to your theatre."

The gentleman smiled and touched his forefinger to his mouth. "Hush, child. All that may be true and I'll not say it is uninteresting but I must talk to that boy, the one who flew into the clouds."

"You're going to make trouble for him, is that it?" asked Jerome, now so relieved at Auguste's success he was ready to defend him right to the gate of any prison.

"Trouble?" The man frowned. "Is that what you imagine? Goodness, no! I want him in my school!"

"But he hasn't any money," said Astair.

"Oh? Well, I wasn't thinking of money, though poor Madame Louva would have to stretch her budget if I gave her another mouth to feed."

"Oh, no, sir! Not really!" Astair flushed with a sudden solution. "You see, I do things for Madame Louva, and if you'd take Auguste into your school I'd give up doing errands for her and let him do them instead."

"I'm becoming a bit confused," said Monsieur Bernard, "but I'm certain my housekeeper will work something out. She always does. But what are we standing about for? Get that boy for me."

Before any of them could so much as turn to look around, Auguste appeared.

"Where were you?" demanded Jerome.

Monsieur Bernard made a gesture, brushing aside the question. Then he placed his hand on Auguste's shoulder. "I want you to come to my house at precisely eleven tonight. I will be back from the theatre by then and waiting. Knock softly. The rest of the household will be asleep. I will let you in and show you to your room. In the morning you will make the acquaintance of Madame Louva and the others. Agreed?"

Auguste blinked very rapidly as he nodded his head. His throat was tight with tears.

Monsieur Bernard reached into his pocket and drew out a large bill. He handed it to Astair. "This will buy all of you a good dinner, though I will be scolded for my generosity." He shook hands with each of them, and when he came to Auguste he smiled and said, "Thank you, my child, for your performance. We'll talk later."

Their dinner that evening was a feast with roast chicken, fried potatoes, salad and cheese and, last, two pastries apiece. But underneath their gaiety was a layer of sadness that Astair expressed for them all. "We'll miss you," she said. "We'll miss you a lot."

So when the last of the food was eaten they trooped out of the cafe-restaurant, separating with many reassurances to Auguste that they would see him again soon.

But Astair wasn't so sure. As she left him at the front door of the Ecole[5] Bernard she felt lonely. She wanted to kiss him on both cheeks to show how she felt, but there was distance between them now, as though he had already gone down a road she couldn't travel. So it was with a handshake and a "*Bonsoir*"[6] that they said good-bye. Then Auguste knocked at the door of Ecole Bernard. The door opened and he stepped through it and away.

[5]Ecole (ā kōl')
[6]Bonsoir (bōng swar')

♦ LIBRARY LINK ♦

*You might like to read the entire book,* The Silent Voice *by Julia Cunningham, to find out what happens to Auguste when he becomes a student at Ecole Bernard.*

## *Reader's Response*

What did you learn from reading Auguste's story of courage and determination?

## Thinking It Over

1. Why did the name Le Théâtre Maritain mean so much to Auguste?
2. Explain why Auguste felt an aching sadness when he first saw Monsieur Bernard in rehearsal.
3. Find two or three details from the story that show the kind of person Monsieur Bernard was. How did you go about selecting these details?
4. Why did Jerome want Auguste to leave the group?
5. Why do you think Auguste was able to mime so successfully at the bird market?
6. If Monsieur Bernard had not invited Auguste to live with him, what other ending might there have been for the story?

## Appreciating Literature

A *symbol* is anything that stands for or represents something else. For example, a river may symbolize a person's journey through life. In this story, how does the closing image of Auguste stepping through an open door symbolize what is happening to him?

## Writing to Learn

**Think and Imagine** What might have happened to Auguste after he knocked at the door of Ecole Bernard? Imagine that five years later, Astair wrote him a letter. Read the beginning of the letter.

**Write** Imagine that you are Astair, and finish the letter. Try to suggest what may have happened to Auguste.

# Print, Stage, and Song

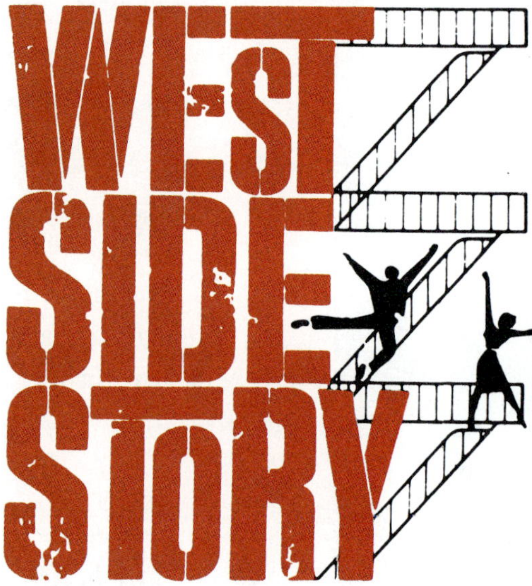


The captivating musical *West Side Story* is based on *Romeo and Juliet.*

If someone mentioned William Shakespeare, one of the last things you would think about would be disputes among youths in New York City. In fact, though, the musical play *West Side Story* is based on Shakespeare's great drama *Romeo and Juliet*. Ever since *West Side Story* was produced on Broadway in 1957 and then as an Academy Award-winning movie in 1961, it has been one of the most popular musicals every made. It remains popular as a videocassette.

Shakespeare is far from being the only author whose works have inspired other artists. Film directors, producers of musical plays, and composers have all turned frequently to classics of literature for ideas. In these classics they have found powerful stories and memorable characters.

Scene from *Porgy and Bess.*

The American composer George Gershwin, for example, based his famous opera, *Porgy and Bess*, on the novel *Porgy* by Dubose Heyward. That book is about life in a small black community. A story about the love of a poor, disabled man for a beautiful woman who could not return his love may not sound like the subject for an opera, but Gershwin was very moved by the story. To make it into an opera, he had to express the entire

Tchaikovsky wrote the *Nutcracker* ballet from a story by E. T. Hoffman called "Nutcracker."

***Certain stories are so powerful that they are used over and over again.***

novel in music, since operas have no spoken words. The result was one of the most profoundly American works of music.

There are certain writers whose stories are so powerful that they are used over and over again. One such writer is Charles Dickens. His *Oliver Twist*, for instance, has been successfully adapted into both a play and a film. The musical play *Oliver!* enjoyed a long run on Broadway. One of its songs, "Food, Glorious Food," has become a part of American popular culture.

Another such writer is Mark Twain. His novel *The Adventures of Huckleberry Finn* was the source of the musical play *Big River*. There are a number of differences between the book and the play, because each genre imposes its own requirements on a story. Many events and characters from the book don't appear in the musical version. However, the growing friendship between Huck and Jim is still central to the musical—as it was central to the novel.

The musical *Cats* is based on *Old Possum's Book of Practical Cats* by T. S. Eliot.

Knowing the original version of a play or a musical gives another dimension to your enjoyment of the version you are seeing.

***If you want to read a book that has been made into a musical, a movie, or a play, ask your librarian for assistance. The librarian can help you use the card catalog to find the original source, the script, or the musical score.***

TIME OUT FOR BOOKS

Newbery Medal 1944

Best Books for Children

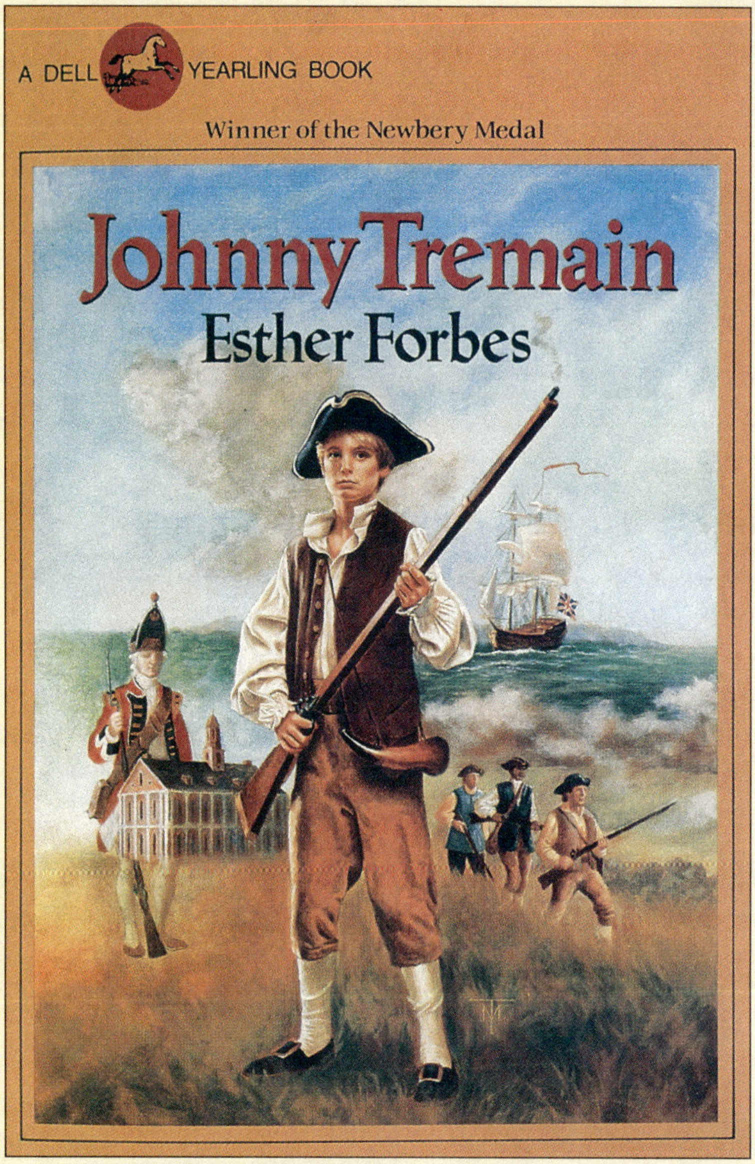


# "*A* man can stand up…"

from *Johnny Tremain* by Esther Forbes

What might have caused an ordinary teenager to become involved in the events leading to the Revolutionary War? People today can never know how it felt to live then. But one way you can begin to imagine life in those trying times is to read vibrant and accurately written stories like *Johnny Tremain*. Esther Forbes, the author, presents a gripping novel based on historical events.

*Johnny Tremain* is a story about a sixteen-year-old boy in Boston at the beginning of the Revolutionary War. Johnny dreams of becoming a great silversmith, but his artistic hopes are cut short by an unfortunate accident. He becomes bitter and self-absorbed. However, these personal problems must be put aside for a more urgent cause—his personal freedom and his nation's survival, without which nothing else matters. He describes himself as "a boy in time of peace and a man in time of war."

As you read *Johnny Tremain*, try to imagine yourself as a teenager living in Colonial America. Would you be able to put aside your dreams for something greater?

# SOMEDAY

by Isaac Asimov

*Long ago, bards sang and told stories. The bard in this story is a twentieth-century computer. He, too, tells stories, until one day . . .*

Niccolo Mazetti lay stomach down on the rug, chin buried in the palm of one small hand, and listened to the Bard disconsolately. There was even the suspicion of tears in his dark eyes, a luxury an eleven-year-old could allow himself only when alone.

The Bard said, "Once upon a time in the middle of a deep wood, there lived a poor woodcutter and his two motherless daughters, who were each as beautiful as the day is long. The older daughter had long hair as black as a feather from a raven's wing, but the younger daughter had hair as bright and golden as the sunlight of an autumn afternoon.

"Many times while the girls were waiting for their father to come home from his day's work in the wood, the older girl would sit before a mirror and sing—"

Reading CORNER

What she sang, Niccolo did not hear, for a call sounded from outside the room: "Hey, Nickie."

And Niccolo, his face clearing on the moment, rushed to the window and shouted, "Hey, Paul."

Paul Loeb waved an excited hand. He was thinner than Niccolo and not as tall, for all he was six months older. His face was full of repressed tension which showed itself most clearly in the rapid blinking of his eyelids. "Hey, Nickie, let me in. I've got an idea and a *half*. Wait till you hear it." He looked rapidly about him as though to check on the possibility of eavesdroppers, but the front yard was quite patently empty. He repeated, in a whisper, "Wait till you hear it."

"All right. I'll open the door."

The Bard continued smoothly, oblivious to the sudden loss of attention on the part of Niccolo. As Paul entered, the Bard was saying, ". . . Thereupon, the lion said, 'If you will find me the lost egg of the bird which flies over the Ebony Mountain once every ten years, I will—' "

Paul said, "Is that a Bard you're listening to? I didn't know you had one."

Niccolo reddened and the look of unhappiness returned to his face. "Just an old thing I had when I was a kid. It's not much good." He kicked at the Bard with his foot and caught the somewhat scarred and discolored plastic covering a glancing blow.

The Bard hiccupped as its speaking attachment was jarred out of contact a moment, then it went on: "—for a year and a day until the iron shoes were worn out. The princess stopped at the side of the road. . . ."

Paul said, "Boy, that *is* an old model," and looked at it critically.

Despite Niccolo's own bitterness against the Bard, he winced at the other's condescending tone. For the moment, he was sorry he had allowed Paul in, at least before he had restored the Bard to its usual resting place in the basement. It was only in the desperation of a dull day and a fruitless discussion with his father that he had resurrected it. And it turned out to be just as stupid as he had expected.

Nickie was a little afraid of Paul anyway, since Paul had special courses at school and everyone said he was going to grow up to be a Computing Engineer.

Not that Niccolo himself was doing badly at school. He got adequate marks in logic, binary manipulations, computing and elementary circuits; all the usual grammar school subjects. But that was it! They were just the usual subjects and he would grow up to be a control-board guard like everyone else.

Paul, however, knew mysterious things about what he called electronics and theoretical mathematics and programming. Especially programming. Niccolo didn't even try to understand when Paul bubbled over about it.

Paul listened to the Bard for a few minutes and said, "Have you been using it much?"

"No!" said Niccolo, offended. "I've had it in the basement since before you moved into the neighborhood. I just got it out today—" He lacked an excuse that seemed adequate to himself, so he concluded, "I just got it out."

Paul said, "Is that what it tells you about: woodcutters and princesses and talking animals?"

Niccolo said, "It's terrible. My dad says we can't afford a new one. I said to him this morning—" The memory of the morning's fruitless pleadings brought Niccolo dangerously near tears, which he repressed in a panic. Somehow, he felt that Paul's pink cheeks never felt the stain of tears and that Paul would have only contempt for anyone else less strong than himself. Niccolo went on, "So I thought I'd try this old thing again, but it's no good."

Paul turned off the Bard, pressed the contact that led to a nearly instantaneous reorientation and recombination of the vocabulary, characters, plot lines, and climaxes stored within it. Then he reactivated it.

The Bard began smoothly, "Once upon a time there was

a little boy named Willikins whose mother had died and who lived with a stepfather and a stepbrother. Although the stepfather was very well-to-do, he begrudged poor Willikins the very bed he slept in so that Willikins was forced to get such rest as he could on a pile of straw in the stable next to the horses—"

"Horses!" cried Paul.

"They're a kind of animal," said Niccolo. "I think."

"I know that! I mean imagine stories about *horses.*"

"It tells about horses all the time," said Niccolo. "There are things called cows, too. You milk them but the Bard doesn't say how."

"Well, gee, why don't you fix it up?"

"I'd like to know how."

The Bard was saying, "Often Willikins would think that if only he were rich and powerful, he would show his stepfather and stepbrother what it meant to be cruel to a little boy, so one day he decided to go out into the world and seek his fortune."

Paul, who wasn't listening to the Bard, said, "It's *easy.* The Bard has memory cylinders all fixed up for plot lines and climaxes and things. We don't have to worry about that. It's just vocabulary we've got to fix so it'll know about computers and automation and electronics and real things about today. Then it can tell interesting stories, you know, instead of about princesses and things."

Niccolo said despondently, "I wish we could do that."

Paul said, "Listen, my dad says if I get into special computing school next year, he'll get me a *real* Bard, a late model. A big one with an attachment for space stories and mysteries. And a visual attachment, too!"

"You mean *see* the stories?"

"Sure. Mr. Daugherty at school says they've got things like that, now, but not for just everybody. Only if I get into computing school, Dad can get a few breaks."

Niccolo's eyes bulged with envy. "Gee. *Seeing* a story."

"You can come over and watch any time, Nickie."

"Oh, boy. Thanks."

"That's all right. But remember, I'm the guy who says what kind of story we hear."

"Sure. Sure." Niccolo would have agreed readily to much more onerous conditions.

Paul's attention returned to the Bard.

It was saying, " 'If that is the case,' said the king, stroking his beard and frowning till clouds filled the sky and lightning flashed, 'you will see to it that my entire land is freed of flies by this time day after tomorrow or—' "

"All we've got to do," said Paul, "is open it up—" He shut the Bard off again and was prying at its front panel as he spoke.

"Hey," said Niccolo, in sudden alarm. "Don't break it."

"I won't break it," said Paul impatiently. "I know all about these things." Then, with sudden caution, "Your father and mother home?"

"No."

"All right, then." He had the front panel off and peered in. "Boy, this *is* a one-cylinder thing."

He worked away at the Bard's innards. Niccolo, who watched with painful suspense, could not make out what he was doing.

Paul pulled out a thin, flexible metal strip, powdered with dots. "That's the Bard's memory cylinder. I'll bet its capacity for stories is under a trillion."

"What are you going to do, Paul?" quavered Niccolo.

"I'll give it vocabulary."

"How?"

"Easy. I've got a book here. Mr. Daugherty gave it to me at school."

Paul pulled the book out of his pocket and pried at it till he had its plastic jacket off. He unreeled the tape a bit, ran it through the vocalizer, which he turned down to a whisper, then placed it within the Bard's vitals. He made further attachments.

"What'll that do?"

"The book will talk and the Bard will put it all on its memory tape."

"What good will that do?"

"Boy, you're silly! This book is all about computers and automation and the Bard will get all that information. Then he can stop talking about kings making lightning when they frown."

Niccolo said, "And the good guy always wins anyway. There's no excitement."

"Oh, well," said Paul, watching to see if his setup was working properly, "that's the way they make Bards. They've got to have the good guy win and make the bad guys lose and things like that. I heard my father talking about it once. He says that without censorship there'd be no telling what the younger generation would come to. He says it's bad enough as it is. . . . There, it's working fine."

Paul brushed his hands against one another and turned away from the Bard. He said, "But listen, I didn't tell you my idea yet. It's the best thing you ever heard, I bet. I came right to you, because I figured you'd come in with me."

"Sure, Paul, sure."

"Okay. You know Mr. Daugherty at school? "

"Sure, I know him."

"He says I'm going to be entering computer school and he wants to encourage me and things like that. He says the world needs more people who design advanced computer circuits and do proper programming."

"Oh?"

Paul might have caught some of the emptiness behind that monosyllable. He said impatiently, "Programming! I told you a hundred times. That's when you set up problems for the giant computers like Multivac to work on. Mr. Daugherty says it gets harder all the time to find people who can really run computers. He says anyone can keep an eye on the controls and check off answers and put through routine problems. He says the trick is to expand research and figure out ways to ask the right questions, and that's hard.

"Anyway, Nickie, he showed me his collection of old computers. It's kind of a hobby of his to collect old computers. He had a tiny computer you had to push with your hand, with little knobs all over it. And he had a hunk of wood he called a slide rule with a little piece of it that went in and out. And some wires with balls on them. He even had a hunk of paper with a kind of thing he called a multiplication table."

Niccolo, who found himself only moderately interested, said, "A paper table?"

"It wasn't really a table like you eat on. It was different. It was to help people compute. Mr. Daugherty tried to explain but he didn't have much time and it was kind of complicated anyway."

"Why didn't people just use a computer?"

"That was before they had computers," cried Paul.

"Before?"

"Sure. Do you think people always had computers? Didn't you ever hear of cavemen?"

Niccolo said, "How'd they get along without computers?"

"I don't know. Mr. Daugherty says they just did anything that came into their heads whether it would be good for everybody or not. They didn't even know if it was good or not. And farmers grew things with their hands and people had to do all the work in the factories and run all the machines."

"I don't believe you."

"That's what Mr. Daugherty said. He said it was just plain messy and everyone was miserable. . . . Anyway, let me get to my idea, will you?"

"Well, go ahead. Who's stopping you?" said Niccolo, offended.

"All right. Well, the hand computers, the ones with the knobs, had little squiggles on each knob. And the slide rule had squiggles on it. And the multiplication table was all squiggles. I asked what they were. Mr. Daugherty said they were numbers."

"What?"

"Each different squiggle stood for a different number. For 'one' you made a kind of mark, for 'two' you make another kind of mark, for 'three' another one and so on."

"What for?"

"So you could compute."

"What for? You just tell the computer—"

"Jiminy," cried Paul, his face twisting with anger, "can't you get it through your head? These slide rules and things didn't talk."

"Then how—"

"The answers showed up in squiggles and you had to know what the squiggles meant. Mr. Daugherty says that, in the olden days, everybody learned how to make squiggles when they were kids and how to decode them, too. Making squiggles was called 'writing' and decoding them was 'reading.' He says there was a different kind of squiggle for every word and they used to write whole books in squiggles. He said they had some at the museum and I could look at them if I wanted to. He said if I was going to be a real computer programmer I would have to know about the history of computing and that's why he was showing me all these things."

Niccolo frowned. He said, "You mean everybody had to figure out squiggles for every word and remember them? . . . Is this all real or are you making it up?"

"It's all real. Honest. Look, this is the way you make a 'one.' " He drew his finger through the air in a rapid downstroke. "This way you make 'two,' and this way 'three.' I learned all the numbers up to 'nine.' "

Niccolo watched the curving finger uncomprehendingly. "What's the good of it?"

"You can learn how to make words. I asked Mr. Daugherty how you made the squiggle for 'Paul Loeb' but he didn't know. He said there were people at the museum who would know. He said there were people who had learned how to decode whole books. He said computers could be designed to decode books

# BOOKS TO ENJOY

***The Way of the Storyteller*** by Ruth Sawyer *(Penguin, 1976)* Drawing upon her own background, the author gives a lively account of her development as a storyteller, as well as practical suggestions for the novice.

***The Sword and the Circle*** by Rosemary Sutcliff *(Dutton, 1981).* The author recounts the fantastic adventures of King Arthur and the Knights of the Round Table, based chiefly on Sir Thomas Malory's *Morte d'Arthur.*

***Sweet and Sour—Tales from China*** retold by Carol Kendall and Yao-wen Li *(Seabury, 1978)* These ancient folk tales are filled with wisdom, wit, and humor.

***The People Could Fly*** by Virginia Hamilton *(Knopf, 1985)* This retelling of twenty-four Black American folk tales includes animal tales, tall tales, fantasy, and tales of freedom, including true slave narratives.

***Dragons and Dreams*** edited by Jane Yolen, Martin H. Greenberg, and Charles G. Waugh *(Harper, 1986)* Here is a collection of ten stories, both fantasy and science fiction, that are fun to read and full of surprises.

UNIT TWO

# When Buffalo Roamed

*Going west has been the American dream.*

*Why has the West captured people's imaginations?*

*detail of* PROSPECTING FOR CATTLE RANGE, *oil on canvas by Frederic Remington, American, 1889*

# SAYING Goodbye

by Marilyn Cram Donahue

*In the mid-1800s, thousands of people traveled vest in search of a better life. Yet the decision to embark on this exciting journey was never an easy one.*

That very afternoon Luanna Hamilton had to go tell Miss Wilson her school plans had changed. It was only fitting, her mother told her, when Miss Wilson had gone to so much trouble for her. Luanna found the teacher in the schoolhouse, dusting and cleaning the one big room, getting ready for opening day.

"Luanna—what a nice surprise! Are you excited about starting at the academy?"

"I—I was, but not anymore. Oh, Miss Wilson, Pa says we're going to California in the spring."

Miss Wilson's smile faded and disappeared. "Are you sure? I mean, is it definite?"

Luanna nodded. "I don't want to go. Pa says it's not the end of the world, but it is for mc. Oh, Miss Wilson, I'd do anything to stay here in Midford Falls."

Miss Wilson put her arm around Luanna's shoulders. "What a waste," she murmured. "What a terrible waste."

It was even worse when Luanna told her friend Nancy, who started to cry and wouldn't stop. "What will I do without you?" she sobbed. "Nothing will ever be the same again."

Nobody had to tell Luanna that—or that it was a wilderness out West. But Nancy did. And then she said a very strange thing. "I—I wish I was going with you, Lu."

There was no figuring people out, Luanna decided. They all seemed to want what they couldn't get. She walked along the dusty path that wound through a field of red clover and was the shortest route home from the Addison farm. She stopped along the way to pick a dandelion puff and blow the little seeds to kingdom come. But she didn't make a wish. There didn't seem to be any use.

She was almost home when she heard the voice. There was no mistaking the sound of Aunt Prue. She sounded for all the world like a crow. Luanna rounded the last curve where the path went through a stand of tamarack trees and ended at the side of the vegetable garden near the back door.

"Well, there's Luanny," Aunt Prue shrieked. "Pick up your feet, girl, and you won't raise so much dust when you walk."

Luanna sighed. They had come early again. Aunt Prue always claimed it gave them a few extra days to visit, but Luanna knew it was because she liked to come upon people unawares. Luanna had seen her slip into the parlor and run her finger over the back of a chair. She was always looking for somebody else's dust, and never happy unless she found some.

The next two weeks were long ones. When Aunt Prue found out about California, she pointed her finger right under Mrs. Hamilton's nose. "If my Fisk started talking foolish, I'd put a stop to it right off."

"That's the difference between you and me, Prue. I don't think Daniel talks foolish."

That stopped Aunt Prue for a minute, but only until she realized that she was going to have Great-aunt Clara full time. "I don't know how I'll manage," she complained. "After all, Rebecca, my house isn't near as roomy as yours." She stopped short. "But you won't be needing this big house any longer, will you?" Luanna thought her eyes began to gleam right then.

She must have gone to work on Uncle Fisk that very day. The first thing anybody knew, he was offering to sell out at Vergennes and buy Mr. Hamilton's cooperage as well as the house and farm. They would move down here in the spring and take right over.

"Isn't it lucky?" Aunt Prue crowed. "Things are working out dandy for everyone."

Not everyone, Luanna thought. And she wasn't the only one who felt that way. Late one night, after all the company had left, she heard voices in the parlor and crept to the stairs to listen.

She knew she was eavesdropping, but the old rules didn't seem to count for much these days.

"Prue dresses fancy and thinks big," her mother was saying, "but she's common, Daniel. I won't have that woman living in my house."

"Rebecca." His voice was gentle. "It won't be your house when she's living in it."

Luanna felt as if someone had pulled a rug out from under her and sent her spinning. Even when she knew Aunt Prue would be living here after they were gone, she had never thought of this as Aunt Prue's house. The voices went on, but Luanna couldn't stand to hear another word.

She crept to her bed and pulled the covers over her ears. *Won't be your house . . . won't be your house. . . .* In a few months, this wouldn't be Luanna's house either. Then where would home be? Not one of these wagons her father was building. She squeezed her eyes shut. Never, never would she call a wagon home!

Just before school started in September, Miss Wilson came to call. Mrs. Hamilton took her into the parlor, and Luanna's father went in after them, closing the door behind him. Luanna didn't even hesitate. She put her ear close to the crack the way she had seen her brother Ben do, and listened.

"If you would let her stay with me for a year or two—" Miss Wilson was saying.

Mr. Hamilton didn't even let her finish. He cleared his throat the way he always did when he was about to say something final. "I know you mean well, Miss Wilson, but Luanna is my daughter. I don't intend leaving her behind."

"Then won't you at least let her start school next week and continue her studies until spring?"

"The academy is expensive. I'm afraid we're going to need all the cash we can save."

"Is that your final word, Mr. Hamilton?"

"It is."

"Then I have one last request. Will you allow me to gather together some lessons for Luanna? A few things she can read and study along the way—some books, perhaps, that will—"

"Books are expensive, Miss Wilson. Luanna can't possibly accept such a—"

"Of course she can." It was her mother's voice. "We're grateful to you, Miss Wilson, for your thoughtfulness. Luanna will be, too."

Luanna's mother did that sometimes—stepped in just in time when her father was about to say no. But she never did it unless it really mattered. And when she did, Mr. Hamilton let her have her say.

So Miss Wilson brought the books and Luanna packed them carefully away. There were pens, too, and two bottles of ink and a thick package of paper, just like they used over at the academy. Luanna held the paper, feeling it with her fingers, then packed it away too, remembering that school had started this year without her.

One afternoon the stage brought the news that California had become a state. It had happened on September 9, 1850, but when word came to Midford Falls the following month, you would have thought it was another Fourth of July, the way Luanna's brothers carried on, hopping up and down and cheering as if they'd won a war. "At least you won't be leaving the country, Lu," Nancy told her. Sometimes Luanna thought Nancy was missing the whole point.

When Thanksgiving came, Luanna couldn't see that there was much to be thankful for. Especially when Aunt Prue and Uncle Fisk made the trip from Vergennes to spend a week with them.

"Isn't this nice?" Aunt Prue exclaimed. "It gives me a chance to look around and see what I want to change. Rebecca, dear, you know you can't take all this with you. Let's go through the house together and decide what you want to leave."

"Humph!" said Aunt Clara. "Don't you have any manners at all, Prue?"

Luanna guessed her aunt didn't, and she was glad when Uncle Fisk finally took her home. Christmas was coming, and she didn't think she could stand to have Aunt Prue around for that. To her surprise, she found that Aunt Clara agreed with her.

"That woman," she snorted, "will be the death of me! I'd almost rather go to California than spend another day in her house." Luanna looked at her in surprise. "Almost," Aunt Clara snapped.

The winter brought heavy snowfalls, and the weather was icy cold. "The sun shines all the year round in California," her brother Nathaniel told her. Well, there was some merit to that, she thought, as she tried to thaw her frozen fingers by the fire. But not a lot.

She thought of the skating pond, the feel of stepping in fresh soft snow clear up to her knees, the crunch of it beneath her feet, the slipping and sliding down the hill above Long Meadow. She looked out the window at the lacy patterns of ice on the trees, and she thought she had never seen anything so beautiful.

But when she went to the mill pond to watch the men cut ice to store for the summer, she realized that her father was cutting it for Uncle Fisk and Aunt Prue. She stood there only a few minutes, then turned and walked away. There were parts of Midford Falls that weren't hers anymore. For the first time, she began to feel as if she didn't belong.

In January, Luanna turned fourteen. "It's my last birthday in Midford Falls," she told Nancy. "I just wish I could die right now so you could bury me here."

"Please don't talk like that, Lu. Look, I brought you a present." Nancy was holding a package wrapped in white paper. "Go on, open it."

It was a metal box with a hinged lid. It looked like a miniature trunk, and was about as large as the family Bible that lay on the table by the front window. Luanna lifted the latch and opened it. Inside were two crimson leaves that had been pressed flat, a small paperweight of polished red marble, and a rolled-up piece of paper tied with a bit of red ribbon saved from the Fourth of July.

"It's a memory box," Nancy told her. "The autumn leaves and red marble are to remind you of Midford Falls. You can add whatever you like, but you have to promise not to open the letter until you reach Illinois."

They were stopping in Illinois to spend the next winter. Then they would push on to Independence, Missouri, early in the spring and join a wagon train moving west. That way they wouldn't be greenhorns when they began the hardest part of the trip.

"We need some experience on the road," Mr. Hamilton explained. "We'll take it slow," he promised. "From Midford Falls to Illinois will seem like a vacation. Think of it, Rebecca, you won't have any housework to do."

Luanna's mother gave him a long look, but she didn't say a word. After that, whenever she dusted the furniture Luanna saw her run her fingers over each piece, slowly, lovingly. And Luanna knew that most of it was going to be left behind for Aunt Prue.

February came and went, and Aunt Clara stayed on. "There's plenty I can help with here," she said, "and I'll be living with Prue soon enough."

Luanna hated the way Aunt Clara bustled around all day, putting her nose where it didn't belong. Even in the evenings she sat there telling them what they should do.

Sugaring began the first week of March, and the air was sweet with the smell of maple sap cooking until the syrup thickened. Mrs. Hamilton boiled most of it down and poured it into wooden tubs to harden into sugar that they would take with them on the trip. But there was plenty of syrup left over to pour in swirling streams over clean white snow. Luanna and Nancy wound the sticky candy on flat, wooden spoons and ate it with sour pickles and fresh wheat doughnuts. Luanna wondered if she would ever taste anything that good again.

It seemed to her that they spent the whole long winter getting ready to leave. They made more soap than Luanna had ever seen. Tallow candles were dipped and packed away. When the cobbler came through town on his circuit, everybody got

shoes—sturdy ones that would stand some walking. Luanna hated them because the soles were pegged with wooden pegs and both feet were alike, but her father said they would be easy to mend on the trail.

There were clothes to be made—out of common homespun, which Luanna thought was ugly compared with the silks they could order from Boston. Mrs. Hamilton dyed her yarn with butternut bark instead of indigo, which was expensive. Pokeberry would have made a beautiful shade of vermilion, but Aunt Clara said butternut-dyed homespun was more practical for where they were going.

Spring seemed to arrive suddenly, and the wild passenger pigeons flew over Midford Falls like great clouds with beating wings. Luanna walked through the fields looking for the first red-winged blackbird, hunting for the first golden crocuses poking up out of thin patches of melting snow. She paid a last visit to the schoolhouse and the mill pond, and she walked around the green, passing her father's cooperage and the general store. One morning she stood on the old covered bridge listening to the sound of Otter Creek as it swelled and ran over its banks. In the afternoon, she and Nancy hiked past the sawmill and climbed the winding trail to the top of Snake Mountain. They could see the long sweep of Lake Champlain on the west with the Adirondacks beyond, and on the east were the Green Mountains.

"What's the matter with everybody, talking about room to see?" she asked Nancy. "We can see in Vermont, for pity's sake!"

Nancy sighed. "Oh, Lu, you're going to see so much more than this. I do wish I could go with you!"

"Don't say that!" Luanna told her. "You've got to stay here. If you were to leave, who would I come home to?"

Nancy stared at her. "Come home to?"

"Yes, I've made up my mind. Somehow I'm going to come back, even if I have to come all the way from California by myself. I can live with you, can't I?"

"Of course you can, Lu, but—"

"Don't you go *anywhere*, Nance. You're my only hope. Promise me right now that you'll be here when I come home."

"But—but what if it takes years and years?"

Luanna made an impatient face. "Don't worry, it won't. And when I come back, I'm going to stay forever."

As the weather warmed, the packing began. Trunks were filled, and decisions were made. Someone had to choose which books, and dishes, and mementoes, and furniture to leave behind. "I can't leave everything," Mrs. Hamilton moaned. "I have to take some part of civilization with me."

"I wish you'd leave me," Luanna muttered. She expected to be scolded and was surprised when her mother stopped what she was doing and put both arms around her and held her tight.

The two wagons were finished and canvas hoods were stretched high over bent hickory bows to make a tall, protective covering. They were sturdy-looking wagons with heavy sideboards, and the wheels were rimmed with iron. Luanna hated the sight of them and kept as far away from them as she could. "They make me feel awful," she confided to Nancy. "When I look at them, I can't pretend we're not going anymore."

Unfortunately, Aunt Clara heard her. "You're a very stubborn girl," she said. "It's a trait that may stand you in good stead on the trip. But you must learn that there are times when you have to give over and accept a situation you can't change."

Luanna glared at her and didn't answer, so Aunt Clara marched her out to the side yard and made her take a good long look at the wagons. "You'd better get acquainted," she said. "You're going to be seeing a lot of each other." Then she walked around each one, showing her where the butter churn would hang, where the water barrels were already strapped on, and where Mr. Hamilton's plow would be attached at the side of one wagon. "Everything that can't hang on the outside goes in here." Aunt Clara lifted a canvas flap and pointed to the wagon boxes. "All your furniture, clothes, and food. See where your ma sewed big pockets and such on the inside of the canvas so you can store more?"

Luanna sniffed. "There isn't enough room for all that and us, too. Where are we going to sit?"

Aunt Clara stared at her. "You have two good legs, don't you? You can right well walk!"

Luanna clamped her mouth shut tight. There wasn't any use telling Aunt Clara she was crazy. They'd be rid of her soon enough. It was about the only good thing Luanna could see about going to California. They would be leaving Aunt Clara behind, and Aunt Prue could deal with her sharp tongue forever and ever.

But that night at dinner, Aunt Clara made an announcement. "If you'll have me," she said, "I'm coming with you. This house won't be the same without all of you in it. I know I'm an old woman, but I'm strong, and I won't hold anybody back. Anyway, I'll likely live longer on the trail than sitting here listening to Prue."

Luanna's father smiled. "We'll be happy to have you," he said. "Won't we, everybody?"

Luanna was the only one who didn't say a word. She didn't trust herself to open her mouth.

At last the day came in early May when the roads were passable and the grass in the fields was green enough to feed the stock. "We'll load the wagons today," said Mr. Hamilton, "and start out first thing tomorrow morning."

Their extra eggs were packed in cornmeal, and thick slabs of bacon were layered in a barrel of bran. Heavy trunks and pieces of furniture went in the wagons first, and everything else had to fit around and on top of those. Food supplies and Mrs. Hamilton's Dutch oven had to be placed where they could be easily unpacked. At the last moment Luanna's mother decided to pack the cherrywood clock that sat on the mantel and the tea set with the moss rose design. Luanna knew it was because she couldn't bear the thought of Aunt Prue telling time by the one or drinking tea out of the other.

A seat was fixed for Aunt Clara in the back of one wagon. Luanna noticed with satisfaction that she would be packed in tight between the bacon and the beans. Maybe when she saw

how shc was going to have to travel, she'd change her mind and stay.

But she didn't. The next morning she climbed in all by herself, slapping Mr. Hamilton's hand when he tried to help her. Mrs. Hamilton swept out the parlor for the last time and closed the front door. She took one long look at the house, then turned away. Mr. Hamilton helped her onto the wagon seat. He had hitched three yoke of oxen to each wagon. Two cages of cackling chickens hung beneath each wagon bed. Luanna's brothers were herding a dozen bleating sheep and trying to keep an eye on Molly and Min, the milk cows. Two of their best horses were tethered to the back of the wagon where Aunt Clara was sitting. The boys climbed up on the seat of that wagon and waited. Aunt Clara had been right about one thing—Luanna was going to walk.

"Until you get tired," her mother had promised. Luanna intended to get tired very quickly.

"Well," Mr. Hamilton said, "I guess this is it. We're to meet the Douglases and the Crawfords out by the Low Pond south of town. Might as well get moving." He cracked his whip high over the animals' heads. "Gee! Haw!" he shouted. The oxen strained at their yokes, and the wagons moved slowly forward.

Luanna stood in the rising dust and looked around her. It was really happening. All her wishing hadn't stopped this day from coming. It seemed to her that her world stood still—her real world—Midford Falls. Only the wagons moved slowly away, leaving her behind.

"Luanna! Luanna!" It was Nancy, running through the tamarack trees into the clearing and around the side of the house. "Oh, Luanna, I had to come to say good-bye again."

Luanna felt Nancy's arms around her. She heard her voice. But none of it seemed real. "Look, Lu, I've brought you a diary. It's just a little one, but you can write in it every night. When you come back home, we can read it together! Oh . . . Lu!"

A tear from Nancy's cheek fell on Luanna's hand. It felt warm and wet. It felt real. This was good-bye, Luanna thought. There wasn't anything she could do to change it. Her own tears mixed with Nancy's. "I have to go now," she said softly. "But I'll be back, Nance. I'll be back someday."

She looked once at the house. It was Aunt Prue's house now. Then she turned and walked along the still-dusty road behind the wagons.

### ♦ Library Link ♦

*This story was taken from the book* Straight Along a Crooked Road *by Marilyn Cram Donahue. You might like to read the entire book to follow the Hamilton family on their journey west.*

## Reader's Response

If you had to leave your home and your community for a part of the world that you do not know, would you object? Explain your answer.

## *Thinking It Over*

1. Why do you think Luanna was opposed to moving?
2. What incident made Luanna realize for the first time that she no longer belonged in Midford Falls?
3. Why did Luanna make Nancy promise not to move?
4. Do you think Mrs. Hamilton wanted to move to California? Cite one example to prove your point.
5. Why do you think families like Luanna's moved west in the 1800s? What thought process did you go through to reach your conclusion?
6. Do you think Luanna kept her promise and returned to Midford Falls? Explain your response.

## *Appreciating Literature*

In this selection the author has chosen to tell the story through a third-person narrator, but the narrator tells only Luanna's thoughts, feelings, and observations. Think about the effect this limited point of view has on the reader. If Luanna herself were the narrator, what different effect might that have on the reader?

## *Writing to Learn*

**THINK AND DECIDE** The word list below is from a story that takes place in the mid-1880s. Brainstorm with a study partner and add other words that describe pioneer life.

**WRITE** Fill in a page in Luanna's diary. Tell about one day in her life as she travels west. If appropriate, use words from the list to make your account sound realistic.

Thinking ◆ Reading ◆ Writing

# Stepping into an Event

When you read historical writing, it's sometimes difficult to imagine or visualize the events being described. It can also be difficult to understand the importance of a historical event because history deals with the past—and the past can sometimes seem remote and unrelated to the concerns of our own day. To understand and appreciate history, it is important to be able to personalize it—to understand how people like you lived, to imagine how you would have felt and acted in the same circumstances, and to compare past times and events to your own life in the present time.

One way to personalize historical writing is to imagine that you are one of the participants in a historical event. By using your own experience and details from what you are reading, you can infer some of the feelings and thoughts of the actual participants in the event.

## *Learning the Strategy*

Read the following account of a historical event. Try to step into the event and imagine that you are Belle Boyd or one of the Union soldiers.

> When eighteen-year-old Belle Boyd, a spy for the Confederate army during the Civil War, found out about the Union army's plans to burn bridges during their retreat, she decided to alert the Confederate troops. In her memoirs, she wrote, "I did not stop to reflect...[but] started at a run down the street, which was thronged with Federal officers and men. I soon

cleared the town and gained the open fields." Union troops opened fire and "the rifle-balls flew thick and fast about me, and more than one struck the ground so near my feet as to throw the dust in my eyes."

How would you feel if you were Belle Boyd? Would you be scared? Or would you be too charged with energy to be frightened by the bullets? If you imagine yourself as a Union soldier, what would you be thinking as you raised your rifle at Belle? Would she remind you of your sister, or would you see her as an enemy and a spy? By putting yourself in the minds of people from the distant past, you can get a better feeling for the events they experienced.

## *Using the Strategy*

Read the following passage from "Saying Goodbye." Imagine yourself in Luanna's place. Then, write a paragraph that describes what you think Luanna is thinking and feeling.

> He cracked his whip high over the animals' heads. . . . The oxen strained at their yokes, and the wagons moved slowly forward.
>
> Luanna stood in the rising dust and looked around her. It was really happening. All her wishing hadn't stopped this day from coming.

## *Applying the Strategy to the Next Story*

The next story, "The Long Road West," is a historical account about traveling west by wagon train in the 1840s. At several points in the story, you will be asked to step into the story and imagine the thoughts and feelings of one of the characters.

The writing connection can be found on page 247.

# THE LONG ROAD WEST

by Russell Freedman

*Today, a plane can take you from the East Coast to the West Coast in a few hours. In the mid-1800s, that same journey took almost half a year, as wagon trains crept across the mountains, deserts, and prairies.*

American Library Association
*1983*

It was a typical wagon train of the 1840s. The swaying wagons, plodding animals, and walking people stretched out along the trail for almost a mile.

Near the end of the train, a boy holding a hickory stick moved slowly through the dust. He used the stick to poke and prod the cows that trudged beside him, mooing and complaining.

Step into this event. What do you think the boy is thinking or feeling?

"Get along!" he shouted. "Hey! Hey! Get along!"

Dust floated in the air. It clogged the boy's nose, parched his throat, and coated his face. His cheeks were smeared where he had brushed away the big mosquitoes that buzzed about everywhere.

Up ahead, his family's wagon bounced down the trail. He could hear the *crack* of his father's whip above the heads of the oxen that pulled the wagon. The animals coughed and snorted. The chains on their yokes rattled with every step they took.

His mother sat in the front seat of the wagon, holding the baby on her lap. His sisters had gone off with some other girls to hunt for wild herbs along the road.

The family was traveling west along the Oregon Trail in what someday would be the state of Wyoming. They followed the sandy banks of the North Platte River past rocky hills dotted with sagebrush and greasewood. This was the land of the Oglala Sioux.

Back in Missouri, their wagon had been a brand-new prairie schooner with red wheels, a blue body, and a fresh white canvas top. Now the top was stained and patched, the paint faded and crusted with mud. The wagon creaked and groaned, but it was still sturdy. On this hot July afternoon, the canvas cover had been rolled back and bunched so that any breezes could blow through the wagon.

The wagon was crammed with the family's possessions—with food, clothing, and furniture; with tools, bedding, kitchenware, and tent supplies. Tied to its side were a plow and a hoe. Hanging from a rope was a sealed pail of milk that bounced steadily as the wagon jolted along. By evening, the milk would be churned into butter.

There were forty wagons in the party, and nearly two hundred men, women, and children. A few of the pioneers rode saddle horses,

**A wagon train pauses for a moment in Dakota Territory before continuing its long journey west.**

but most of them walked. The only ones riding inside the wagons were little children with their mothers, and people who were sick or injured. Following the wagons were herds of milk cows and beef cattle, along with extra oxen, mules, and horses.

The pioneers had been up since four that morning, when the sentries started the day by firing their rifles. Hurrying about in the darkness, they had kindled fires, put on kettles of water, milked cows, pulled down tents, loaded wagons, and fixed breakfast. By seven, they were ready to roll. The train captain gave the signal to move out. Slowly the lead wagons rolled forward, and the others fell into line.

At noon they stopped for an hour's rest. The teams of oxen and mules were turned loose from the wagons but were not unyoked. Blankets and buffalo robes were spread out beside the trail. The pioneers ate a cold lunch, relaxed a bit, then rolled down the trail again.

As they moved along, they passed the splintered wreck of an abandoned wagon. Every two or three miles, they saw wooden grave markers where pioneers had been laid to rest beside the trail. As the day wore on, children began to climb aboard the wagons, finding nooks and corners where they could curl up and nap.

Late that afternoon, near a grove of willows, the train captain gave the signal to stop for the night. One after another, the wagons pulled off the trail and began to form a large circle, or corral. The wagons were locked together, front to rear, with chains; the front tongue of one wagon reached under the rear wheels of the next. A gateway was left open to admit the livestock. Then the last wagon was rolled into place, sealing the corral.

Safely inside, the pioneers tended their cattle, pitched tents, and started campfires for the evening meal. Families sat together eating beans, dried buffalo meat, and camp-baked bread from tin plates.

**What would you be thinking about if you were eating dinner around this campfire?**

By 8 P.M., sentries had taken their posts around the corral. Children ran past playing tag. Some girls sat in a circle, sharing secrets and laughing. A boy lay sprawled on his belly beside a campfire, studying a tattered copy of the *Emigrants Guide to Oregon and California.* Grown-ups stood in small groups, chatting and planning the day ahead.

Gradually the pioneers drifted off to their tents and wagons, where they huddled under blankets and fell asleep. Even in July, the night was chilly at this high altitude. They had traveled perhaps fifteen miles that day, nearly seven hundred miles since leaving Missouri in May. They still had more than twice that distance to go.

The first pioneers to travel west by wagon train had set out from Missouri in the spring of 1841. Each year after that, emigrants streamed westward in ever-increasing numbers. By 1869, when the first transcontinental railroad was completed, more than 350,000 pioneers had followed the ruts of the Oregon Trail across the continent.

At the beginning, most of them headed for the Pacific Coast. They went west to claim free land in the Oregon and California territories, to strike it rich by mining gold and silver, to settle in a new country where there was plenty of elbowroom and boundless opportunity.

They called themselves "emigrants" because, as they started their journey, they were actually leaving America. During the early 1840s, the United States ended at the banks of the Missouri River. The region that later would be Kansas and Nebraska had been set aside by the United States government as Native American territory. California was still a northern province of Mexico. The vast wilderness of the Oregon country was claimed jointly by the United States and Great Britain. Gradually these western territories would become part of the United States. But when the first emigrants set out, they were entering a foreign land.

Their journey started in one of the raw frontier towns along the Missouri River known as the "jumping-off places." Wagons rumbled through the muddy streets of these towns. Fur trappers and Native Americans mingled with westbound emigrants on sagging wooden sidewalks. Each year the wagon trains started rolling in late April or early May. Timing was crucial. If the emigrants started too early, they might not find enough spring grass on the prairie to graze their livestock. If they started too late, they might be stranded in the western mountains by early winter blizzards.

Several trails led west. The best-known and most popular by far was the Oregon Trail. It led across the Great Plains, climbed over the Rockies, then branched off toward Oregon in one direction and California in the other.

For most of its route, the Oregon Trail was little more than a pair of wheel ruts cutting across 2,400 miles of prairie sod, mountain rocks, and desert sand. When the trail came to a river, the ruts stopped at the water's edge. If the river was not too deep, the emigrants could ford it with their wagons. Otherwise they had to lift the wagons off their wheels and float them across on rafts, as their horses and cattle swam alongside.

(Above) Pioneers relax to a fiddler's tune during a mid-day break.
(Below) Struggling against heavy loads, oxen are urged onward.

What would you be thinking on the nice days? What about the stormy days?

The first weeks on the trail were always the easiest. Their wagons were packed with fresh supplies; their animals were sleek and healthy. The land was flat, the weather often mild. The rippling grass of the Kansas prairie was sprinkled with wildflowers, and hummingbirds shimmered above the fields of clover.

The emigrants enjoyed balmy days along the trail, but when they were caught in prairie storms, then they were miserable. Violent rainstorms came suddenly. Driving sheets of rain drilled against the canvas tops of wagons and tents and rose in a spray from the ground. Campfires fizzled out. Cooking was impossible. At times, top-heavy wagons were blown over and tents were uprooted by screaming prairie winds. Lightning flashed across the sky, and with the *crack* of thunder, the livestock sometimes broke away in terror. Riders had to gallop out and round them up. They came back drenched.

As the emigrants entered the foothills of the Rockies, the trail began to climb steadily uphill. Oxen and mules struggled against their loads. Teamsters shouted and lashed their whips to urge on their tired teams. To lighten the load, the emigrants began to dump cherished household possessions. Massive oak bureaus and mahogany claw-foot tables were left beside the road to crack and scorch under the western sun.

**At this point the Oregon Trail leaves the Platte River for the Sweetwater.**

By now, hardship and fatigue showed on the emigrants' faces. At times it seemed that half of them were ill. Adults and children bounced along in wagons, burning with high temperatures or shivering with chills.

Gradually the trail climbed the Rockies. It crossed the continental divide at South Pass, a windy upland valley that cut through the mountains. Beyond the Rockies, the trail branched off. One branch led northwest toward the coast of Oregon. The other veered southwest toward California. At this point the emigrants were only about halfway to their destinations.

Emigrants bound for California had to cross the treacherous deserts of Utah and Nevada, then pull their wagons over the rugged Sierra Nevada. If they kept on schedule, they could make it across the mountains before the first winter snowfall. The road to Oregon followed the twisting Snake River along steep, boulder-strewn ledges. It passed through a desolate plateau, then climbed west over the Blue Mountains and the Cascades.

As the emigrants pressed forward, oxen and mules were overcome by heat and exhaustion. Animals stumbled in their tracks and dropped dead in the yoke. Their bleached bones became a common sight along the trail. Once past the deserts, wagons had to be hoisted up steep

mountain slopes with chains and pulleys and ropes, then eased down with their wheels locked. Sometimes chains snapped and wagons broke loose, careening down hills and toppling over mountain ledges.

If food supplies ran low, the emigrants had to slaughter their oxen and mules and eat them. Some pioneers were forced to abandon their wagons altogether and cross the mountains on horseback or on foot.

Babies were born during the westward journey, and many emigrants died. Some were killed in skirmishes with Native Americans, but that did not happen often. Accidents and disease killed far more emigrants than the Native Americans did. Epidemics of cholera and typhoid swept through wagon trains. People drowned during river crossings in plain sight of their families and friends. Children were bitten by snakes and caught in stampedes. They fell out of wagons and under the wheels or the oxen's hooves. One out of every seventeen emigrants who started the trip was buried beside the Oregon Trail.

**What would you be thinking as you arrived in a fertile valley that marked the end of your westward journey?**

Many emigrants spent six to eight months on the trail. Often it was November or December before they finally came down from the mountains into the fertile valleys of Oregon and California.

## *Reader's Response*

Suppose your family had decided to emigrate west in the 1800s. If you knew ahead of time the kind of information presented in this article, would you have tried to persuade your family not to make the trip? Explain why or why not.

## Thinking It Over

1. Compare a wagon at the beginning of its journey westward with one toward the end of the journey.
2. Tell, in correct order, the main events of a typical day in the pioneers' journey westward.
3. Why do you think the pioneers formed a corral of wagons at the end of each day?
4. Give three reasons the pioneers had for going west.
5. Why were the first wagon-train pioneers called emigrants?
6. If families traveling westward had gone alone, and not as part of a wagon train, in what ways would the journey have been more difficult? How did you figure out your answer?

## Appreciating Literature

The illustrations that accompany an article often play a role in the reader's enjoyment of the piece. This article has three different types of illustrations—a famous painting by Albert Bierstadt, old photographs, and engravings. What do you think these illustrations add to the article? Which do you prefer?

## Writing to Learn

**THINK AND DECIDE** List five problems that almost every pioneer had to face. Arrange these problems in order, according to your own opinion, from most serious to least serious.

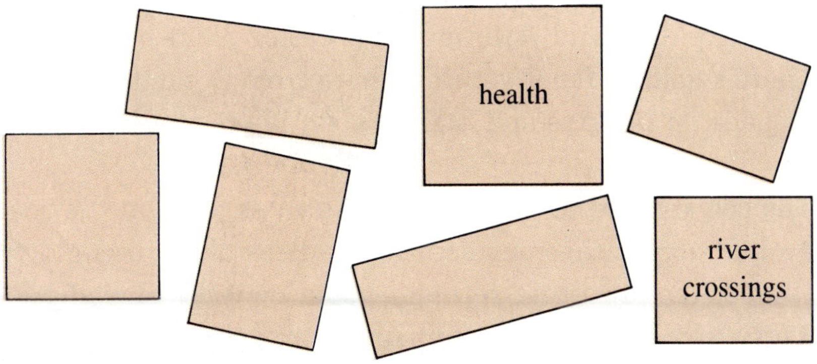


**WRITE** In a paragraph, explain why the problem you placed at the beginning of your list was the most serious, and why the one you placed at the end was the least serious.

AWARD WINNING Author

# WESTERN WAGONS

They went with axe and rifle, when the trail was still to blaze,
They went with wife and children, in the prairie-schooner days,
With banjo and with frying pan—Susanna, don't you cry!
For I'm off to California to get rich out there or die!

We've broken land and cleared it, but we're tired
of where we are.
They say that wild Nebraska is a better place by far.
There's gold in far Wyoming, there's black earth in Ioway,
So pack up the kids and blankets, for we're moving out today!

The cowards never started and the weak died on the road,
And all across the continent the endless campfires glowed.
*We'd taken land and settled—but a traveler passed by—*
*And we're going West tomorrow—Lordy, never ask us why!*

THE OLD SCOUT'S TALE, *oil on canvas by William Tylee Ranney, Thomas Gilcrease Institute, Tulsa, Oklahoma*

We're going West tomorrow, where the promises can't fail.
O'er the hills in legions, boys, and crowd the dusty trail!
We shall starve and freeze and suffer. We shall die,
  and tame the lands.
But we're going West tomorrow, with our fortune in our hands.

STEPHEN VINCENT BENÉT

*As cold winds howl and wind-driven snow darkens the sky for days at a time, a young pioneer woman and her baby face a winter alone on the prairie.*

# WEATHERING THE STORM

## from *Let the Hurricane Roar*
## by Rose Wilder Lane

*A young pioneer couple, David and Molly, and their infant son have just experienced the destruction of their crops by grasshoppers. Unwilling to forfeit their claim, David returns East to earn money to keep their homestead going. Molly chooses to remain behind. When David is detained by an accident, Molly must face the winter alone in their sodhouse.*

Three days and nights the winds did not cease to howl, and when Molly opened the door she could not see the door ledge through swirling snow. How cold it was she could not guess. At sight of the cloud she had hurriedly begun cramming every spare inch of the dugout with hay. Twisted hard, it burned with a brief, hot flame. Her palms were soon raw and bleeding from handling the sharp, harsh stuff, but she kept on twisting it; she kept the dugout warm.

READERS' CHOICE AWARD

In the long dark hours—for she was frugal with kerosene; a wavering light came from the drafts and the broken lid of the stove—she began to fight a vague and monstrous dread. It lay beneath her thoughts; she could not grasp it as a whole; she was always aware of it and never able to defeat it. It lay shapeless and black in the depths of her. From time to time it flung up a question:

What if the baby gets sick?

"He won't be sick!" she retorted. "He's a strong, healthy baby. If he's sick, I'll take care of him. I'd take care of him anyway; there's no doctor in town."

Suppose something has happened to David? Suppose he never comes back?

"Be still! I won't listen."

That was like a wolf's howl in the wind. Wolves?

"Nonsense, I have the gun. How could a wolf get through the door?"

When you go out—If a wolf sprang suddenly—What of the baby, alone in the dugout?

"Why am I scaring myself with horrible fancies? Nothing like that will happen."

She could never conquer the shapeless, nameless dread itself. Silenced, it did not leave her. It would begin again.

What if the baby gets sick?

"Oh, stop, stop! I can't stand this!" her spirit cried out in anguish. And she asked herself angrily, "What is the matter with you? Brace up and show a little decent spunk! It's only a storm; there'll be lots of them before spring." She tried to conquer the shapeless, dark thing by ignoring it.

The wind howled, gray darkness pressed against the paper pane, a little hard snow, dry as sand, was forced through the crack beneath the door.

On the fourth morning Molly was awakened by an immense, profound silence. The frosty air stung her nostrils; the blanket was edged with rime from her breath. Snug in the hollow of her body the baby slept cozily. The window was a vague gray in the dark. She lighted the lamp and started a fire in the cold stove.

She was not perturbed until she tried to open the door. Something outside held it against her confident push. And suddenly wild terror possessed her. She felt a Thing outside, pressed against the door.

It was only snow. She said to herself that it was only snow. There was no danger; the ledge was narrow. She flung all her strength and weight against the door. The stout planks quivered; they pressed against a crunching and a squeaking, and from top to bottom of them ran a sound like a derisive scratch of claws. Then snow fell down the abrupt slope below the ledge, and sunlight pierced Molly's eyes.

Taking the shovel, she forced her body through the narrow aperture she had gained. For an instant the pain in her eyes blinded her. Then she saw the immensity of whiteness and dazzling blue. She confronted space.

Under the immeasurably vast sky, a limitless expanse of snow refracted the cold glitter of the sun. Nothing stirred, nothing breathed; there was no other movement than the ceaseless interplay of innumerable and unthinkably tiny rays of light. Air and sun and snow were the whole visible world—a world neither alive nor dead, and terrible because it was alien to life and death, and ignorant of them.

In that instant she knew the infinite smallness, weakness, of life in the lifeless universe. She felt the vast, insensate forces against which life itself is a rebellion. Infinitely small and weak was the spark of warmth in a living heart. Yet valiantly the tiny heart continued to beat. Tired, weak, burdened by its own fears and sorrows, still it persisted, indomitably it continued to exist, and in bare existence itself, without assurance of victory, even without hope, in its indomitable existence among vast, incalculable, lifeless forces, it was invincible.

Molly was never able to say, even in her own thoughts, what she knew when she first came out of the dugout after the October blizzard. It was a moment of inexpressible terror, courage and pride. She was aware of human dignity. She felt that she was alive. She could feel what David felt, singing: "Let the hurricane roar! We'll weather the blast."

She drew a deep breath, and with her shovel she attacked the snow. The winds had packed it hard as ice against the door and the creek bank. The path was buried under a slanting drift. Inch by inch, pounding, digging, scraping, lifting, she made a way on which she could safely walk, and that scratch on the illimitable waste of trackless snow was a triumph.

A blizzard of such severity so early in October seemed to predict an unusually hard winter. She could not know when the next storm might strike, and her first care was fuel. She dug into the snow-covered stacks by the barn, and tying a rope around big bundles of hay, she dragged them one by one down the path and into the dugout.

When she threw out the water in which she washed her hands, she noticed that its drops tinkled on the ice crust. They had frozen in the air. Startled, she looked into the mirror. Her nose and ears were white, and she had to rub them with snow till they painfully thawed.

Then for three weeks the weather was mild, the snow was melting. There were days when the door stood open and the air was like spring. From above the dugout she could see the town; she could, indeed, see fifty miles beyond it.

In early November the winter settled down. Blizzard followed blizzard out of the northwest. Sometimes there was a clear day between them, sometimes only a few hours. As soon as the winds ceased their howling and the snow thinned so that she could see, she went out with the shovel.

The wind would be steadily blowing, driving a low scud of snow before it. She worked sometimes waist deep in blown snow so thick that she could not see her feet. The whole world seemed covered with white spray flying under the cold sunshine. Her eyes were bloodshot and her skin burned red and blistered, and she never came into the dugout without looking to see if face and ears were frozen.

On the dark days of the blizzards she twisted hay; she lighted the lamp for cleaning and cooking and washing. And she played with the baby.

He was older now; he watched the gleams of firelight and clapped his hands, and his soft little palms hardly ever missed each other. His blue eyes looked into Molly's; his firm little body had a will of its own. He could hold up his own head proudly; he could straighten his backbone; all by himself he could sit up, and he could crawl. Kicking and crowing, he burbled sounds almost like words. "Mama," she could hear him say.

"Papa," she urged him. "Say it, baby dumpling! Say 'papa.' "

"Blablub!" he replied triumphantly, giving her a roguish glance that melted her heart. Kneeling by the bunk, she squeezed his wiggling body between her raw hands, she rolled and tumbled him and buried her rough face in his softness, in the warm perfume of his baby body. His fist tugged painfully at her hair and she laughed, teasing his nose with the loosened ends. She had begun to be almost as lighthearted as David. She wondered, "Is David that way because he's frightened, because he has to be brave?"

There was always the ache of incompleteness without him. The shapeless dread might at any moment stab her with a question. But day by day the baby and she survived, and in the dugout the howling

winds, the cold and snow and dark could not touch them. Her lightheartedness was a defiance.

Then came the seven days' blizzard. There had been only a few hours of clear weather, but Molly had worked desperately; she had enough hay for three days and she had never known a blizzard to last longer. On the third day she burned the hay sparingly, but she was not alarmed. On the fourth day she broke up and burned a box, keeping the stove barely warm. On the fifth day she burned the remaining box. The heavy benches and table were left, and the cradle; in her folly she had left the ax in the barn.

She sat wrapped in blankets on the edge of the bunk. When the fire went out there was no light at all. The window was obscurely gray, a dim and unnaturally square eye, looking in upon her. The stout door shook to the pounding and prying of yelling winds. And time was lost, so that she did not know whether this were day or night, nor how long those winds had possessed all space. She had so long hoped to hear their energy exhausted that it seemed to her inexhaustible. The tiny pocket of still air in the dugout was increasingly cold.

If she and the baby lay close together under blankets, they could exist for some time in the warmth of their own bodies. If this were to go on forever—It could not, of course. Feebly she gave up the problem of the heavy benches, which she could not break up with her hands. It must be the cradle. But she feared to burn it so soon.

During the seventh day she smashed and frugally burned the cradle. The birds that David had carved helped to boil tea and potatoes. She mashed a potato in a little hot water and fed it with a spoon to the baby. Then she put out the lamp and lay down with him under all the bedding.

A change in the sound of the wind awakened her. She did not know whether it was night or day, but when she forced the door open she saw a whiteness of driven snow. A fierce north wind was driving the flakes steadily before it, and Molly's relief was like a shout of joy. The snow was not swirling; the blizzard was over!

When next she opened the door, the storm had diminished so that she could see vaguely into it. She was able to clear the path, and when she reached its top she could see dim shapes of barn and haystacks. The wind almost took her off her feet, and when she had a bundle of hay and was dragging it through the soft drifts, she had to fight it as though it were a live thing struggling to get away.

After she had filled the dugout with hay, she stretched a rope from the barn to the top of the path, so that she could fetch fuel, if necessary, during a blizzard.

Vaguely through the storm she seemed to see a dark patch on the opposite bank of the creek. It troubled her, for she could not imagine what it might be; perhaps an illusion of eyes weeping in the wind, perhaps some danger against which she should defend herself. She shut the door against it hurriedly and gave herself to the marvel of warmth and rest.

In the morning, in dazzling glitter of sun on snow, she saw across the creek a herd of cattle. Huddled together, heads toward the south and noses drooping to their knees, they stood patiently enduring the

cold. In terror she thought of the haystacks. The creek bank hid them from the cattle now, but if the herd moved southeast, across the slough, and saw that food, would all the strength of the wind prevent them from turning and destroying her fuel?

She put on her wraps and took the pistol. Not with pitchfork or ax, she knew, could she keep starving cattle from food. Nor did she dare risk facing the stampede. She could only try to turn it with shots, and, failing, take refuge in the barn. If the fuel were lost—

The cattle did not move. It came to her, while she watched, that for a long time they had not moved. Yesterday she had seen the herd, huddled motionless in the storm. This prodigy, this incredible fact of cattle not moving before a storm, chilled her thought. She stared at them—gaunt sides and ridged backbones, dropped necks and lax tails, motionless as if carved. Were they dead—frozen? No; breath came white from their nostrils.

The thought that they might be dead had brought a vision of meat.

Her courage quailed. There was something monstrous, something that gave her an unreasoning terror, like a breath of the supernatural, in this herd of motionless cattle. Her jaw clenched against the cold, she went slowly, kneedeep in drifts, down the bank and across the frozen creek. Was this too great a risk? Leaving the baby in the dugout and venturing into she knew not what? The cattle did not move. She went within ten yards of them, five, two. They did not even lift their heads.

Over their eyes—thick over their eyes and hollowed temples—were cakes of ice. When she saw this, she understood. Their own breath, steaming upward while they plodded before the storm, had frozen and blinded them.

In a rage of pity, an outbursting cry against the universal cruelty, she plunged through the snow to the nearest patiently dying creature; she wrenched the ice from its eyes. The steer snorted; he flung up his head in terror, and ran, staggering. The herd quivered. A few yards away, the steer stopped, hesitated in fear of the loneliness around him, and turned back uncertainly toward the herd. A long bawl of misery came from his throat. Then he, too, let his head droop.

Molly knew what she must do. She thought of the baby, drawing his strength from hers. She held all thought, all feeling, firmly to the baby, and walking to the nearest young steer, she put the pistol to his temple, shut her eyes and fired. The report crashed through her.

She felt the shudder of all the beasts. When she opened her eyes they had not moved. The steer lay dead, only a little blood trickling, freezing, from the wound. And perhaps it had been merciful to kill him.

Then, like an inspiration, a revival of all hope, she thought of a cow. The cow! Why not? In the herd there were many cows. Alas, they belonged to somebody. To whom? She did not know; that might never be known; impossible to guess how many miles—hundreds, perhaps—they had been driven by the storm. But they were branded. She could not steal. Yet, if she did not take one of these cows, would it not die? The whole blinded herd was helpless and dying. To kill for food was permissible, but to steal? Was she a cattle thief? But a cow—to have a cow! Milk for the baby. To surprise David, when he came home, with a cow!

She thought that perhaps there was a yearling that was not branded.

In her excitement she was almost laughing. Clumsy in boots and coat and shawls, she pushed into the harmless herd. The heifers, she knew, would be in the center. The old bull grumbled in his throat, shaking his blind head, but he did not move; he did not even paw the snow. There was a young heifer, unbranded, almost plump, a clear red all over. Molly marked it for her own, for their own cow.

This incredible marvel of good fortune filled her with joy. What a triumph, what a joke—to take a cow from the blizzard, to take it from the very midst of a dangerous herd! And to have a cow—after so many calamities, in spite of calamities, to have a cow—this was a vindication of all confidence and hope.

She struggled through the drifts, across the creek, up the bank, to the dugout. She fed the stove with hay, she nursed the baby, dressed him warmly, wrapped him in blankets like a cocoon. Then she went to the barn for a rope.

The short winter day gave her not too much time. The sun was overhead before she had succeeded in prodding and tugging the terrified, wild, blinded heifer out of the herd. It clung with desperation to the safety of the herd, and she had still to get it across the creek, up the bank and into the barn. Its strength—greater than hers—wore her out. In one frantic plunge and leap it undid the work of half an hour. Its blindness was her only help and she thanked God for the continued bitter cold. But often she stopped to rub face and ears with snow, and beating her numb hands on her chest did not keep the feeling in them.

It was near sunset before she got the heifer into the barn. She put hay into the manger and tore the ice from the heifer's eyes. With the rope and ax she went back to the herd. She cut the best parts of meat from the half-frozen carcass, and tied the pieces together. Then, trembling in her weariness, she went from animal to animal, tearing off the blinding ice. The cattle snorted and plunged; each one ran staggering a little way and waited, bawling. Slowly the herd drifted before the wind. The sun sank in coldness, the glow faded from the snow, and in the dusk she released the old bull. He lifted his head, bellowed weakly, and plunged staggering after the herd.

In the dark they would not see her hay. The wind was blowing toward the town site; let the townspeople deal with the survivors who reached it. Molly had given the cattle a chance for their lives, and she felt she had earned her cow.

The blizzard that came that night lasted only a day. Molly lay cozily in bed. The baby gurgled and kicked in exuberance of spirits; a great beef stew simmered on the stove, filling the air with its fragrance. The snowy hay in the manger would suffice the heifer for both food and water. The howling of the blizzard did not disturb Molly; she felt the braggart joy of Samson, hugging in secret his triumph. "A lion stood in the way; but out of the eater I have taken meat; out of the strong I have taken sweetness."

If only David could know that they had a cow! But now she was confident that David would come home strong and well; this winter would end, they would be together in the spring. And how good to lie on a soft hay tick, under warm blankets; how good to feel the heartening strength of meat stealing drowsily all through one's body; how good to be warm and to rest. She felt she had never been thankful enough for all her blessings.

### ♦ Library Link ♦

*If you would like to know about other struggles that young homesteaders had to face, read* Let the Hurricane Roar *by Rose Wilder Lane.*

## Reader's Response

How do you explain Molly's ability to survive and endure formidable difficulties?

## Thinking It Over

1. What was the shapeless, nameless dread that haunted Molly?
2. Describe what Molly realized about life when she first emerged from the October blizzard.
3. What became Molly's most immediate crisis after the week-long blizzard?
4. Summarize how Molly handled this crisis and even improved her situation. How did you decide what events to include in your summary?
5. What did the episode with the cow symbolize for Molly?

## Appreciating Literature

In this story, there is both internal and external conflict. Molly's internal conflict is with "a vague and nameless dread" as she anticipates all the awful things that might happen. Her external conflict is with the forces of nature as she struggles to keep herself and the baby warm and nourished. How does Molly's success with her external conflict help her resolve her internal conflict?

## Writing to Learn

**THINK AND EVALUATE** Make a contrast chart like the one below. At the left, write words or phrases to describe what Molly was like at the beginning of the story. At the right, describe what she was like at the end.

| Molly's Contrast Chart | |
|---|---|
| **Before** | **After** |
| | |
| | |

**WRITE** Molly was a person who felt weak but acted strong. Why? Using the contrast chart as a guide, write a paragraph describing the change in Molly and explaining why you think she changed so much.

# Memorial Ode

*Chant*
Now, listen, Ye who established the Great League,
Now it has become old,
Now there is nothing but wilderness.

Ye are in your graves who established it.
Ye have taken it with you and have placed it under you,
And there is nothing left but desert.
There you have taken your great minds.
That which you established, you have taken with you
Ye have placed under your heads what ye have established,
The Great League.

*Refrain*
Woe, woe! Hearken ye!
  We are diminished
Woe, woe!
  The land has become a thicket.
Woe, woe!
  The clear places are deserted
  They are in their graves who established it.
Woe, the Great League!
  Yet they declared it should endure.
The Great League, Woe!
  Their work has grown old
  We are become wretched. Woe!

CHIEF JOHN BUCK

THE HIAWATHA BELT,
*commemorating the founding of the League of the Iroquois.*

AWARD WINNING Author

# Buffalo Dusk

The buffaloes are gone.
And those who saw the buffaloes are gone.
Those who saw the buffaloes by thousands and how they
pawed the prairie sod into dust with their hoofs, their great
heads down pawing on in a great pageant of dusk,
Those who saw the buffaloes are gone.
And the buffaloes are gone.

CARL SANDBURG

THE BUFFALO TRAIL, *oil on canvas by Albert Bierstadt, 1867–1868.*

# The EAGLE and the ORIOLE

by Jamake Highwater

*For Yesa, a Native American boy, the skills and courage of a warrior would be necessary in his adult life. But Yesa's grandmother felt that more than that would be necessary.*

He fell in love with the wings of birds, the bright light of spring dancing upon them in the morning. Without looking up he knew that the sparrows were bathing in the hot Sun. Just from the happy voices of the children, he knew that the willows grew greener. And with every gust of wind the butterflies changed places in the branches, beating their translucent wings into color.

These were the most wonderful days. But they were also days of much learning, for Yesa was no longer a boy. Now that he had earned a name for himself, he left behind the games of children—the mock battles against the bees, the wrestling, and the make-believe hunting parties. Now all the battles were real, and the search for food was a serious business that demanded skill and wisdom.

"You have much to learn, Yesa, before you will be truly a man," Mysterious Medicine told him. "And you must listen carefully to all that I tell you."

His uncle was his teacher until his fifteenth winter. He was strict and solemn, but Yesa admired his knowledge and gave great attention to the lessons given to him by Mysterious Medicine.

"Yesa," his uncle would say, "look closely at everything you see. Do not let anything miss your attention."

And in the evening, when Yesa returned to the lodge, his uncle questioned his observations.

"On which side of the trees is the lighter bark? On which side do the branches grow most regularly?"

Then Mysterious Medicine would ask Yesa to describe all the new birds that he had seen during the day. The young man would speak of their color or the shape of their bill or their song. And then his uncle would give each its proper name, and Yesa repeated it until he had committed it to memory.

"Yesa," Mysterious Medicine would ask, "how do you know if there are fish in a lake?"

Anxious to please his uncle, Yesa blurted out the first thing that came into his head. "Because they jump out of the water for flies!"

Mysterious Medicine smiled patiently and then he said, "What do you think of the little pebbles grouped together under the shallow water? And what has made the pretty curved marks in the sandy bottom, and the little sandbanks? Where do you often see the birds that eat fish?"

"Ah," murmured the young man apologetically, ". . . now I understand. These are all the signs that tell us that fish live in a lake."

The old man nodded slowly. "You must follow the example of the *Shunktokecha*—the wolf, my child. Even when he is chased and must run for his very life, he will always pause for just a moment to take one more look at you before he dashes away. So you too, Yesa, must learn to take a second look at everything you see. You can learn much from the animals. But you should watch them silently and unobserved. I have been a witness to their courtships and their quarrels and have learned many of their secrets in this way. I once saw a terrifying battle between a pair of grizzly bears and three buffalos—a very foolish fight for the bears, for it was then the Moon of strawberries, when the buffalo sharpen and polish their big horns for the bloody contests they wage among themselves. From these observations of the four-legged ones you learn to be a hunter and a warrior, for the animals know more than we will ever know and it is the wise person who learns as much from them as he can. Do you understand?" Mysterious Medicine asked in a whisper.

Yesa nodded as he watched every gesture and grimace of his uncle.

"In hunting," the old man continued solemnly, "you will be guided by the habits of the animal you seek. Always remember that a moose stays in a swampy, low land or between high mountains near a spring or a lake. When you are confronted by a bear or a wildcat who shows signs of attacking you, you must make him understand that you have seen him and are aware of what he intends to do. If you rush such an animal with a sharp spear he will turn and run, for no beast will face such an attack unless he is cornered and wounded. There is, however, one exception: the gray wolf will attack fiercely when he is very hungry. But their courage depends entirely upon their numbers. In this they are much like white men. One or two wolves will never attack a man. But a pack of wolves is deadly, because each cowardly wolf takes his courage from the group. This is a failure of the wolves, for a creature must take courage from himself."

These were the teachings of Mysterious Medicine, a man widely known as one of the greatest hunters of the tribe. And it was from this uncle that Yesa learned much of warring and hunting and the quest of manhood.

All boys were expected to endure hardship as part of their education. A young man had to be strong and fit; he had to be able to go without food and water without displaying weakness; he had to be capable of long-distance running, and he was required regularly to traverse a pathless and alien countryside without losing his way by either day or night. All these abilities were required of any young man who hoped to be a warrior.

Sometimes Mysterious Medicine would abruptly awaken Yesa, in the early morning before the sun had arisen, and challenge his nephew to fast with him all day. Yesa had no choice; he was expected to accept such contests as part of the ordeal of becoming an adult. He and his uncle would blacken their faces with charcoal so everyone in the village would know they were fasting, and then they would go out among the people, who tempted them with delicacies. Poor Yesa was especially taunted with food and water until he was ready to lose his temper or give in to temptation. But mercifully the sun would finally reach the western hills, and the difficult fast would be over.

Often, no sooner had the exhausted Yesa fallen to sleep than he would be suddenly awakened by loud war whoops.

"Wha . . . wha . . . what's happening!" he would yelp as he leaped to his feet.

It was Mysterious Medicine who had sneaked up on Yesa and shouted the war cries. He expected his nephew to awaken with perfect presence of mind, always ready to grasp a weapon and to give a shrill whoop in reply. If Yesa failed to respond properly, if he were startled or sleepy or confused, then Mysterious Medicine would ridicule him and say that he would never become a warrior.

No sooner had Yesa accustomed himself to being roused from a sound sleep by war cries than his crafty uncle changed his tactics and would shoot off his gun just outside the lodge. But eventually Yesa managed to respond with alertness to every trick his uncle could devise. And finally Mysterious Medicine smiled proudly at his nephew. Yesa smiled back, knowing his uncle's pleasure meant he was becoming stronger and wiser each day and that soon he would be old enough and skillful enough to join a war party.

Whenever the Indians of the Plains went on the warpath, it was the custom to test the young warriors, putting them through many ordeals before they ever came face to face with the enemies. And so it happened that Yesa and his brother, Chatanna, were put to the test by their elders. When they were near a hostile Indian camp, the brothers were selected to go after the water, though the creek was dangerously close to the enemies.

Yesa was ready for the challenge. Together with Chatanna, he picked his way through the dark woods, dipped the pail into the water as quickly and as quietly as possible, and then hurried back to camp. The two brothers' hearts leaped at every crackling twig, every hoot of the owls, until at last they reached the tipi of their uncle.

Mysterious Medicine smiled proudly at both of them, and they breathed a sigh of relief as they turned to join the men around the fire. But their uncle was not finished with their test. Slowly he turned the bucket on its side and spilled the contents on the ground.

"Yes, Yesa and Chatanna, it is true. I think you are going to be very brave men," he said as he emptied out the precious contents of the pail. "And so now you will fill the bucket a second time and show twice as much courage."

By the time the brothers returned to the encampment of their people the second time, they were so exhausted they could not eat. Chatanna slouched off to the lodge of his uncle, while Yesa returned to the tipi of his grandmother, Uncheedah.

"Ai!" she exclaimed as she embraced him. "But do not forget. To be a warrior is good," she murmured as she led Yesa to his bed, "but to be wise and generous is also good!"

And then, as she put wood on the fire and squatted over the kettle, rocking to and fro on her heels, she gazed lovingly at her grandson. "Close your eyes, my strong-hearted child," she whispered, "and I will tell you a marvelous story. This is the tale of the *Hetunkala*—the field mice who live in the sky. Each night the mice saw the little sliver of the Moon grow larger. Yes, each night they saw the Moon hanging in the enormous black sky, growing so heavy that she began to fall. It was then, many years ago, that the mice nibbled gently upon her sides until she was small enough to rise once again . . . high into the deepest heavens! But one terrible night," Uncheedah murmured, "the *Hetunkala* nibbled too eagerly, leaving scars upon the silver Moon. And so they were hurled down to the Earth, and they lost their special place in the sky. And ever since that day, they have gathered when the Moon is full, trying to find their way back among the Stars."

The grandmother smiled and touched Yesa's black hair. "Be strong of heart . . . be patient!" she whispered as he drifted to sleep. "But above all, Yesa, learn to dream, for there is no secret and no power in a man who does not know how to dream."

The wings of birds fluttered to the moonlight. The willows grew greener. And with every gust of wind the butterflies changed places in the branches of his mind, beating their translucent wings into colors and dreams as he slept.

And then it was morning.

Chatanna was the brother with whom Yesa now passed all his days. Though they had lived with different grandmothers ever since the death of their mother, they were now constant companions as they approached manhood. Their two older brothers had perished with their father. Of the four sons, they were the last, and they naturally shared many problems and secrets. They played together, slept together, and ate together. They also shared many dreams. And as Chatanna was three summers older, Yesa looked up to him and often sought his advice on the many mysteries of the world.

Yesa also had a cousin who was four summers younger than he, and though he had known her all his life, it was not until these years of his initiation into manhood that he began to take notice of her.

She was called Oesedah.

Although Oesedah had a mother who looked after her with great affection and care, it was Uncheedah who had become her chaperone and teacher. And so during the same days that Mysterious

Medicine attended to the education of Yesa, Uncheedah taught little Oesedah all the knowledge that young women were expected to know before they could become wives. From a small and awkward little girl, Oesedah was being transformed daily into a very handsome woman.

When Yesa was not out in the woods with Chatanna, he would sit at home with Oesedah. His beautiful cousin always had a hundred urgent questions ready for him. Some of these inquiries were simple for Yesa to answer because they dealt with everyday tribal matters, but some of his cousin's questions were very mysterious and to answer them took considerable wisdom.

Uncheedah had skillfully dodged these difficult questions by telling Oesedah: "Yesa ought to know that—he is a man and I am not. You should ask him."

The truth of the matter, however, was that Uncheedah had herself already explained the answers to many of these "manly" questions to Yesa. It was Grandmother's way of encouraging the young people to talk to each other and to try to understand and solve their problems by themselves. Often Uncheedah quizzed Yesa, Chatanna, and Oesedah together, urging them to answer her questions together, and in this way learn how much power there could be in acting as a group rather than as individuals. "What bird shows most judgment in caring for its young?" Uncheedah asked.

At once Chatanna exclaimed: "The eagle!"

Yesa, on the other hand, was silent for a long time. He was confused—so many birds came into his mind all at once. He couldn't decide upon an answer. Finally he declared: "It is the oriole!"

"Ai . . ." Uncheedah said with a grin. "Now tell me, Chatanna, what proof do you have that the eagle is the best parent?"

Chatanna spoke with complete confidence. "The eagle is the wisest of all birds. Its nest is made in the safest possible place, upon a high and inaccessible cliff. It provides its young with much fresh meat. And in its mountaintop nest it has the freshest of air. The eagle is brought up under the spell of the grandest scenes and inspired with lofty feelings and great bravery. It sees that all other beings live beneath it and that eagles are the children of the king of the birds. A young eagle shows the spirit of a warrior while still in its nest. Being

exposed to the weather the young eagle becomes hardy and strong. It is accustomed to the voice of the Thunderbird and the sighing of the Great Mystery. The eagle cannot help being noble because its parents select the most lofty place in which it is born. Isn't that so, Uncheedah?" Chatanna concluded with great excitement in his voice.

"Ai," she murmured as she smiled at Chatanna and then slowly looked at Yesa and awaited his speech on behalf of the orioles.

At first Yesa was staggered by the nobility of Chatanna's fine speech, and he could not bring himself to speak. But soon he recovered his confidence with the help of Oesedah, who said: "Wait until Yesa tells us about the loveliness of the oriole's home!"

"My grandmother, it was you who said that a mother who has a gentle voice will have children of a good disposition. I think the oriole is that kind of parent. It provides both sunshine and shadow for its young. Its nest is suspended from a bough where it is rocked by every gentle wind; and this nest is lined with soft things both deep and warm so that the featherless little birds do not suffer the cold."

"That is just like white people," Chatanna interrupted with annoyance. "That's just like them! And who cares about them! The eagle teaches its young to survive hardships. That is the Indian way!"

"Ai! Chatanna," Yesa exclaimed, "you have interrupted me before I have finished. Grandmother, surely I have the right to say what I wish to say."

"Ai," Uncheedah agreed, "you have that right and your brother should be ashamed for a discourtesy we would not even offer an enemy, for each person must be heard. *That,* Chatanna, is the true Indian way!"

Chatanna lowered his head with embarrassment as Yesa continued to speak. "You would not have lived, Chatanna, if you had been exposed to the snow and the wind when you were a baby!" he said reproachfully to his brother. "The oriole shows wisdom in providing its children with a warm home. It also offers them love when they are young and need much love. Of all the birds the oriole has been the wisest, for it has created a nest unlike any other nest. It is love of their children that has inspired the oriole to invent such a marvelous nest, while it is only pride that makes the eagle raise its children in the freezing heights of the mountains!"

The brothers peered anxiously at Uncheedah for her decision. "You are good boys and you have learned to think and to speak your minds, and that is more important than being right."

"But which of us speaks the truth?" Chatanna insisted.

Grandmother laughed and touched both of her grandsons with a loving gesture. Then she said: "When we are wise and when we ponder many questions, it is not truth that we are seeking, my children. What we are seeking is meaning. And meaning and truth are not the same things."

To this remark Oesedah smiled brightly, for she seemed to grasp things that the brothers had great difficulty understanding. She was an odd little creature, with a heart so generous and good that she seemed at times more like one of the four-legged creatures than a young woman.

When autumn arrived Oesedah began living with Uncheedah and Yesa, for it was a difficult season, and her family was so large there was not enough meat to go around. Mysterious Medicine was a great hunter and there was always enough food for everyone. And so Oesedah would come to the lodge of Uncheedah and stay through the fall months. The girl was lonely, however, as she was the only young female in the family. She often played by herself while Yesa and Chatanna were hunting with their uncle. There was one willow in particular that Oesedah visited regularly, holding long conversations with it, a portion of which she would afterward repeat to Yesa.

"That's ridiculous!" Chatanna would mutter. "Talking to a willow tree!"

But Yesa believed in such things, for he had often spoken to the animals. "What did the willow say?" he asked his cousin.

She blushed and explained that the willow was her husband. Some curious magic spell had compelled the young warrior she loved to assume the shape of a tree.

"But you must not tell Chatanna," she insisted, "because he cannot understand such things."

So Yesa never spoke of Oesedah's secret to Chatanna.

But for all of his bad temper and stubbornness Chatanna was a good and loyal friend, and Yesa loved him dearly. They shared many secrets and they depended upon each other's allegiance. They had pledged eternal friendship in Yesa's thirteenth summer. And they had sworn that they would go on their first warpath together and either win, or die, side by side.

Then one spring morning Mysterious Medicine took Chatanna with him to the Canadian trading post on the Assiniboine River, where the people often went to trade off furs for ammunition and supplies.

When Mysterious Medicine returned to camp, Chatanna was not with him!

Yesa was terrified that his brother had been killed, but his uncle quickly explained what had taken place. A white Canadian at the post with whom Mysterious Medicine did some trading had six daughters but no sons. When he saw how handsome and intelligent Chatanna was, he at once offered to adopt him.

"What?" Yesa exclaimed in sorrow. "Do you mean that you have given my brother away?"

Uncheedah gave Yesa a stern look. He was not allowed to speak to his uncle discourteously no matter how unhappy he might be.

"The trader promised that we can go to see him whenever we wish," Mysterious Medicine said. "And, as you know, by giving this trader Chatanna we have greatly strengthened our friendship, for now our families are one."

Yesa turned away and could not speak.

He silently left the lodge and stood in the darkness, looking into the north with a terrible pain in his heart.

For many long weeks he could not be consoled. Uncheedah did everything to gladden her grandson, but a black shadow hung over his face. His only companion was little Oesedah, with whom he whispered beneath the willow on the river's narrow bank.

"How could Chatanna desert me like that?" Yesa muttered.

"He did not want to do it," Oesedah insisted. "I know how much he loved you! He would have come back to us if it were possible. But he could not return. He has been changed into a white man just as my husband was turned into a willow!"

Yesa did not speak. He sat sadly with his cousin under the wide branches of the tree until Uncheedah could no longer bear his silence.

"What is there to be done?" she murmured. "I too mourn the loss of that precious boy, but what can be done? Your uncle is a strong man with an unyielding will of his own, and neither you nor I can argue with him."

"But what will become of Chatanna?" Yesa cried out in pain.

For a moment the old woman's eyes filled with tears and she shook her head helplessly. "All the sons are lost but you, my pitiful last. And there is nothing Uncheedah can do about it. I would rather that he had been taken away by the Ojibwa. I would rather that he had been stolen by an enemy than by that trader, for now he will be taught the ways of the white man!" And again Uncheedah bowed her head and wept.

As the dark days passed, Grandmother became so despondent that she would not speak or eat. The gloom of the lodge became unbearable, and at last Mysterious Medicine, shamed by the disapproving glances of his family, relented.

"Ai!" he groaned peevishly. "I will take him back! I will take him back! The next time I visit the trading post I will bring Chatanna home again, if only the three of you will bring this dismal behavior to an end!"

Yesa was delighted and warmly embraced his befuddled uncle.

"None of that . . . none of that!" Mysterious Medicine exclaimed. "You are too old to be fondling your uncle! So behave yourself and understand that you should be punished for having questioned my decision!"

"He is still a boy. . . ." Uncheedah softly protested, touching her angry son on the shoulder.

"No," Mysterious Medicine countered sternly, "he is a man, and if he wishes to be a warrior he must learn to obey his elders! That is the first thing that a brave must learn. To weep and mourn your losses is beneath a true warrior. Yesa, you must learn to accept the commands of your elders! Never again will I permit you to contest my word!"

With these angry words, Mysterious Medicine left the lodge. Yesa's heart was crushed, for his uncle had never spoken to him so harshly, and despite his joy over the promised return of Chatanna, he was still deeply mortified.

But the reunion was not to be. The white trader was a cunning man. No sooner had he taken Chatanna into his family than he moved to a remote region of Canada.

Yesa never saw Chatanna again.

### ♦ Library Link ♦

*You can read more about Yesa and his friends in Jamake Highwater's* Eyes of Darkness, *from which this selection was taken.*

## Reader's Response

Do you think that the lessons that Yesa, Chatanna, and Oesedah learned were valuable? Explain your response.

## Thinking It Over

1. Describe the abilities that were required of a young man who hoped to be a warrior.
2. Based on Mysterious Medicine's words and actions, how would you describe the kind of person he was?
3. Explain how you felt about Mysterious Medicine's dumping of the water that Yesa and Chatanna brought from the creek.
4. How did Yesa and Chatanna differ in the way they viewed the world?
5. What qualities did Yesa possess that caused Oesedah to trust and admire him so much? Explain how you reached your conclusion.

## Appreciating Literature

Mysterious Medicine tells Yesa to follow the example of the wolf and pause to take a second look. Taking a second look at literature is also important. The first time we look at a story, we find out what happens. The second time, we can think about what the author might be telling us through the story. Take a second look at the contrast between the eagle and the oriole. What message about values and growing up does Highwater seem to be conveying?

## Writing to Learn

**Think and Elaborate** To elaborate means to expand or add to. Read the story quotations listed below. "Elaborate" by discussing each quotation in your own words.

| Quotations | Restatements |
|---|---|
| 1. "A creature must take courage from himself." | 1. a person must look inside for bravery. |
| 2. "Be strong of heart. Be patient." | |
| 3. "Learn to dream. There is no power and no secret in a man who does not know how to dream." | |

**Write** Select one of the quotations. Write a paragraph telling why you agree or disagree with the ideas it represents.

# The Story of the Gold at Sutter's Mill

by R. Conrad Stein

*One day in 1848, there was a surprising discovery at John Sutter's mill in California. When the news reached the East, the "Rush" westward was on!*

For thousands of years, streams in central California wound peacefully through the hills. Native Americans paused at those streams to drink the crystal-clear water. Now and then they saw glints of yellow in the streambeds. They nodded and passed on. The tribes of old California had no use for gold.

Other men, however, were willing to risk their lives for gold. When they learned of the rich deposits in California, they headed west like stampeding cattle.

The great race to California began in 1849. The first traces of gold had been found a year earlier on the property of John Augustus Sutter.

Sutter was an unlikely figure to be remembered in history books. In 1832 he had left his native Switzerland to come to the United States. At the time, he had no money and was escaping his many debts at home. After drifting from state to state, Sutter decided to go to California. He arrived there in 1839.

California then belonged to Mexico. It was a huge area where few people lived. The Mexican settlements amounted to a dozen or so missions that were strung out between the struggling village of Los Angeles and the shores of San Francisco Bay.

Giving away large pieces of land to settlers was common in early California. Sutter talked the governor into giving him 50,000 acres in the rich Sacramento Valley. In the past, he had tried and failed at many different businesses. But with so much land, Sutter believed he could now become as wealthy and powerful as the noblemen he had admired while growing up in Switzerland.

In 1846 war broke out between Mexico and America. Because of that war, California became a territory of the United States.

Sutter paid little attention to the war. A dream churned in his mind. He hoped to acquire still more land and establish his own empire in California. Already he had built a fort near the American River, and now called himself "Captain Sutter."

One day in January, 1848, Sutter's foreman hurried inside Sutter's office and shut the door. Then he showed Sutter two pieces of yellow metal about the size of unpopped popcorn.

Sutter rolled them in his fingers. "Gold?" he asked.

The foreman nodded.

Sutter smiled. Gold on his property would make him even richer and more powerful than he had dared to dream.

Neither Sutter nor his foreman knew they were sitting on top of enough gold to turn sleepy California into a booming territory almost overnight.

At first Sutter tried to keep the discovery a secret, but the news soon leaked out. A ten-year-old boy, a son of Sutter's cook, found a tiny gold lump on the riverbank. He proudly showed it to passersby. One of them was a man who delivered goods by horse and wagon to the scattered farms in the Sacramento Valley. In a few weeks the valley was buzzing with the news that gold had been found at Sutter's Mill.

About a month after the find, a small newspaper called the *Californian* reported:

> GOLD MINE FOUND—In the newly made raceway of the sawmill erected by Captain Sutter on the American fork, gold has been found in considerable quantities.

The newspaper article was incorrect. So far, only a tiny amount of gold had been found. But the mention of gold can bring forth feelings of excitement and greed in the most sensible of men. So the article was read closely by everyone in California.

Those first few specks of gold were the germs of what became a new disease. Gold fever struck at Sutter's Mill and swept through California like an epidemic.

Men dropped what they were doing and rushed to the mill. Farmers left plows in the fields. Store owners bolted their doors shut. Workers put aside their tools.

The newspaper that broke the story had to shut down. The reporters and pressmen ran off to dig for gold. The newspaper's last editorial said:

> The whole country from San Francisco to Los Angeles resounds with the sordid cry of gold! GOLD! GOLD! GOLD! While the field is left half planted, the house half built, and everything neglected but the manufacturers of shovels and pickaxes.

Suddenly everyone in California became a gold miner. And some of them were very lucky. A man named Joe Dye collected $40,000 in gold in just seven weeks. Two partners, William Daylor and Perry McCoon, made $17,000 in one week. A boy named Davenport, who claimed to be twelve years old but looked even younger, found $2,700 worth of gold in just two days.

As in many other enterprises, the people who were there first got the most.

**John Sutter and his property, Sutter's Mill, became the focus for the California Gold Rush.**

A year later an army of miners descended on California. Then gold mining became hard work. Only a lucky few made quick fortunes.

News of the gold find spread east. Hunters and traders crossing the Great Plains talked to settlers on the Mississippi. They said that in California huge chunks of gold covered the ground like stones. Sailors who had shipped out of San Francisco brought stories of California gold to eastern cities. They told of men in California who had become overnight millionaires. Most of the stories were exaggerated, but they were based on truth.

The gold found at Sutter's Mill caused one of the wildest mass movements of people the world had ever seen—the Great California Gold Rush.

From the farms, small towns, and cities of the eastern United States, men headed to California.

Many of them carried washbowls. They hoped to use these to "wash" or "pan" gold out of the sand. A popular song in the East was sung to the tune of "Oh! Susanna!"

> Oh! California! That's the land for me!
> I'm bound for California with my washbowl on my knee.

In the year 1849, some 85,000 gold seekers swarmed to California. Those early arrivals were called "forty-niners."

Most forty-niners were young men in their teens and early twenties. They were looking for adventure, as well as a fortune. Other forty-niners were older men. Many of them had deserted their families because of the lure of gold.

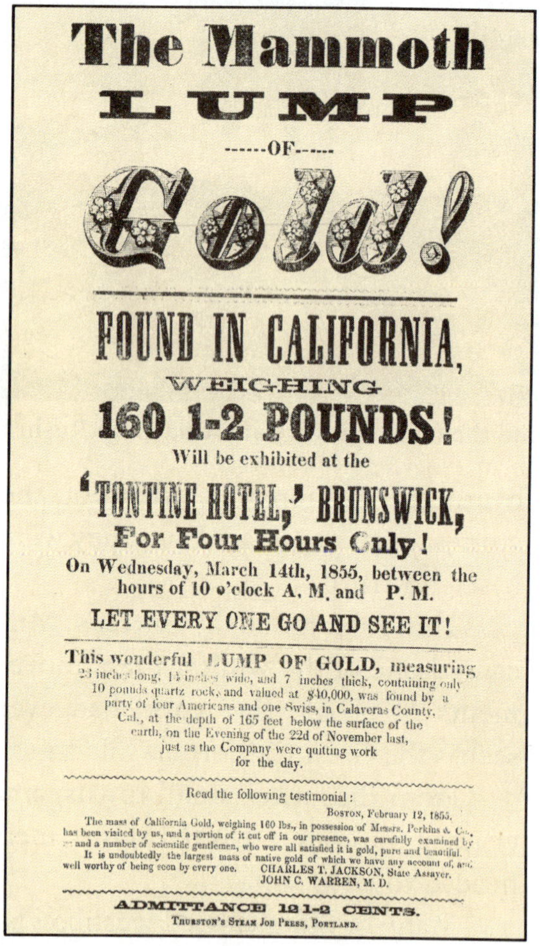


**The mention of gold filled many people with excitement and greed.**

The first decision a forty-niner faced was how to get to California. He could choose one of three ways. One was to take a ship out of an Atlantic port, sail around Cape Horn at the tip of South America, and then go up to the Pacific Coast to San Francisco. A second route was to go overland by horse and wagon or on foot. A third was a combination of the first two—take a ship to Mexico or Panama, cross overland, and then take another ship heading north to California.

The route by sea appealed to men from the East Coast. Sleek new clipper ships were fast, but they mainly carried cargo. So most of the forty-niners who took this route sailed on older, slower ships. It took these ships six or eight months to go from the East Coast to San Francisco. Greedy ship captains took as many passengers as they could cram on board. So in the holds, the gold seekers slept three to a bed. The beds were stacked one on top of the other. They were so close together that the passengers had no room to sit up. The food they were served was a dreadful mixture of salt pork and beans. One forty-niner later wrote that "there were two bugs for every bean." Sometimes the quality of the food didn't matter. Most passengers lost their appetites while rounding Cape Horn. Violent storms there tossed ships about like toy boats in a bathtub. Many forty-niners became so seasick they cursed the day they decided to seek gold.

The most popular route to the gold fields was the one that ran overland. Forty-niners gathered in groups at frontier settlements such as St. Joseph on the Missouri River. From there—by horse, wagon, mule, and on foot—they headed west. They followed almost the same route explorers Lewis and Clark had taken some fifty years earlier. The gold seekers soon encountered Native Americans, but most of them wanted only to trade. After passing through the Great Plains, the forty-niners had trouble finding water and grass for their animals. Near the Sierra Nevada Mountains, the travelers faced a hellish stretch of land called the Forty-Mile Desert. One forty-niner wrote to a friend who was about to take the trip, "Expect to find the worst desert you ever saw, and then find it worse than you expected."

Many gold seekers thought the best route to California was the one that ran over both land and water. Most of them crossed overland at Panama. This meant a long trip through mosquito-infested swamps. Dozens of miners caught malaria there and died—still more than a thousand miles from California. To cross Panama, miners hired native boatmen to paddle them through the maze of rivers that cut from one side of the country to the other. The boatmen found that they could charge whatever fee they wished. The price of a passage for two men rose from $10 to $50 in just a few months. The Panamanians liked to sing as they rowed through the jungle rivers. They spoke no English, but because of the forty-niners their favorite songs became "Oh! Susanna!" and "Yankee Doodle."

When he finally arrived in the gold fields, the forty-niner faced shocking prices. A horse that a year before had sold for $6 in California now cost a whopping $300. The price of food was enough to make a miner cry. A loaf of bread—$2. A pound of butter—$6. One egg—$3. A tin of sardines (a treat for the miner)—$16.

At the very start of the gold rush, merchants discovered they could charge miners outrageous prices and get away with it. When gold fever first struck California, a store owner named Sam Brannan learned that iron pans were needed to take gold from streambeds. At twenty cents apiece, Brannan bought practically every iron pan in California. He then resold the pans to forty-niners for eight to ten dollars each. Before the end of the gold rush, Brannan became a millionaire.

New arrivals at the fields learned immediately that gold mining is hard work.

**Prospectors brought with them a wide variety of equipment and supplies.**

Among the forty-niners the most popular method of mining gold dust was by using the wash pan. It looked like a pie plate and was usually made of tin or iron. The miner filled his wash pan with dirt or gravel and held it under the water while swirling it gently. Gold is a heavy metal. So the flowing water would wash the light dirt away and leave the heavier gold dust behind.

To pan for gold dust, a miner had to spend back-breaking hours squatting in an ice-cold stream. His hands were under water most of the time. At the end of a long day, his arms felt numb all the way up to his elbows.

Despite the hard work and sky-high prices, new miners splashed into streams, scooped up gravel, and prayed. A few were lucky. "Eureka! Oh how my heart beat!" wrote one miner after he discovered gold in his pan for the first time. "I sat still and looked at it for some minutes before I touched it."

During the gold rush, men used the phrase "seeing the elephant" to describe the feeling of discovering gold. The phrase came from an old story about a Midwestern farmer who all his life had wanted to see an elephant. Finally, a circus came to town and the farmer hitched up his horses and wagon and rode to see it. He was fascinated by his first sight of an elephant, but his horses panicked. They galloped away, dragging the wagon behind them. The wagon broke loose, tumbled down a hill, and was completely destroyed. "I don't care," said the farmer looking at the wreckage of his wagon. "I've seen the elephant."

"Seeing the elephant" became the most popular words spoken by forty-niners. The story of the farmer summed up why they had joined the gold rush. They were willing to risk their health, their money, and their lives for the thrill of finding gold.

One of those who hoped to "see the elephant" was John Augustus Sutter. His 50,000 acres crawled with miners. They had trampled his crops, muddied his streams, and slaughtered his cattle for food. "The country swarmed with lawless men," Sutter later wrote. "Talking with them did no good. I was alone and there was no law."

**Prospectors soon discovered that gold mining was back-breaking work.**

Since he could not fight the waves of miners, Sutter decided to join them. Forgetting his dreams of an empire, he bought mining gear and set out for the hills. His Native American friends told him that gold was bad medicine. They claimed the gold belonged to a demon who lived far away in the hills and would put a curse on those who took the gold away. Sutter dismissed those warnings as superstition.

Often forty-niners found gold in the form of nuggets. Nuggets are a miner's dream. They are lumps of gold that can be as large as marbles. On rare occasions, huge nuggets were found that weighed ten, twelve, and fourteen pounds. The largest single nugget ever found in the United States was dug out of the California gold fields in the mid-1850s. It was a monster that weighed an undreamed-of one hundred and ninety-five pounds.

A lucky miner could stumble on a nugget practically anywhere. Around the campfires at night, forty-niners loved to tell stories about men chancing upon gold nuggets. In one story a miner sat on a rock cursing his luck because he had not found a speck of gold in a month. In anger the man kicked a stone. Beneath it was a shining gold nugget. Another story told of two miners working together in a narrow canyon. For some reason they got into a fistfight. One miner swung at the other, missed, and hit the canyon wall. A gold nugget fell out. Both miners forgot their fight and began scratching at the wall with their hands. And it was said that near Sacramento a little farm girl found a rock she thought was pretty. She brought it to her mother who wiped it off and discovered it was a seven-pound nugget.

As the gold rush stretched into the 1850s, the richest deposits became mined out. But a man could still find a stream where he could pan enough gold to earn about thirty dollars a day. This was a good wage—even in California where prices were so high.

## *Reader's Response*

If you had lived in the East at the time gold was discovered at Sutter's Mill, would you have gone west?

## Thinking It Over

1. List the events of the gold rush as narrated in this account. Begin with the discovery of gold and end with the mid-1850s.
2. What was the most important change brought about by the discovery of gold at Sutter's Mill?
3. If you had been a "forty-niner," which of the three routes to California would you have taken? Why?
4. Describe three disappointments that were in store for most "forty-niners" once they reached California. What influenced your decisions most—things that you have read or feelings that you have had?
5. How did the newspaper the *Californian* promote "gold fever"?

## Appreciating Literature

In informational articles, you may sometimes find that the author expresses his or her own viewpoint on the subject. This viewpoint may be revealed in things the author says, by the choice of words, or by the selection of facts and events the author writes about. Find evidence of the author's viewpoint in "The Story of the Gold at Sutter's Mill."

## Writing to Learn

**THINK AND IMAGINE** What were the characteristics of the people who caught "gold fever"? On a sheet of paper, list the characteristics you believe they had.

**WRITE** Write a paragraph describing how these characteristics might have changed after a few months.

# LITERATURE LINK

## *How can an author's use of symbols enrich your reading ?*

America's bald eagle—what an impressive sight! Wings spread wide, it soars powerful and free, dominant over all it surveys. You can see why the eagle was chosen as the standard of the ancient Roman leaders. With its invincible spirit and strength, it stood for everything an emperor or king wanted to be. But for the early citizens of the United States, who chose the bald eagle as their symbol, the bird stood for more than power. Fearless in flying the skies, the eagle came to represent the freedom they all desired as citizens in their new democracy.

## *Why Symbols?*

From the example of the eagle, you can see that a symbol is something physical that can stand for an abstract idea such as power or freedom. Many things—statues, animals, flowers, even colors—can have symbolic meaning. Authors use symbols to enrich the meaning of stories and to draw out a reader's emotions.

In "The Eagle and the Oriole," the brothers debate which of their chosen birds makes the best parent. What does each bird symbolize? Read these passages to find out.

> Chatanna spoke with complete confidence. "The eagle is the wisest of all birds. Its nest is made in the safest possible place, upon a high and inaccessible cliff. It provides its young with much fresh meat. And in its mountaintop nest it has the freshest of air. The eagle is brought up under the spell of the grandest scenes and inspired with lofty feelings and great bravery. It sees that all other beings live beneath it and that eagles are the children of the king of the birds…"

Later Yesa speaks:

> "My grandmother, it was you who said that a mother who has a gentle voice will have children of good disposition. I think the oriole is that kind of parent. It provides both sunshine and shadow for its young. Its nest is suspended from a bough where it is rocked by every gentle wind; and this nest is lined with soft things both deep and warm so that the featherless little birds do not suffer the cold."

The eagle symbolizes the teachings of the boys' uncle who wants them to be bold warriors. What qualities does the eagle embody? How does the oriole symbolize the teachings of the grandmother, who wants the boys to be wise and generous?

Understanding the use of symbols will help you understand the deeper meaning of a poem or story. It can also enrich your writing.

**Y**ou will soon read the poem "Nothing Gold Can Stay." Look for clues the author provides to discover what idea or hidden truth gold represents.

WORLD OF READING

# Magazine

News About Reading

## The Pony Express: Letters from Home

"He rode fifty miles without stopping, by daylight, moonlight, starlight, or through the blackness of darkness."
—Mark Twain, *Roughing It*

Everyone knows about the Pony Express, but what people know is often a mixture of fact and fancy.

The Pony Express really existed; it wasn't just invented in Western movies. It played a critical role in the rapid expansion of the west. In fact, before the days of the Pony Express, weeks would pass before settlers received mail from family and friends or news of current events. It was to fill this void that the Pony Express was created. Letters, newspapers, and other written materials brought by the Pony Express helped settlers feel they were still connected to home.

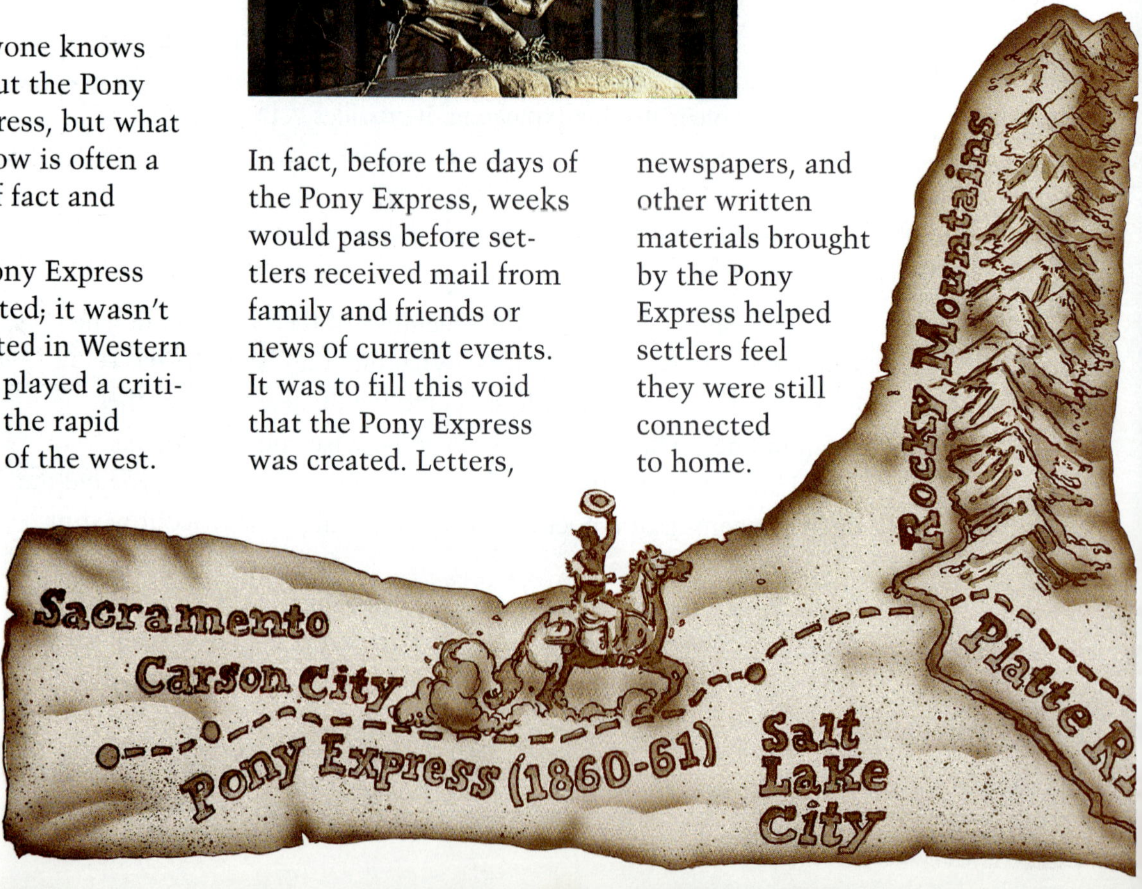

Originally Pony Express mail was canceled by handstamps. The first Pony Express gummed stamps were issued by Wells, Fargo & Company after April, 1861. Pony Express stamps are rare and are collector's items.

***Before the days of the Pony Express, weeks would pass before settlers received mail . . . or news of current events.***

To make all this happen, the Pony Express was set up in a systematic, but harsh way. Riders covered seventy-five to one hundred miles a day changing horses about every ten or fifteen miles. Often a rider would finish his run bleeding from the mouth and nose. There were eighty riders who covered the 2,000 mile route from St. Joseph, Missouri, to Sacramento, California.

Pony Express riders were such heroic figures that people think the Pony Express lasted for many years. In reality it lasted, from start to finish, a total of eighteen months. No sooner was it started on April 3, 1860, than telegraph wires were strung across the plains. The telegraph could transmit news and information much more quickly and cheaply than the Pony Express. Thus, on October 24, 1861, the Pony Express system of 190 stations, four hundred horses, four hundred keepers and assistants, and eighty riders was quickly dismantled.

Financially, the Pony Express was a failure; but to the pioneers who received their news and letters from home through the "Pony," it was a great success. Although the Pony Express was in existence for only a short time, it lives on in the legends and lore of the Old West.

***Did you know that the first gummed postage stamp was issued in England in 1840? Philately is the hobby of those who are fond of studying and collecting postage stamps. There are so many different subjects depicted on stamps that many collectors specialize in a particular subject, such as birds, sports figures, or Civil War stamps. To find out more about stamps and stamp collecting, ask your librarian to help you find philatelic journals, magazines, and books.***

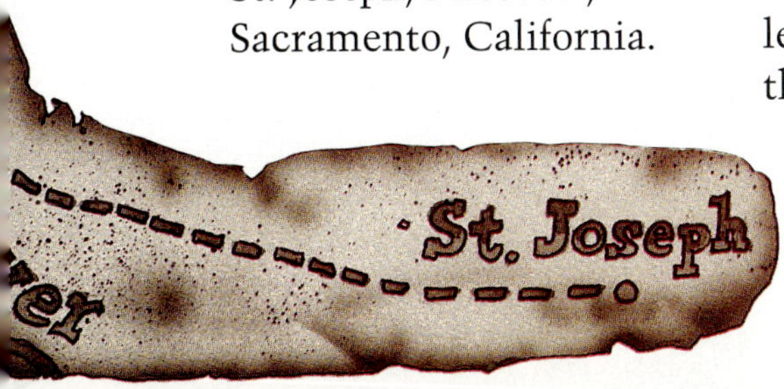

AWARD WINNING *Author*

Historic Picture Service

# A PECK OF GOLD

Dust always blowing about the town,
Except when sea fog laid it down,
And I was one of the children told
Some of the blowing dust was gold.

All the dust the wind blew high
Appeared like gold in the sunset sky,
But I was one of the children told
Some of the dust was really gold.

Such was life in the Golden Gate:
Gold dusted all we drank and ate,
And I was one of the children told,
"We all must eat our peck of gold."

ROBERT FROST

# NOTHING GOLD CAN STAY

Nature's first green is gold,
Her hardest hue to hold.
Her early leaf's a flower;
But only so an hour.
Then leaf subsides to leaf.
So Eden sank to grief,
So dawn goes down to day.
Nothing gold can stay.

ROBERT FROST

GOLD MINING IN CALIFORNIA, *lithograph by Currier & Ives, 1871.*

# All That Glitters

## from *Roughing It*
## by Mark Twain

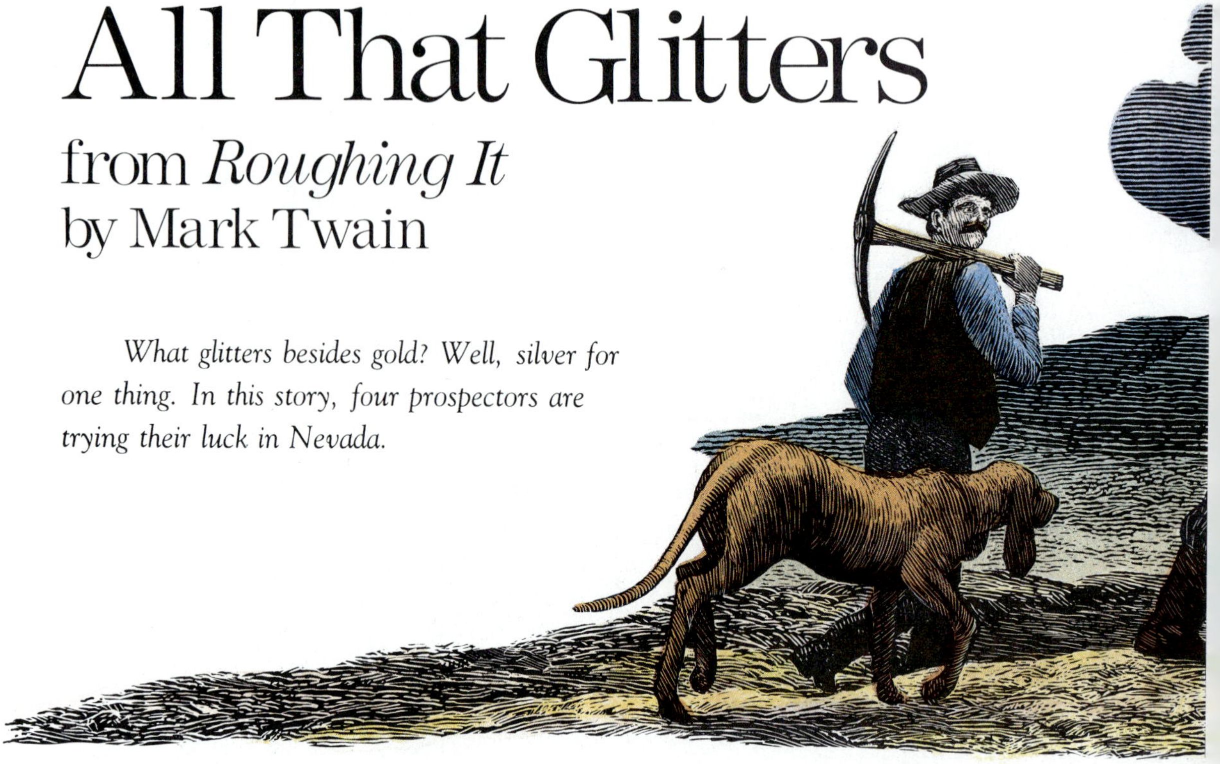

*What glitters besides gold? Well, silver for one thing. In this story, four prospectors are trying their luck in Nevada.*

Hurry, was the word! We wasted no time. Our party consisted of four persons—a blacksmith sixty years of age, two young lawyers, and myself. We bought a wagon and two miserable old horses. We put eighteen hundred pounds of provisions and mining tools in the wagon and drove out of Carson on a chilly December afternoon. The horses were so weak and old that we soon found that it would be better if one or two of us got out and walked. It was an improvement. Next, we found that it would be better if a third man got out. That was an improvement also. It was at this time that I volunteered to drive, although I had never driven a harnessed horse before, and many a man in such a position would have felt fairly excused from such a responsibility. But in a little while it was found that it would be a fine thing if the driver got out and walked also. It was at this time that I resigned the position of driver, and never resumed it again. Within the hour, we found that it would not only be better, but was absolutely necessary, that we four, taking turns, two at a time, should put our hands against the end of the wagon and push it through the sand, leaving the feeble horses little to do but keep

out of the way and hold up the tongue. Perhaps it is well for one to know his fate at first, and get reconciled to it. We had learned ours in one afternoon. It was plain that we had to walk through the sand and shove that wagon and those horses two hundred miles. So we accepted the situation, and from that time forth we never rode. More than that, we stood regular and nearly constant watches pushing up behind.

We made seven miles, and camped in the desert. Young Claggett (now member of Congress from Montana) unharnessed and fed and watered the horses; Oliphant and I cut sagebrush, built the fire and brought water to cook with; and old Mr. Ballou, the blacksmith, did the cooking. This division of labor, and this appointment, was adhered to throughout the journey. We had no tent, and so we slept under our blankets in the open plain. We were so tired that we slept soundly.

We were fifteen days making the trip—two hundred miles—thirteen, rather, for we lay by a couple of days, in one place, to let the horses rest. We could really have accomplished the journey in ten days if we had towed the horses behind the wagon, but we did

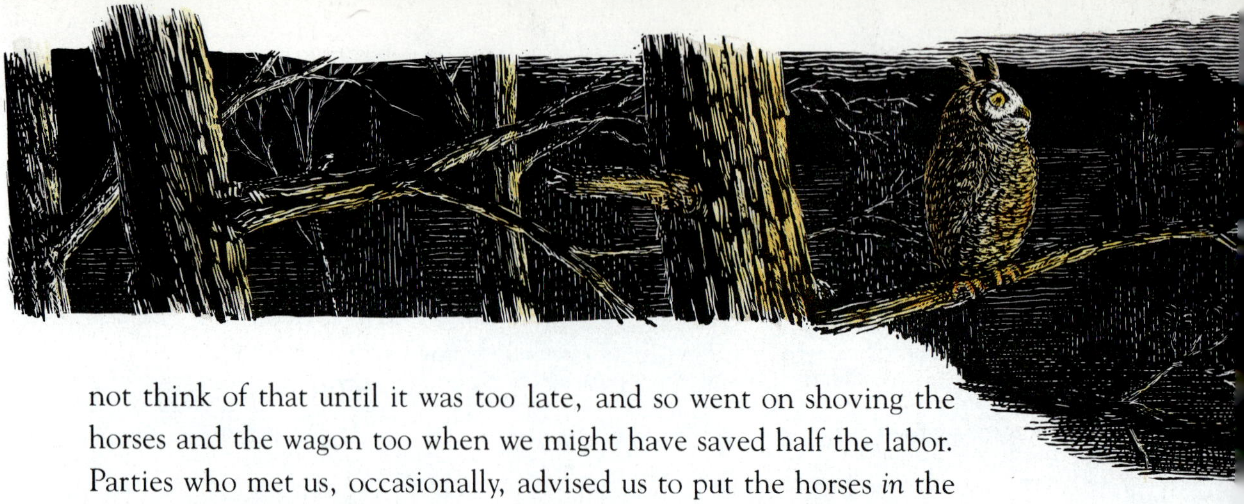

not think of that until it was too late, and so went on shoving the horses and the wagon too when we might have saved half the labor. Parties who met us, occasionally, advised us to put the horses *in* the wagon, but Mr. Ballou, through whose iron-clad earnestness no sarcasm could pierce, said that that would not do, because the provisions were exposed and would suffer, the horses being "bituminous from long deprivation." The reader will excuse me from translating. What Mr. Ballou customarily meant, when he used a long word, was a secret between himself and his Maker. He was one of the best and kindest-hearted men that ever graced a humble sphere of life. He was gentleness and simplicity itself—and unselfishness, too. Although he was more than twice as old as the eldest of us, he never gave himself any airs, privileges, or exemptions on that account. He did a *young* man's share of the work; and did his share of conversing and entertaining from the general standpoint of *any* age—not from the arrogant, overawing summit-height of sixty years. His one striking peculiarity was his Partingtonian fashion of loving and using big words *for their own sakes*, and independent of any bearing they might have upon the thought he was purposing to convey. He always let his ponderous syllables fall with an easy unconsciousness that left them wholly without offensiveness. In truth, his air was so natural and so simple that one was always catching himself accepting his stately sentences as meaning something, when they really meant nothing in the world. If a word was long and grand and resonant, that was sufficient to win the old man's love, and he would drop that word into the most out-of-the-way place in a sentence or a subject, and be as pleased with it as if it were perfectly luminous with meaning.

We four always spread our common stock of blankets together on the frozen ground, and slept side by side; and finding that our foolish, long-legged hound pup had a deal of animal heat in him, Oliphant got to admitting him to the bed, between himself and Mr.

Ballou, hugging the dog's warm back to his breast and finding great comfort in it. But in the night the pup would get stretchy and brace his feet against the old man's back and shove, grunting complacently the while; and now and then, being warm and snug, grateful and happy, he would paw the old man's back simply in excess of comfort; and at yet other times he would dream of the chase and in his sleep tug at the old man's back hair and bark in his ear. The old gentleman complained mildly about these familiarities, at last, and when he got through with his statement he said that such a dog as that was not a proper animal to admit to bed with tired men, because he was "so meretricious in his movements and so organic in his emotions." We turned the dog out.

It was a hard, wearing, toilsome journey, but it had its bright side; for after each day was done and our wolfish hunger appeased with a hot supper of fried bacon, bread, molasses, and black coffee, song-singing, and yarn-spinning around the evening camp-fire in the still solitudes of the desert was a happy, care-free sort of recreation that seemed the very summit and culmination of earthly luxury. It is a kind of life that has a potent charm for all men, whether city or country-bred. We are descended from desert-lounging Arabs, and countless ages of growth toward perfect civilization have failed to root out of us the nomadic instinct. We all confess to a gratified thrill at the thought of "camping out."

Once we made twenty-five miles in a day, and once we made forty miles (through the Great American Desert), and ten miles beyond—fifty in all—in twenty-three hours, without halting to eat, drink, or rest. To stretch out and go to sleep, even on stony and frozen ground, after pushing a wagon and two horses fifty miles, is a delight so supreme that for the moment it almost seems cheap at the price.

We camped two days in the neighborhood of the "Sink of the Humboldt." We tried to use the strong alkaline water of the Sink, but it would not answer. It was like drinking lye, and not weak lye, either. It left a taste in the mouth, bitter and every way execrable, and a burning in the stomach that was very uncomfortable. We put molasses in it, but that helped it very little, we added a pickle, yet the alkali was the prominent taste, and so it was unfit for drinking. The coffee we made of this water was the meanest compound humans have yet invented. It was really viler to the taste than the unameliorated water itself. Mr. Ballou, being the architect and builder of the beverage, felt constrained to endorse and uphold it, and so drank half a cup, by little sips, making shift to praise it faintly the while, but finally threw out the remainder, and said frankly it was "too technical for him."

But presently we found a spring of fresh water, convenient, and then, with nothing to mar our enjoyment, and no stragglers to interrupt it, we entered into our rest.

After leaving the Sink, we traveled along the Humboldt River a little way. People accustomed to the monster mile-wide Mississippi, grow accustomed to associating the term "river" with a high degree of watery grandeur. Consequently, such people feel rather disappointed when they stand on the shores of the Humboldt or the Carson and find that a "river" in Nevada is a sickly rivulet which is just the counterpart of the Erie Canal in all respects save that the canal is twice as long and four times as deep. One of the pleasantest and most invigorating exercises one can contrive is to run and jump across the Humboldt River till he is overheated, and then drink it dry.

On the fifteenth day we completed our march of two hundred miles and entered Unionville, Humboldt County, in the midst of a driving snowstorm. Unionville consisted of eleven cabins and a liberty pole. Six of the cabins were strung along one side of a deep cañon,[1] and the other five faced them. The rest of the landscape was made up of bleak mountain walls that rose so high into the sky from both sides of the cañon that the village was left, as it were, far down in the bottom of a crevice. It was always daylight on the mountain tops a long time before the darkness lifted and revealed Unionville.

[1] cañon (kan′yən): noun. a canyon

We built a small, rude cabin in the side of the crevice and roofed it with canvas, leaving a corner open to serve as a chimney, through which the cattle used to tumble occasionally, at night, and mash our furniture and interrupt our sleep. It was very cold weather and fuel was scarce. Indians brought brush and bushes several miles on their backs; and when we could catch a laden Indian it was well—and when we could not (which was the rule, not the exception), we shivered and bore it.

I confess, without shame, that I expected to find masses of silver lying all about the ground. I expected to see it glittering in the sun on the mountain summits. I said nothing about this, for some instinct told me that I might possibly have an exaggerated idea about it, and so if I betrayed my thought I might bring derision upon myself. Yet I was as perfectly satisfied in my own mind as I could be of anything, that I was going to gather up, in a day or two, or at furthest a week or two, silver enough to make me satisfactorily wealthy—and so my fancy was already busy with plans for spending this money. The first opportunity that offered, I sauntered carelessly away from the cabin, keeping an eye on the other boys, and stopping and contemplating the sky when they seemed to be observing me; but as soon as the coast was manifestly clear, I fled away as guiltily as a thief might have done and never halted till I was far beyond sight and call. Then I began my search with a feverish excitement that was brimful of expectation—almost of certainty. I crawled about the ground, seizing and examining bits of stone, blowing the dust from them or rubbing them on my clothes, and then peering at them with anxious hope. Presently I found a bright fragment and my heart bounded! I hid behind a boulder and polished it and scrutinized it with a nervous eagerness and a delight that was more pronounced than absolute certainty itself could have afforded. The more I examined the fragment the more I was convinced that I had found the door to fortune. I marked the spot and carried away my specimen. Up and down the rugged mountainside I searched, with always increasing interest and always augmenting gratitude that I had come to Humboldt and come in time. Of all the experiences of my life, this secret search among the hidden treasures of silver-land was the nearest to unmarred ecstasy. It was a delirious revel. By and by, in the bed of a shallow rivulet, I

G.M. DENTCH

found a deposit of shining yellow scales, and my breath almost forsook me! A gold-mine, and in my simplicity I had been content with vulgar silver! I was so excited that I half believed my overwrought imagination was deceiving me. Then a fear came upon me that people might be observing me and would guess my secret. Moved by this thought, I made a circuit of the place, and ascended a knoll to reconnoiter. Solitude. No creature was near. Then I returned to my mine, fortifying myself against possible disappointment, but my fears were groundless—the shining scales were still there. I set about scooping them out, and for an hour I toiled down the windings of the stream and robbed its bed. But at last the descending sun warned me to give up the quest, and I turned homeward laden with wealth. As I walked along I could not help smiling at the thought of my being so excited over my fragment of silver when a nobler metal was almost under my nose. In this little time the former had so fallen in my estimation that once or twice I was on the point of throwing it away.

The boys were as hungry as usual, but I could eat nothing. Neither could I talk. I was full of dreams and far away. Their conversation interrupted the flow of my fancy somewhat, and annoyed me a little, too. I despised the sordid and commonplace things they talked about. But as they proceeded, it began to amuse me. It grew to be rare fun to hear them planning their poor little economies and sighing over possible privations and distresses when a gold-mine, all our own, lay within sight of the cabin, and I could point it out at any moment. Smothered hilarity began to oppress me, presently. It was hard to resist the impulse to burst out with exultation and reveal everything; but I did resist. I said within myself that I would filter the great news through my lips calmly and be serene as a summer morning while I watched its effect in their faces. I said:

"Where have you all been?"

"Prospecting."

"What did you find?"

"Nothing."

"Nothing? What do you think of the country?"

"Can't tell, yet," said Mr. Ballou, who was an old gold-miner, and had likewise had considerable experience among the silver-mines.

"Well, haven't you formed any sort of opinion?"

"Yes, a sort of a one. It's fair enough here, maybe, but overrated. Seven-thousand-dollar ledges are scarce, though. That Sheba may be rich enough, but we don't own it; and, besides, the rock is so full of base metals that all the science in the world can't work it. We'll not starve, here, but we'll not get rich, I'm afraid."

"So you think the prospect is pretty poor?"

"No name for it!"

"Well, we'd better go back, hadn't we?"

"Oh, not yet—of course not. We'll try it a riffle, first."

"Suppose, now—this is merely a supposition, you know—suppose you could find a ledge that would yield, say, a hundred and fifty dollars a ton—would that satisfy you?"

"Try us once!" from the whole party.

"Or suppose—merely a supposition, of course—suppose you were to find a ledge that would yield two thousand dollars a ton—would that satisfy you?"

"Here—what do you mean? What are you coming at? Is there some mystery behind all this?"

"Never mind. I am not saying anything. You know perfectly well there are no rich mines here—of course you do. Because you have been around and examined for yourselves. Anybody would know that, that had been around. But just for the sake of argument, suppose—in a kind of general way—suppose some person were to tell you that two-thousand-dollar ledges were simply contemptible—contemptible, understand—and that right yonder in sight of this very cabin there were piles of pure gold and pure silver—oceans of it—enough to make you all rich in twenty-four hours! Come!"

"I should say he was as crazy as a loon!" said old Ballou, but wild with excitement, nevertheless.

"Gentlemen," said I, "I don't say anything—I haven't been around, you know, and of course don't know anything—but all I ask of you is to cast your eye on that, for instance, and tell me what you think of it!" and I tossed my treasure before them.

There was an eager scrabble for it, and a closing of heads together over it under the candlelight. Then old Ballou said:

"Think of it? I think it is nothing but a lot of granite rubbish and nasty glittering mica that isn't worth ten cents an acre!"

So vanished my dream. So melted my wealth away. So toppled my airy castle to the earth and left me stricken and forlorn.

Moralizing, I observed, then, that "all that glitters is not gold."

Mr. Ballou said I could go further than that, and lay it up among my treasures of knowledge, that nothing that glitters is gold. So I learned then, once for all, that gold in its native state is but dull, unornamental stuff, and that only lowborn metals excite the admiration of the ignorant with an ostentatious glitter. However, like the rest of the world, I still go on underrating men of gold and glorifying men of mica. Commonplace human nature cannot rise above that.

### ♦ Library Link ♦

*Mark Twain is one of America's most popular writers. If you enjoyed reading this humorous selection from his novel* Roughing It, *you will also enjoy his classic novels,* The Adventures of Tom Sawyer *and* The Adventures of Huckleberry Finn.

## Reader's Response

Do you agree with the narrator that it is human nature to underrate men of gold and glorify men of mica? Explain your response.

## Thinking It Over

1. What "fate" did the four people realize was theirs in the beginning of the story?
2. Describe Mr. Ballou. How did you decide what details to use in your description?
3. What was the men's primary reason for taking the journey?
4. Why do you think the narrator described his experience of searching for silver as almost one of ecstasy?
5. Describe the part of the story that you found most humorous, and explain why you felt it was funny.

## Appreciating Literature

This selection was first published in 1872—more than a hundred years ago. There were many writers at that time, publishing many works; yet only a few of these writers are still read today. Mark Twain is one of these few. Why do you suppose his work has endured? What is there about it that makes it appealing to people today?

## Writing to Learn

**Think and Analyze** No one in the world writes exactly like Mark Twain. Yet sometimes it is difficult to describe his style. The words below show characteristics of authors' styles. On your paper, list the characteristics you think represent Twain's style.

| | | |
|---|---|---|
| realistic<br>fanciful<br>humorous<br>serious | hard vocabulary<br>easy vocabulary | slang<br>no slang<br>dialogue<br>no dialogue |

**Write** Compose a "Mark Twainian" sentence that fits into a paragraph in the story that you just read. Copy the paragraph with your new sentence in it. Challenge a classmate to read the new paragraph and find your original "Twain-like" sentence.

# Literature Link

## *How can you figure out facts and feelings that are left unstated by an author?*

If you were the artist, what title would you give this painting? Look carefully at the details: the position of the two people in relation to each other, the expressions on their faces, the careful way the child holds the banjo, the curl of the man's fingers around the neck of the instrument. Use these details and your own knowledge to infer just what is happening in the painting. You can easily figure out that the man is teaching the boy to play the banjo. So it won't surprise you to learn that the great American painter Henry Tanner entitled this painting *The Banjo Lesson.*

This is a very simple example of a process that can sometimes be quite complex. It is this process of inferring, also called making inferences, that is at the heart of much of your reading. Just as you figured out the title of the painting, you often make inferences when you read.

## *Reading Between the Lines*

What's happening? Who are these people? What are they doing? Where are they going? When is it happening? These are the questions that probably came into your mind the first time you read this beginning of "All That Glitters":

> Hurry, was the word! We wasted no time. Our party consisted of four persons—a blacksmith sixty years of age, two young lawyers, and myself. We bought a wagon and two miserable old horses. We put eighteen hundred pounds of provisions and mining tools in the wagon and drove out of Carson on a chilly December afternoon.

Mark Twain is doing what many authors like to do. He brings you into the middle of things to get you involved in the action. Then you begin wondering what is happening. He's caught your attention, so you read on to find the answers. But there are important clues to help answer your questions right there in the opening sentences, if you can only read between the lines.

The words that *are* there are telling you that the narrator, who is one of the characters, is in a hurry to get started. But started with what? Much is left unstated. By thinking about the words *wagon* and *drove out of Carson*, you most likely inferred that Twain is describing a journey, and the *eighteen hundred pounds of provisions* tells you that it will be a long one. Did you notice that he never once states that a journey is beginning? You inferred this important point by putting these clues together. You most likely also inferred that the setting of this journey is a time and place in the past. What clues helped you to infer this? Maybe the fact that *you* know Twain lived in the last century helped you. Maybe Twain's reference to a *blacksmith* and traveling by *horse and wagon* also helped you to realize that you are not reading a description of a contemporary event. What else can you infer about the nature of the journey using clues from the passage together with facts from your own storehouse of knowledge?

## *Filling in the Gaps*

When you make an inference, you figure out information that the author does not state directly in a passage. To read between the lines, you have to fill in the gaps between *what is stated* and *what is left unstated*. Here are some tips to help you fill in the gaps:

- Read the stated facts and descriptions thoughtfully.
- Allow your natural questions to help you identify what has been left unstated.
- Using clues from your own experience and word clues from the narrative, come to your own conclusion about what the unstated facts are.
- Read on to see if you are right and to learn more.

As you read on, if your inference seems to be wrong, your mind will naturally keep trying to fill in the gaps. You will find that as you continue reading in this way, you will have a clearer understanding of all that was left unstated at the start. As you get better at using this strategy, you will be more and more captivated by narratives that challenge you to fill in the gaps and read between the lines.

Now read more from the beginning of "All That Glitters." In this passage, what inferences can you draw about the character who is the narrator?

> The horses were so weak and old that we soon found that it would be better if one or two of us got out and walked. It was an improvement. Next, we found that it would be better if a third man got out. That was an improvement also. It was at this time that I volunteered to drive, although I had never driven a harnessed horse before, and many a man in such a position would have felt fairly excused from such a responsibility. But in a little while it was found that it would be a fine thing if the driver got out and walked also. It was at this time that I resigned the position of driver, and never resumed it again. Within the hour, we found that it would not only be better, but was absolutely necessary, that we four, taking turns, two at a time, should put our hands against the end of the wagon and push it

through the sand, leaving the feeble horses little to do but keep out of the way and hold up the tongue. Perhaps it is well for one to know his fate at first, and get reconciled to it. We had learned ours in one afternoon.

What can you conclude about the personality and motive of the narrator? You might infer that he wanted to do everything possible to avoid walking, since when it became clear that three men had to walk, he volunteered to drive. And he didn't know how to drive! Read the passage again. This time, think about all the characters. Do you think the men are experienced travelers? What clues can you use to infer an answer? At this point in the narrative, can you infer what kind of a story this is? Do you think it will be serious, sad, or humorous? What clues do you have to support this conclusion?

See how making inferences enriches reading about the adventures of Lo Tung in the next selection, "It's Not the Great Wall, but It Will Last Forever."

# It's Not the Great Wall, but It Will Last Forever

## by Eve Bunting

*Completing a railroad across a vast continent—across mountains, deserts, and rivers—once seemed impossible. The story of how the transcontinental railroad was finally built is a story worth knowing.*

Lo Tung leaned against the rattling wall of the freight car. Beneath him the floor moved as the wheels clacked over the rails. It was a long time since he'd sat or walked on anything steady. First there had been the long days and nights on the Pacific Mail Steamship that had brought him from China, then the riverboat from San Francisco to Sacramento, then the train, waiting on the levee.

He hadn't had time for more than a glimpse of the strange, iron monster belching smoke before the boss man had hustled them aboard. It was hard to believe that he was here now, in this freight car along with other Chinese workers, rolling eastward across America.

Lo Tung looked sideways at his friend, Wei. Wei was fifteen years old, too, and as small and thin as Lo Tung.

"Not more than a hundred pounds, either of you," the agent had said in disgust. "You two will not be able to do the heavy railroad work."

"Don't worry. We are strong," Lo Tung had said. He had not added "Ho Sen was strong, the strongest man in our village. And he was killed building the American railway." Now Ho Sen's bones lay somewhere in this strange country. And Chen Chi Yuen. He had gone and never been heard from again.

Sitting now in the freight car, thinking about the work, Lo Tung flexed his muscles. Strong for the work. Of course, strong and fearless.

It was growing dark. They had been closed in here together for hours, so many of them from the ship. The air was used up and the smells were bad.

"The train must stop soon," Wei said. "At the place where the rails end. Then our work will begin."

"And our wages," Lo Tung added.

Why had they been brought all the way from China to help build this railroad? "Is the job so big that they've run out of workers in America?" Wei had whispered. "Or have they run out of Americans who want this work?"

"Perhaps a wage that seems generous to us does not seem that way to them," Lo Tung suggested.

Everyone in their hungry village had read the notices pasted to the walls.

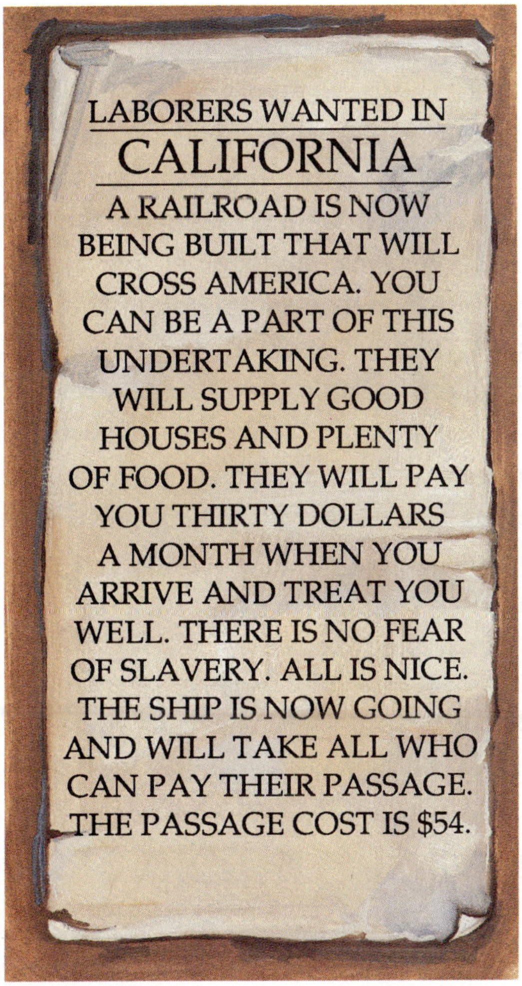


"Aiya!" Lo Tung said. Fifty-four dollars was a fortune, and impossible for his mother! The agent had allowed them to borrow from him. That was when he'd complained of Lo Tung's size.

"Not a penny of your wages will be yours till you pay me back," he had warned.

Lo Tung had agreed. He would have agreed to almost anything. Not that he wanted to go to America. The thought of leaving his home brought tears to his eyes. But it was clearly his duty. He was, after all, the eldest son. Since his father's death the family responsibility had been his. If he went, his debt to the agent would be cleared in two months. Then he could begin sending money home for his mother and his sisters, and his little brother. He had to believe that he could save enough to go home himself some day.

Thinking of home here in the heat of the freight car made loneliness rise in him like water in a swamp. Fear was bad, but loneliness was worse. He would not allow himself to remember.

"We are slowing," Wei said. "I can see through a crack."

Someone else said, "We are here."

Tired men and boys staggered up, swaying, hoisting their bedrolls. As the train chugged to a stop they waited quietly for what was to come.

When the doors opened Lo Tung saw that it was night outside, the sky filled with a million crystal stars.

"American stars," he whispered to Wei, pointing upward.

"Are they the same that shine over China or . . . "

"Out! Everyone out!" Men waited beside the train, big, bulky men who cast massive shadows.

"Hurry! Get a move on!"

The words were not in Lo Tung's language but he understood the tone. He jumped down to the ground with the others.

"Quickly now! Over here!"

The yellow lanterns the men carried swung as they moved, shining on the big faces under the wide brimmed western hats, dropping pools of light on their muddy boots.

Lo Tung looked back at the train. It puffed and groaned like a tired dragon. How strange it was, and how strange the darkness beyond. That was the great breadth of America. That was where the rails would go.

"Chop chop!" the big men yelled, and the lanterns swung in impatient arcs.

The Chinese moved forward, their slippers soundless on the dirt.

Lo Tung saw now that there were trees all around them, giant trees that crowded the track and stretched up to the starry sky. There was a nose-tickling smell of pine and fresh cut wood and for a moment he thought he heard the rush of a river. But when he tipped his head back he saw that the noise came from the wind in the tops of the trees. The trees are whispering, he thought. What do they say? Here are more of these men, come to cut us down, come to build their railroad? Could trees feel fear, too? It was colder outside than it was in the train and Lo Tung shivered.

A man came to stand in front of them. He was Chinese and when he spoke he used their language.

"I am the head man here," he said, and Wei whispered to Lo Tung: "See? He is the head man and he is one of us. He came before we did, that is all. One could do well here."

"My name is Chu Wen. You may call me Mr. Chu. I work for the big boss men and I am in charge of you. The Central Pacific Railway welcomes you. On the other side of the country workers lay rails from East to West. One day these rails will meet and we will have a great connection that will bring everyone together."

He pointed to the ground that had been cleared close to the tracks, and through the darkness Lo Tung saw the pale outline of tents. "This is where you will live. As you make progress each day, the tents will move with you. There will be plenty of food and hard work. Get yourselves settled for the night. Tomorrow your new lives will begin."

There was rice and dried cuttlefish, as much as they could eat. Then there was sleep. Rolled in his bedroll, listening to the whispers of the trees, in spite of his loneliness Lo Tung slept.

By sunrise they were at work, hacking the ground with picks and shovels, clearing the land in front of the shining rails so that new shining rails could be added.

Three times that first day the cook's aide brought kegs of tea, balanced on a bamboo pole across his shoulders. Then Lo Tung took a moment to look into the blue emptiness of the sky and to remind himself how fortunate he was to be able to help his mother. He would labor well, show no fear, and bring only honor to his family's name.

Quickly he discovered that there was little honor to being Chinese in this new land. Their jobs were the lowest and their wages, too. The workers who were not Chinese mocked their clothes, their straw hats and baggy cotton pants.

"What is that you're eating?" they'd ask, wrinkling up their noses. "Is that seaweed?"

The Chinese ate silently, their eyes lowered to their bowls, only their chopsticks moving.

One night, Big John O'Donnell, the largest and most ill-mannered of the work gang, cut off Tang Yin's long queue. The next morning Lo Chung saw it hanging from Big John's belt. Lo Chung's heart wept for Tang Yin's loss.

"Be wise and tolerant," Mr. Chu told them. "It is hard for these others. Many of them have come from countries as hungry as our own. We are unusual to them, strangers. They see how well we work. They fear for their jobs. There is talk that the bosses will bring in still more Chinese. That is why these others say that we are too small, too weak, too foolish to build a railroad."

"Do they not know that our people built the Great Wall of China?" Lo Chung asked. "What is a railroad compared to that?"

"Keep to yourselves," Mr. Chu advised. "Say little. Work hard."

They did. And the tracks grew another five miles, and another five.

When a tree stood in their way they chopped it down.

"I am sorry, tree," Lo Chung whispered then. But he axed as fiercely as anyone. When a root would not come free it was blasted free. And always, it seemed, the Chinese did the blasting.

"Everyone knows you are good with gunpowder," Big John said. "Pretend it's New Year."

Men were killed as the railroad grew.

"Sometimes I think these rails ride high on Chinese bones," Wei said sadly. But the rails rode on all kinds of bones. The work went on.

At night there were baths in wooden barrels, clean clothes and rest. There were campfires and talk of the mighty railroad, and home.

And always before he slept, Lo Chung weighed his money pouch in his hand. In spite of what he sent home the pouch grew heavier. Sometimes he watched the moon float in its bed of darkness and he wondered if his mother watched it too. Sometimes, in secret, he cried.

They were moving high into the Sierra now, blasting tunnels through granite rocks. They built wooden trestles to span the canyons, crawling on them like flies, putting down ties, laying the rails. They chipped and chiselled and clawed. Then they were in the gorge of the American River and the work stopped. On either side were sheer walls of granite that stretched for twelve miles. No place for a foothold on those cliffs. No place for even a mountain goat to climb.

"Aiya!" the Chinese said, staring in wonder.

"The end of the line," the others whispered. "The end of the Central Pacific."

It was the Chinese who thought of the solution. Wasn't there a saying that for every question there is an answer? And hadn't their ancestors built impossible roads that hung from mountains for thousands of years? There was a way.

Quickly they took reeds and wove from them baskets, each wide enough and deep enough to hold two men. Two small men.

"We will tie ropes to the baskets," they said. "You will lower us over the cliff and we will take picks and make holes where there are no holes, and we will plant gunpowder. This cliff will not be as smooth as glass when we have finished.

"It is not possible," the bosses said. "If those ropes break. . . . "

Big John shook his head. "Reed baskets! Craziness!"

"We have made the baskets strong," the Chinese told him.

"My people know about such things," Mr. Chu added proudly.

Good fortune signs were painted on the four sides and the ropes secured. The baskets were ready.

"Lo Tung! Wei! You will go first. You weigh the least. You will be the test."

"If we come back we have passed the test?" Lo Tung asked.

The head man nodded. "And if not, you have failed."

Lo Tung took off the new boots that he'd bought at the company store. The boots were heavy and might tear the bottom of the basket. He allowed himself to look once at the emptiness below.

Someone touched his shoulder. "Good luck, Lo Tung," Big John said. "I'll say one thing for you. You have guts."

Lo Tung lowered his eyes. He had not known that Big John knew his name.

He climbed into the basket where Wei waited and he saw the shake of fear in Wei's knees. His own shook, too. But only a fool would not be afraid. The important thing was that they would go.

One second the basket rested on the edge of the cliff, the next second it swung out into space.

Lo Tung heard the creak of the pulley, and when he looked back he saw that Big John was holding the rope, too.

Already they were moving jerkily down the side of the cliff. Wind caught the basket, spun it like a top, made it dance in the air. Birds screamed from their nests and flapped at their heads. The basket bumped the rock sides, bumped again, and shreds of reeds drifted down toward the silver thread of river.

A person would fall faster, Lo Tung thought and quickly threw the thought away. He strained to see above him. He could see only the smooth gray walls of the cliff, the clouds turning in the sky like sailing junks on a lake, the ropes snaking up. Faces, small as beans, lined the top of the cliff where men lay peering down.

"Lo Tung?" Wei's voice was lost in the emptiness. "Lo Tung, will we go home one day? And will we talk strong about what we did, here in America?"

"Yes," Lo Tung said. "And we will tell how we built this railroad. It is not the Great Wall, but it will last forever."

The basket had stopped now. Far, far above them arms waved. It was the signal. This was where they must work.

Lo Tung and Wei stood and leaned over the side of the basket toward the cliff face. The sides were only waist high. Easy to topple over, Lo Tung thought. Easy to fall, like the shreds of reeds. He grabbed for a twig that grew from a crack in the rock, holding it to keep himself steady. But it pulled free in his hand. Dirt loosened, blew in his mouth and eyes. The sun swung dizzily above them; wind sang in his nose. When they worked together the basket tilted, ready to throw them out, so they took turns, one to poke at the hard, smooth wall, one to balance the weight on the other side.

So much work to make one small hole.

So much work to make another.

Six holes now and the sun moving across the sky.

"Gunpowder," Lo Tung said. He took it from Wei, packed it in the six holes. Wei waved his arms to give the signal. When the answering shake came on the ropes, Lo Tung lit the fuses.

"Now," he yelled. "Now!"

The basket rose in quick jolts and stops, swinging back and forth like the pendulum on a clock.

Below him Lo Tung saw the glow of the fuses as the sparks crept closer and closer to the powder. He wanted to jump from the basket and haul himself up the rope, hand over hand to safety.

"Hurry! Hurry!" they called, straining upward, standing on their toes to put as much space as possible between them and the explosives.

Rising now so fast that his ears hurt.

"Faster," they called. "Hurry!"

Below them the fuses had disappeared and Lo Tung knew that they had reached the holes where the gunpowder waited.

"Hurry! Please hurry!"

And now they were up, hands helping them to scramble from the basket, to lie flat along the earth as the explosions came.

They came in short, quick cracks. Puffs of smoke shot like rifle fire from the cliffs. Lo Tung heard the rumble as the chunks of granite broke away, sliding and tumbling to the gorge below. There would be footholds now . . . toe holds . . . places to stand to hack out the path that would carry the precious railway.

Western hats and straw hats were tossed together into the air.

"You did it!"

Lo Tung and Wei were tossed in the air, too.

It was when they shook hands that Lo Tung saw the burns, raw on Big John's palms and wrists. He'd held that rope so fast, and pulled so mightily that the skin had rubbed away through his gloves.

"Good job," he told Lo Tung. "Now more baskets can go down. But you two were the first. You showed us something about courage."

Lo Tung nodded, smiling, not recognizing the words but understanding anyway. He had a sense of all of them, a team, working together, the rails stretching into far distance behind them.

"In my country there is a saying," he told Big John. "Make a stranger your friend and together you can plant a field. Or build a railroad," he added.

Big John smiled as if he, too, understood.

Lo Tung thought that true understanding would be slow, like the building of a railroad. But that perhaps, today, it had begun.

## *Reader's Response*

How do you feel about the quotation "Make a stranger your friend, and together you can plant a field"?

## Thinking It Over

1. Why did Lo Tung go to America?
2. State three problems that Chinese workers had to face in America.
3. Compare Big John's attitude toward the Chinese at the beginning of the story with his attitude at the end of the story.
4. Based on what you know of Lo Tung's qualities, goals, and dreams, what do you think Lo Tung did when his job on the railroad was finished?
5. What two Chinese sayings were mentioned in the story, and how were they significant? How did you work out your answer to this question?

## Appreciating Literature

This story is an example of historical fiction in which fictional characters participate in real historical events. How can reading historical fiction enrich our understanding of the past? What kinds of things would an author have to research in order to create an accurate picture of the past?

## Writing to Learn

**Think and Imagine** How would you feel if you were in Lo Tung's place? Step into the story and imagine how he might have felt and what he might have thought. Making a diagram of his thoughts and feelings may help you. Complete this diagram on your own paper.

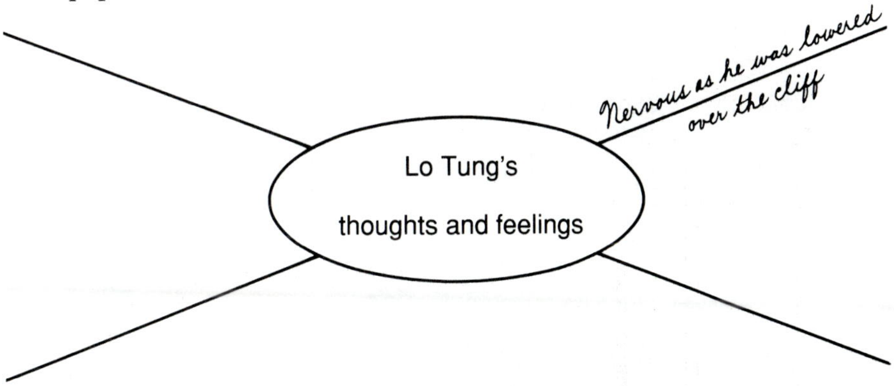


**Write** Using your diagram, write a paragraph describing how you think Lo Tung thought and felt.

Using Maps

# Reading Social Studies

In social studies books, maps and written information are used together to convey information. Maps are helpful because some information is easier to understand in graphic form than in written form.

When you see a map in your social studies book, ask yourself what information the author is giving you in the map. Then, read the title, the labels on the map, the key or legend, and any captions that might be provided. These map details help you understand the map itself as well as the accompanying written material.

Study the map below and read the passage from a social studies book on the next page.

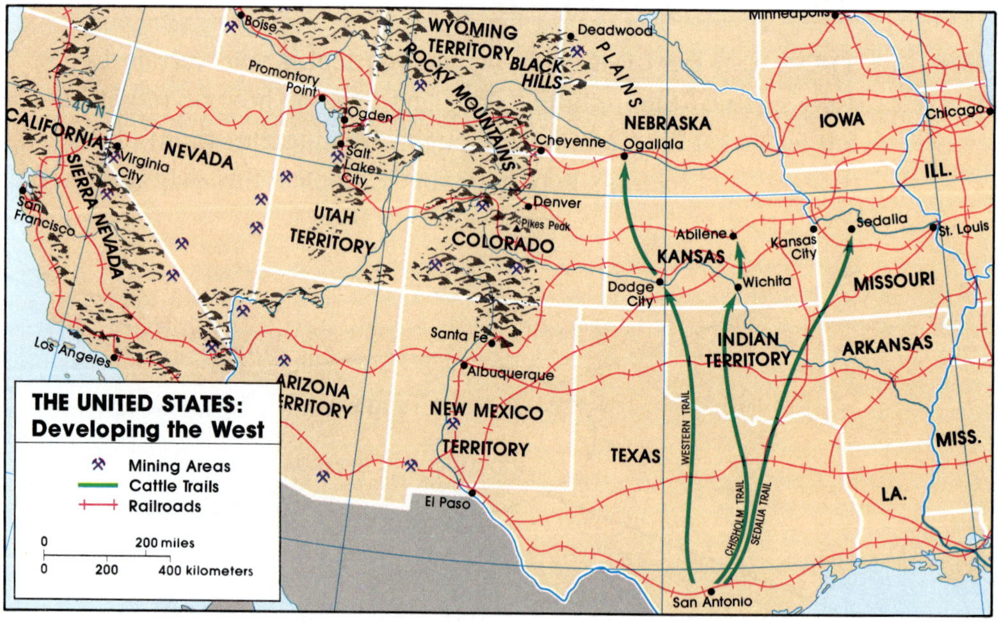

In the 1860s, while the mining towns of the West were booming, Texas ranchers were profiting by raising cattle for shipment to eastern markets. Cowhands herded the cattle long distances to the railroad. In 1867, the nearest railroad was in Abilene, Kansas, hundreds of miles away from any Texas ranch. During the next twenty years, about six million cattle reached market along such trails as the Chisholm Trail to Abilene.

By 1850, most railroads in the East had been built. As travel by rail was faster and safer than travel by wagon train, it became a national priority to connect the East and the West by rail. In 1862, Congress funded the first transcontinental railroad. The Union Pacific Railroad was built in a westward direction from Nebraska. The Central Pacific Railroad was built in an eastward direction beginning in California. The two railroads were joined with a golden spike at Promontory Point on May 10, 1869.

By looking at the map, you can see the exact location of the mining areas mentioned in the first paragraph of the passage. It also shows the location of the trails along which the cowhands herded cattle. By using the scale of distance found in the key to the map, you can verify that the Chisholm Trail was more than six hundred miles long. You can also see that the cowhands used the Western Trail and the Sedalia Trail to herd cattle to railroads.

The map also helps you see the route of the first transcontinental railroad. Use the map to find Promontory Point, where the two sections of the transcontinental railroad were joined.

Although the written material in the chapter does not specifically discuss the distances and hardships involved in developing the West, the physical features on the map help you visualize the vast expanse of the continent, the extensive mountains, and the difficulty of the trip west. This helps you understand the nation's compelling interest in connecting the East and the West by railroad.

**As You Read** Read the following pages from a social studies textbook, and study the maps. Answer the questions on page 253.

CHAPTER 13

# Spanning the Continent

1820–1853

## On to Oregon

***How did the Oregon Country become part of the United States?***

**VOCABULARY**

| | |
|---|---|
| **Great American Desert** | **"Fifty-four forty or fight!"** |
| **Mountain Men** | **49th parallel** |
| **Oregon Trail** | |
| **provisional government** | |

**Major Long's Mistake** Major Stephen Long was chiefly responsible for a great mistake in American geography. In the 1820s this army officer led an expedition in the lands between the Missouri River and the Rocky Mountains. The official maps of the expedition labeled the region the **Great American Desert**. Major Long wrote of this region: "It is wholly unfit for cultivation and . . . uninhabitable by people depending on agriculture for their subsistence."

For 50 years mapmakers copied Long's maps with their misleading labels. Settlers crossed the "desert" without stopping, on their way to the more desirable lands west of the Rockies. Much of the land was a great treeless plain. Today these plains support millions of people. But to those pioneers it must have seemed like an endless desert.

**Trails West** During Major Long's explorations he discovered routes through the trackless Great Plains. Another army officer, Captain John C. Frémont, also roamed through the West. He and his guide, Kit Carson, discovered suitable routes for the westward migration that would soon follow.

It was Frémont's wife, Jessie Benton Frémont, who carried the story of her husband's explorations to people in the East. She took his official reports of two exploring expeditions of the 1840s and turned them into popular books. Persons planning to venture to the west coast eagerly read the books and studied the maps and the descriptions of the western trails.

By the early 1840s experienced and capable guides were ready to lead wagon trains of settlers and traders over the best routes into the far western lands. Many of these guides were men who had spent their early lives trapping and trading for furs in the Rockies. They have become known in history as the **Mountain Men**.

**Mountain Men** The Mountain Men were highly resourceful and wise in the ways of the wilderness. Many of them guided exploring parties that were sent out by the army. They led groups that brought goods to trade with the Indians for furs.

**During the 1840s, hundreds of families headed west, traveling by covered wagon.**
**■ When did Americans settle in Texas?**

They also hired out as guides to the wagon trains of pioneers heading west.

Jim Bridger was a famous Mountain Man. He discovered many of the principal landmarks between the Rockies and the Sierra Nevada. Like most of the Mountain Men, Bridger got along well with the Indians. His first wife was the daughter of a chief of the Flathead tribe. They had two children before she died. His second wife was a Ute. She died in childbirth on July 4, 1849. It is said that Jim Bridger raised his motherless baby on buffalo milk.

James Beckwourth was another famous Mountain Man. He was born in Virginia, probably into slavery, but he grew up in St. Louis as a free man. After joining a fur-trading expedition to the Rocky Mountains, Beckwourth lived for 11 years with the Crow Indians. They gave him the name of Morning Star. Later, Beckwourth became an army scout and discovered a pass through the Sierra Nevada. This route is today called Beckwourth Pass.

**During the 1840s Easterners poured into the fertile Oregon Country.**
**■ What fort was built at the point at which the Snake River joins the Columbia River?**

## The Oregon Country

In the late 1700s, American ships visited the Oregon coast. Captain Robert Gray discovered the mouth of the Columbia River in 1792. Little more than 10 years later, the Lewis and Clark expedition gave the United States a further claim to the Oregon Country. In 1811, John Jacob Astor founded Astoria, a fur-trading post near the mouth of the Columbia River. Great Britain also claimed the region. It based its claims on the explorations of Sir Francis Drake in 1579, Captain James Cook in 1778, and Captain George Vancouver in 1792. In 1818, the treaty between Great Britain and the United States that set the northern border of the Louisiana Purchase (see page 328) allowed citizens of both nations to settle in Oregon. But no decision was made about which nation owned the country.

The Oregon Country was much larger than the present state of Oregon. It extended west from the Rocky Mountains to the Pacific Ocean. Its northern boundary was 54°40′ north latitude. This boundary, which touched the southern tip of Alaska, was established by a treaty between the United States and Russia in 1824. In the south the Oregon Country touched the northern border of California. Both American and British fur traders spread the word about the richness of the land.

Christian missionaries also played a prominent part in attracting settlers to Oregon. In 1834, Jason Lee led a party of Methodist missionaries to the Oregon Country. Father De Smet, a Jesuit missionary, also established several missions in Oregon. Marcus Whitman, a young New York doctor, was still another pioneer missionary. In 1836 he and his wife built their

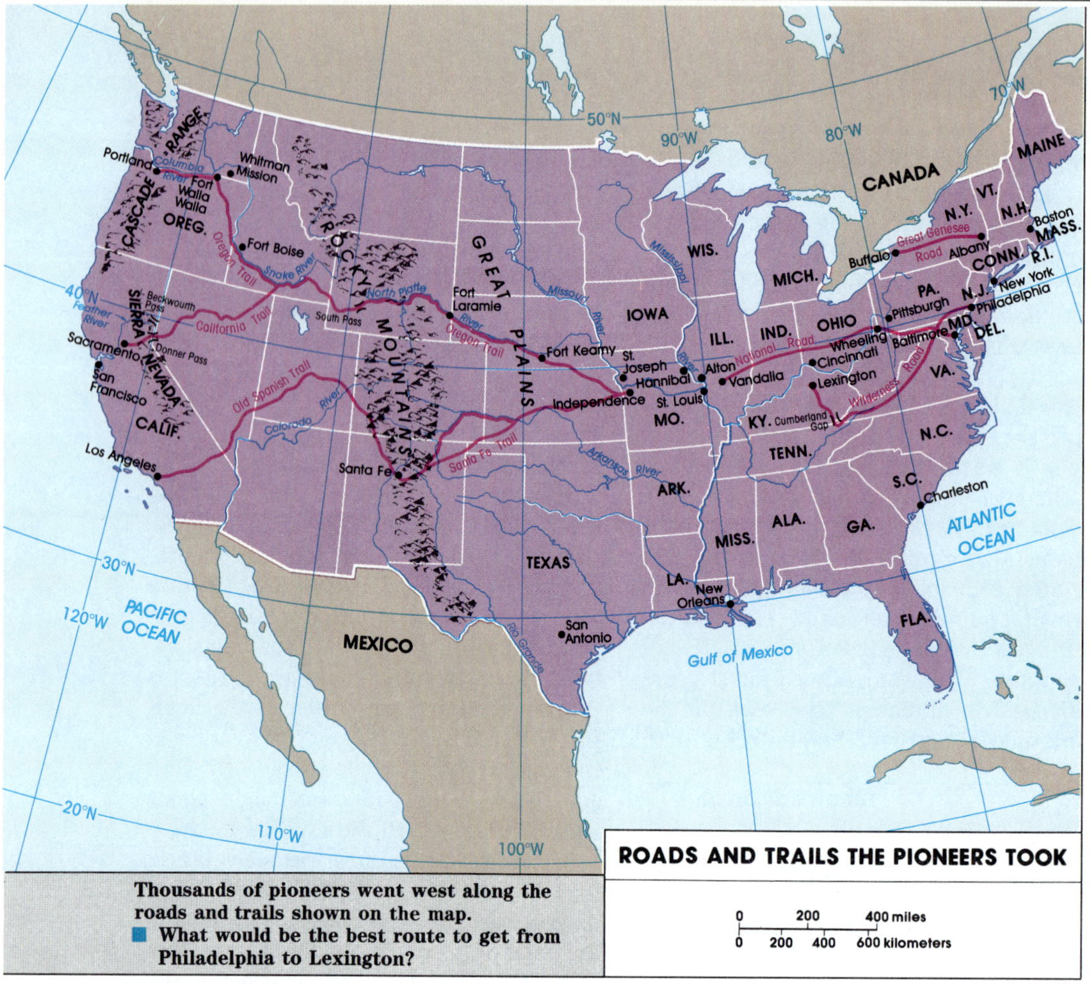


**ROADS AND TRAILS THE PIONEERS TOOK**

**Thousands of pioneers went west along the roads and trails shown on the map.**

■ **What would be the best route to get from Philadelphia to Lexington?**

mission near the site of present-day Walla Walla, Washington. Narcissa Prentiss Whitman was one of the first white women to settle west of the Rockies.

**"Oregon Fever"** The reports of the missionaries created great interest in the Oregon Country. By the 1840s the interest in moving to this northwestern region was so intense that it began to be called "Oregon fever." People talked of the great crops of wheat one could raise in Oregon. Stories of the rich soil and the good climate were told. One account declared that

> out in Oregon the pigs are running about under the great acorn trees, round and fat, and already cooked, with knives and forks sticking in them so that you can cut off a slice whenever you are hungry.

After hearing tales like this, it is no wonder that thousands of people planned to move to the Oregon Country. The first large group to travel the **Oregon Trail** left Independence, Missouri, in the spring of 1843. It included about 1,000 men, women, and children. They had loaded their possessions into huge covered wagons pulled by oxen.

Starting from Independence, the trail to Oregon covered nearly 2,000 miles (3,200 km). The slow-moving caravans went northwest to the Platte River.

## *Using What You Have Learned*

1. The material you read tells you that the Oregon Trail covered nearly two thousand miles. How could you use the map on page 252 to verify this distance?

2. How was the Oregon Country different in size from the present state of Oregon? Use the maps on page 251 and 252 to help you answer this question.

3. Two passes through the Sierra Nevada Mountains are shown on page 252. Which pass is mentioned in the lesson? What is the name of the other pass?

4. Approximately how long, in miles, was the northern boundary of the Oregon Country? What map feature did you use to figure out the answer?

5. Which map would you use to see the region Major Stephen Long mistakenly labeled? What is the appropriate label for this region?

6. Construct a key for the map on page 252 that shows symbols for cities, trails, and international borders. Use colors.

7. In addition to the Oregon Trail discussed in the reading material, what other major trail connected the East and the West? Which map gives you this information?

8. Answer the question under the map on page 252. Explain your answer.

9. Based on the map on page 252, describe three experiences pioneers might have had as they traveled west.

# THE ETERNAL FRONTIER

by Louis L'Amour

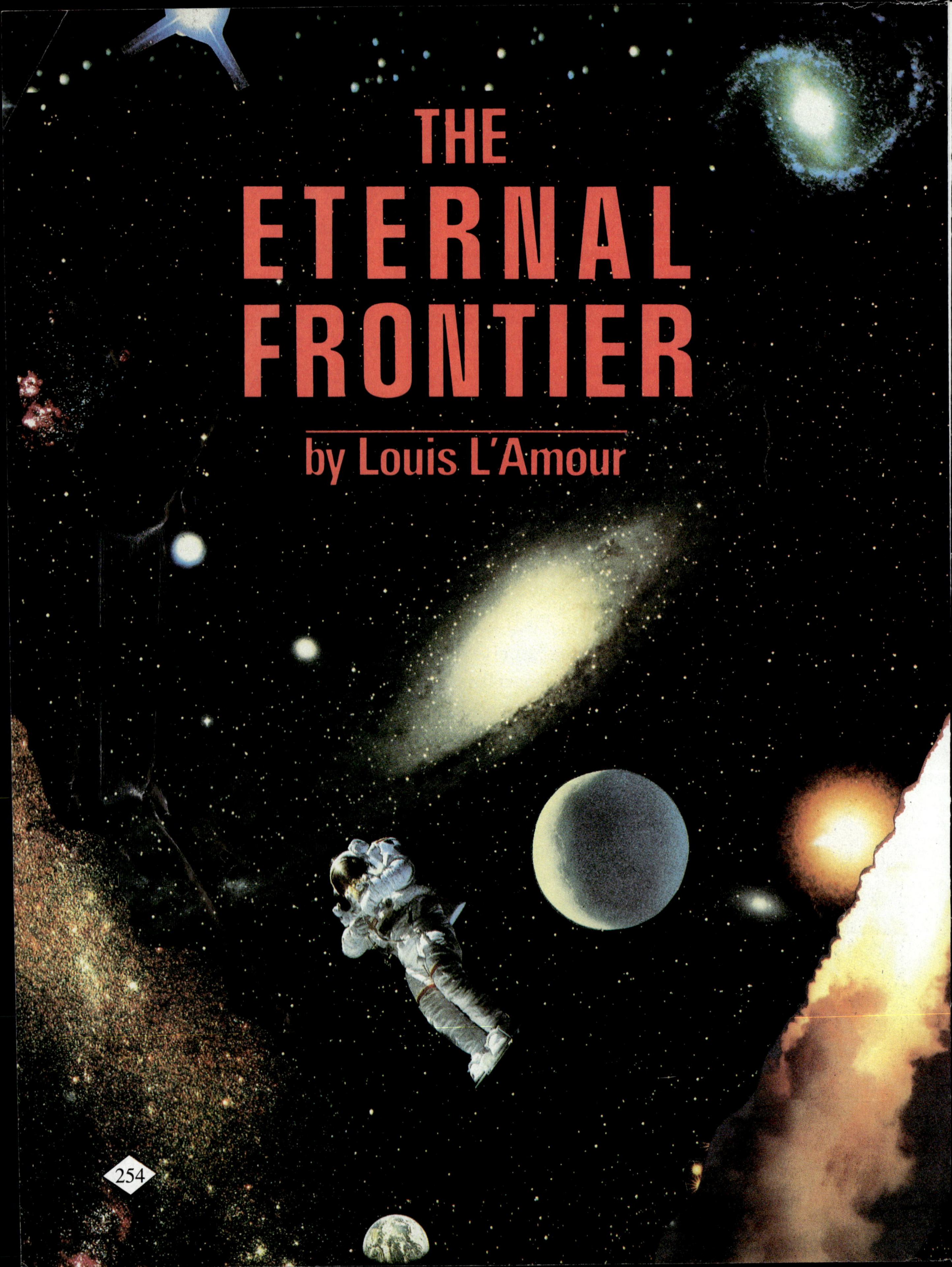

*Do you hate to sit still? Do you long for adventure? Don't worry. There are still some frontiers to conquer.*

The question I am most often asked is, "Where is the frontier now?"

The answer should be obvious. Our frontier lies in outer space.

The moon, the asteroids, the planets, these are mere stepping stones, where we will test ourselves, learn needful lessons, and grow in knowledge before we attempt those frontiers beyond our solar system. Outer space is a frontier without end, the eternal frontier, an everlasting challenge to explorers not only of other planets and other solar systems but also of the human mind.

All that has gone before was preliminary. We have been preparing ourselves mentally for what lies ahead. Many problems remain, but if we can avoid a devastating war we shall move with a rapidity scarcely to be believed. In the past seventy years we have developed the automobile, radio, television, transcontinental and transoceanic flight, and the electrification of the country, among a multitude of other such developments. In 1900 there were 144 miles of surfaced road in the United States. Now there are over 3,000,000. Paved roads and the development of the automobile have gone hand in hand, the automobile being the civilized person's antidote to overpopulation.

What is needed now are leaders with perspective; we need leadership on a thousand fronts but they must be men and women who can take the long view and help to shape the outlines of our future. There will always be the nay-sayers, those who cling to our lovely green planet as a baby clings to its mother, but there will be others like those who have taken us this far along the path to a limitless future.

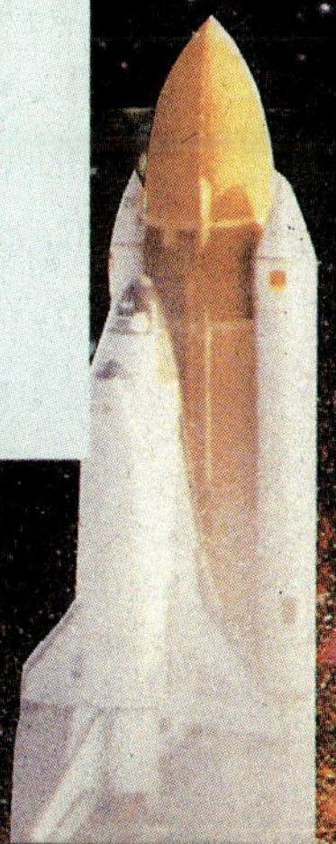

We are a people born to the frontier. It has been a part of our thinking, waking, and sleeping since people first landed on this continent. The frontier is the line that separates the known from the unknown wherever it may be, and we have a driving need to see what lies beyond. It was this that brought people to America, no matter what excuses they may have given themselves or others.

Freedom of religion, some said, and the need for land, a better future for their children, the lust for gold, or the desire to escape class restrictions—all these reasons were given. The fact remains that many, suffering from the same needs and restrictions, did not come.

Why then did some cross the ocean to America and not others? Of course, all who felt that urge did not come to America; some went to India, Africa, Australia, New Zealand, or elsewhere. Those who did come to America began almost at once to push inland, challenging the unknown, daring to go beyond the thin line that divides the known and the unknown. Many had, after landing from the old country, developed good farms or successful businesses; they had become people of standing in their communities. Why then did they move on, leaving all behind?

I believe it to be something buried in their genes, some inherited trait, perhaps something essential to the survival of the species.

They went to the edge of the mountains, then they crossed the mountains and found their way through impassable forests to the Mississippi. After that the Great Plains, the Rocky Mountains, and on to Oregon and California. They trapped fur, traded with Native Americans, hunted buffalo, ranched with cattle or sheep, built towns, and farmed. Yet the genes lay buried within them, and after a few months, a few years, they moved on.

Each science has its own frontiers, and the future of our nation and the world lies in research and development, in probing what lies beyond.

A short time ago we moved into outer space. We landed men on the moon; we sent a vehicle beyond the outer limits of the solar system, a vehicle still moving farther and farther into that limitless distance. If our world were to die tomorrow, that tiny vehicle would go on and on forever, carrying its mighty message to the stars. Out there, someone, sometime, would know that once we existed, that we had the vision and we made the effort. People are not bound by the earth's atmospheric envelope or by its gravitational field, nor is the human mind bound by any limits at all.

One might ask—why outer space, when so much remains to be done here? If that had been the human spirit we would still be hunters and food gatherers, growling over the bones of carrion in a cave somewhere. It is our destiny to move out, to accept the challenge, to dare the unknown. It is our destiny to achieve.

Yet we must not forget that along the way to outer space whole industries are springing into being that did not exist before. The computer age has arisen in part from the space effort, which gave great impetus to the development of computing devices. Transistors, chips, integrated circuits, Teflon, new medicines, new ways of treating diseases, new ways of performing operations, all these and a multitude of other developments that enable people to live, and to live better, are linked to the space effort. Most of these developments have been so incorporated into our day-to-day lives that they are taken for granted, their origin not considered.

If we are content to live in the past, we have no future. And today is the past.

## *Reader's Response*

There are many frontiers to explore, including the frontiers of knowledge. What frontier interests you most?

## Thinking It Over

1. Why did the author call outer space the "eternal frontier"?
2. What do you think the author meant when he said that the automobile is the "civilized person's antidote to overpopulation"?
3. According to the author, what was the real reason people emigrated to America? What evidence did you find that led you to your answer?
4. According to the author, why do people have an urge to probe and move beyond frontiers?
5. Did the last sentence of "The Eternal Frontier" state a fact or an opinion? Explain your answer.

## Appreciating Literature

In this essay, Louis L'Amour is seeking to inspire us. How does he make use of history to inspire us? How does he make use of language to inspire us?

## Writing to Learn

**Think and Evaluate** Do you agree with Louis L'Amour's ideas? Make an evaluation chart. Rate your agreement or disagreement.

| | |
|---|---|
| Agree Strongly | 4 |
| Agree | 3 |
| Agree Partially | 2 |
| Agree Slightly | 1 |
| Do not agree | 0 |

| EVALUATION CHART | |
|---|---|
| 1. Our frontier lies in outer space. | ____ |
| 2. The future of our nation and the world lies in research and development, in probing what lies beyond. | ____ |
| 3. It is our destiny to achieve. | ____ |
| 4. If we are content to live in the past, we have no future. And today is the past. | ____ |

**Write** Express an opinion. Write an explanation of why you agree or disagree with Louis L'Amour. Respond to any part of the article that interests you.

TIME OUT FOR BOOKS

Newbery Honor Book 1971

Best Books for Children

***We were like animals who hear the hunter approach but from terror cannot flee.***

from *Sing Down the Moon* by Scott O'Dell

Scott O'Dell received many awards for his writing, but in 1982 he created his own award, the Scott O'Dell Award for Historical Fiction. He felt strongly that young people should know about the lives of people who had come before.

In the historical novel *Sing Down the Moon*, Bright Morning, a fifteen-year-old Navaho girl, and her people have been evicted from their homes. We learn about the Navahos in 1864 when the U.S. government ordered them to leave their homeland in Arizona. Soldiers forced the Navahos to march 300 miles to Fort Sumner, New Mexico, where they were imprisoned for four years. This journey, known as "The Long Walk" is a tragic part of every Navaho child's heritage. O'Dell felt that it was important for every American to know the history and courage of the Navaho people.

When you read *Sing Down the Moon*, you might feel as though you are walking the long road to New Mexico beside Bright Morning, learning firsthand how the Navahos lost their homes but were determined to hold onto their heritage.

Reading CORNER

*Once settled in their new land, pioneers like the Bergsons found that the challenges were far from over. . . .*

# Holding On

## from O Pioneers! • by Willa Cather

*Alexandra Bergson, her mother and three brothers, Oscar, Lou, and Emil, are enduring the hardships of farmsteading in Nebraska. Neighbors and friends are giving up the struggle and moving to towns, where life will be easier. The time has come for Alexandra, the oldest of the Bergson children, to decide whether to stay or go.*

For the first three years after John Bergson's death, the affairs of his family prospered. Then came the hard times that brought every one on the Divide to the brink of despair; three years of drouth and failure, the last struggle of a wild soil against the encroaching plowshare. The first of these fruitless summers the Bergson boys bore courageously. The failure of the corn crop made labor cheap. Lou and Oscar hired two men and put in bigger crops than ever before. They lost everything they spent. The whole country was discouraged. Farmers who were already in debt had to give up their land. A few foreclosures demoralized the county. The settlers sat about on the wooden sidewalks in the little town and told each other that the country was never meant for men to live in; the thing to do was to get back to Iowa, to Illinois, to any place that had been proved habitable. The Bergson boys, certainly, would have been happier with their Uncle Otto, in the bakery shop in Chicago. Like most of their neighbors, they were meant to follow in paths already marked out for them, not to break trails in a new country. A steady job, a few holidays, nothing to think about, and they would

have been very happy. It was no fault of theirs that they had been dragged into the wilderness when they were little boys. A pioneer should have imagination, should be able to enjoy the idea of things more than the things themselves.

The second of these barren summers was passing. One September afternoon Alexandra Bergson had gone over to the garden across the draw to dig sweet potatoes—they had been thriving upon the weather that was fatal to everything else. But when Carl Linstrum came up the garden rows to find her, she was not working. She was standing lost in thought, leaning upon her pitchfork, her sunbonnet lying beside her on the ground. The dry garden patch smelled of drying vines and was strewn with yellow seed-cucumbers and pumpkins and citrons. At one end, next to the rhubarb, grew feathery asparagus, with red berries. Down the middle of the garden was a

row of gooseberry and currant bushes. A few tough zinnias and marigolds and a row of scarlet sage bore witness to the buckets of water that Mrs. Bergson had carried there after sundown, against the prohibition of her sons. Carl came quietly and slowly up the garden path, looking intently at Alexandra. She did not hear him. She was standing perfectly still, with that serious ease so characteristic of her. Her thick, reddish braids, twisted about her head, fairly burned in the sunlight. The air was cool enough to make the warm sun pleasant on one's back and shoulders, and so clear that the eye could follow a hawk up and up, into the blazing blue depths of the sky. Even Carl, never a very cheerful boy, and considerably darkened by these last two bitter years, loved the country on days like this, felt something strong and young and wild come out of it, that laughed at care.

"Alexandra," he said as he approached her, "I want to talk to you. Let's sit down by the gooseberry bushes." He picked up her sack of potatoes and they crossed the garden. "Boys gone to town?" he asked as he sank down on the warm, sun-baked earth. "Well, we have made up our minds at last, Alexandra. We are really going away."

She looked at him as if she were a little frightened. "Really, Carl? Is it settled?"

"Yes, father has heard from St. Louis, and they will give him back his old job in the cigar factory. He must be there by the first of November. They are taking on new men then. We will sell the place for whatever we can get, and auction the stock. We haven't enough to ship. I am going to learn engraving with a German engraver there, and then try to get work in Chicago."

Alexandra's hands dropped in her lap. Her eyes became dreamy and filled with tears.

Carl's sensitive lower lip trembled. He scratched in the soft earth beside him with a stick. "That's all I hate about it, Alexandra," he said slowly. "You've stood by us through so much and helped father out so many times, and now it seems as if we were running off and leaving you to face the worst of it. But it isn't as if we could really ever be of any help to you. We are only one more drag, one more thing you look out for and feel responsible for. Father was never meant for a farmer, you know that. And I hate it. We'd only get in deeper and deeper."

"Yes, yes, Carl, I know. You are wasting your life here. You are able to do much better things. You are nearly nineteen now, and I wouldn't have you stay. I've always hoped you would get away. But I can't help feeling scared when I think how I will miss you—more than you will ever know." She brushed the tears from her cheeks, not trying to hide them.

"But, Alexandra," he said sadly and wistfully, "I've never been any real help to you, beyond sometimes trying to keep the boys in a good humor."

Alexandra smiled and shook her head. "Oh, it's not that. Nothing like that. It's by understanding me, and the boys, and mother, that you've helped me. I expect that is the only way one person ever really can help another. I think you are about the only one that ever helped me. Somehow it will take more courage to bear your going than everything that has happened before."

Carl looked at the ground. "You see, we've all depended so on you," he said, "even father. He makes me laugh. When anything comes up he always says, 'I wonder what the Bergsons are going to do about that? I guess I'll go and ask her.' I'll never forget that time, when we first came here, and our horse had the colic, and I ran over to your place—your father was away, and you came home with me and showed father how to let the wind out of the horse. You were only a little girl then, but you knew ever so much more about farm work than poor father. You remember how homesick I used to get, and what long talks we used to have coming from school? We've somehow always felt alike about things."

"Yes, that's it; we've liked the same things and we've liked them together, without anybody else knowing. And we've had good times, hunting for Christmas trees and going for ducks and making our plum wine together every year. We've never either of us had any other close friend. And now—" Alexandra wiped her eyes with the corner of her apron, "and now I must remember that you are going where you will have many friends, and will find the work you were meant to do. But you'll write to me, Carl? That will mean a great deal to me here."

"I'll write as long as I live," cried the boy impetuously. "And I'll be working for you as much as for myself, Alexandra. I want to do something you'll like and be proud of. I'm a fool here, but I know I can do something!" He sat up and frowned at the red grass.

Alexandra sighed. "How discouraged the boys will be when they hear. They always come home from town discouraged, anyway. So many people are trying to leave the country, and they talk to our boys and make them low-spirited. I'm afraid they are beginning to feel hard toward me because I won't listen to any talk about going. Sometimes I feel like I'm getting tired of standing up for this country."

"I won't tell the boys yet, if you'd rather not."

"Oh, I'll tell them myself, to-night, when they come home.

They'll be talking wild, anyway, and no good comes of keeping bad news. It's all harder on them than it is on me. Lou wants to get married, poor boy, and he can't until times are better. See, there goes the sun, Carl. I must be getting back. Mother will want her potatoes. It's chilly already, the moment the light goes."

Alexandra rose and looked about. A golden afterglow throbbed in the west, but the country already looked empty and mournful.

A dark moving mass came over the western hill, the Lee boy was bringing in the herd from the other half-section. Emil ran from the windmill to open the corral gate. From the log house, on the little rise across the draw, the smoke was curling. The cattle lowed and bellowed. In the sky the pale half-moon was slowly silvering. Alexandra and Carl walked together down the potato rows. "I have to keep telling myself what is going to happen," she said softly. "Since you have been here, ten years now, I have never really been lonely. But I can remember what it was like before. Now I shall have nobody but Emil. But he is my boy, and he is tender-hearted."

That night, when the boys were called to supper, they sat down moodily. They had worn their coats to town, but they ate in their striped shirts and suspenders. They were grown men now, and, as Alexandra said, for the last few years they had been growing more and more like themselves. Lou was still the slighter of the two, the quicker and more intelligent, but apt to go off at half-cock. He had a lively blue eye, a thin, fair skin (always burned red to the neckband of his shirt in summer), stiff, yellow hair that would not lie down on his head, and a bristly little yellow mustache, of which he was very proud. Oscar could not grow a mustache; his pale face was as bare as an egg, and his white eyebrows gave it an empty look. He was a man of powerful body and unusual endurance; the sort of man you could attach to a corn-sheller as you would an engine. He would turn it all day, without hurrying, without slowing down. But he was as indolent of mind as he was unsparing of his body. His love of routine amounted to a vice. He worked like an insect, always doing the same thing over in the same way, regardless of whether it was best or not. He felt that there was a sovereign virtue in mere bodily toil, and he rather liked to do things in the hardest way. If a field had once been in corn, he couldn't bear to put it into wheat. He liked to begin his corn-planting at the same time every year, whether the season were backward or forward. He seemed to feel that by his own irreproachable regularity he would clear himself of blame and reprove the weather. When the wheat crop failed, he threshed the straw at a dead loss to demonstrate how little grain there was, and thus prove his case against Providence.

Lou, on the other hand, was fussy and flighty; always planned to get through two days' work in one, and often got only the least important things done. He liked to keep the place up, but he never got round to doing odd jobs until he had to neglect more pressing work to attend to them. In the middle of the wheat harvest, when the grain was over-ripe and every hand was needed, he would stop to mend fences or to patch the harness; then dash down to the field and overwork and be laid up in bed for a week. The two boys balanced each other, and they pulled well together. They had been good friends since they were children. One seldom went anywhere, even to town, without the other.

To-night, after they sat down to supper, Oscar kept looking at Lou as if he expected him to say something, and Lou blinked his eyes and frowned at his plate. It was Alexandra herself who at last opened the discussion.

"The Linstrums," she said calmly, as she put another plate of hot biscuits on the table, "are going back to St. Louis. The old man is going to work in the cigar factory again."

At this Lou plunged in. "You see, Alexandra, everybody who can crawl out is going away. There's no use of us trying to stick it out, just to be stubborn. There's something in knowing when to quit."

"Where do you want to go, Lou?"

"Any place where things will grow," said Oscar grimly.

Lou reached for a potato. "Chris Arnson has traded his half-section for a place down on the river."

"Who did he trade with?"

"Charley Fuller, in town."

"Fuller the real estate man? You see, Lou, that Fuller has a head on him. He's buying and trading for every bit of land he can get up here. It'll make him a rich man, some day."

"He's rich now, that's why he can take a chance."

"Why can't we? We'll live longer than he will. Some day the land itself will be worth more than all we can ever raise on it."

Lou laughed. "It could be worth that, and still not be worth much. Why, Alexandra, you don't know what you're talking about.

Our place wouldn't bring now what it would six years ago. The fellows that settled up here just made a mistake. Now they're beginning to see this high land wasn't never meant to grow nothing on, and everybody who ain't fixed to graze cattle is trying to crawl out. It's too high to farm up here. All the Americans are skinning out. That man Percy Adams, north of town, told me that he was going to let Fuller take his land and stuff for four hundred dollars and a ticket to Chicago."

"There's Fuller again!" Alexandra exclaimed. "I wish that man would take me for a partner. He's feathering his nest! If only poor people could learn a little from rich people! But all these fellows who are running off are bad farmers, like poor Mr. Linstrum. They couldn't get ahead even in good years, and they all got into debt while father was getting out. I think we ought to hold on as long as we can on father's account. He was so set on keeping this land. He must have seen harder times than this, here. How was it in the early days, mother?"

Mrs. Bergson was weeping quietly. These family discussions always depressed her, and made her remember all that she had been torn away from. "I don't see why the boys are always taking on about going away," she said, wiping her eyes. "I don't want to move again; out to some raw place, maybe, where we'd be worse off than we are here, and all to do over again. I won't move! If the rest of you go, I will ask some of the neighbors to take me in, and stay and be buried by father. I'm not going to leave him by himself on the prairie, for cattle to run over." She began to cry more bitterly.

The boys looked angry. Alexandra put a soothing hand on her mother's shoulder. "There's no question of that, mother. You don't have to go if you don't want to. A third of the place belongs to you by American law, and we can't sell without your consent. We only want you to advise us. How did it use to be when you and father first came? Was it really as bad as this, or not?"

"Oh, worse! Much worse," moaned Mrs. Bergson. "Drouth, chince-bugs, hail, everything! My garden all cut to pieces like sauer-kraut. No grapes on the creek, no nothing. The people all lived just like coyotes."

Oscar got up and tramped out of the kitchen. Lou followed him. They felt that Alexandra had taken an unfair advantage in turning their mother loose on them. The next morning they were silent and reserved. They did not offer to take the women to church, but went down to the barn immediately after breakfast and stayed all day. When Carl Linstrum came over in the afternoon, Alexandra winked to him and pointed toward the barn. He understood her and went down to play cards with the boys. They believed that a very wicked thing to do on Sunday, and it relieved their feelings.

Alexandra stayed in the house. On Sunday afternoon Mrs. Bergson always took a nap, and Alexandra read. During the week she read only the newspaper, but on Sunday, and in the long evenings of winter, she read a good deal; read a few things over a great many times. She knew long portions of the "Frithjof Saga" by heart, and, like most Swedes who read at all, she was fond of Longfellow's verse—the ballads and the "Golden Legend" and "The Spanish Student." To-day she sat in the wooden rocking-chair with the Swedish Bible open on her knees, but she was not reading. She was looking thoughtfully away at the point where the upland road disappeared over the rim of the prairies. Her body was in an attitude of perfect repose, such as it was apt to take when she was thinking earnestly. Her mind was slow, truthful, steadfast. She had not the least spark of cleverness.

All afternoon the sitting-room was full of quiet and sunlight. Emil was making rabbit traps in the kitchen shed. The hens were clucking and scratching brown holes in the flower beds, and the wind was teasing the prince's feather by the door.

That evening Carl came in with the boys to supper.

"Emil," said Alexandra, when they were all seated at the table, "how would you like to go traveling? Because I am going to take a trip, and you can go with me if you want to."

The boys looked up in amazement; they were always afraid of Alexandra's schemes. Carl was interested.

"I've been thinking, boys," she went on, "that maybe I am too set against making a change. I'm going to take Brigham and the buckboard to-morrow and drive down to the river country and spend a few days looking over what they've got down there. If I find anything good, you boys can go down and make a trade."

"Nobody down there will trade for anything up here," said Oscar gloomily.

"That's just what I want to find out. Maybe they are just as discontented down there as we are up here. Things away from home often look better than they are. You know what your Hans Andersen book says, Carl, about the Swedes liking to buy Danish bread and the Danes liking to buy Swedish bread, because people always think the bread of another country is better than their own. Anyway, I've heard so much about the river farms, I won't be satisfied till I've seen for myself."

Lou fidgeted. "Look out! Don't agree to anything. Don't let them fool you."

Lou was apt to be fooled himself. He had not yet learned to keep away from the shell-game wagons that followed the circus.

After supper Lou put on a necktie and went across the fields to court Annie Lee, and Carl and Oscar sat down to a game of checkers, while Alexandra read "The Swiss Family Robinson" aloud to her mother and Emil. It was not long before the two boys at the table neglected their game to listen. They were all big children together, and they found the adventures of the family in the tree house so absorbing that they gave them their undivided attention.

Alexandra and Emil spent five days down among the river farms, driving up and down the valley. Alexandra talked to the men about their crops and to the women about their poultry. She spent a whole day with one young farmer who had been away at school, and who was experimenting with a new kind of clover hay. She learned a great deal. As they drove along, she and Emil talked and planned. At last, on the sixth day, Alexandra turned Brigham's head northward and left the river behind.

"There's nothing in it for us down there, Emil. There are a few fine farms, but they are owned by the rich men in town, and couldn't be bought. Most of the land is rough and hilly. They can always scrape along down there, but they can never do anything big. Down there they have a little certainty, but up with us there is a big chance. We must have faith in the high land, Emil. I want to hold on harder than ever and when you're a man you'll thank me." She urged Brigham forward.

When the road began to climb the first long swells of the Divide, Alexandra hummed an old Swedish hymn, and Emil wondered why his sister looked so happy. Her face was so radiant that

he felt shy about asking her. For the first time, perhaps, since that land emerged from the waters of geologic ages, a human face was set toward it with love and yearning. It seemed beautiful to her, rich and strong and glorious. Her eyes drank in the breadth of it, until her tears blinded her. Then the Genius of the Divide, the great, free spirit which breathes across it, must have bent lower than it ever bent to a human will before. The history of every country begins in the heart of a man or a woman.

Alexandra reached home in the afternoon. That evening she held a family council and told her brothers all that she had seen and heard.

"I want you boys to go down yourselves and look it over. Nothing will convince you like seeing with your own eyes. The river land was settled before this, and so they are a few years ahead of us, and have learned more about farming. The land sells for three times as much as this, but in five years we will double it. The rich men down there own all the best land, and they are buying all they can get. The thing to do is to sell our cattle and what little old corn we have, and buy the Linstrum place. Then the next thing to do is to take out two loans on our half-sections, and buy Peter Crow's place; raise every dollar we can, and buy every acre we can."

"Mortgage the homestead again?" Lou cried. He sprang up and began to wind the clock furiously. "I won't slave to pay off another mortgage. I'll never do it. You'd just as soon kill us all, Alexandra, to carry out some scheme!"

Oscar rubbed his high, pale forehead. "How do you propose to pay off your mortgages?"

Alexandra looked from one to the other and bit her lip. They had never seen her so nervous. "See here," she brought out at last. "We borrow the money for six years. Well, with the money we buy a half-section from Linstrum and a half from Crow, and a quarter from Struble, maybe. That will give us upwards of fourteen hundred acres, won't it? You won't have to pay off your mortgages for six years. By that time, any of this land will be worth thirty dollars an acre—it will be worth fifty, but we'll say thirty; then you can sell a garden patch anywhere, and pay off a debt of sixteen hundred dollars. It's not the principal I'm worried about, it's the interest and taxes. We'll have to strain to meet the payments. But as sure as we are sitting here to-night, we can sit down here ten years from now independent landowners, not struggling farmers any longer. The chance that father was always looking for has come."

Lou was pacing the floor. "But how do you *know* that land is going to go up enough to pay the mortgages and—"

"And make us rich besides?" Alexandra put in firmly. "I can't explain that, Lou. You'll have to take my word for it. I *know*, that's all. When you drive about over the country you can feel it coming."

Oscar had been sitting with his head lowered, his hands hanging between his knees. "But we can't work so much land," he said dully, as if he were talking to himself. "We can't even try. It would just lie there and we'd work ourselves to death." He sighed, and laid his calloused fist on the table.

Alexandra's eyes filled with tears. She put her hand on his shoulder. "You poor boy, you won't have to work it. The men in town who are buying up other people's land don't try to farm it. They are the men to watch, in a new country. Let's try to do like the shrewd ones, and not like these stupid fellows. I don't want you boys always to have to work like this. I want you to be independent, and Emil to go to school."

Lou held his head as if it were splitting. "Everybody will say we are crazy. It must be crazy, or everybody would be doing it."

"If they were, we wouldn't have much chance. No, Lou, I was talking about that with the smart young man who is raising the new kind of clover. He says the right thing is usually just what everybody don't do. Why are we better fixed than any of our neighbors? Because father had more brains. Our people were better people than these in the old country. We *ought* to do more than they do, and see further ahead. Yes, mother, I'm going to clear the table now."

Alexandra rose. The boys went to the stable to see to the stock, and they were gone a long while. When they came back Lou played on his *dragharmonika* and Oscar sat figuring at his father's secretary all evening. They said nothing more about Alexandra's project, but she felt sure now that they would consent to it. Just

before bedtime Oscar went out for a pail of water. When he did not come back, Alexandra threw a shawl over her head and ran down the path to the windmill. She found him sitting there with his head in his hands, and she sat down beside him.

"Don't do anything you don't want to do, Oscar," she whispered. She waited a moment, but he did not stir. "I won't say any more about it, if you'd rather not. What makes you so discouraged?"

"I dread signing my name to them pieces of paper," he said slowly. "All the time I was a boy we had a mortgage hanging over us."

"Then don't sign one. I don't want you to, if you feel that way."

Oscar shook his head. "No, I can see there's a chance that way. I've thought a good while there might be. We're in so deep now, we might as well go deeper. But it's hard work pulling out of debt. Like pulling a threshing-machine out of the mud; breaks your back. Me and Lou's worked hard, and I can't see it's got us ahead much."

"Nobody knows about that as well as I do, Oscar. That's why I want to try an easier way. I don't want you to have to grub for every dollar."

"Yes, I know what you mean. Maybe it'll come out right. But signing papers is signing papers. There ain't no maybe about that." He took his pail and trudged up the path to the house.

Alexandra drew her shawl closer about her and stood leaning against the frame of the mill, looking at the stars which glittered so keenly through the frosty autumn air. She always loved to watch them, to think of their vastness and distance, and of their ordered march. It fortified her to reflect upon the great operations of nature, and when she thought of the law that lay behind them, she felt a sense of personal security. That night she had a new consciousness of the country, felt almost a new relation to it. Even her talk with the boys had not taken away the feeling that had overwhelmed her when she drove back to the Divide that afternoon. She had never known before how much the country meant to her. The chirping of the insects down in the long grass had been like the sweetest music. She had felt as if her heart were hiding down there, somewhere, with the quail and the plover and all the little wild things that crooned or buzzed in the sun. Under the long shaggy ridges, she felt the future stirring.

### ♦ Library Link ♦

*The selection you just read is a chapter from the novel* O Pioneers! *by Willa Cather.*

## Reader's Response

If Alexandra had asked your opinion regarding the land purchase, what would you have advised her to do?

# Writing about Reading

## *Writing from Another Place and Time*

The stories in this unit related the experiences of pioneers who met the challenges of the Old West. For example, you read about Molly, a young mother who found the stamina to brave a raging blizzard. You also read about a railroad worker who planted gunpowder in walls of solid granite.

Imagine that you are a pioneer. Choose one of the pioneers in this unit, a real pioneer from history, or one from your own imagination. Write a journal entry about one day in your life. Record what happened during that day and how you felt about it.

### *Prewriting*

To prepare for your imaginary step into history, make notes on these questions about your "pioneer" self.

- What is your name?
- Why and how did you travel to the Old West?
- What problems or adventures have you had?
- Where do you live?
- What is your job?
- What year is it?

Next make a chart in which you sketch out one day's major events and note your feelings and comments. As an example, study Molly's chart on the next page.

**Molly from "Let the Hurricane Roar" makes a chart.**

| *What happened?* | *Comment* | *Feeling* |
| --- | --- | --- |
| I see a herd of frozen cattle. | Will they eat my hay stacks? | anxious |
| I discover the cattle are blinded by ice and snow. | Could I kill one for meat? | hopeful |
| I kill a steer for food, steal a heifer for milk. | Am I a thief? | guilty |
| I place heifer in barn. | My baby will have milk! | joyful |

### *Writing*

Date your journal and write a brief introduction of yourself. Use information from your chart to write a journal entry. Relate the incident in enough detail to create the feeling that you really were in the Old West. Be sure to describe how you felt during and after those incidents.

### *Revising*

Read your journal entry to yourself. How can you improve your entry?

### *Proofreading*

Correct any errors. Make a clean copy.

### *Publishing*

Combine your entries with those of some of your classmates to create a magazine entitled *Pioneer Times*. Include pictures and advertisements.

# WORKING TOGETHER

## *Writing Letters Home*

In this unit, you learned about how the Old West was settled. The pioneers, forty-niners, and railroad workers left behind relatives, friends, neighbors, and the comfort of familiar surroundings to start a new life. Your group will now pretend to be one of the story characters from this unit and write letters to people back home.

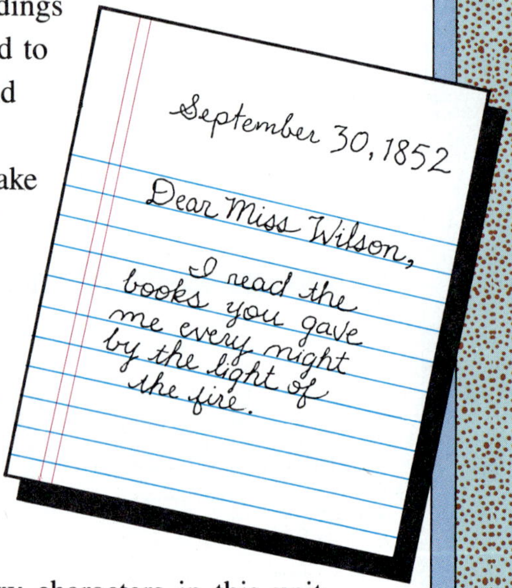


To help your group work well together, make sure you take responsibility for one or more of these tasks:

- Contributing to the group's discussions
- Sharing your own feelings about the stories
- Working quietly as you write
- Expressing appreciation for others' work

Begin by recalling and discussing the story characters in this unit. Who had the most difficult or exciting time? Which character would you have liked to meet most? Together, agree on one character for whom you will write letters home. Talk about the things that person would be likely to write home about. Include their feelings and experiences, the people they met, and the way they might describe their new surroundings. List the people back home to whom the story character might write, such as relatives, neighbors, or friends. Each of you should then write a short letter from the story character to one of the people on the back-home list. When everyone has finished, exchange letters. Take turns reading out loud the letter you received and telling the group how you think the person receiving the letter might feel.

# BOOKS TO ENJOY

***On the Way Home*** by Laura Ingalls Wilder *(Harper, 1962)* This 1894 diary records the author's trip with her family from South Dakota to Missouri and gives an accurate view of the prairie frontier that characterizes her work.

***Old Yeller*** by Fred Gipson *(Harper, 1956)* A homely yellow dog is companion to a fourteen-year-old boy on a Texas homestead. The dog helps and hinders Travis in the exciting events of family life in the 1860s.

***The Horsecatcher*** by Mari Sandoz *(Westminster, 1957)* Determined to become a horsecatcher, a Cheyenne youth struggles to attain freedom from group tradition and learns a valuable lesson about responsibility.

***Beyond the Divide*** by Kathryn Lasky *(Macmillan, 1983)* In 1849 a fourteen-year-old Amish girl and her father join the Gold Rush, leaving their close-knit community for a wagon train, with a group of colorful emigrants.

***Samurai of Gold Hill*** by Yoshiko Uchida *(Creative Arts, 1985)* In 1869 a Japanese boy and his samurai father journey to California to establish a tea and silk farm.

Jackson Pollock

UNIT THREE

# FLIGHTS OF FANCY

*From the Loch Ness Monster to aliens from outer space— what is real and what is not, and how can you be sure?*

THE MOON-WOMAN CUTS THE CIRCLE,
*oil on canvas by Jackson Pollock, American, 1943*

# BIGGER THAN LIFE

by Edward Edelson

*Do you wear Mickey Mouse's picture on your shirt, hope Bugs Bunny's troubles will never end, and feel sorry for King Kong? If you do, you are not alone. There is something that makes these imaginary creatures seem so real.*

The powerful hold of imaginary film animals on the American consciousness was demonstrated vividly in 1978, when the fiftieth anniversary of Mickey Mouse was celebrated. The events included a White House appearance in which the President's daughter, Amy Carter, met with Mickey; a ninety-minute television special; a cross-country whistle-stop train tour featuring an actor dressed in a Mickey Mouse costume; installation of a plaque in the Broadway theater where the first Mickey Mouse short was shown; an exhibition of Mickey Mouse memorabilia in the Library of Congress; and a month-long Mickey Mouse retrospective at the prestigious Museum of Modern Art in New York. All these marks of respect for Mickey were accompanied by a brisk sale of Mickey Mouse merchandise, from the familiar wristwatches to drinking glasses, place mats, and posters. And all of this for a character whose last film was made in 1953, long before today's child fans were born.

Beginnings are everything. Mickey Mouse was born during a long, despondent train ride that Walt Disney took from New York to California early in 1928. Disney had been making a series of cartoons about a character called Oswald the Rabbit, and he had been told in New York that Oswald had been wrested away from him in a corporate power play by his partners.

In a magazine article issued many years later, Walt Disney told a romantic story of how the idea of another cartoon animal began to emerge from his thoughts, and of how the concept finally arrived of

READERS' CHOICE AWARD

making the animal "a romping, rollicking little mouse." According to the article, even the train whistle screeched, "A m-m-owause." By the time the train was in the Middle West, the article went on, Disney had decided to dress the mouse in a pair of red velvet pants with two pearl buttons.

Disney first named the character Mortimer Mouse, but quickly changed the first name to Mickey. The character that appeared in the first Mickey Mouse film short to be screened, *Steamboat Willie,* was designed to be simple, because Disney's studio had to push out a lot of film in a hurry. The head was a circle, the nose was an oblong circle, the ears were two big circles, the body was pear-shaped, the arms and legs were lines, and the feet were boxlike.

Mickey had one huge break: he appeared just at the time when the screen had discovered sound. In fact, *Steamboat Willie,* in which Mickey made his screen debut, was the third Mickey Mouse cartoon that Disney made, but the first to have sound—an ingenious musical sound track that was written to accentuate the animals' gags in the film. The first two cartoons, *Plane Crazy* and *Gallopin' Gaucho,* had no takers until they, too, were given sound tracks after the success of *Steamboat Willie*.

Mickey Mouse was a success at every level. Arturo Toscanini saw a Mickey Mouse cartoon, *The Band Concert*, in 1935, and asked for it to be rerun because the great conductor enjoyed Mickey's parody of Toscanini's behavior on the podium. That same year, the New York *Times* reported that "the King of England won't go to the movies unless Mickey Mouse is on the bill." President Roosevelt showed Mickey Mouse cartoons in the White House.

Over the years, Mickey's appearance changed as the animators tinkered with their drawings. He became rounder, smoother, more suave. His character also changed. Originally, Mickey was a troublemaker. As the Disney studio developed more cartoon animal characters, Mickey became a straight man, setting up gags for Goofy, the clumsy dog, and for irascible Donald Duck. Mickey now was the good guy who had a romantic interest, Minnie Mouse.

The hallmark of Disney cartoons during the peak years of Mickey Mouse and his gang was a painstaking dedication to quality. Disney is credited with setting new standards for color fidelity on film. His cartoonists were an elite group, handpicked from a mob of applicants and put through training that lasted for years. Careful attention was paid to every last detail, with both music and speech being synchronized to the characters' movements. Technically, the Disney shorts, lasting only seven to eight minutes, usually were far ahead of the main features on the same bill.

In all, 118 Mickey Mouse cartoons were released between 1928 and 1953. The changing nature of the entertainment business was blamed for bringing the series to an end. The cartoons were made primarily to be shown as part of an evening-long double feature. When television arrived, the double feature faded out and so did cartoon shorts. One other factor was involved. Cartoon shorts never were really big moneymakers, and the Disney studio (The Mouse House, as insiders called it) was devoting most of its effort to full-length cartoon features, such as *Snow White and the Seven Dwarfs*.

Before the series ended, Mickey Mouse had lost a lot of the favor he enjoyed with the critics. There were learned articles complaining that Mickey's world had become too goody-goody, and that Mickey's gang had been robbed of their sharpness by prosperity, respectability, and complacency. As Mickey's star fell in critical esteem, more reviewers began saying that first place had been taken over by a much more abrasive character, the star of Warner Brothers Looney Tunes and Merrie Melodies: Bugs Bunny.

Bugs Bunny made his first appearance in a 1940 cartoon

**In 1933, Walt Disney was awarded a medal from educators for his distinguished service to children.**

called *The Happy Hare*, and Mel Blanc, the voice behind the cartoon, said he provided Bugs with the toughest accent he could provide—mostly Brooklyn, but with a mixture of the Bronx.

There are differing stories of how Bugs got his celebrated tag line, "What's up, doc?" Some said that the line came from a young animator, who used to go around the studio saying, "What's up, doc?" so often that they finally wrote it into the script. But Blanc maintained that the studio originally wanted Bugs to say, "Hey, what's cookin'," but the phrase didn't sound modern enough for an up-to-date rabbit like Bugs. "At the time, 'What's up, doc?' was a very popular expression, so I suggested that Bugs use it," Blanc recalled.

Cartoon animals multiplied through the 1940s. There were Sylvester the Cat and Tweety Pie the Canary (whose line was, "I taut I taw a puddy tat"), Tom and Jerry (Tom was the cat and Jerry was the mouse), and many others. The animators who worked in those days agree on two things today. Walt Disney is given the credit for establishing the animated cartoon, not only because Disney created the very concept of a cartoon animal with a real personality but also because he—aided chiefly by a genius named Ub Iwerks, who has little fame outside the business but is renowned by insiders—set new technical standards for cartoons.

Is it mere nostalgia that makes movie fans think that the imaginary animals of the past were better? Posing that question invites the same endless debate you can start by asking whether the baseball players of yesteryear were better than today's high-priced stars. But it is certain that one film animal of the past has established a position that is virtually unchallenged.

That animal is King Kong—and one hastens to add that it is the original King Kong of the 1933 film. Like the original Mickey Mouse films, *King Kong* established a new standard for the movies—in this case, a standard for special effects. In the decades to follow, others were to improve upon some of the techniques used in *King Kong*, but those techniques were the starting point for virtually every effort in the field.

The story of the giant ape, who is worshiped as a god on a mysterious island, is captured by an ambitious filmmaker, breaks free to terrorize a city and kidnap the girl with whom the ape apparently has fallen in love, and finally is shot down by airplanes from the top of the Empire State Building, was produced and directed by Merian C. Cooper, using methods developed by Willis H. O'Brien.

O'Brien was the pioneer in the use of models to create realistic-looking but imaginary creatures. The original King Kong, for example, never existed in full size. Most of the film was made by using eighteen-inch-high models with ball-and-socket joints. O'Brien would shoot one frame of film, move the model a fraction of an inch, shoot another frame, and so on until the picture of a real, moving ape was achieved. Days were needed to get only a few feet of film, and more time was needed for the special techniques by which the actors were included in the action.

Parts of Kong were built for special scenes. A giant hand was built for the shots in which King Kong grabbed the actress Fay Wray and carried her away. And a model of Kong's head and shoulders, twenty-feet high, was built for close-ups, including the frightening scene in which Kong's face suddenly appears outside Fay Wray's hotel room. But

(Above) Godzilla, the giant lizard, terrorizes Tokyo, while King Kong (right) fights off airplanes atop the Empire State Building.

otherwise, "the eighth wonder of the world," as Kong was introduced in the film, was no more than a handful of models covered with fur. Still, Cooper had created a new kind of film character: an outsized ape with personality.

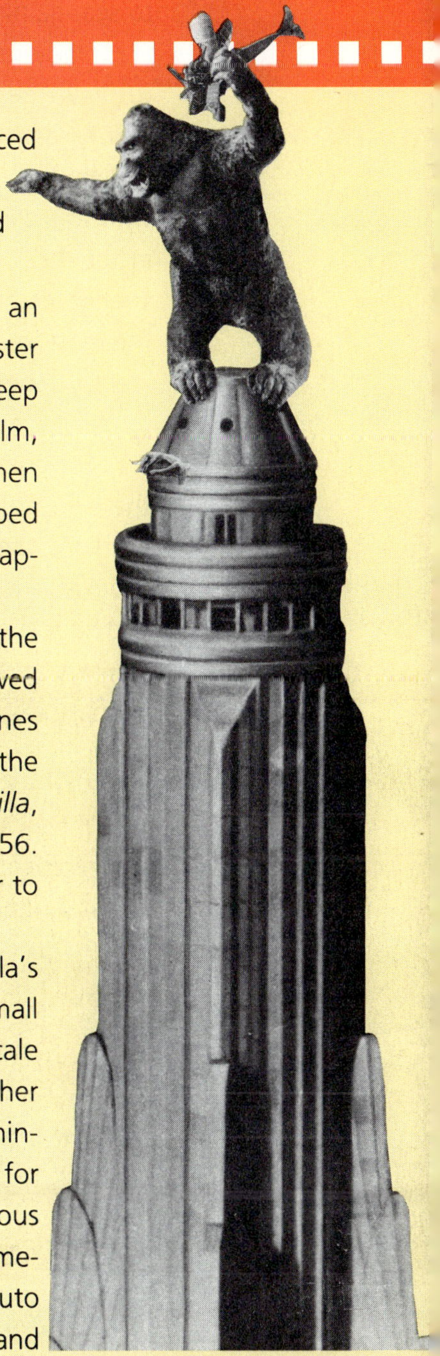

A rival for Kong did emerge, in an unexpected form and from an unanticipated source. In 1954, the Japanese studio Toho made a monster movie about a giant lizard who is awakened from his prehistoric sleep by an American nuclear bomb test off the coast of Japan. In the film, the monster destroys some ships by simply breathing on them, then comes ashore to level much of Tokyo. The lizard eventually is stopped by a secret weapon called the "oxygen destroyer," developed by a Japanese scientist.

The film was a hit in Asian cities, and Toho decided to try it in the American market. They hired Raymond Burr (in the days before he achieved wealth and fame as television's Perry Mason), spent a day shooting scenes of him as an American reporter named Steve Martin who covers the monster story, changed the name of the film from *Gojira* to *Godzilla, King of the Monsters*, and released the film in the United States in 1956. It hit the jackpot. Indeed, *Godzilla* was the first Japanese movie ever to succeed outside the art-house circuit in America.

Special-effects work was one of the major reasons for Godzilla's success. The Japanese used their own method. Rather than building small models of the animal, they used actors inside rubber suits and built scale models of the cities. The Tokyo through which Godzilla and the other monsters rampaged so often was actually an exquisitely designed miniature metropolis that covered two full city blocks. Another reason for the box-office appeal of Godzilla was the variety of his enemies. In various films, Godzilla has fought Ghidrah the Three-Headed Monster, something called the Smog Monster (which feeds on factory fumes and auto exhausts), a giant bird that created typhoons by flapping its wings, and none other than King Kong. With tact, the Japanese filmed two endings to *King Kong vs. Godzilla* (1963). In the version that was shown in Japan, Godzilla beat King Kong to a pulp. But in the film that appeared in the United States, King Kong struggled to his feet and threw Godzilla out to sea, gaining victory by a TKO.

One question about the imaginary animals of the movies is where to draw the line. For example, should the apes in *Planet of the Apes* (1967), and the four sequels that it inspired, be included in the roster? And how about Chewbacca, the monkey-faced, furry, blue-eyed Wookie who was copilot on a spaceship with Han Solo (played by Harrison Ford) in the 1977 smash hit *Star Wars*? For that matter, how about all the strange creatures who congregated in the spaceport cantina in one of the most imaginative scenes of *Star Wars*? Those creatures were almost literally indescribable, but they were supposed to be as intelligent as human beings.

Fortunately, it isn't necessary to draw the line too clearly. One of the enjoyable things about the movies is that they can erase many of the lines that exist in real life, so that audiences can enjoy blue-eyed Wookies and humanoid apes, giant lizards who come to the aid of people and huge gorillas who fall in love with young girls, mice who wear velvet trousers and rabbits who talk with a Brooklyn accent. With imaginary animals, relax and enjoy.

### ♦ Library Link ♦

*This selection by Edward Edelson came from his full-length book* Great Animals of the Movies.

## Reader's Response

Do you share people's fascination with animated film characters? In what ways?

## Thinking It Over

1. Describe how the idea of Mickey Mouse came about.
2. Why was *King Kong* considered a landmark film?
3. Compare the way special effects were used in *King Kong* to the way they were used in *Godzilla*. How did you decide what factors to include in your comparison?
4. State two reasons for the success of the Godzilla movies.
5. Why do you think animated film animals have such a powerful hold on people's imaginations?

## Appreciating Literature

One mark of good writing is a smooth flow or transition from one topic to another. In this selection, Edward Edelson leads the reader very smoothly from the discussion of one imaginary creature to another. Look at the last two paragraphs on page 289. Here the author shifts from discussing Mickey Mouse to describing Bugs Bunny. How does the author make the transition work so smoothly? Find other examples of transitions and explain how they work.

## Writing to Learn

**THINK AND IMAGINE** Draw a strip of film containing six squares on your paper. In each square, list the name of a film creature from this article.

**WRITE** Now that you have read about unusual creatures, introduce your classmates to an imaginary one that you invent. Your creature could star in a cartoon or a movie. Give your creature a name and tell the kind of role that best suits its talents.

Thinking ◆ Reading ◆ Writing

# Changing Perspectives

In the previous selection, "Bigger Than Life," you read about the original King Kong character. A famous scene from the 1933 movie shows the giant ape straddling the Empire State Building, swatting at planes with one hand while holding the kidnapped girl in the other. For decades, movie fans have watched this dramatic scene and experienced terror from a safe distance.

Suppose you were asked to retell the story of King Kong from the point of view of one of the characters in the film, perhaps even Kong himself. Changing perspectives in this way would require you to rethink the story and to put it together in a new way.

By assuming the perspective of different characters in a story, you can become an active reader and leave the role of onlooker behind. It's also a good way to try to summarize a story.

## *Learning the Strategy*

One way to explore a story from a different perspective is to prepare a point-of-view report. Consider, for example, how things might have looked to King Kong from atop the Empire State Building.

**My Adventure in New York**
by King Kong

Airplanes were shooting things at me, and there was unbearable noise all around me. I thought I'd be free near the clouds, but I found myself trapped on a strange kind of tree with no branches.

Now consider how one of the pilots in the attacking planes might have viewed the scene.

> **Kong's Siege of New York**
> by Ernest Officer
>
> The enormous beast had grappled its way to the top of the Empire State Building, causing great damage. He waved his arms wildly, showing no regard for his screaming victim. He had to be stopped!

## *Using the Strategy*

Choose any of the other film characters described in "Bigger Than Life." Feel free to use any event you remember from the character's movies or cartoons. Give your report a title and let the character you chose be the author. Imagine, for example, how Godzilla might describe his meeting with King Kong, or how Mickey Mouse might describe his creation by Walt Disney:

> **The Story of My Life**
> by Mickey Mouse
>
> Sure, Walt says he thought me up all by himself. The truth is . . .

## *Applying the Strategy to the Next Story*

As you read the next selection, "Pegasus and Bellerophon," you will be asked to adopt different points of view. Then you will write a point of view report about an event in the story.

The writing connection can be found on page 343.

# PEGASUS AND BELLEROPHON

by Margaret Evans Price

*One of the most beloved of ancient myths is this one about a young prince and his magical winged horse.*

Pegasus was a wonderful winged horse that belonged to Minerva, the gray-eyed goddess who watched over heroes and gave wisdom and skill to all those who truly wished it.

Now it happened that after Minerva had caught and named Pegasus, the winged horse, she did not care to ride him herself, but knew no human who deserved to own him. So Minerva gave Pegasus to the nymphs to care for until she could find a youth brave enough and wise enough to ride him.

The nymphs were happy caring for Pegasus. They brushed him, combed his mane, and fed him, but they knew that some day he would belong to a mortal master who would come and ride him away.

At last in Corinth there was born a little prince named Bellerophon. Glaucus, his father, had more skill in handling horses than any other man. As Bellerophon grew up, his father trained him and taught him all he knew, so that while Bellerophon was still very young he understood the ways of horses and learned to ride them.

All this time the winged horse was without a master.

When Bellerophon was sixteen he began to long for travel and adventure in other lands, so he set out to visit a neighboring king.

Many friends came to bid the gallant young man goodbye and wish him well, but there was one, named Proetus, who pretended to be Bellerophon's friend, but who really wished for him the worst that might happen. Proetus was jealous of Prince Bellerophon, and hoped that the young hero would not return from the journey.

It happened that Proetus was the son-in-law of Iobates, King of Lycia, and so, pretending friendship, Proetus gave Bellerophon a letter to carry to the king. Bellerophon, knowing nothing of the wicked words that were in this letter, put it carefully in the pocket of his tunic and rode gaily away.

When he reached Lycia, the home of Iobates, he found great sorrow in the land and all the people mourning. Each night a monster called the Chimaera came down into the valley and carried off women and children, sheep and oxen. The mountain where he lived was white with the bones of his victims.

**Imagine that you were a victim of the Chimaera who had a narrow escape. How would you describe your encounter?**

Bellerophon rode through the mourning city and came to the palace of the king. He presented himself to Iobates and gave him the letter.

As the king read, his face darkened and he seemed troubled, for the letter asked that Bellerophon should be put to death. The king did not like to heed the request in this strange letter, yet he wished to please his son-in-law. He knew that to kill a guest would be a wicked deed and against the laws of kindness to a visitor, and might also bring war on him from the land where the young prince lived. So he decided to send Bellerophon to slay the Chimaera, thinking he never could come back alive.

Bellerophon was not the least bit afraid, because he longed for adventure, and his heart was filled with a great desire to overcome this dark and evil monster, free the kingdom from fear, and make the mourning people happy.

But before starting out he found the oldest and wisest man in the whole kingdom and asked his advice. This aged man was named Polyidus. When he saw that Bellerophon was young and full of courage, yet humble enough to ask help from someone older, Polyidus told him a secret that no one else in the kingdom knew.

He told him of Minerva's winged horse, which he had once seen drinking at a spring deep in the forest.

"If you sleep all night in Minerva's temple," said the old man, "and offer gifts at her altar, she may help you to find the horse."

Bellerophon went to the temple, and as he slept he dreamed that he saw Minerva, clad in silver armor, her gray eyes shining as if they held sparks of fire. Plumes of blue and rose and violet floated from her helmet. She carried a golden bridle in her hand and told Bellerophon how he might reach the well where Pegasus came to drink.

When Bellerophon awakened, he saw the golden bridle on the temple floor beside him, and knew Minerva really had visited him. Then with the bridle over his arm he set out on his journey through the forest. When he found the well, he hid himself among the bushes nearby to watch for the coming of the winged horse. Soon Bellerophon saw the winged horse flying far up in the sky. Nearer and nearer he wheeled until his silver feet touched the green grass beside the spring.

As Pegasus bent his head to drink, Bellerophon sprang from his hiding place and caught him by the mane. Before Pegasus knew what had happened, the golden bridle was slipped over his head, and Bellerophon had leaped to his back and was sitting between his outspread wings.

Imagine that you are a citizen of Corinth, walking to work in the morning. You look up to the sky. How would you report what you see?

Pegasus rose into the air and darted wildly through the sky, now flying high among the clouds, now diving swiftly toward the earth. He reared and plunged, trying to shake Bellerophon from his back. He flew wildly over the sea and the mountains all the way to Africa and back. He flew over Thebes and over Corinth, and people looking up into the sky thought they saw some strange bird passing overhead.

But Bellerophon understood how to handle fierce horses, for he remembered the things his father had taught him. At last Pegasus knew he had found his master and, tired and panting, sank down to the grass beside the well.

After Pegasus had rested, Bellerophon armed himself with a long spear and rode toward the mountain where the Chimaera lived.

There on a ledge of rock outside his cave the monster lay basking in the sunlight. He was partly like a lion and partly like a dragon. He lay with his lion's head resting between his paws and his long green tail, like that of a lizard, curled around him.

Bellerophon rode his horse as near as he dared to the ledge on which the dragon lay, then raised his spear to strike at the Chimaera, but the great beast blew out clouds of smoke and fire, and Pegasus drew back in terror.

As the monster drew in his breath for another puff, Bellerophon rode close to the ledge and with one strong thrust sent his spear through the heart of the Chimaera.

When the young prince came back to the palace, riding the winged horse and carrying the head of the dreadful Chimaera, there was wild rejoicing in Lycia. Everyone admired and praised Bellerophon, and crowded around the wonderful horse, amazed at his wings and his silver feet.

**The Chimaera might view things a bit differently. How do you suppose he would describe these events?**

The young daughter of King Iobates, who came out on the portico of the palace to see the hero and his horse, fell in love with Bellerophon the moment she saw the young warrior sitting so proudly between the white wings of Pegasus. King Iobates led her to Bellerophon and gave her to him for his bride.

For a long time they were happy together. Bellerophon and Pegasus went on many adventures, and when Iobates died Bellerophon became King.

At last one day Bellerophon thought of a most daring adventure. He decided he would try to ride Pegasus to Mount Olympus and visit the gods.

Minerva appeared and warned him that the gods would be angry, but he mounted his horse and rose high into the clouds, urging Pegasus up toward the summit of Mount Olympus.

You have thought about the tale of Pegasus and Bellerophon from several points of view. Did changing your perspective add to your understanding of the story? How?

Jupiter, chief of the gods, looked down and, seeing the horse approaching, was angry to think that any mortal should dare approach the home of the gods. He caused a gadfly to light on Pegasus and sting his neck, his shoulders, and his nose.

Pegasus was so startled by this that at once he reared and wheeled among the clouds, leaping wildly in the air, and Bellerophon was thrown from his back and dropped down to earth.

Minerva, causing him to land where the ground was soft, spared his life, but as long as he lived Bellerophon wandered, crippled and lonely, seeking all over the earth for his wonderful winged horse.

But Pegasus never again returned to him.

## ♦ Library Link ♦

*If you would like to read other Greek myths, try* Greek Gods and Heroes *by Robert Graves.*

## Reader's Response

How would you use this story to teach a lesson to younger children?

## Thinking It Over

1. Why were the people of Lycia in mourning?
2. What personal qualities did Bellerophon reveal in the story?
3. Find examples to show that Pegasus was not pleased when Bellerophon first leaped on his back.
4. How did Pegasus know he had found his master?
5. Why do you think Bellerophon wanted to visit the gods? On what do you base your opinion?
6. Do you think Minerva treated Bellerophon fairly?

## Appreciating Literature

For centuries, writers and artists have used myths for inspiration. In fact, one reason for studying myths is to understand how they are used in literature and art. Think about the lesson that the story of Pegasus and Bellerophon teaches and explain how writers and artists might use the story in their work.

## Writing to Learn

**Think and Predict** As a reader, how well do you feel you know Bellerophon? Will he ever again know the joy of owning a winged horse?

Name three things that could happen to Bellerophon.

For example:

1. He could seek advice from the wisest person he knows.
2. Bellerophon may decide to apologize for his rash behavior.
3. He may ask Minerva for help.

**Write** Select the best response from above or from your own choices. Write an addition to this story, telling how Bellerophon handles his defeat.

# PEGASUS in POUND

Once into a quiet village,
Without haste and without heed,
In the golden prime of morning,
Strayed the poet's wingèd steed.

It was Autumn, and incessant
Piped the quails from shocks and sheaves,
And, like living coals, the apples
Burned among the withering leaves.

Thus, upon the village common,
By the school-boys he was found;
And the wise men, in their wisdom,
Put him straightway into pound.

Then the sombre village crier,
Ringing loud his brazen bell,
Wandered down the street proclaiming
There was an estray to sell.

And the curious country people,
Rich and poor, and young and old,
Came in haste to see this wondrous
Wingèd steed, with mane of gold.

Thus the day passed, and the evening
Fell, with vapors cold and dim;
But it brought no food nor shelter,
Brought no straw nor stall, for him.

Patiently, and still expectant,
    Looked he through the wooden bars,
Saw the moon rise o'er the landscape,
    Saw the tranquil, patient stars;

Till at length the bell at midnight
    Sounded from its dark abode,
And, from out a neighboring farm-yard,
    Loud the cock Alectryon crowed.

Then, with nostrils wide distended,
    Breaking from his iron chain,
And unfolding far his pinions,
    To those stars he soared again.

On the morrow, when the village
    Woke to all its toil and care,
Lo! the strange steed had departed.
    And they knew not when nor where.

But they found, upon the greensward
    Where his struggling hoofs had trod,
Pure and bright, a fountain flowing
    From the hoof-marks in the sod.

From that hour, the fount unfailing
    Gladdens the whole region round,
Strengthening all who drink its waters,
    While it soothes them with its sound.

HENRY WADSWORTH LONGFELLOW

COIN, *Corinth, Greece, 5th century B.C.*

# Literature Link

## *How can you figure out the unfamiliar meaning of a familiar word?*

Soon Bellerophon saw the winged horse flying far up in the sky. Nearer and nearer he wheeled until his silver feet touched the green grass beside the spring.

Suppose when you were reading "Pegasus and Bellerophon" you got confused by the use of the word *wheeled* in this passage. What clues could help you figure out the meaning? Maybe you pictured Pegasus, a horse with wings, "flying far up in the sky." Perhaps you then realized that the author couldn't be referring to wheels. *Wheeled* must refer to the horse "circling" lower and lower, like a bird does before landing on the ground.

### *What's the Story?*

Keeping in mind the *kind* of story you're reading can help you figure out the meanings of new words or even familiar words with unfamiliar meanings. Then if you are confused by the meaning of a word, you can try these tips:

- Look for context clues. The words that come before and after the confusing word might give you valuable clues.

- Think about the kind of story you're reading. Is it a myth? A fantasy? A sports story? For example, in a baseball story, would you expect the word *bullpen* to have anything to do with bulls?
- Consider context clues and overall story context together.
- If you're still confused, use a dictionary.

Try using these tips as you reread a passage from the beginning of the selection "All That Glitters."

> Within the hour, we found that it would not only be better, but was absolutely necessary, that we four, taking turns, two at a time, should put our hands against the end of the wagon and push it through the sand, leaving the feeble horses little to do but keep out of the way and hold up the tongue. ...We could really have accomplished the journey in ten days if we had towed the horses behind the wagon, but we did not think of that until it was too late, and so went on shoving the horses and the wagon too when we might have saved half the labor. Parties who met us, occasionally, advised us to put the horses *in* the wagon, but Mr. Ballou, through whose iron clad earnestness no sarcasm could pierce, said that it would not do....

Did the author's use of the word *tongue* confuse you? Look again, and think about the context clues. You might not be able to figure out exactly what *tongue* means here, but the context clues tell you that it's some part of the wagon that the horses are holding up. And since the horses are in front of the wagon, you know that that's where the tongue must be.

*Parties* is a word that has more than one meaning. Do you think the author means the kind of parties with noisemakers and balloons? Probably not. Using the context of the story, which is about prospectors in Nevada, you could figure out that *parties* is used to mean "groups of people doing something together."

If you get stuck on any words as you read "Aerin's Dragon," stop and think about what kind of story it is. Then use context clues to figure out the unfamiliar meaning of familiar words. Later, you can confirm the meaning in a dictionary.

*In the land of Damar, a dragon is on the loose. Only one person has the courage to try to slay the dragon and that person is the least likely dragonslayer in the kingdom.*

# Aerin's Dragon

by Robin McKinley
from The Hero and the Crown

*Aerin, the daughter of the king of Damar, has perfected an ointment called "kenet" that will make her fireproof. Now Aerin needs a chance to prove the protective power of kenet—and to prove her own worth.*

*As the story opens, Aerin, her cousin Tor, and her father, Arlbeth, are together at the breakfast table.*

So it was the three of them lingering over third cups of malak one morning when the first petitioner of the day came to speak to the king.

The petitioner reported a dragon, destroying crops and killing chickens. It had also badly burned a child who had accidentally discovered its lair, although the child had been rescued in time to save its life.

Arlbeth sighed and rubbed his face with his hand. "Very well. We will send someone to deal with it."

The man bowed and left.

NEWBERY MEDAL
1985

"There will be more of them now, with the trouble at the Border," said Tor. "That sort of vermin seems to breed faster when the North wind blows."

"I fear you are right," Arlbeth replied. "And we can ill spare anyone just now."

"I'll go," said Tor.

"Don't be a fool," snapped the king, and then immediately said, "I'm sorry. I can spare you least of all—as you know. Dragons don't kill people very often any more, but dragon-slayers rarely come back without a few uncomfortable burns."

"Someday," said Tor with a wry smile, "when we have nothing better to do, we must think up a more efficient way to cope with dragons. It's hard to take them seriously—but they are a serious nuisance." Aerin sat very still.

"Yes." Arlbeth frowned into his malak. "I'll ask tomorrow for half a dozen volunteers to go take care of this. And pray it's an old slow one."

Aerin also prayed it was an old slow one as she slipped off. She had only a day's grace, so she needed to leave at once; fortunately she had visited the village in question once on a state journey with her father, so she knew more or less how to get there. It was only a few hours' ride.

Her hands shook as she saddled Talat and tied the bundles of dragon-proof suit, kenet, sword, and a spear—which she wasn't at all sure she could use, since, barring a few lessons from Tor when she was eight or nine years old, she was entirely self-taught—to the saddle. Then she had to negotiate her way past the stable, the castle, and down the king's way and out of the City without anyone trying to stop her; and the sword and spear, in spite of the long cloak she had casually laid over them, were a bit difficult to disguise.

Her luck—or something—was good. She was worrying so anxiously about what she would say if stopped that she gave herself a headache; but as she rode, everyone seemed to be looking not quite in her direction—almost as if they couldn't quite *see* her, she thought. It made her feel a little creepy. But she got out of the City unchallenged.

The eerie feeling, and the headache, lifted at once when she and Talat set off through the forest below the City. The sun was shining, and the birds seemed to be singing just for her. Talat lifted into a canter, and she let him run for a while, the wind slipping through her hair, the shank of the spear tapping discreetly at her leg, reminding her that she was on her way to accomplish something useful.

She stopped at a little distance from the dragon-infested village to put on her suit—which was no longer quite so greasy with the kenet; it had reached its saturation point, perhaps, and then adapted, as well-oiled boots adapt to the feet that wear them. Her suit still quenched torches, but it had grown as soft and supple as cloth, and almost as easy to wear. She rubbed ointment on her face and her horse, and pulled on her long gloves. Shining rather in the sunlight then and reeking of pungent herbs, Aerin rode into the village.

Talat was unmistakably a warhorse, even to anyone who had never seen one before, and her red hair immediately identified her as the first sol. A little boy stood up from his doorstep and shouted: "They're here for the dragon!" and then there were a dozen, two dozen folk in the street, looking at her, and then looking in puzzlement for the five or six others that should have been riding with her.

"I am alone," said Aerin; she would have liked to explain, not that she was here without her father's knowledge but

that she was alone because she was dragon-proof (she hoped) and didn't need any help. But her courage rather failed her, and she didn't. In fact what the villagers saw as royal pride worked very well, and they fell over themselves to stop appearing to believe that a first sol (even a half-foreign one) couldn't handle a dragon by herself, and several spoke at once, offering to show the way to where the dragon had made its lair, all of them careful not to look again down the road behind her.

She was wondering how she could tell them delicately that she didn't want them hanging around to watch, since she wasn't at all sure how graceful (or effective) her first encounter with a real dragon was likely to be. But the villagers who accompanied her to show her the way had no intention of getting anywhere near the scene of the battle; a cornered dragon was not going to care what non-combatant bystanders it happened to catch with an ill-aimed lash of fire. They pointed the way, and then returned to their village to wait on events.

Aerin hung her sword round her waist, settled the spear into the crook of her arm. Talat walked with his ears sharply forward, and when he snorted she smelled it too: fire, and something else. It was a new smell, and it was the smell of a creature that did not care if the meat it ate was fresh or not, and was not tidy with the bones afterward. It was the smell of dragon.

Talat, after his warning snort, paced onward carefully. They came soon to a little clearing with a hummock of rock at its edge. The hummock had a hole in it, the upper edge of which was rimed with greasy smoke. The litter of past dragon meals was scattered across the once green meadow, and it occurred to Aerin that the footing would be worse for a horse's hard hoofs than a dragon's sinewy claws.

Talat halted, and they stood, Aerin gazing into the black hole in the hill. A minute or two went by and she wondered, suddenly, how one got the dragon to pay attention to one in the first place. Did she have to wake it up? Yell? Throw water into the cave at it?

Just as her spearpoint sagged with doubt, the dragon hurtled out of its den and straight at them: and it opened its mouth and blasted them with its fire—except that Talat had never doubted, and was ready to step nimbly out of its way as Aerin scrabbled with her spear and grabbed at Talat's mane to keep from falling off onto the dragon's back. It spun round—it was about the height of Talat's knees, big for a dragon, and dreadfully quick on its yellow-clawed feet—and sprayed fire at them again. This time, although Talat got them out of the worst of it, it licked over her arm. She saw the fire wash over the spear

handle and glance off her elbow, but she did not feel it; and the knowledge that her ointment did accomplish what it was meant to do gave her strength and cleared her mind. She steadied the spear-butt and nudged Talat with one ankle; as he sidestepped and as the dragon whirled round at them again, she threw her spear.

It wouldn't have been a very good cast for a seasoned dragon-hunter, but it served her purpose. It stuck in the dragon's neck, in the soft place between neck and shoulder where the scales were thin, and it slowed the dragon down. It twitched and lashed its tail and roared at her, but she knew she hadn't given it a mortal wound; if she let it skulk off to its lair, it would eventually heal and re-emerge, nastier than ever.

It bent itself around the wounded shoulder and tried to grip the spear in its teeth, which were long and thin and sharp and not well suited for catching hold of anything so smooth and hard and narrow as a spearshaft. Aerin dismounted and pulled out her sword, and approached it warily. It ignored her, or appeared to, till she was quite close; and then it snapped its long narrow head around at her again and spat fire.

It caught her squarely; and dragonfire had none of the friendliness of a woodfire burning by the side of a river where she had first tested her fireproof suit. The dragonfire pulled at her, seeking her life; it clawed at her pale shining skin, and at the supple leather she wore; and while the heat of it did not distress her, the heat of its malice did; and as the fire passed over her and disappeared she stood still in shock, and stared straight ahead of her, and did not move.

The dragon knew it had killed her. It was an old dragon, and had killed one or two human beings, and knew that it had caught this one well and thoroughly. It had been a bit puzzled that she did not scream when it burned her arm, and that she did not scream now and fall down writhing on the earth; but this did not matter. She would not trouble it further, and it could attend to its sore shoulder.

Aerin took half a dozen stiff steps forward, grasped the end of the spear and forced the dragon to the ground, swung her sword up and down, and cut off the dragon's head.

Then there was an angry scream from Talat, and she whirled, the heat of the dead dragon's fresh-spilled blood rising as steam and clouding her vision: but she saw dragonfire, and she saw Talat rear and strike with his forefeet.

She ran toward them and thought, gods, help me, it had a mate; I forgot, often there are two of them; and she chopped at the second dragon's tail, and missed. It swung around, breathing fire, and she felt the heat of it across her throat, and then Talat struck at it again. It lashed her with its tail when it whirled to face the horse again, and Aerin tripped and fell, and the dragon was on top of her at once, the claws scrabbling at her leather tunic and the long teeth fumbling for her throat. The smoke from its nostrils hurt her eyes. She yelled, frantically, and squirmed under the dragon's weight; and she heard something tear, and she knew if she was caught in dragon fire again she would be burned.

Then Talat thumped into the dragon's side with both hind feet, and the force of the blow lifted them both—for the dragon's claws were tangled in leather laces—and dropped them heavily. The dragon coughed, but there was no fire; and Aerin had fallen half on top of the thing. It raked her with its spiked tail, and something else tore; and its teeth snapped together inches from her face. Her sword was too long; she could not get it close enough for stabbing, and her shoulder was tiring. She dropped the sword and struggled to reach her right boottop, where she had a short dagger, but the dragon rolled, and she could not reach it.

Then Talat was there again, and he bit the dragon above its small red eye, where the ear hole was; and the dragon twisted its neck to spout fire at him, but it was still dazed by its fall, and only a little fire came out of its mouth. Talat plunged his own face into the trickle of smoke and seized the dragon by the nostrils and dragged its head back; and still farther back. Its forefeet and breast came clear of the ground and as the dragon thrashed, Aerin's leg came free, and she pulled the dagger from her boot and thrust it into the dragon's scaleless breast. The dragon shrieked, the noise muffled by Talat's grip on its nose, and Aerin stumbled away to pick up her sword.

Talat swung the dying dragon back and forth, and slashed at its body with one forefoot, and the muscles of his heavy stallion's neck ran with sweat and smudges of ash. Aerin lifted up the sword and sliced the dragon's belly open, and it convulsed once, shuddered, and died. Talat dropped the body and stood with his head down, shivering, and Aerin realized what she had done, and how little she had known about what it would involve, and how near she had come to failure, and her stomach rebelled, and she lost what remained of her breakfast over the smoking mutilated corpse of the second dragon.

She walked a few steps away till she came to a tree, and with her hands on its bole she felt her way to the ground, and sat with her knees drawn up and her head between them for a few minutes. Her head began to clear, and her breathing slowed, and as she looked up and blinked vaguely at the leaves overhead, she heard Talat's hoofbeats behind her. She put out a hand, and he put his bloody nose into it, and so they remained for several heartbeats more, and then Aerin sighed and stood up. "Even dragons need water. Let's look for a stream."

Again they were lucky, for there was one close at hand. Aerin carefully washed Talat's face, and discovered that most of the blood was dragon's, although his forelock was singed half away. "And to think I almost didn't bother to put any kenet on your head," she murmured. "I thought it was going to be so easy." She pulled Talat's saddle off to give him a proper bath, after which he climbed the bank and found a nice scratchy bit of dirt and rolled vigorously, and stood up again mud-colored. "Oh dear," said Aerin. She splashed water on her face and hands and then abruptly pulled off all her dragon-tainted clothing and submerged. She came up again when she needed to breathe, chased Talat back into the water to wash the mud off, and then brushed and rubbed him hard till she was warm and dry with the work and he was at least no more than damp.

She dressed slowly and with reluctance, and they returned to the battlefield. She tried to remember what else she ought to have thought of about dragons. Eggs? Well, if there were eggs, they'd die, for new-hatched dragons depended on their parents for several months. And if there were young dragons, surely we'd have seen them—?

With much greater reluctance she tied together some dry brush and set fire to it from her tinder box, and approached the dark foul-smelling hole in the rock. She had to stoop to get inside the cave at all, and her torch guttered and tried to go out. She had an impression of a shallow cave with irregular walls of rock and dirt, and a pebbly floor; but she could not bear the smell, or the knowledge that the grisly creatures she had just killed had lived here, and she jerked back outside into the sunlight again, and dropped her torch, and stamped out the fire. She didn't think there were any eggs, or dragon kits. She'd have to hope there weren't.

She thought: I have to take the heads with me. The hunters always bring the heads—and it does prove it without a lot of talking about it. I don't think I can talk about it. So she picked up her sword again and whacked off the second dragon's head, and then washed her sword and dagger in the stream, resheathed them, and tied her spear behind the saddle. The dragons looked small now, motionless and headless, little bigger and no more dangerous than rabbits; and the ugly heads, with the long noses and sharp teeth, looked false, like masks in a monster-play for the children during one of the City holidays, where part of the fun is to be frightened—but not very much. Who could be frightened of a dragon?

I could, she thought.

She tied the heads in the heavy cloth she'd carried her leather suit in, and mounted Talat, and they went slowly back to the village.

The villagers were all waiting, over a hundred of them, gathered at the edge of town; the fields beyond the village were empty, and men and women in their working clothes, looking odd in their idleness, all stood watching the path Aerin and Talat had disappeared down only an hour ago. A murmur arose as the front rank caught sight of them, and Talat raised his head and arched his neck, for he remembered how it should be, coming home from battle and bearing news of victory. The people pressed forward, and as Talat came out of the trees they surrounded him, looking up at Aerin: Just the one girl and her fine horse, surely they have not faced the dragon, for they are uninjured; and they were embarrassed to hope for a sol's burns, but they wished so sorely for the end of the dragon.

"Lady?" one man said hesitantly. "Did you meet the dragon?"

Aerin realized that their silence was uncertainty; she had suddenly feared that they would not accept even the gift of dragon-slaying from the daughter of a foreigner, and she smiled in relief, and the villagers smiled back at her, wonderingly. "Yes, I met your dragon; and its mate." She reached behind her and pulled at the cloth that held the heads, and the heads fell to the ground; one rolled, and the villagers scattered before it as if it still had some power to do them harm. Then they laughed a little sheepishly at themselves; and then everyone turned as the boy who had announced Aerin's arrival said, "Look!"

Seven horsemen were riding into the village as Aerin had ridden in. "You weren't supposed to get here till tomorrow," she murmured, for she recognized Gebeth and Mik and Orin, who were cousins of hers a few times removed and members of her father's court, and four of their men. Gebeth and Orin had been on many dragon hunts before; they were loyal and reliable, and did not consider dragon-hunting beneath them, for it was a thing that needed to be done, and a service they could do for their king.

"Aerin-sol," said Gebeth; his voice was surprised, respectful—for her father's sake, not hers—and disapproving. He would not scold her in front of the villagers, but he would certainly give Arlbeth a highly colored tale later on.

"Gebeth," she said. She watched with a certain ironic pleasure as he tried to think of a way to ask her what she was doing here; and then Orin, behind him, said something, and pointed to the ground where the small dragons' heads lay in the dust. Gebeth dropped his gaze from the unwelcome sight of his sovereign's young daughter rigged out like a soldier boy who has seen better days, realized what he was looking at, and yanked his eyes up again to stare disbelievingly at red-haired Aerin in her torn leather suit.

"I—er—I've gotten rid of the dragons already, if that's what you mean," said Aerin.

Gebeth dismounted, slowly, and slowly stooped down to stare at her trophies. The jaws of one were open, and the sharp teeth showed. Gebeth was not a rapid nor an original thinker, and he remained squatting on his heels and staring at the grisly heads long after he needed only to verify the dragonness of them. As slowly as he had stooped he straightened up again and bowed, stiffly, to Aerin, saying, "Lady, I salute you." His fingers flicked out in some ritual recognition or other, but Aerin couldn't tell which salute he was offering her, and rather doubted he knew which one he wanted to give. "Thank you," she said gravely.

Gebeth turned and caught the eye of one of his men, who dismounted and wrapped the heads up again; and then, as Gebeth gave no further hint, hesitated, and finally approached Talat to tie the bundle behind Aerin's saddle.

"May we escort you home, lady?" Gebeth said, raising his eyes to stare at Talat's pricked and bridleless ears, but carefully avoiding Aerin's face.

"Thank you," she said again, and Gebeth mounted his horse, and turned it back toward the City, and waited, that Aerin might lead; and Talat, who knew about the heads of columns, strode out without any hint from his rider.

The villagers, not entirely sure what they had witnessed, tried a faint cheer as Talat stepped off; and the boy who announced arrivals ran forward to pat Talat's shoulder, and Talat dropped his nose in acknowledgment and permitted the familiarity. A girl only a few years older than the boy stepped up to catch Aerin's eye, and said clearly, "We thank you." Aerin smiled and said, "The honor is mine." The girl grew to adulthood remembering the first sol's smile, and her seat on her proud white horse.

### ♦ Library Link ♦

*You can read more about Aerin and the Land of Damar in Robin McKinley's* The Hero and the Crown, *from which this selection was taken.*

## ***Reader's Response***

What do you think are the enjoyable qualities of this kind of fantasy?

## Thinking It Over

1. What troubles had the dragon created in the kingdom?
2. Why did Aerin decide to try slaying the dragon?
3. In what ways did Talat help Aerin achieve her goal?
4. Who were the noncombatant bystanders?
5. In your opinion, why was Aerin so quiet and modest about her triumph? What evidence led you to your opinion?

## Appreciating Literature

In traditional literature, a *stock character* is one we instantly recognize (for example, the wicked stepmother, the beautiful princess, or the noble dragon slayer). Stock characters are predictable and uncomplicated. In what ways would you say that Aerin is a stock character? In what ways is she different from a stock character? How do these differences affect the reader?

## Writing to Learn

**Think and Summarize** Aerin excites our imagination as we follow her adventures. Copy the chart below. Identify five incidents, in sequence, from the story. Chart the interest value of each incident. A *5* indicates the highest peak of interest. A *1* shows the lowest measure of interest.

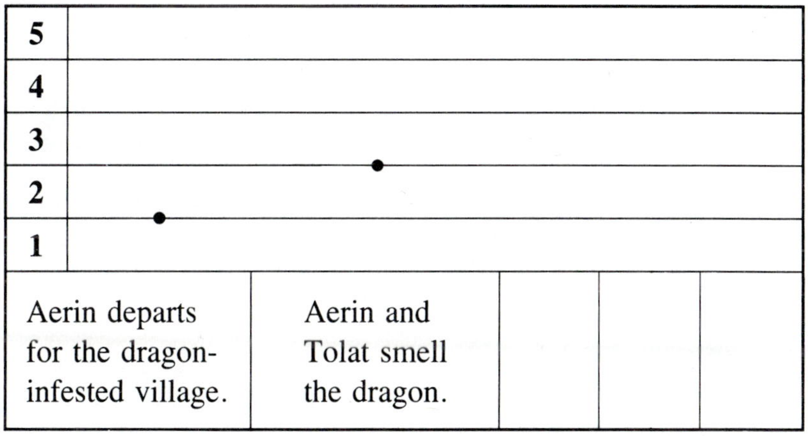


**Write** Imagine you are an observer assigned to report on Aerin's adventures. Write a narrative about the incident that was most interesting to you.

Lee Bennett Hopkins
INTERVIEWS

# Robin McKinley

Jennifer Carolyn Robin Turrell McKinley was born in her mother's hometown, Warren, Ohio. She grew up, however, all over the world because her father was serving in the United States Navy.

"As an only child, I grew up feeling that books, which you could take with you when your father was reassigned halfway around the world, were more reliable friends than human beings, who stayed behind or whose fathers were posted in some other direction," she stated. "I discovered early the world of books and reading."

One of her favorite childhood books was Frances Hodgson Burnett's *A Little Princess*. "I can't remember the first time I read *A Little Princess*, but this particular story about Sara Crewe, a little girl who told stories so wonderful that she believed them herself, fascinated me. I never quite lived up to Sara Crewe's standards, but I tried awfully hard."

Ms. McKinley attended school in Pennsylvania, spent some time zipping around Washington, D.C. on a motorcycle, and went to Maine's Bowdoin College, where she graduated with honors.

At the age of twenty-four, she wrote her first book, *Beauty: A Retelling of the Story of Beauty and the Beast*. She sent the manuscript to a publisher, who accepted it immediately and published the novel in 1978. Widely read, *Beauty* established Ms. McKinley as an important new voice in young adult literature.

Following *Beauty*, she created such works as *The Door in the Hedge*, a collection of four original and retold fairy tales; *Imaginary Lands: A Collection of Short Stories*, which she conceived and edited; *The Blue Sword*, which brought her a 1983 Newbery Honor Book citation; and *The Hero and the Crown*, which was awarded the Newbery Medal in 1985.

I asked Ms. McKinley if and how winning the Newbery Award changed her life. She replied, "It paid the bills for two years. Writers tend to live, slightly hysterically, from one advance or royalty check to the next. The Newbery Award lets you relax a little, fiscally. It also means that you are taken more seriously as a writer, which is pleasant. Personally, however, I didn't like the bright lights and the attention I received during the award year itself. It's a two-edged sword, like just about everything else in life."

About writing she explained, "Writing has always been the other side of reading for me; it never occurred to me not to make up stories. Once I got old enough to realize that one might aspire to be an author, I knew it was for me. I even majored in English literature in college, a good indication of my fine, bold disdain for anything so trivial as earning a living. I was going to be a writer, like Dickens and Hardy and Conrad—and Kipling and H. Rider Haggard and J. R. R. Tolkien."

I asked her what advice she gives to young adults who think they would like to write professionally one day. She answered, "I advise them to study veterinary medicine, which is easier. You don't want to be a writer unless you have no choice—and if you have no choice, good luck to you. You read as much as you can and write as much as you can. You don't have to be very organized about it unless you're an organized sort of person. But you *do* have to do it compulsively, convulsively, constantly, and you have to love it—be unable to live without it. Neither the reading nor the writing is more important. You read to feed your own story-telling faculty; you write to learn how, so that when the story presents itself to you, you'll be ready. Well, you'll never be ready. The story in your head will always be better than the one you write, which is one of the brutal facts about being a writer. But you can make yourself as ready as you can be."

Among her various pastimes are riding horses and listening to music. She said, "About the only irresistible attraction that reality has ever exerted on me is horses and riding. There are few things more real than mucking out stalls or falling on your head when you've forgotten to wear your hard hat."

Ms. McKinley's passion for horses has sometimes backfired. "Shortly before I was due to turn in *The Blue Sword* to my editor, a horse fell on me and broke my hand, thus bringing the book to a brutal halt for about six weeks."

As for her taste in music, she explains that one of her passions is rock music. "People fall back with cries of horror when I say this, but I believe my passion for it derives from the same source as my passion for opera; they're both about the excesses of human feeling, and they're both best loud. With that said, my desert island composer is still Giuseppe Verdi. There's music going fourteen or sixteen hours a day wherever I am."

Ms. McKinley describes herself as being clumsy, somewhat resembling her character Aerin in *The Hero and the Crown*. "During my childhood I was covered with bruises resulting from constant battles with intransigent door frames and pieces of furniture. About a month before I was supposed to turn in *The Hero and the Crown*, I fell on *myself* and broke my ankle. This was actually good for the book because for nine weeks I could do very little but type. I now suffer from an interesting new desire to withdraw into a padded room with my typewriter when a new book is coming to an end.

"I can't answer that inevitable question about where I get my ideas. Somehow or other, some of these pictures in my head, which

more responsible people call daydreams, turn themselves into stories. I am not an organized writer. When a story wants to get out of my skull and onto paper, it lets me know; it keeps me awake at night, makes me forget to pay overdue bills, renders me incapable of holding rational conversations with old friends. However, I have learned some survival skills to get the bills paid before my electricity is turned off. I can't complain. I love writing even though it is exhausting and frustrating."

Ms. McKinley reads compulsively and travels a great deal. She owns a little house in a village on the coast of Maine, which she considers home, but she also has an apartment in New York City.

"I shuttle cheerfully between the two places when I'm not flying to Seattle or London or plotting to get to Australia or back to the Far East. I lead at least two separate lives—possibly three. In New York I'm out every night. In Maine, weeks go by without anything of a social nature occurring at all, barring picking up the mail at the post office every morning and going to bed faithfully at nine o'clock every night. I spend hours at the typewriter and on the phone in both places, but the phone bills are much worse in Maine since I'm usually talking to people in New York. In both places I wear a lot of leather and rhinestones. My schedule at present is to spend winter in Maine and summer in New York, which makes me sound like a lunatic. But I love the simplicity and isolation of Maine in the winter, and I'll take the heat, even Manhattan heat, over the sidewalks cluttered with summer people who are looking for—nay, insisting on—'quaint'! Real life only comes out of hiding again after the summer people leave. But while my lilac-covered cottage in Maine is the light of my life, I still want a castle in Scotland," she said.

## *Reader's Response*

How do you feel about Ms. McKinley's opinion that reading is just as important as writing for a writer?

## Thinking It Over

1. What do you think motivated McKinley to become a writer?
2. Describe Robin McKinley's advice to young adults who think they would like to write professionally.
3. Do you agree with McKinley that the story in your head is always better than the one you write? How did you arrive at your answer?
4. If McKinley had not become a writer, what else do you think she might have become?

## Appreciating Literature

When a writer interviews someone, the purpose of the interview is to obtain information about the person. However, a good interviewer prepares by finding out as much as possible *before* the interview. Why do you think such preparation would be important? What things do you think Lee Bennett Hopkins may have known about Robin McKinley before he interviewed her?

## Writing to Learn

**Think and Analyze** As you read the interview with Robin McKinley, you can almost read between the lines and know what questions the interviewer must have asked her to elicit this information. Complete the chart below by listing four questions the interviewer may have asked Ms. McKinley.

| Questions |
| --- |
| 1. When was your first book published? |
| 2. |
| 3. |
| 4. |
| 5. |

**Write** Examine your list of questions. Find those that you could answer about yourself. Write a short autobiographical sketch that includes your answers to the questions you chose.

maggie and milly and molly and may
went down to the beach(to play one day)

and maggie discovered a shell that sang
so sweetly she couldn't remember her troubles,and

milly befriended a stranded star
whose rays five languid fingers were;

and molly was chased by a horrible thing
which raced sideways while blowing bubbles:and

may came home with a smooth round stone
as small as a world and as large as alone.

For whatever we lose(like a you or a me)
it's always ourselves we find in the sea

e. e. cummings

SMALL YACHT RACING, *oil on canvas by Samuel Carr, 1881.*

CHARLES AND ROBERT'S FIRST ASCENT IN A HYDROGEN BALLOON IN PARIS, DECEMBER 1, 1783, *color lithograph, French.*

*who knows if the moon's*
*a balloon,coming out of a keen city*
*in the sky—filled with pretty people?*
*(and if you and i should*

*get into it,if they*
*should take me and take you into their balloon,*
*why then*
*we'd go up higher with all the pretty people*

*than houses and steeples and clouds:*
*go sailing*
*away and away sailing into a keen*
*city which nobody's ever visited,where*

*always*
  *it's*
   *Spring)and everyone's*
*in love and flowers pick themselves*

*e. e. cummings*

# LITERATURE LINK

## *How does an author use unexpected twists in a story to surprise and entertain you?*

In the land of Damar, a dragon is on the loose. Only one person has the courage to try to slay the dragon and that person is the least likely dragonslayer in the kingdom. Is it any wonder that the dozen or so townspeople assembled to greet the dragonslayer stare at Aerin in puzzlement? They keep looking for the five or six other dragonslayers they are expecting.

### *What Do You Expect?*

The townspeople in "Aerin's Dragon" quickly find out that things in life don't always turn out the way they expect. A sudden turn of events catches them completely off guard. The same thing can be true when you are reading. Events in stories can suddenly twist around and surprise you.

This kind of literary twist, or unexpected turn of events, is called irony. Irony causes you to rethink your expectations. An author may use irony to entertain you or to make a very serious point. For example, do you remember the ending of "The Boy and the Piano Tuner," a story you read in Unit 1? You can reread it below; it may help you understand how an author uses irony and the effect it can have on you.

> The minutes slipped by unnoticed, and then, inevitably, it was time to come back to reality. To say goodbye. The happy and enraptured youngster spoke up boldly:
>
> "When I grow up, I'm going to be like you!"
>
> The maestro was moved and placed his long, slender fingers on the perspiring little head. Proud and satisfied that he had conveyed such a favorable impression of his profession, he asked, "Then you're going to be a piano tuner?"
>
> "No," said the little boy confidently. "I'm going to talk with children."

That wasn't what you expected to hear the boy say, was it? You probably thought, as did the piano tuner, that the boy was talking about a future in piano tuning or about how he wanted to have an important job like the piano tuner's. The author was using irony here to make a point about another skill of the piano tuner, one he probably never thought about. What point do you think the author is making?

Ironic statements or events are not always easy to identify at first. Often you realize that the author is being ironic only after you've thought about the story awhile. When you *do* identify irony, you are able to enjoy a story on several levels at once: You'll be entertained, gain insight into characters, and perhaps even learn a lesson. You can also learn to enhance your own writing by using irony. Here's how you can identify irony in a story.

- Look for a surprise—the opposite of what you expect to happen.
- Look for a contrast between what is *said* and what is *meant.*
- Look for understatement or exaggeration.

**B**e on the lookout for irony while reading the next selection, "Playing for Keeps." How do you think this device affects the author's telling of the story?

by Jack C. Haldeman II

*Johnny is in his backyard when he confronts a visitor who has traveled a long distance . . . a very long distance.*

Johnny Russell was playing in his backyard when the aliens landed. He was Tarzan in a land of giant ferns while they invaded Philadelphia, but had shifted over to Superman before Baltimore fell. Johnny was eight years old and easily bored. By the time his mother called him in for dinner, the aliens were all over Washington, D.C. Things were a mess. Ugly green monsters were everywhere. Lots of people were real upset, especially Johnny. They were having spinach for dinner.

Johnny hated spinach more than anything else in the world, except maybe brussels sprouts and creamed corn.

He made such a fuss at the table, trying to slip the dog his spinach, that his parents sent him to bed early. That was too bad, because there was a lot of neat stuff on television that night. Eight years old is just the right age for appreciating a good monster or two.

Johnny slept through it all, dreaming that he was flying his tree house over the ocean in search of lost continents.

His parents, on the other hand, were totally immersed in aliens of the real sort. There was no escaping them. Even the twenty-four-hour sports network was full of monsters. Specials followed specials all night long. Bert and Sara stayed glued to the tube, afraid they might miss something. It was an exciting time to watch television, even better than the time the dam burst at Fort Mudge. A good crisis brought out the best in the electronics media, no doubt about that.

They watched the national news for a while and then switched over to the local news. They even tuned in PBS and watched a panel of distinguished professors pointing sticks at an alien's picture. It was exciting. Sara made popcorn and Bert got some soda from the fridge.

"Don't you think we ought to wake up Johnny?" asked Sara, salting the popcorn.

Bert opened his soda. "No," he said. "We've got to teach him not to play with his food. A parent has certain obligations, you know." Bert had always been the strict one.

"But isn't that a little severe?" asked Sara. "After all, he's very fond of hideous beasts."

"No," said Bert. "Remember what he did with the brussels sprouts?"

Sara turned pale. "I thought I'd never get it all out. The air conditioning hasn't worked right since."

"And the creamed corn?"

Sara shuddered at the memory of the bomb squad marching through their living room in knee-deep water. "You're right," she said, passing him the popcorn.

They settled back and watched the early news, the special news, the update news, the fast-break news, the late news, and the late-late news. In between, they watched the news in brief and the news in detail. They were saturated with news and popcorn and all they got out of it was indigestion and no news at all. Nobody knew much of anything about the aliens except they were crawling all over the place and were meaner than junkyard dogs.

Their silver, cigar-shaped spaceships had simply appeared out of nowhere with a shimmering colorful splash of glitter not unlike the special effects of a once-popular TV show still in reruns. It was horrible. People fled in panic, especially when the monsters started coming out of the spaceships.

The aliens stood about eight feet tall with thick, stocky bodies. Their four arms had too many elbows and not enough fingers. Folds of wrinkled green skin covered their neckless heads, and their three unblinking eyes held what could only be interpreted as malice and contempt for the entire human race.

At first it was hoped that they might be a congenial star-roving race of beings, eager as puppy dogs to give humans all sorts of marvelous inventions. These hopes were quickly dashed. The aliens seemed far more interested in vaporizing people. Helicopters and airplanes that approached the hovering ships vanished in white-hot explosions. People who were foolish enough to make threatening gestures or stray too close went up in smoke. It made for good television footage, but did little to aid any kind of mutual understanding.

Mutual understanding, as a matter of fact, didn't seem to be the aliens' strong suit. They just didn't appear to be interested. Some of the best minds on Earth had attempted to establish communication with the aliens. Some of the best minds on Earth had been vaporized, too. The aliens were obviously intelligent, but they didn't have much to say.

Bert and Sara were about ready to turn in, having watched the instant replay of the destruction of Washington for the fourth or fifth time. It was impressive, but not really all that great. The Japanese had done it better in that movie about the radioactive frog. Sara washed the popcorn bowls.

"I'll bet Johnny will be excited when he wakes up," she said. "Channel Four said they've even seen a couple aliens right here in town. Imagine that."

"I don't think we ought to tell the boy about them," said Bert. "At least not yet."

"For goodness sakes, honey. Why not?"

"The child has an active enough imagination as it is. There's no sense in getting him all riled up. Remember the time he thought he saw that UFO down by the river?"

Sara nearly dropped the bowl she was drying. That had been a near thing. Johnny had pulled every fire alarm in town, and only their friendship with the judge had kept their names out of the paper.

"Besides," said Bert. "What does a kid know about monsters? He's only eight years old."

Sara nodded. He was right, as always.

But Johnny wasn't completely fooled. When little Freddy Nabors didn't show up by twelve o'clock, he knew something was wrong. He and Freddy always messed around together on Saturday afternoon. Sometimes they went on dangerous secret missions, but usually they just played. By twelve-fifteen Johnny had decided a plague must have killed all the kids on Earth but him so he went out into the backyard to play.

He wasn't allowed to go out behind the garage, so naturally it was his favorite place. It was full of old lumber and rusty nails. Lumber was more fun to play with than almost anything. Sometimes he built boats out of the scraps, and sometimes spaceships. Today he built a Grand Prix car. It was low and sleek, faster than a bat. He pretended it was orange with black trim. Since he couldn't find any wheels, he used cinder blocks for racing tires.

Diving into the hairpin turn, he had just passed Fangio and was gaining on Andretti when he saw the monster. Johnny was not impressed. He'd seen better ones on television. Sticking his tongue out between his lips and making a rude noise, he downshifted with a raspberry and pulled to the side of the road. After taking off his imaginary helmet and racing gloves, he got out of his fabricated car and stared at the alien. The alien stared back. Three eyes to two, the alien had an edge; but Johnny never flinched. The Lone Ranger wouldn't have backed down, and neither would he.

In the distance Johnny could see one of their spaceships hovering over the river. It looked just like the one he'd seen before. He

knew better than to head for the fire alarms this time, though.

The alien grunted and pointed at his ship and then to himself. Johnny stood as firm as Wyatt Earp, his jaw set like Montgomery Clift's, playing for keeps, his body held with the stern pride of John Wayne. He didn't nod; he didn't blink. He stared at the monster with Paul Newman's baby-blue eyes, hard as ice. He wished he'd worn long pants, though. Shorts just didn't cut it when you were staring down a monster.

The alien started waving all its arms in the air, grunting like crazy. Johnny was frightened, but he didn't give an inch. He could have been Gary Cooper standing alone in the middle of a dusty street facing an angry mob with only the badge on his chest and the goodness in his heart to protect him. Johnny could almost hear the people scurrying for cover. The helmet and racing gloves were useless. He should have had his six-shooter.

The alien kicked at the dust, smoothing out an area between them. He bent over and Johnny hunkered down to join him. At least now he knew what to expect. They were about to talk, or *palaver*, as Slim Pickins would say.

The alien picked up a stick and drew a large circle in the dirt. From a fold in his tunic he removed a small golden globe, which he placed precisely in the center. He pointed to the sun and then to the globe. Johnny nodded, his face as deadpan as if he were trying to fill an inside straight.

The monster drew three concentric circles around the golden globe and placed another globe on the third circle. It was smaller than the first and covered with blue and white swirls. He patted the dirt, waved his arms in circles all around them, and pointed to the globe. Johnny bit his lip. This was getting complicated.

The alien continued drawing circles in the dust and setting down the small globes. When he had finished, nine of them surrounded the larger yellow one. With a flourish he took one more from his tunic. This one was special; it was silver and seemed to glow with a light from within. He set it outside the farthest circle and pointed first to himself, then to the spaceship, and finally to the silver sphere.

Slowly he began rolling the sphere into the ring of circles. As he passed the outermost globe, he snarled and crushed it into the dirt beneath one of his massive thumbs. He continued rolling the silver sphere toward the center, snarling and crushing as he demolished each of the small globes. When he reached the third globe from the center, his lips drew back in a hideous sneer and he rose to his full height, towering over the crouching boy. The alien gloated, roaring with bone-chilling laughter as he crushed the small blue globe under his foot, grinding it into the dirt with a vengeance.

This, at last, was something Johnny could understand. It was a challenge. Without rising, he reached around to his back pocket. It was still there, as he knew it would be. He'd won it from Freddy

Nabors two years ago and he never went anywhere without it. It was his talisman, his good luck piece. It was also his weapon and had never let him down. He gritted his teeth and took it reassuringly in his hand. It was blue with milky white bands, a perfect agate.

He dropped and took quick aim, oblivious to the ranting and raving of the alien. He'd been under pressure before. This was nothing new. With a flick of his thumb the aggie sailed across the dust, crashing into the silver ball, sending it careening out of orbit into the yellow one. They both flew outside the circle.

He stood—as a man would stand after battle—and retrieved all the marbles. He held them high above his head.

"Keepsies," he said and slipped them into his pocket.

The alien backed away in horror, babbling wildly. With a shimmer and a pop, he disappeared. An instant later the spaceship vanished in a similar fashion, as did all the spaceships and all the aliens all over the world.

Johnny climbed back into his Grand Prix car and accelerated through the gears. He was nearly a lap behind by now and would have to do some fancy driving to catch up. Besides, his mother was fixing creamed corn tonight, and the boy who had saved the world had important things on his mind.

As he took the checkered flag he wondered how Conan would have handled creamed corn.

### ♦ Library Link ♦

*If you enjoyed "Playing for Keeps," which appears in* Tales from Isaac Asimov's Science Fiction Magazine, *you might want to read Art Vesity's* The First Day, *another story in that collection.*

## ◆ *Reader's Response*

If one of the aliens in "Playing for Keeps" landed in your backyard, how would you respond?

## Thinking It Over

1. What was unusual about Bert and Sara's reaction to the news about the aliens?
2. Compare Johnny's personal qualities with those of other eight-year-old children.
3. Summarize Johnny's reactions when the alien first approached him.
4. What did the silver globe symbolize?
5. What was the alien trying to communicate to Johnny? What makes you think so?
6. Why do you think the alien fled in horror after Johnny had collected all the globes?
7. What "important" issue was on Johnny's mind after he saved the world?

## Appreciating Literature

The title of this story involves a play on words. Before you read the story, what did you think the title meant? What additional meaning did it have after you read the story?

## Writing to Learn

**Think and Imagine** This imaginative story introduces us to Johnny Russell and an unusual creature from space. Complete the following flowchart of story events on your own paper. Add as many boxes as you choose.

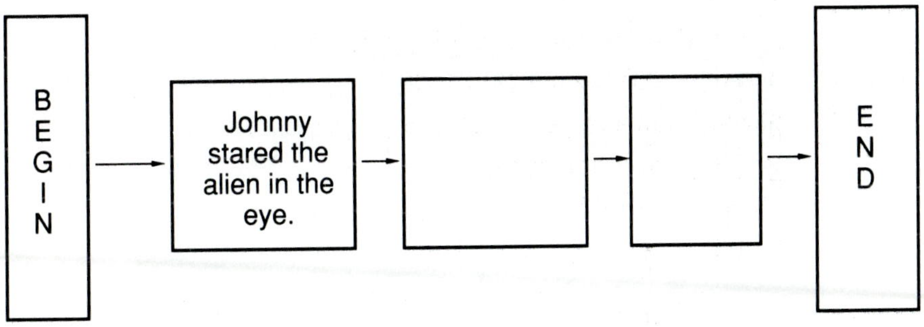


**Write** Take Johnny's point of view and use the ideas from the flowchart to write a report about the encounter with the alien.

# The Night the Martians Landed

**by Howard Koch**

*Sometimes it's fun to listen to a scary story, but once a major segment of the American public listened to such a story and did not know it wasn't true. What happened then has become a legend.*

In 1898 H. G. Wells published a novella entitled *The War of the Worlds* about an invasion of the earth by creatures from the planet Mars which I dramatized in the form of news bulletins and the diary of a survivor. On the Eve of Hallowe'en, October 30, 1938, this radio play was broadcast over CBS by Orson Welles and the Mercury Theatre with some startling and unforeseen results. Between nine o'clock eastern standard time and dawn of the next day men, women and children in scores of towns and cities across the nation were in flight from objects that had no existence except in their imaginations.

In the course of forty-five minutes of actual time—as differentiated from subjective or fictional time—the invading Martians were presumably able to blast off from their planet, land on the earth, set up their destructive machines, defeat our army, disrupt communications, demoralize the population and occupy whole sections of the country. In forty-five minutes!

For days following the Martian broadcast headlines screamed and newspapers around the world tried to recreate the atmosphere of terror that spread over America on that October night. Even some years later the event is vividly recalled by an editor of the *New York Times*.

> *"The panic came in the night. Here, there and everywhere people suddenly dropped to their knees and began to moan and babble. Housewives wept, tore their hair and fell into swoons. Grown men wept, too, and dashed about the streets. College students trembled and prayed. Telephone lines were clogged with calls. In a few hours more the Red Cross and the National Guard would have had to be mobilized."*

During and after the broadcast frantic telephone calls flooded the switchboards of radio stations, newspapers and police headquarters. Some radio stations reported increases as much as five hundred percent over the usual Sunday night volume. Naturally it was CBS that received the full impact. I was not at the studio during the broadcast but John Houseman, co-producer of the show, was there and gives the following eyewitness account:

> *"At the height of the drama, around 8:31 the fictional Secretary of the Interior was on the air with an exhortation to the American people. Toward the end of this speech (circa 8:32 E.S.T.) Davidson Taylor, supervisor of the broadcast for the Columbia Broadcasting System, received a phone call in the control room, creased his lips, and hurriedly left the studio. By the time he returned a few moments later—pale as death—clouds of heavy smoke were rising from Newark, New Jersey, and the Martians, tall as skyscrapers, were astride the Pulaski Skyway preparatory to wading the Hudson River. To us in the studio, the show seemed to be progressing splendidly—how splendidly Davidson Taylor had just learned outside. For several minutes now a kind of madness had seemed to be sweeping the continent—somehow connected with our show. The CBS switchboards had been swamped into uselessness but from outside sources vague rumors were coming in of deaths and suicides and panic injuries. . . . I remember during the playing of the final theme, the phone started to ring in the control room and a shrill voice through the receiver announcing itself as the mayor of some Midwestern city, one of the big ones. He is screaming for Welles. Choking with fury, he reports mobs in the streets of the city, women and children huddled in churches, violence and looting . . . Orson hangs up quickly. For we are now off the air and the studio door bursts open. The following hours are a nightmare. The building is suddenly full of people and dark blue uniforms. We are hurried out of the studio, downstairs, into a back office. Here we sit, incommunicado, while network employees are busily collecting, destroying or locking up all scripts and records of the broadcast. . . . Hours later, instead of arresting us, they let us out a back way. We scurry down to the theater like hunted animals to their holes. It is surprising to see life going on as usual in the midnight streets."*

The brunt of public outcry fell on Orson. For days he was pursued by reporters and threatened by outraged citizens. Lawsuits for injuries and damages were filed against CBS and Mercury Theatre, running into millions of dollars, but none of these came to trial since there

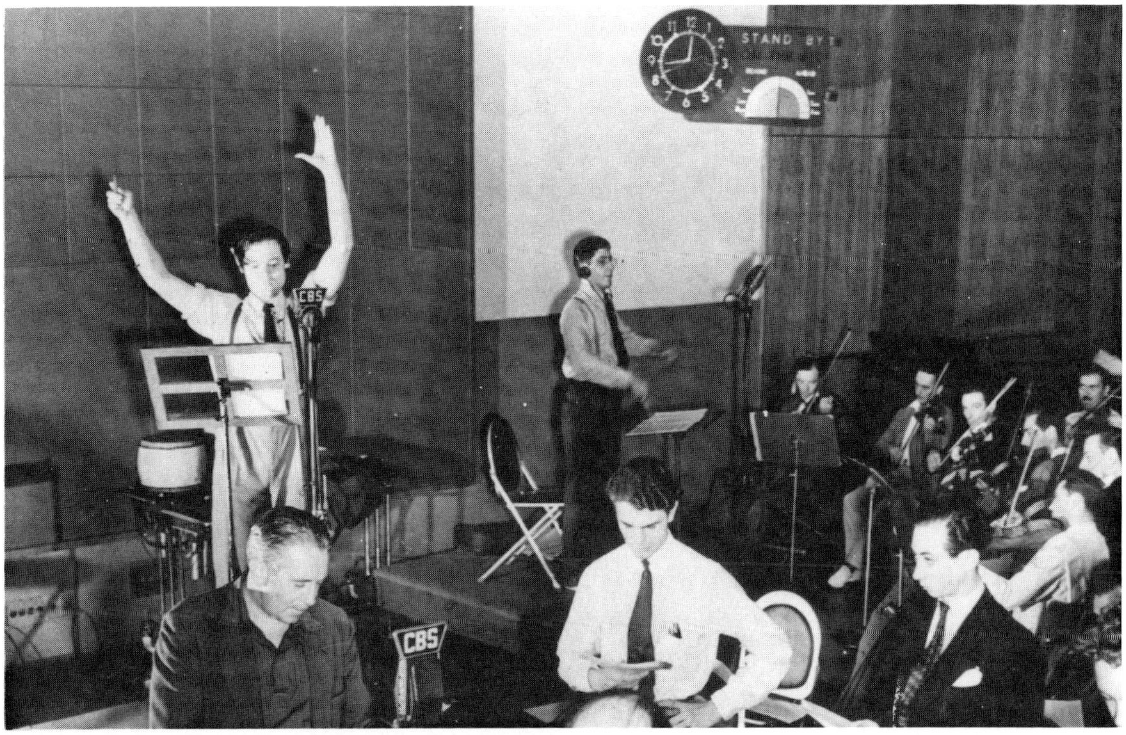

The Mercury Theatre presents the radio broadcast *Invasion From Mars*.

Orson Welles (center) is interviewed by reporters following the "panic broadcast".

was no similar example for such actions under those circumstances. As the shock was absorbed and the excitement died down, the tide of public opinion reversed itself. Mail continued to pour into radio stations but the vast majority were favorable, even congratulatory. Stories of individual experiences during the panic are recounted to this day like the reminiscences of people who have lived through an actual war.

> *"I tuned in when the weather reports were given. I was with my little boy. My husband was at the movies. I thought it was all up with us. I grabbed my boy and just sat and cried."*

This reaction of a mother living in a crowded New Jersey tenement was typical of many in several important respects. She saw certain death facing not only herself and her family but the "us" included the whole human race. It was tragedy on an incomprehensible scale. Over aeons of time people had survived the long and perilous climb from prehistoric origins to a relatively civilized state. Having gained control over the earth, people were beginning to dream of reaching other planets. In one night their illusions of mastery were shattered. Creatures infinitely more advanced in technology were arriving from the reddish-hued planet their ancestors had named for the god of war and these formidable strangers were taking over the earth. Little wonder that this woman "sat down and cried."

After the broadcast almost everyone I met had a story to tell, either a personal experience or something that happened to someone he knew. Many of these accounts told of frantic efforts to reach absent members of their family before the end came. The head of the location department at Warner Brothers studio told me his experience in these words as nearly as I can recall them:

> *"My wife and I were driving through the redwood forest in northern California when the broadcast came over our car radio. At first it was just New Jersey but soon the things were landing all over, even in California. There was no escape. All we could think of was to try to get back to L.A. to see our children once more. And be with them when it happened. We went right by gas stations but I forgot we were low in gas. In the middle of the forest our gas ran*

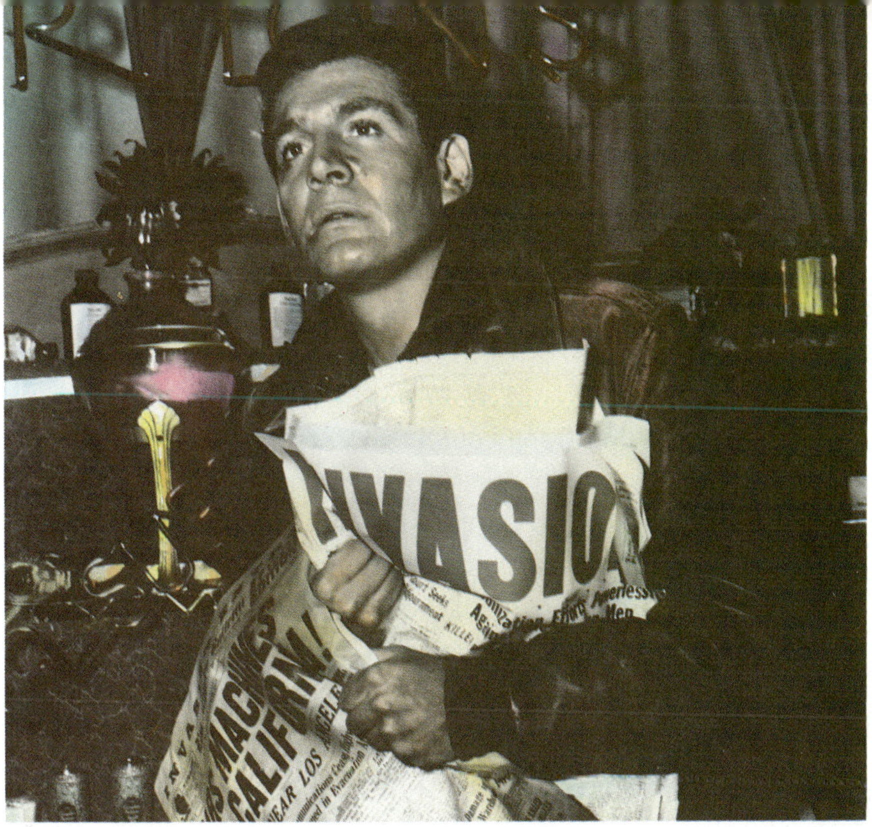

**Actor Gene Barry is shown in the 1953 movie version of** *The War of the Worlds*.

*out. There was nothing to do. We just sat there holding hands expecting any minute to see those Martian monsters appear over the tops of the trees. When Orson said it was a Hallowe'en prank, it was like being reprieved on the way to the gas chamber."*

Some of the stories had their humorous aspect—at least in retrospect. This account came from a young college student:

*"My girlfriend and I were at a party in the village. Someone turned on the radio. It was just when the Martians were spraying the people at Grovers Mill with the heat ray. At first we couldn't believe it was happening but it was so real we stayed glued to the radio getting more scared every minute. My girl began to cry. She wanted to be with her family. The party broke up in a hurry, our friends scattering in all directions. I drove like crazy up Sixth Avenue. I don't know how fast—fifty, maybe sixty miles an hour. The traffic cops at the street crossings just stared at us, they couldn't believe their eyes, whizzing right past them going through the red lights. I didn't care if I got a ticket. It was all over anyway. Funny thing, none of the cops chased us. I guess they were too flabbergasted. My apartment was*

*on the way so I stopped just long enough to rush in and shout up to my father that the Martians had landed and we were all going to be killed and I was taking my girl home. When we got there, her parents were waiting for us. My father had called them. Told them to hold me there until he could send a doctor as I'd gone out of my mind."*

Professor Hadley Cantril of Princeton and his research staff did a thorough study into the causes of the panic reactions, which was published by the Princeton University Press under the title, *Invasion from Mars*. They estimated that approximately 6,000,000 people listened to the program and, of that number, at least 1,200,000 took the broadcast literally and reacted according to their natures and circumstances. In addition an unknown number who were not tuned into the broadcast were caught up in the mass hysteria.

Why were so many Americans ready to believe such a fantastic tale and why did they behave in such an irrational manner? A mere switch of the radio dial to another station broadcasting in a normal manner would have shattered the illusion of a world catastrophe. Some listeners did switch over but a surprising number of people failed to make this simple check.

**The movie version of the invasion used special effects to grip moviegoers.**

*"Living in a troublesome world, anything is liable to happen. We hear so much news every day. So many things we hear are unbelievable. For instance, all of a sudden six hundred children burned to death in a school fire, or a lot of people are thrown out of work. Everything seems to be a shock to me."*

A troublesome world. Those words, spoken by one of the women interviewed, say a great deal. High on the list of causes for the panic cited by the Princeton study is insecurity. Insecurity of all kinds—personal, economic and political. Life is insecure at best. We are here briefly, surrounded by the mysteries of our origin and significance, with only a slight hold on our environment—hostages to the fates both outside and within ourselves. Beside the uncertainties that are part of our lives are those we needlessly inflict on each other. In our highly productive but haphazard economic system we are able to produce all that we need, yet the wealth it creates is so unevenly distributed, much into wasteful channels, that poverty is a permanent state for a large part of the world's population. In our so-called wealthy society even this lopsided prosperity is anything but stable. Either we are just emerging from a depression or being cautioned by bankers and politicians that one is approaching.

Many responses of those interviewed showed a definite connection between their economic insecurity and their susceptibility to panic as in the following cases:

*"Ever since my husband lost his job a few years ago, things seem to have gone from bad to worse. I don't know when everything will be all right again."*

*"I haven't been employed for four years on account of the depression and I don't know how long my brother's job will last."*

In 1938, the year of the broadcast, the deep depression of the early thirties was still vivid in the memories of all adults. They had experienced the shock of losing their jobs or their businesses or their farms overnight. Many saw their families hungry and, some, homeless as the banks foreclosed mortgages on a vast scale. The solid rock of our social structure turned out to be quicksand.

*"The announcer said a meteor had fallen from Mars and I was sure he thought that but in the back of my head I had an idea that the meteor was just a camouflage. It was really an airplane like a zeppelin that looked like a meteor and the Germans were attacking us with gas bombs."*

Add to all the other anxieties the shadow of war creeping toward us during the thirties. As we know, war is the building of forces already at work during times of peace like humidity gathering before a storm. When the fighting actually starts, it often comes as a relief since we have already endured the suspense. The Martians were on the move long before the night of the symbolic invasion. Many listeners translated the monstrous creatures into Germans. They assumed that Hitler had developed a secret devastating weapon and was taking over the whole world. In one terror-filled night all our fears and insecurities came home to roost.

*"When those things landed, I thought the best thing to do was to go away, so I took $3.25 out of my savings and bought a ticket. After I'd gone sixty miles, I heard it was a play. Now I don't have any money left for the shoes I was saving up for. Would you please have someone send me a pair of black shoes, size 9 B."*

This pathetic letter addressed to Orson from a laborer illustrates another factor in one's susceptibility to a panic reaction. Although college graduates were not immune, the Cantril study showed that the response to the broadcast varied in proportion to the level of education a person had. In general, those with more schooling had acquired a more reliable critical standard which enabled them to weigh the credibility of the events in the radio play against their knowledge of the world. An invasion from another planet was too fantastic to believe, it didn't concur with their conception of reality. Besides, too many things happened in too short a time. Also to many educated listeners the voice of Orson Welles was a familiar one. They knew Orson as a man of many attainments but not the astronomer he portrayed as Professor Pierson in the broadcast.

In some cases coincidence added fuel to the imaginary fires that were spreading over cities and countrysides. In the small town of

Concrete, Washington, there was a local power failure at the very moment when the Martians in the play were supposedly disrupting the nation's communication and power sources. To the local listeners, suddenly plunged into darkness as the lights went out all over town, it seemed a confirmation of what they believed was happening all over the country. The result was mass hysteria, families fleeing wildly in the night, isolated from any information source that might calm their terror.

> *"I believed the broadcast as soon as I heard the professor from Princeton and the officials in Washington. I knew it was an awfully dangerous situation when all those military men were there and the Secretary of State spoke."*

Average net paid circulation for September exceeded Daily---1,800,000 Sunday-3,150,000

DAILY NEWS

Copyright 1938 by News Syndicate Co., Inc. Reg. U. S. Pat. Off. NEW YORK'S PICTURE NEWSPAPER Entered as 2nd class matter, Post Office, New York, N. Y.

FINAL

Vol. 20. No. 109 New York, Monday, October 31, 1938* 48 Pages 2 Cents IN CITY LIMITS | 3 CENTS Elsewhere

# FAKE RADIO 'WAR' STIRS TERROR THROUGH U.S.

Story on Page 2

**Newspaper headlines reflect one night's terror.**

Unfortunately, we are ready to believe almost anything if it comes from a recognized authority. This man gave complete credibility to the "news bulletins" from the nonexistent Intercontinental Radio News because important people were supposedly making the announcements. He mentioned the "Secretary of State" although it was actually the fictional Secretary of the Interior whose Rooseveltian voice came over the air. Instead of hearing what was actually said, the listener heard what matched his own beliefs. However, it is interesting to note that while people believed the "information" government officials were giving out about the gravity of the situation, they were not ready to take their advice to put their trust in the military forces of this nation. It seems that was the moment many listeners chose to drop everything and depart for distant places.

The social and psychological factors which contributed to the panic were not confined to America. A year or so after our program a radio production group in Lima, Peru, obtained the play, translated it into Spanish and broadcast it to their citizens. Again a panic occurred but on a smaller scale since there were fewer radios within the broadcast range. However, the aftermath was even more drastic. Since then, we have tried to keep the Martian genii in a bottle tightly corked with a warning label "open at your peril."

## *Reader's Response*

Do you think a radio station should have the right to broadcast a play like the one described in this selection? Explain.

## Thinking It Over

1. Why did terror grip some people in America on the eve of Hallowe'en, October 30, 1938?
2. What are some psychological and social factors that might have contributed to people's believing the broadcast and panicking?
3. Why did many Americans link the Martian invasion with Germany?
4. Do you agree with the author that people "are ready to believe almost anything if it comes from a recognized authority"? Explain your response.
5. If a radio broadcast of invading Martians occurred today, do you think the response would be the same as it was in 1938? What makes you think it would or would not?

## Appreciating Literature

Nonfiction writers often use quotations from eyewitnesses. In this account of the famous "panic broadcast" of 1938, notice how the author uses quotations throughout the article. How do these quotations make you feel about the people who panicked? How do the quotations help you to understand why they panicked?

## Writing to Learn

**Think and Analyze** In "The Night the Martians Landed," people were interviewed after the broadcast and revealed a variety of reactions. Draw a microphone like the one shown below, and list some of the reactions.

**Write** What would you ask these same people today? Write two questions and their possible answers.

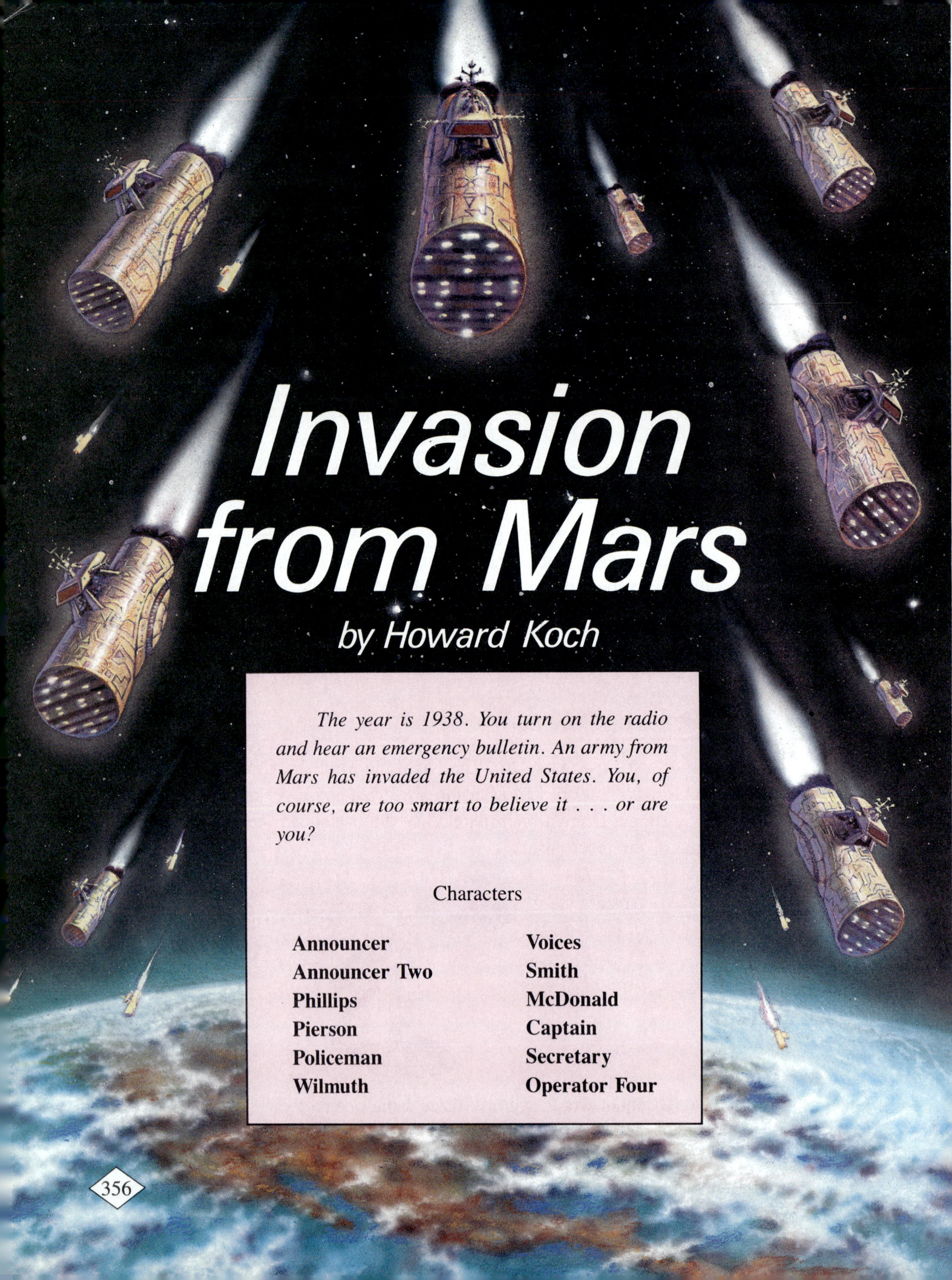

# Invasion from Mars

## by Howard Koch

*The year is 1938. You turn on the radio and hear an emergency bulletin. An army from Mars has invaded the United States. You, of course, are too smart to believe it . . . or are you?*

Characters

| | |
|---|---|
| **Announcer** | **Voices** |
| **Announcer Two** | **Smith** |
| **Phillips** | **McDonald** |
| **Pierson** | **Captain** |
| **Policeman** | **Secretary** |
| **Wilmuth** | **Operator Four** |

**Announcer:** Ladies and gentlemen, here is the latest bulletin from the Intercontinental Radio News. Montreal, Canada: Professor Morse of McGill University reports observing a total of three explosions on the planet Mars, between the hours of 7:45 P.M. and 9:20 P.M., eastern standard time. This confirms earlier reports received from American observatories. Now, nearer home, comes a special announcement from Trenton, New Jersey. It is reported that at 8:50 P.M. a huge, flaming object, believed to be a meteorite, fell on a farm in the neighborhood of Grovers Mill, New Jersey, twenty-two miles from Trenton. The flash in the sky was visible within a radius of several hundred miles and the noise of the impact was heard as far north as Elizabeth.

We have dispatched a special mobile unit to the scene, and will have our commentator, Mr. Phillips, give you a word description as soon as he can reach there from Princeton. In the meantime, we take you to the Hotel Martinet in Brooklyn, where Bobby Millette and his orchestra are offering a program of dance music.

(*Swing band for twenty seconds . . . then cut*)

**Announcer Two:** We take you now to Grovers Mill, New Jersey.

(*Crowd noises . . . police sirens*)

**Phillips:** Ladies and gentlemen, this is Carl Phillips at the Wilmuth farm, Grovers Mill, New Jersey. Professor Pierson and myself made the eleven miles from Princeton in ten minutes. Well, I . . . I hardly know where to begin, to paint for you a word picture of the strange scene before my eyes, like something out of a modern *Arabian Nights*.

Well, I just got here. I haven't had a chance to look around yet. I guess that's it. Yes, I guess that's the . . . thing, directly in front of me, half buried in a vast pit. Must have struck with terrific force. The ground is covered with splinters of a tree it must have struck on its way down. What I can see of the . . . object itself doesn't look very much like a meteor, at least not the meteors I've seen. It looks more like a huge cylinder. It has a diameter of . . . what would you say, Professor Pierson?

**Pierson:** (*Off*) About thirty yards.

**Phillips:** About thirty yards . . . The metal on the sheath is . . . well, I've never seen anything like it. The color is sort of yellowish-white. Curious spectators now are pressing close to the object in spite of the efforts of the police to keep them back. They're getting in front of my line of vision. Would you mind standing on one side, please?

**Policeman:** One side, there, one side.

**Phillips:** While the policemen are pushing the crowd back, here's Mr. Wilmuth, owner of the farm here. He may have some interesting facts to add. . . . Mr. Wilmuth, would you please tell the radio audience as much as you remember of this rather unusual visitor that dropped in your backyard? Step closer, please. Ladies and gentlemen, this is Mr. Wilmuth.

**Wilmuth:** I was listenin' to the radio.

**Phillips:** Closer and louder, please.

**Wilmuth:** Pardon me!

**Phillips:** Louder, please, and closer.

**Wilmuth:** Yes sir—while I was listening to the radio and kinda drowsin', that Professor fellow was talkin' about Mars, so I was half dozin' and half . . .

**Phillips:** Yes, Mr. Wilmuth. Then what happened?

**Wilmuth:** As I was sayin', I was listenin' to the radio kinda halfways . . .

**Phillips:** Yes, Mr. Wilmuth, and then you saw something?

**Wilmuth:** Not first off, I heard something.

**Phillips:** And what did you hear?

**Wilmuth:** A hissing sound. Like this: ssssss . . . kinda like a fourt' of July rocket.

**Phillips:** Then what?

**Wilmuth:** Turned my head out the window and thought I was asleep and dreamin'.

**Phillips:** Yes?

**Wilmuth:** I saw a kinda greenish streak and then zingo! Somethin' smacked the ground. Knocked me clear out of my chair!

**Phillips:** Well, were you frightened, Mr. Wilmuth?

**Wilmuth:** Well, I—I'm not quite sure. I reckon I—I was kinda riled.

**Phillips:** Thank you, Mr. Wilmuth. Thank you.

**Wilmuth:** Want me to tell you some more?

**Phillips:** No . . . That's quite all right, that's plenty.

**Phillips:** Ladies and gentlemen, you've just heard Mr. Wilmuth, owner of the farm where this thing has fallen. I wish I could convey the atmosphere . . . the background of this . . . fantastic scene. Hundreds of cars are parked in a field in back of us. Police are trying to rope off the roadway leading into the farm. But it's no use. They're breaking right through. Their headlights throw an enormous spot on the pit where the object's half buried. Some of the more daring souls are venturing near the edge. Their silhouettes stand out against the metal sheen. (*Faint humming sound*)

One man wants to touch the thing . . . he's having an argument with a policeman. The policeman wins. . . . Now, ladies and gentlemen, there's something I haven't mentioned in all this excitement, but it's becoming more distinct. Perhaps you've caught it already on your radio. Listen: (*Long pause*) . . . Do you hear it? It's a curious humming sound that seems to come from inside the object. I'll move the microphone nearer. Here. (*Pause*) Now we're not more than twenty-five feet away. Can you hear it now? Oh, Professor Pierson!

**Pierson:** Yes, Mr. Phillips?

**Phillips:** Can you tell us the meaning of that scraping noise inside the thing?

**Pierson:** Possibly the unequal cooling of its surface.

**Phillips:** Do you still think it's a meteor, Professor?

**Pierson:** I don't know what to think. The metal casing is definitely extraterrestrial . . . not found on this earth. Friction with the earth's atmosphere usually tears holes in a meteorite. This thing is smooth and, as you can see, of cylindrical shape.

**Phillips:** Just a minute! Something's happening! Ladies and gentlemen, this is terrific! This end of the thing is beginning to flake off! The top is beginning to rotate like a screw! The thing must be hollow!

**Voices:** She's a movin'!

Look, the thing's unscrewing!

Keep back, there! Keep back, I tell you!

Maybe there's men in it trying to escape!

It's red hot, they'll burn to a cinder!

Keep back there. Keep those idiots back! (*Suddenly the clanking sound of a huge piece of falling metal*)

**Voices:** She's off! The top's loose!

Look out there! Stand back!

**Phillips:** Ladies and gentlemen, this is the most terrifying thing I have ever witnessed . . . Wait a minute! *Someone's crawling out of the hollow top*. Some-

one or . . . something. I can see peering out of that black hole two luminous disks . . . are they eyes? It might be a face. It might . . . (*Shout of awe from the crowd*)

**Phillips:** Good heavens, something's wriggling out of the shadow like a gray snake. Now it's another one, and another. They look like tentacles to me. There, I can see the thing's body. It's large as a bear and it glistens like wet leather. But that face. It . . . it's indescribable. I can hardly force myself to keep looking at it. The eyes are black and gleam like a serpent. The mouth is V-shaped with saliva dripping from its rimless lips that seem to quiver and pulsate. The monster or whatever it is can hardly move. It seems weighed down by . . . possibly gravity or something. The thing's raising up. The crowd falls back. They've seen enough. This is the most extraordinary experience. I can't find words. . . I'm pulling this microphone with me as I talk. I'll have to stop the description until I've taken a new position. Hold on, will you please, I'll be back in a minute. (*Fade into piano*)

**Announcer Two:** We are bringing you an eyewitness account of what's happening on the Wilmuth farm, Grovers Mill, New Jersey. (*More piano*) We now return you to Carl Phillips at Grovers Mill.

**Phillips:** Ladies and gentlemen (Am I on?). Ladies and gentlemen, here I am, back of a stone wall that adjoins Mr. Wilmuth's garden. From here I get a sweep of the whole scene. I'll give you every detail as long as I can talk. As long as I can see. More state police have arrived. They're drawing up a cordon in front of the pit, about thirty of them. No need to push the crowd back now. They're willing to keep their distance. The captain is conferring with someone. We can't quite see who. Oh yes, I believe it's Professor Pierson. Yes, it is. Now they've parted. The professor moves around one side, studying the object, while the captain and two policemen advance with something in their hands. I can see it now. It's a white handkerchief tied to a pole . . . a flag of truce. If those creatures know what that means . . . what anything means! . . . *Wait!* Something's happening! (*Hissing sound followed by a humming that increases in intensity*)

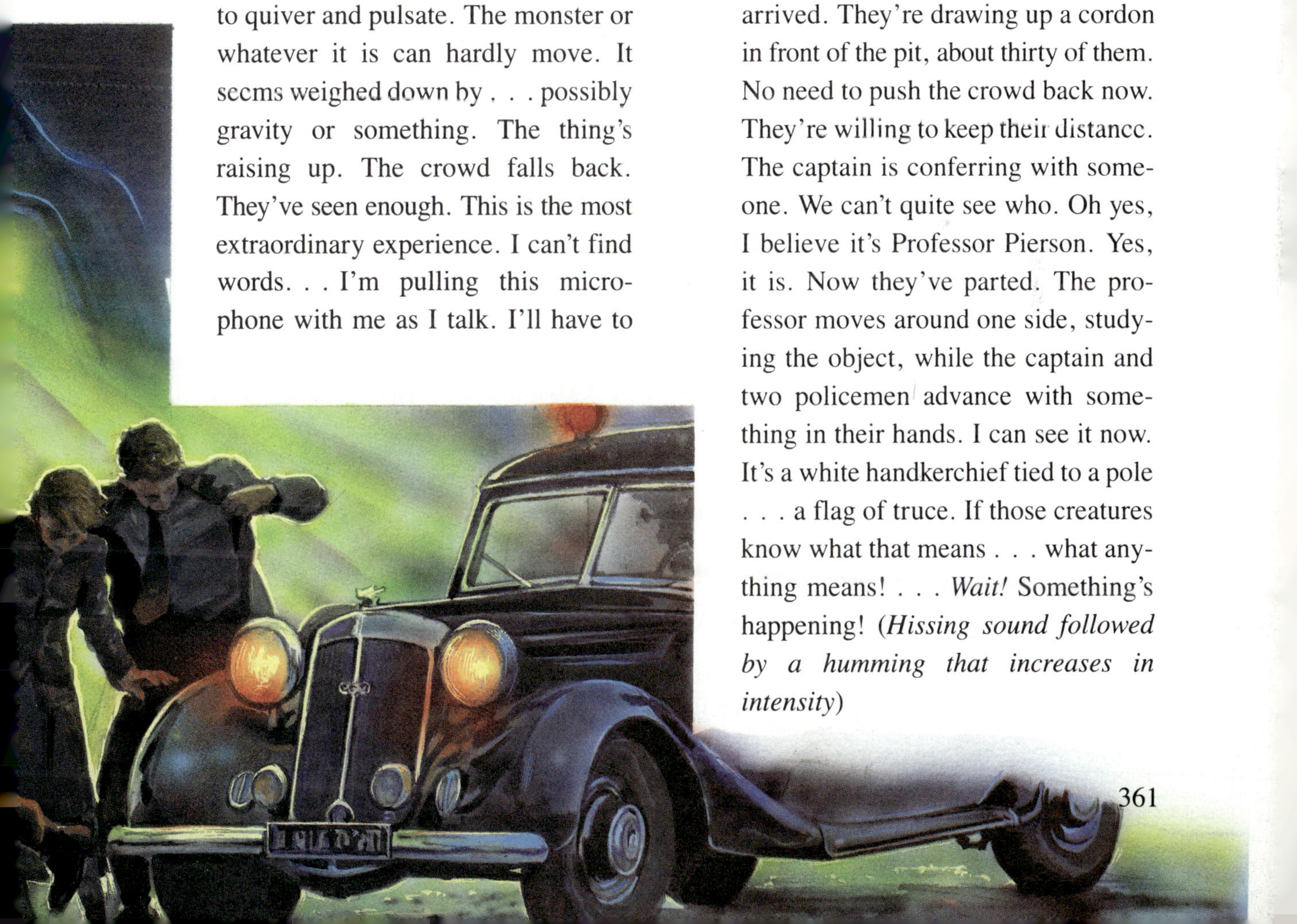

A humped shape is rising out of the pit. I can make out a small beam of light against a mirror. What's that? There's a jet of flame springing from that mirror, and it leaps right at the advancing men. It strikes them head on! Oh no, they're turning into flame! (*Screams and unearthly shrieks*)

Now the whole field's caught fire. (*Explosion*) The woods . . . the barns . . . the gas tanks of automobiles . . . it's spreading everywhere. It's coming this way. About twenty yards to my right . . . (*Crash of microphone . . . then dead silence*)

**Announcer Two:** Ladies and gentlemen, due to circumstances beyond our control, we are unable to continue the broadcast from Grovers Mill. Evidently there's some difficulty with our field transmission. However, we will return to that point at the earliest opportunity. In the meantime, we have a late bulletin from San Diego, California. Professor Indellkoffer, speaking at a dinner of the California Astronomical Society, expressed the opinion that the explosions on Mars are undoubtedly nothing more than severe volcanic disturbances on the surface of the planet. We continue now with our piano interlude. (*Piano . . . then cut*) Ladies and gentlemen, I have just been handed a message that came in from Grovers Mill by telephone. Just a moment. At least forty people including six state troopers lie dead in a field east of the village of Grovers Mill, their bodies burned and distorted beyond all recognition. The next voice you hear will be that of Brigadier General Montgomery Smith, commander of the state militia at Trenton, New Jersey.

**Smith:** I have been requested by the governor of New Jersey to place the counties of Mercer and Middlesex as far west as Princeton, and east to Jamesburg, under martial law. No one will be permitted to enter this area except by special pass issued by state or military authorities. Four companies of state militia are proceeding from Trenton to Grovers Mill, and will aid in the evacuation of homes within the range of military operations. Thank you.

**Announcer:** You have just been listening to General Montgomery Smith, commanding the state militia at Trenton. In the meantime, further details of the catastrophe at Grovers Mill are coming in. The strange creatures, after unleashing their deadly assault, crawled back in their pit and made no attempt to prevent the efforts of the firemen to recover the bodies and extinguish the fire. Combined fire departments of Mercer County are fighting the flames which menace the entire countryside.

We have been unable to establish any contact with our mobile unit at Grovers Mill, but we hope to be able to return you there at the earliest possible moment. In the meantime we take you—uh, just one moment please. (*Long pause*)

(*Whisper*) Ladies and gentlemen, I have just been informed that we have finally established communication with an eyewitness of the tragedy. Professor Pierson has been located at a farmhouse near Grovers Mill where he has established an emergency observation post. As a scientist, he will give you his explanation of the calamity. The next voice you will hear will be that of Professor Pierson, brought to you by direct wire. Professor Pierson.

**Pierson:** Of the creatures in the rocket cylinder at Grovers Mill, I can give you no authoritative information—either as to their nature, their origin, or their purposes here on earth. Of their destructive instrument I might venture some conjectural explanation. For want of a better term, I shall refer to the mysterious weapon as a heat ray. It's all too evident that these creatures have scientific knowledge far in advance of our own. It is my guess that in some way they are able to generate an intense heat in a chamber of practically absolute nonconductivity. This intense heat they project in a parallel beam against any object they choose, by means of a polished parabolic mirror of unknown composition, much as the mirror of a lighthouse projects a beam of light. That is my conjecture of the origin of the heat ray . . .

**Announcer Two:** Thank you, Professor Pierson. Ladies and gentlemen, here is a bulletin from Trenton. It is a brief statement informing us that the charred body of Carl Phillips has been identified in a Trenton hospital. Now here's another bulletin from Washington, D.C.

Office of the director of the National Red Cross reports that ten units of Red Cross emergency workers have been assigned to the headquarters of the state militia stationed outside of Grovers Mill, New Jersey. Here's a bulletin from state police, Princeton Junction: The fires at Grovers Mill and vicinity now under control. Scouts report all quiet in the pit, and no sign of life appearing from the mouth of the cylinder . . . And now, ladies and gentlemen, we have a special statement from Mr. Harry McDonald, vice-president in charge of operations.

**McDonald:** We have received a request from the militia at Trenton to place at their disposal our entire broadcasting facilities. In view of the gravity of the situation, and believing that radio has a definite responsibility to serve in the public interest at all times, we are turning over our facilities to the state militia at Trenton.

**Announcer:** We take you now to the field headquarters of the state militia near Grovers Mill, New Jersey.

**Captain:** This is Captain Lansing of the signal corps, attached to the state militia now engaged in military operations in the vicinity of Grovers Mill. Situation arising from the reported presence of certain individuals of unidentified nature is now under complete control.

The cylindrical object which lies in a pit directly below our position is surrounded on all sides by eight battalions of infantry, without heavy fieldpieces, but adequately armed with rifles and machine guns. All cause for alarm, if such cause ever existed, is now entirely unjustified. The things, whatever they are, do not even venture to poke their heads above the pit. I can see their hiding place plainly in the glare of the searchlights here. With all their reported resources, these creatures can scarcely stand up against heavy machine-gun fire. Anyway, it's an interesting outing for the troops. I can make out their khaki uniforms, crossing back and forth in front of the lights. It looks almost like a real war. There appears to be some slight smoke in the woods bordering the Millstone River. Probably fire started by campers. Well, we ought to see some action soon. One of the companies is deploying on the left flank. A quick thrust and it will be over. Now wait a minute! I see something on top of the cylinder. No, it's nothing but a shadow. Now the troops are on the edge of the Wilmuth farm. Seven thousand armed men closing in on an old metal tube. Wait, that wasn't a shadow! It's something moving . . . solid metal . . . kind of a shieldlike affair rising up out of the cylinder . . . It's going higher and higher. Why, it's standing on legs . . . actually rearing up on a sort of metal framework. Now it's reaching above the trees and the searchlights are on it! Hold on!

**Announcer Two:** Ladies and gentlemen, I have a grave announcement to make. Incredible as it may seem, both the observations of science and the evidence of our eyes lead to the inescapable assumption that those strange beings who landed in the Jersey farmlands tonight are the vanguard of an invading army from the planet Mars. The battle which took place tonight at Grovers Mill has ended in one of the most startling defeats ever suffered by an army in modern times; seven thousand men armed with rifles and machine guns pitted against a single fighting machine of the invaders from Mars. One hundred and twenty known survivors. The rest strewn over the battle area from Grovers Mill to Plainsboro, crushed and trampled to death under the metal feet of the monster, or burned to cinders by its heat ray. The monster is now in control of the middle section of New Jersey and has effectively cut the state through its center. Communication lines are down from Pennsylvania to the Atlantic Ocean. Railroad tracks are torn and service from New York to Philadelphia discontinued except routing some of the trains through Allentown and Phoenixville. Highways to the north, south, and west are clogged with frantic human traffic. Police and army reserves are unable to control the mad flight. By morning the fugitives will have swelled Philadelphia, Camden, and Trenton, it is estimated, to twice their normal population.

At this time martial law prevails throughout New Jersey and eastern Pennsylvania. We take you now to Washington for a special broadcast on the National Emergency . . . the Secretary of the Interior . . .

**Secretary:** Citizens of the nation: I shall not try to conceal the gravity of the situation that confronts the country nor the concern of your government in protecting the lives and property of its people. However, I wish to impress upon you—private citizens and public officials, all of you—the urgent need of calm and resourceful action. Fortunately, this formidable enemy is still confined to a comparatively small area, and we may place our faith in the military forces to keep them there. In the meantime we must continue the performance of our duties each and every one of us, so that we may confront this destructive adversary with a nation united, courageous, and consecrated to the preservation of human supremacy on this earth. I thank you.

**Announcer:** You have just heard the Secretary of the Interior speaking from Washington. Bulletins too numerous to read are piling up in the studio here. We are informed that the central portion of New Jersey is blacked out from radio communication due to the effect of the heat ray upon power lines and electrical equipment. Here is a special bulletin from New York. Cables received from English, French, German scientific bodies offering assistance. Astronomers report continued gas outbursts at regular intervals on planet Mars. Majority voice opinion that enemy will be reinforced by additional rocket machines. Attempts made to locate Professor Pierson of Princeton, who has observed Martians at close range. It is feared he was lost in recent battle. Langham Field,

Virginia: Scouting planes report three Martian machines visible above treetops, moving north towards Somerville with population fleeing ahead of them. Heat ray not in use; although advancing at express-train speed, invaders pick their way carefully. They seem to be making conscious effort to avoid destruction of cities and countryside. However, they stop to uproot power lines, bridges, and railroad tracks. Their apparent objective is to crush resistance, paralyze communication, and disorganize human society.

Here is a bulletin from Basking Ridge, New Jersey: Hunters have stumbled on a second cylinder similar to the first embedded in the great swamp twenty miles south of Morristown. U.S. army fieldpieces are proceeding from Newark to blow up second invading unit before cylinder can be opened and the fighting machine

rigged. They are taking up position in the—foothills of Watchung Mountains. Another bulletin from Langham Field, Virginia: Scouting planes report enemy machines, now three in number, increasing speed northward kicking over houses and trees in their evident haste to form a conjunction with their allies south of Morristown. Machines also sighted by telephone operator east of Middlesex within ten miles of Plainfield. *(Pause)*

**Announcer Two:** I'm speaking from the roof of Broadcasting Building, New York City. The bells you hear are ringing to warn the people to evacuate the city as the Martians approach. Estimated in last two hours three million people have moved out along the roads to the north, Hutchison River Parkway still kept open for motor traffic. Avoid bridges to Long Island . . . hopelessly jammed. All communication with Jersey shore closed ten minutes ago. No more defenses. Our army wiped out . . . artillery, air force, everything wiped out. This may be the last broadcast. We'll stay here to the end. (*Pause*) Now I look down the harbor. All manner of boats, overloaded with fleeing population, pulling out from docks. (*Sound of boat whistles*)

Streets are all jammed. Noise in crowds like New Year's Eve in city. Wait a minute . . . Enemy now in sight above the Palisades. Five great machines. First one is crossing river. I can see it from here, wading the Hudson like a man wading through a brook . . . A bulletin's handed me . . . Martian cylinders are falling all over the country. One outside Buffalo, one in Chicago, St. Louis . . . seem to be timed and spaced . . . . Now the first machine reaches the shore. He stands watching, looking over the city. His steel, cowlish head is even with the skyscrapers. He waits for the others. They rise like a line of new towers on the city's west side . . . Now they're lifting their metal hands. This is the end now. Smoke comes out . . . black smoke, drifting over the city. People in the streets see it now. They're running towards the East River . . . thousands of them, dropping in like rats. Now the smoke's spreading faster. It's reached Times Square. People trying to run away from it, but it's no use. They're falling like flies. Now the smoke's crossing Sixth Avenue . . . Fifth Avenue . . . one hundred yards away . . . it's fifty feet . . .

**Operator Four:** 2X2L calling CQ . . .
2X2L calling CQ . . .
2X2L calling CQ . . . New York.
Isn't there anyone on the air?
Isn't there anyone . . .
2X2L—

**Announcer:** You are listening to a CBS presentation of Orson Welles and the Mercury Theatre on the Air in an original dramatization of *The War of the Worlds* by H. G. Wells. The performance will continue after a brief intermission.

This is the Columbia . . . Broadcasting System. (*Music*)

**Pierson:** As I set down these notes on paper, I'm obsessed by the thought that I may be the last living man on earth. I have been hiding in this empty house near Grovers Mill—a small island of daylight cut off by the black smoke from the rest of the world. All that happened before the arrival of these monstrous creatures in the world now seems part of another life . . . a life that has no continuity with the present, furtive existence of the lonely derelict who pencils these words on the back of some astronomical notes bearing the signature of Richard Pierson. I look down at my blackened hands, my torn shoes, my tattered clothes, and I try to connect them with a professor who lives at Princeton, and who on the night of October 30, glimpsed through his telescope an orange splash of light on a distant planet. My wife, my colleagues, my

students, my books, my observatory, my . . . my world . . . where are they? Did they ever exist? Am I Richard Pierson? What day is it? Do days exist without calendars? Does time pass when there are no human hands left to wind the clocks? . . . In writing down my daily life I tell myself I shall preserve human history between the dark covers of this little book that was meant to record the movements of the stars . . . But to write I must live, and to live I must eat . . . I find moldy bread in the kitchen, and an orange not too spoiled to swallow. I keep watch at the window. From time to time I catch sight of a Martian above the black smoke.

The smoke still holds the house in its black coil . . . But at length there is a hissing sound and suddenly I see a Martian mounted on his machine, spraying the air with a jet of steam, as if to dissipate the smoke. I watch in a corner as his huge metal legs nearly brush against the house. Exhausted by terror, I fall asleep . . . It's morning. Sun streams in the window. The black cloud of gas has lifted, and the scorched meadows to the north look as though a black snowstorm has passed over them. I venture from the house. I make my way to a road. No traffic. Here and there a wrecked car, baggage overturned, a blackened skeleton. I push on north. For some reason I feel safer trailing these monsters than running away from them. And I keep a careful watch. I have seen the Martians feed. Should one of their machines appear over the top of trees, I am ready to fling myself flat on the earth. I come to a chestnut tree. October. Chestnuts are ripe. I fill my pockets. I must keep alive. Two days I wander in a vague northerly direction through a desolate world. Finally I notice a living creature . . . a small red squirrel in a beech tree. I stare at him, and wonder. He stares back at me. I believe at that moment the animal and I shared the same emotion . . . the joy of finding another living being . . . I push on north. I find dead cows in a brackish field.

Beyond, the charred ruins of a dairy. The silo remains standing guard over the wasteland like a lighthouse deserted by the sea. Astride the silo perches a weathercock. The arrow points north. (*Long pause*)

I came at last to the Holland Tunnel. I entered that silent tube anxious to know the fate of the great city on the other side of the Hudson. Cautiously I came out of the tunnel and made my way up Canal Street.

I reached Fourteenth Street, and there again were black powder and several bodies, and an evil ominous smell from the gratings of the cellars of some of the houses. I wandered up through the Thirties and Forties; I stood alone on Times Square. I caught sight of a lean dog running down Seventh Avenue with a piece of dark brown meat in his jaws, and a pack of starving mongrels at his heels. He made a wide circle around me, as though he feared I might prove a fresh competitor. I walked up Broadway in the direction of that strange powder—past silent shopwindows, displaying their mute wares to empty sidewalks—past the Capitol Theatre, silent, dark—past a shooting gallery, where a row of empty guns faced an arrested line of wooden ducks. Near Columbus Circle I noticed models of 1939 motorcars in the showrooms facing empty streets. From over the top of the General Motors Building, I watched a flock of black birds circling in the sky. I hurried on. Suddenly I caught sight of the hood of a Martian machine, standing somewhere in Central Park, gleaming in the late afternoon sun. An insane idea! I rushed recklessly across Columbus Circle and into the Park. I climbed a small hill above the pond at Sixtieth Street. From there I could see, standing in a silent row along the mall, nineteen of those great metal Titans, their cowls empty, their steel arms hanging listlessly by their sides. I looked in vain for the monsters that inhabit those machines.

Suddenly, my eyes were attracted to the immense flock of black birds that hovered directly below me. They

circled to the ground, and there before my eyes, stark and silent, lay the Martians, with the hungry birds pecking and tearing brown shreds of flesh from their dead bodies. Later when their bodies were examined in laboratories, it was found that they were killed by the putrefactive and disease bacteria against which their systems were unprepared . . . slain, after all our human defenses had failed, by the humblest thing put upon this earth.

Before the cylinder fell there was a general persuasion that through all the deep of space no life existed beyond the petty surface of our minute sphere. Now we see further. Dim and wonderful is the vision I have conjured up in my mind of life spreading slowly from this little seedbed of the solar system throughout the inanimate vastness of sidereal space. But that is a remote dream. It may be that the destruction of the Martians is only a reprieve. To them, and not to us, is the future ordained perhaps.

Strange it now seems to sit in my peaceful study at Princeton writing down this last chapter of the record begun at Grovers Mill. Strange to see from my window the university spires dim and blue through an April haze. Strange to see young people strolling on the green, where the new spring grass heals the last black scars of a bruised earth. Strange to watch

the sightseers enter the museum where the dissembled parts of a Martian machine are kept on public view. Strange when I recall the time when I first saw it, bright and clean-cut, hard and silent, under the dawn of that last great day.

(*Music*) This is Orson Welles, ladies and gentlemen, out of character to assure you that *The War of the Worlds* has no further significance than as the holiday offering it was intended to be. The Mercury Theatre's own radio version of dressing up in a sheet and jumping out of a bush and saying Boo! Starting now, we couldn't soap all your windows and steal all your garden gates, by tomorrow night . . . so we did the next best thing. We annihilated the world before your very ears, and utterly destroyed the Columbia Broadcasting System. You will be relieved, I hope, to learn that we didn't mean it, and that both institutions are still open for business. So good-bye everybody, and remember, please, for the next day or so, the terrible lesson you learned tonight. That grinning, glowing, globular invader of your living room is an inhabitant of the pumpkin patch, and if your doorbell rings and nobody's there, that was no Martian . . . it's Hallowe'en.

### ♦ Library Link ♦

*The radio play that you just read was dramatized from a short novel entitled* The War of the Worlds *by H. G. Wells.*

## ◆ *Reader's Response*

Do you think that this play is so realistic you would be convinced of an invasion from Mars? Give reasons for your answer.

## Thinking It Over

1. How did the announcer create a sense of emergency in his opening remarks?
2. List, in order, three developments in the play that led to the conclusion that the United States had been invaded by Martians.
3. Identify the part that you thought was most realistic.
4. At what point in the play does the audience know the broadcast is fantasy? How did you identify this point?

## Appreciating Literature

Howard Koch wrote this radio play by *adapting*, or changing into a different format, the novel *War of the Worlds* by H. G. Wells. What are the elements of a play that are different from those of a novel? How do you think a writer goes about adapting a novel into a radio play?

## Writing to Learn

**Think and Decide** "Invasion from Mars" may have succeeded because of the reality created by the author's use of authentic details. Draw a cylinder on your paper and fill it with detail words that made "Invasion from Mars" seem real.

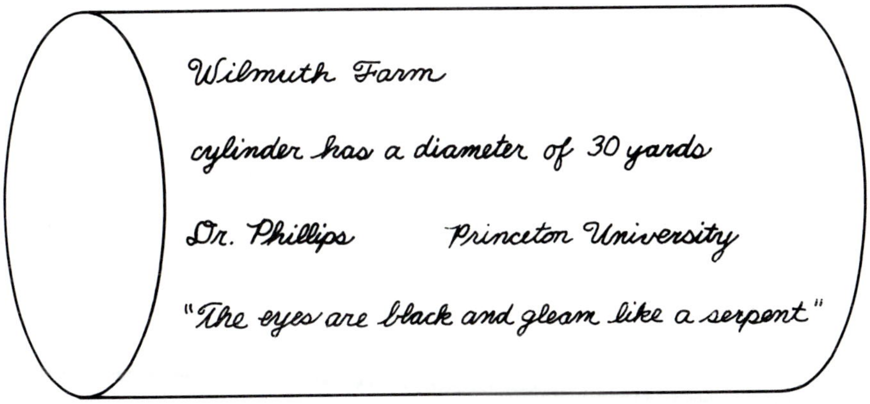


**Write** Think of another story in this unit that has an imaginary creature. Use authentic-sounding details to write a news broadcast about that creature.

# WORLD OF READING Magazine

*News About Reading*

## Illuminated Manuscripts

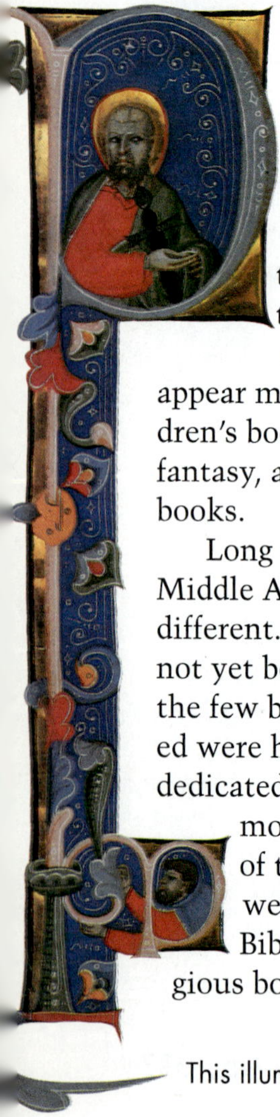

Pictures are rare in adult books today. Illustrations rich in color and detail appear mostly in children's books, books of fantasy, and special art books.

Long ago in the Middle Ages, things were different. Printing had not yet been invented, so the few books that existed were hand copied by dedicated monks in monasteries. Most of these books were, of course, Bibles or other religious books.

This illuminated capital letter appears in a Latin Bible completed in 1342.

This painting shows a monk creating an illuminated manuscript.

### Ancient Assembly Lines

One group of monks would prepare the vellum, a fine parchment used before paper was common. A second group, the scribes, did the writing. A third group were the artists who decorated the manuscripts with vivid colors and gold and silver leaf. The fourth group bound the manuscripts into books. These manuscripts were called "illuminated" because the use of gold and silver made them appear to be lighted from within.

In most illuminated manuscripts, people, monsters, scrolls, and scenes wound around the borders of the pages or intertwined with the text. Different styles of illumination, however, developed in various parts of Europe.

One famous manuscript of the Middle Ages, *The Book of the Marvels of the World*, included pictures of especially vivid serpents, dragons, and strange happenings.

The Celtic monks of Ireland and Britain were famous for elaborately decorating the first letter of a page or passages. (An example is the letter *P*

A man scrapes the stretched skin of a calf to make parchment.

that begins this article.) Sometimes these initial letters covered an entire page. One of the most famous of the Celtic books was *The Book of Kells.*

The Koran, a Moslem holy book, has especially intricate designs and some of the most beautiful calligraphy, or handwriting, of any ancient manuscript.

The parchment on which illuminated manuscripts were written and illustrated was made from animal skins, usually the skins of sheep, goats, or calves. The skins were washed and then dipped in lime to remove fat and hair. Then the skins were stretched on frames and scraped with knives. The last stage of preparation was rubbing the skins with pumice and chalk to make them smooth and white.

### Lasting Treasures

Parchment is extremely durable; parchment scrolls have survived from 1500 B.C. It is the durability of the parchment on which the monks copied and decorated their manuscripts that has allowed these treasures to last for so many years, remaining as beautiful today as they were when the monks created them.

Illuminated manuscripts are such an important legacy and so beautiful that modern technology is being developed to preserve and reproduce them. Complex computer imaging systems are being used to make exact reproductions so that not only scholars but book lovers everywhere can enjoy these exquisite works.

***If you enjoy doodling in the margins of your note paper, you might like to try your hand at calligraphy, the art of decorative lettering. There are many instructional manuals that provide step-by-step guides to the different lettering techniques. Ask your local librarian about them and you'll be on your way to mastering an age-old craft.***

A diary written in the Middle Ages features these pages of illuminated manuscript.

# Literature Link

## *How can you analyze and evaluate the opinions you read?*

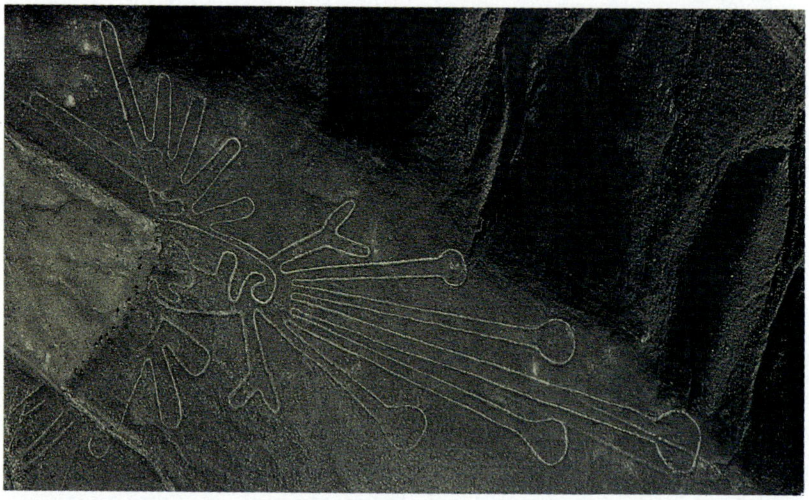

Do you believe everything you read? A better question might be: How can you *know* what to believe? When in doubt, you should always check the facts. But when a writer uses both facts and opinions, your job is twice as hard. Read this paragraph about the mysterious drawings on the Nazca plateau in southwestern Peru. Do you find these facts hard to believe? See if the photograph above helps to convince you. Does the writer include any personal opinions that might confuse your decision?

As travel by airplane became more and more common in the 1920s and 1930s, pilots and passengers who flew over the hills of Peru began to see strange shapes. Huge geometric figures, giant spiders, and enormous horses were etched into the rock. These drawings can only be found in Peru, and there lies the mystery. We will probably never know why or for whom these drawings were created. Studying them, however, is the most fascinating job on earth.

## *Can You Prove It?*

Find the statements in the paragraph that you could prove true or false. These are the facts. But be careful because every factual statement is not always true! For example, you just read that hill drawings like those on the Nazca plateau are found only in Peru. However, similar drawings *have* been found in the Mojave Desert in the United States and in southwestern England. The author's statement, written as fact, is not true. So, as definite and impressive as facts may sound, always check them out.

Now look at the last sentence in the paragraph about the Peruvian drawings. Is there any way the author can prove what the most fascinating job on earth is? Of course not. That's because it's the author's personal opinion. You are free to agree or disagree with an opinion, but you cannot prove it true or false.

Opinions often masquerade as facts, especially when they're surrounded by impressive facts you know to be true. If you can distinguish fact from opinion, you can better evaluate what you read.

In Unit 2, you read "The Eternal Frontier" by Louis L'Amour. Because it is a personal essay, you can be almost sure that it contains the author's opinions. What facts and opinions do you find in L'Amour's argument about why early settlers kept moving farther and farther west?

> Many had, after landing from the old country, developed good farms or successful businesses; they had become people of standing in their communities. Why then did they move on, leaving all behind?
>
> I believe it to be something buried in their genes, some inherited trait, perhaps something essential to the survival of the species.
>
> They went to the edge of the mountains, then they crossed the mountains and found their way through impassable forests to the Mississippi. After that the Great Plains, the Rocky Mountains, and on to Oregon and California. They trapped fur, traded with Native Americans, hunted buffalo, ranched with cattle or sheep, built towns, and farmed. Yet the genes lay buried within them, and after a few months, a few years, they moved on.

## *Is It Valid?*

The phrase *I believe* clearly identifies L'Amour's statement of opinion. What do you think of his idea? Do you believe that some trait inherited by the settlers could have made them move west? Of course, you are free to disagree with this. Remember, there is no true or false opinion. But examine carefully the sentences that precede and follow his opinion statement. What facts do you find in these sentences? Do you see how L'Amour uses the facts to reinforce his opinion and to convince you that his opinion *must* be true?

Although you cannot call an opinion true or false, you can test it to see if it is valid—if it makes sense because it is supported by facts. Using a diagram like the one below can help you organize L'Amour's opinion and the statements he uses to support it. This will help you to test his opinion to see if he has really supported it.

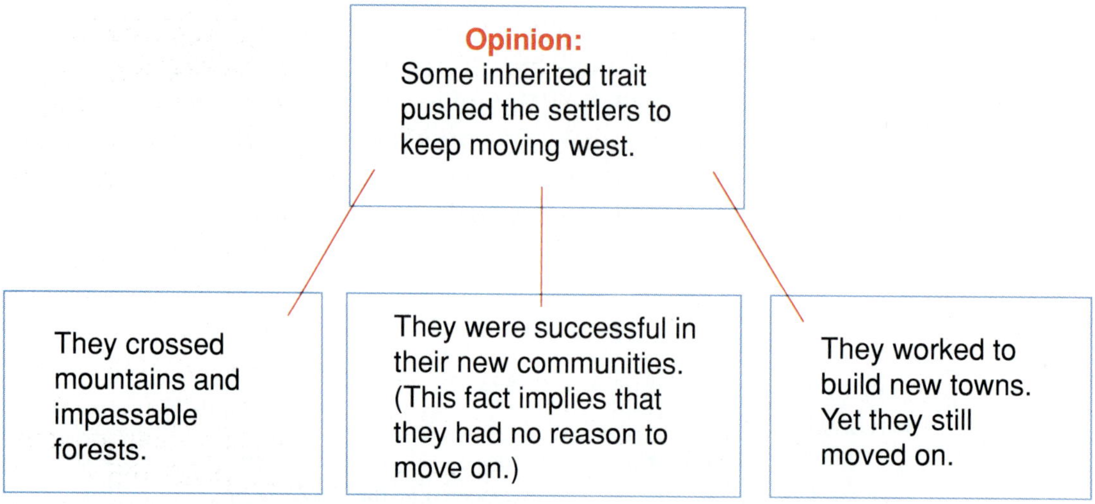


L'Amour lays the facts before you in an effort to make his opinion the only reasonable conclusion. What do you think about this? You might agree that he *does* show that the settlers were determined as they kept moving west. You might even agree that their determination came from something very strong within the people. But what support has he given for the idea that the determination came from some *inherited trait*? Is his opinion valid?

Suppose L'Amour had used the following statements to support his idea. Do you think then that his opinion would be valid?

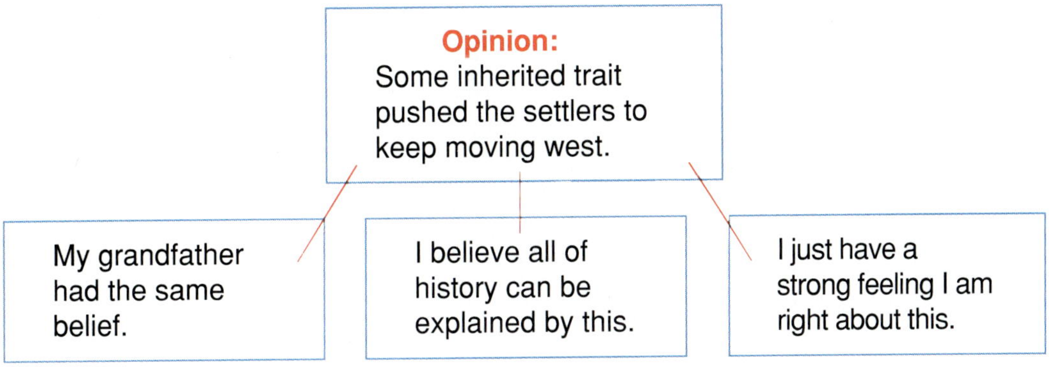


These statements do not give reasonable support because they are not facts. They are just strong statements of opinion filled with emotion. Since no facts at all were used, most people would not consider this opinion valid.

The tips below can help you evaluate articles that contain both facts and opinions.

- When you read a statement, ask yourself: Can this statement be proven true or false?
- If so, the statement is probably a fact. But check it out: Be sure the facts are true. Be wary of absolute statements that contain words such as: *always, never, only, all.*
- To identify an opinion look for a personal judgment, attitude, or feeling that can be neither true nor false. Look for signal words or phrases, such as: *I believe, I think, it seems to me; or fantastic, the worst, the best, the most.*
- Carefully examine opinion statements and supporting facts.
- Decide if the opinion is valid or not; that is, whether or not it is supported well with the facts.

As you read "Mystery of Loch Ness," use what you have learned in this lesson to evaluate the facts and opinions. Is the Loch Ness Monster real? What are the facts? What opinions can you identify? How valid are they? What's *your* opinion?

# Mystery of Loch Ness

by Gerald S. Snyder

*There is a monster in Loch Ness, people say. We know there are no such things as monsters. Still, with so many people believing they have seen* something *there . . .*

Over the years there have been thousands of reports about the Loch Ness monster from people who don't give their word lightly—professional people, engineers, doctors, lawyers, ministers, admirals, abbots, and insurance executives, as well as fishermen, farmers, and housewives. These are people from all walks of life, credible eyewitnesses, not given to making up stories, with no reason to lie or embellish their accounts. There have been at least 3,000 recorded sightings, at least triple that amount of reported sightings, by passersby, vacationers, permanent residents of the loch area, and dedicated loch watchers.

Generally, the sightings of mysterious denizens fall into four main categories: (1) the head and neck; (2) one hump; (3) two or more humps; and (4) disturbances on the loch surface.

If the sightings are all wrong, if there are no Monsters, it may be that the world has seen a remarkable example of popular delusion, the scores of witnesses testifying to the force of human imagination. But is it possible that so many people of integrity could be mistaken? Ruling out, as unlikely, the possibility of a massive hoax, it seems logical to allow for some honest mistakes. The gracefully curved neck of a "creature" could be nothing more than the root of a tree suddenly brought to the surface. The startling "hump" seen to turn up the water could be a large mat of vegetation. An animal with "horns" might simply be a deer swimming. Waves and wakes can take astonishing shapes. Giant eels might account for the occasional reports of giant "worms."

But not all of the sightings can be dismissed, for not only does the Loch Ness Monster continue to appear but to many people it appears repeatedly.

Over a period of some twenty-three years, for instance, Mr. and Mrs. Richard Jenkyns of the English village of Helmsdale, Sutherland, have both had sightings—four in all and ranging "over the whole length of the loch and always in early spring or in the autumn," as Mr. Jenkyns remembers. "On no occasion have either my wife or myself made any effort to search or watch for the appearance and our reasons for being there have been for holiday or residential purposes only."

What kind of phenomena had they seen?

Mr. Jenkyns could not even guess. "Reptilian, mollusk, amphibian, or even paranormal," he said. But "at all events my sightings always gave me an unpleasant feeling, maybe from merely witnessing the unknown."

Over the years the waters of Loch Ness have kept heaving and stirring with new accounts, as the following samples will testify.

- "I definitely saw a dark object which created a wash out in the loch. It was not there for any length of time before it submerged, but I am sure of what I saw."
- "We had a good clear view from the lochside. A long black object like an upturned rowing boat appeared to be part of the body and a little bit in front there was a head which resembled a big seal."
- "The object at first looked like a wave, but afterwards there was no mistaking the arched humpback moving in serpentine fashion. The object came up and down three times."
- "What seemed to be a huge gully appeared in the water and a series of distinct waves were created. We just had the impression of a tremendously powerful long dark object swirling about in the middle of the spray. This lasted for a few seconds only and the loch gradually became calm again."
- "The thing I saw had a large rounded head with a great thick body of tremendous girth."

• "It raised its neck out of the water and shook itself. I then distinctly saw what I took to be a dark-colored mane running about four feet down from the back of the creature's head."

• "I watched it for a minute or so. I was walking to the water's edge and I saw two long, oval humps appear out of the surface about 300 or 400 yards from me. The humps kept dipping below the water and reappearing, all the time moving slowly across the loch."

• "I had a splendid view, but it is difficult to describe exactly what it was. There was a head and neck sticking out above the water, and behind were two parts of the creature's back. I would not describe them as humps, for they were fairly long."

• "I saw it was something alive. It was about twelve feet long and appeared to have one or two slight humps, though I do not think they were really humps but simply the configuration of the body."

• "I saw what looked like a boat speeding towards Drumnadrochit Bay. Our launch followed it into the bay and we began searching near the shore. Suddenly I saw a great wash break out and cut right across our bows. It moved at a terrific rate for a few seconds, and then a black object which may have been a fin or a hump, which I saw sticking out of the middle, disappeared in a terrific flurry of water."

• "I saw the huge beast on the surface nine or ten yards from the shore. It was shining black in the moonlight and created a great swirl. From its movement I should say its head and neck were delving into the water as though in search of food."

In 1976 two policemen witnessed the unknown and their detailed report, previously unpublished, would seem to confirm what the Jenkyns and many others have seen.

It was about 4:40 in the afternoon of April 13. The two officers, Sergeant Donald Nicolson and Constable A. "Sandy" Gray, were patrolling the Inverness to Fort William A82 road which runs for about fifteen miles along the north shore of Loch Ness.

Constable Gray was driving, heading west, when suddenly, near the camping site at Rhuda Bhan, Invermoriston, he noticed a disturbance in the loch between 200 and 250 yards away.

Sergeant Nicolson glanced to where Gray was pointing and saw, he said, "a black object," which he took to be a boat in distress because the water around the object was stirred up.

"Stop quickly," Nicolson ordered, "There's a boat foundering down there!"

Gray stopped the car and both officers hurried out and began running down through the trees separating the road from the loch. Standing on the edge, they stared out across the water. By now the disturbance appeared very clear.

"The only way I can find of describing it was that the water seemed to be boiling," said Gray. "In the 'boiling water', I could see two fins approximately twenty to twenty-five feet

**Former Royal Air Force Pilot Tom Dinsdale displays model of monster he claims to have seen at Loch Ness.**

apart and traveling at a fair speed through the water in an easterly direction towards Inverness." The fins were "about two to three feet out of the water and were silvery-gray in color."

Nicolson spied the same thing. The phenomenon "looked like two fin-like objects cutting through the water at speed."

The objects were moving eastward, toward Inverness "at a speed comparable to that of a fairly fast launch," said Nicolson. "The two objects were moving in unison and obviously had a common origin as during the time we watched, the distance between them did not seem to vary."

"At no time did we see any head or anything that could be the creature's body," Gray added.

For about two or three minutes the two officers stood staring at the strange sight. Then, as Nicolson recalled, "the two objects submerged, again in unison."

While Nicolson remained at lochside, Gray returned to the roadway to try to stop a vehicle in order to get the driver or passengers to corroborate the sighting. But it was April, before the tourist season had begun, and the road was quiet. Gray remained anxiously looking for a car.

Nicolson, meanwhile, kept gazing at the loch's surface. Then all of a sudden he saw the "fins" resurface, and for a short period, "they continued to travel toward Inverness at the same speed as before. When the fins finally submerged for the last time, a wash similar to that of a large boat traveling at speed was created, forming waves which broke on the stony loch shore. This wash was such that I was required to step backwards in a hurry to save my feet from getting wet."

"It was confirmed that there were no submarines or any unusual craft on the loch on that particular day," said Nicolson.

Finally, Gray managed to stop a car. But by then "the creature had vanished and the loch was quite peaceful."

In his opinion, he said, "the creature in Loch Ness must be of considerable size to create the disturbance it was causing. The loch at the time of our sighting was calm, it was a cool, dry day, and there was not a boat in sight on Loch Ness."

In the police records at Fort Augustus the sighting was duly recorded, under the heading: "Unidentified object seen on Loch Ness." And there it remains today, for anyone to see.

Who is to doubt the sincerity of this and other reports? Some of the observations are bound to be invalid—bobbing logs and dark waves taken for "humps," for instance. And the mind can work ahead of, or influence, what the eye can see. Numerous eyewitnesses have claimed to see two and three-humped Monsters in the loch, moving with great speed, when the loch's mirror-like surface easily could have been reflecting the movement of low-flying ducks, casting dark reflections upon the water. They would not have seen the ducks blend in with the background or trees and rocks on the opposite shore.

What is puzzling, however, is that there have been so many sightings, so many apparently honest accounts given. This makes it very difficult to ascribe to simple mistakes or optical illusions or mass hysteria the cumulative evidence of what has been reported. Eyewitness observations are not to be ignored. Far from it, in fact, for it is mainly because of them that other, more scientific methods of determination have been pursued. Surely, the investigators reason, everyone can't be wrong. There must be *something* unusual in Loch Ness.

If the case for the Loch Ness Monster could be put to a jury—to a group of average men and women with no preconceived ideas on the subject—it would probably surprise no one if the decision brought in, after due deliberation, was, "Yes, there is a Loch Ness Monster" or "Yes, there are Loch Ness Monsters." For so much *testimonial* and *circumstantial* evidence is there on the subject—so much evidence, that is, which tends to establish a conclusion indirectly by inference from facts otherwise hard to explain—that a jury hardly could be expected to bring in a verdict of any other kind.

In courts of law, people have been tried and convicted on circumstantial evidence. Without absolute proof of a deed done or crime committed, juries are forced to consider both kinds of proof, and no one would question the right to do so.

**Monster hunters searching Loch Ness for the fabled creature use cameras capable of photographing in total darkness.**

When it comes to the Loch Ness Monster, however, paleontologists ask for bones. Others ask for tissue samples or even a whole Monster. For either dead, stuffed, or alive, they say, they must have positive proof. Whereas in legal cases criminals are almost always judged on the basis of witnesses and unproven, circumstantial evidence, the scientist frowns upon presumption. He or she must have proof.

Because there is no positive proof, the case for the Loch Ness Monster is completely testimonial and circumstantial.

Beginning, first of all, with the world of reputable eyewitnesses—persons whose word there is no reason to doubt, people like Constable Gray and Sergeant Nicolson, for instance—we have hundreds of sightings which cannot be treated lightly. We cannot exclude the possibility that many of the sightings may be erroneous no matter how honest or sincere the reports, but the frequency and number of sightings over the years demand that some attention be paid to them. Of the 10,000 or so reported sightings, and the 3,000 or so recorded sightings, in books, magazines, newspapers, and official and unofficial reports, a great many seem to confirm that *something* strange has been occurring in Loch Ness.

The sightings do not appear to fit any particular pattern, and the observers often confuse shape, size, and speed, and sometimes can't tell the head from the tail, but there is an uncanny similarity to the way the said animals are described as moving—with, for example, bursts of speed and side splashing, as might be produced by those flipper-like "appendages." And at the same time, so many of the eyewitness reports agree on color (generally black or gray) and on the location of sightings (around the mouths of rivers running into the loch).

Next in the circumstantial case for the Loch Ness Monster are the pictures, which have been of all kinds, still and motion picture, color and black and white, made on and beneath the surface. Although only two dozen or so pictures have survived to fit the label "Loch Ness Monster," and although all—without exception—are controversial, they all have been taken by seemingly reputable people. Some of the photographers have been amateurs, it is true, but some, such as Harold Edgerton, the MIT [Massachusetts Institute of Technology] professor who is world-renowned for his skill at designing underwater photographic equipment, are highly skilled professionals.

Similarly, there is no reason to doubt the integrity of the most persistent Nessie-hunting group, the Academy of Applied Science, or to question the sincerity of its belief that a breeding population of large animals inhabit Loch Ness. Its data, so painstakingly gathered and so well-documented, cannot simply be explained away as a series of inanimate "objects." Accumulating each year, bit by bit, the Academy evidence has served to renew the enthusiasm of all the faithful and has encouraged the Academy itself to again and again, year in and year out, ponder the challenge of uncovering the mystery. It has

Harold Edgerton inspects his underwater photographic equipment.

**Sophisticated equipment is used in the Nessie Hunt.**

found, analyzed, and corrected deficiencies in equipment. It has improved photographic techniques. Many of the underwater cameras are arranged, for instance, stereoscopically—set at different angles—so that animals coming into view can be measured precisely. It has adapted for better underwater use television cameras and videotape recorders, as well as instant cameras.

On the basis of eyewitness reports and photographic evidence alone, our hypothetical jury might easily bring in a verdict for *Nessiteras rhombopteryx.*[1]

But even there the evidence doesn't end, for there is now sophisticated *acoustic* evidence, involving highly reliable techniques of underwater surveillance utilizing sound waves which have detected unusual large objects in the depths of Loch Ness.

Are the "objects" really animals?

Can they, at least, be presumed to be animate?

Is there a Loch Ness Monster?

[1]*Nessiteras rhombopteryx* (ne′ sē te′ rəs räm bôp′ ter iks′)

To all of these questions the combined evidence seems to be saying there is reality to the observations—there is proof of unusual occurrences in the Scottish loch.

In the quest for knowledge (a simple but good definition for science), scientists must wade through dazzling masses of evidence to find positive proof. They must see actual carcass samples or the bones of dead creatures. Their minds, of necessity, must screen out the superstitions, the superficially intriguing, the hearsay, the unproved, the unscientific speculations.

Formal scientific attitudes are subject to change, and interpretations of evidence are subject to varying views, but in the scientific mind there is a need for much more than just circumstantial evidence. Tantalizing clues are not enough. The scientist wants material evidence, facts he or she can deal with, or things observable. He or she also seeks independent corroborative evidence, and this must be strong if it is to carry scientific respectability. Most important, the evidence must be available for scientific inspection and analysis—which the Loch Ness Monster is not.

By and large, therefore, the scientific community has yet to accept the phenomena of Monsters in Loch Ness. While some eminent scientists have gone on record as saying there is ample proof of something strange in Loch Ness, the vast majority of those questioned have voiced skepticism, attempting to explain away the mystery as natural phenomena.

In late 1975, at the height of interest in the latest Nessie photographs made by the Academy of Applied Science, Dr. John Shields of Britain's Natural History Museum rose at a press conference to say there was no evidence to prove that any of the photographs were of animate creatures or were even of the same object. The scientific name given Nessie, he maintained, was spreading a "false notion of reality." This remark received little notice in the press, and one journalist gave as his explanation "The fact that some newspapers had paid an agency for the right to reproduce the maligned pictures (the current asking price then was about $400 each) and in some cases had added artists' impressions to help readers decide what they were all about may also have had something to do with the fact that Dr. Shields's attack was largely ignored."

In response, the Nessie-hunters point to the "stodginess" of traditional, old-school scientists—those who must have bones to prove the existence of an animal—and assert that new methods for producing evidence, such as sonar, call for a more open-minded approach to judging that evidence. The Nessie faithful charge it is arrogant for scientists, no matter how learned, to avoid all of the reasonable and cumulative evidence. As one Monster supporter put it many years ago: "If medical science had shown as little enterprise and as little courage in its various fields as marine zoologists have shown in regard to the Loch Ness animal, appendicitis would still be a fatal illness and tuberculosis would be killing millions every year."

Generally, however, it is the expertise of the scientist that puts Nessie down. The vertebrate animal theory is strong, for instance, but just try telling a zoologist that the humps so often reported may be the effect of a vertebrate animal undulating vertically through the water, and the scientist is apt to fire back, correctly, that vertebrates "don't move like caterpillars."

There never has been a full survey of scientists on the Loch Ness phenomena. And even if on a worldwide basis a poll were attempted, most scientists could probably be expected to decline a judgment, giving as their reason lack of evidence upon which to base an accurate opinion.

What we do have, from the limited number of scientists who have made their view public, is a consensus which seems to be saying there *may* be something unusual in the loch. There *is* enough evidence to warrant further examination.

That is why the search continues. The hunters are still hunting, with cameras and sonar trying to turn up tangible evidence. The reports of sightings are open to interpretation and so are not conclusive. The surface photographs have not been clear enough and therefore have done little more than stir the imagination. The underwater pictures have had to be computer enhanced and have led to so much speculation and controversy. No bones or animal tissue have been produced. The sonar searches have contributed little to actual identification of the phenomena. The answer to the question "Is There a Loch Ness Monster?" is still unanswered.

What *can* be concluded?

While nothing definite can be proved about the existence or identity of the Loch Ness Monster, other significant conclusions can be drawn to help in future investigations. For example, the sonar searches have proved beyond doubt that

**A life-size model of the elusive Loch Ness monster captures one's imagination. Could it be real?**

the walls of Loch Ness are steep, with sharp ridges beneath which large creatures could hide. There is no proof of the existence of underwater caves, but the evidence does indicate the likelihood of their existence.

Also, it is known for sure as a result of the new sonar "eyes," that the loch contains enough large schools of fish to adequately feed a whole colony of Monsters. Any fisherman might have told us this years ago, it is true, but the sonar traces offer conclusive proof.

Going one step farther, the sonar experts tell us their tracings prove the existence of "large, moving objects" in the loch. From this we are tempted to conclude the objects are "Monsters," be they giant aquatic amphibians or thick-bodied eels, which at least one scientist (Roy Mackal) suspects the creatures to be.

There is perhaps one sure way of solving the enigma—drain the loch.

Or capture a live animal.

No one seriously expects this to happen, however, and so it looks as though the Loch Ness Monster will continue to remain mysterious and elusive.

♦ LIBRARY LINK ♦

*If you enjoyed reading about "Nessie," you might also like to read about other legendary creatures. Nonfiction books on this subject include* Science Looks at Mysterious Monsters *by Thomas Aylesworth.*

## *Reader's Response*

Based on the evidence presented in this selection, do you believe that the Loch Ness monster exists? Why or why not?

## Thinking It Over

1. What four types of sightings of the Loch Ness monster do most eyewitnesses report?
2. What alternative explanations could there be for these sightings?
3. Why don't many scientists believe the monster exists?
4. Compare the kind of evidence needed to convict a person in a court of law with the kind of evidence needed to prove scientifically the existence of the Loch Ness monster.
5. Is there any area of agreement between scientists and "Nessie-hunters"? Explain how you arrived at your conclusion.

## Appreciating Literature

An author makes certain assumptions about his or her audience. What assumptions do you think Gerald Snyder makes about his audience's belief or lack of belief in the Loch Ness monster? How do assumptions about the audience shape Snyder's article?

## Writing to Learn

**THINK AND DECIDE** What is the Loch Ness monster? Find six different answers to this question and write them in a chart like the one below.

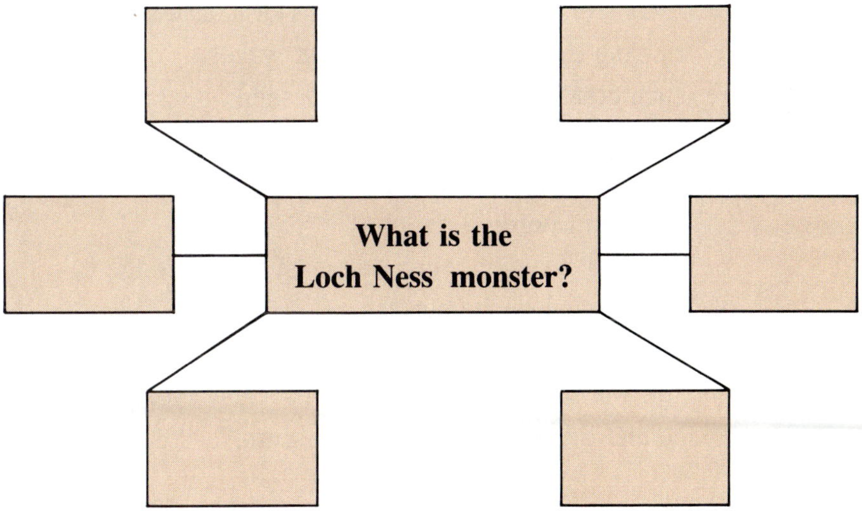


**WRITE** Decide which of the above answers is most likely to be true. Write an explanation of your choice.

# Conversation By Loch Ness

"Monster, with the head of a horse,
what are you, troubling quiet waters?"
"I am the unknown.
I live under all quiet waters.
I am the thing beyond your calculations,
below them,
above them,
alone.
I come from an earlier era of the earth and sea,
and live close and deep.
You will dream of me in your sleep.
Explain me away if you can,
you will not be rid of me."

"Monster, with the maned neck of a snake,
rippling the quiet water without waves,
such creatures as you we have seen
in carboniferous graves.
Your race is long extinct."
"Yet am I here.
The past lives on when you least acknowledge it,
lives on below the surface
in the depths below quiet waters.
You will see it back of your sons' clear eyes,
behind the smiles of your daughters."

ELIZABETH COATSWORTH

AWARD WINNING
*Author*

*Urquehart Castle and Loch Ness, Scotland*

TIME OUT FOR BOOKS

*Best Books For Children*

***As he approached the village he met a number of people, but none of whom he knew, which somewhat surprised him…***

from "Rip Van Winkle" by Washington Irving

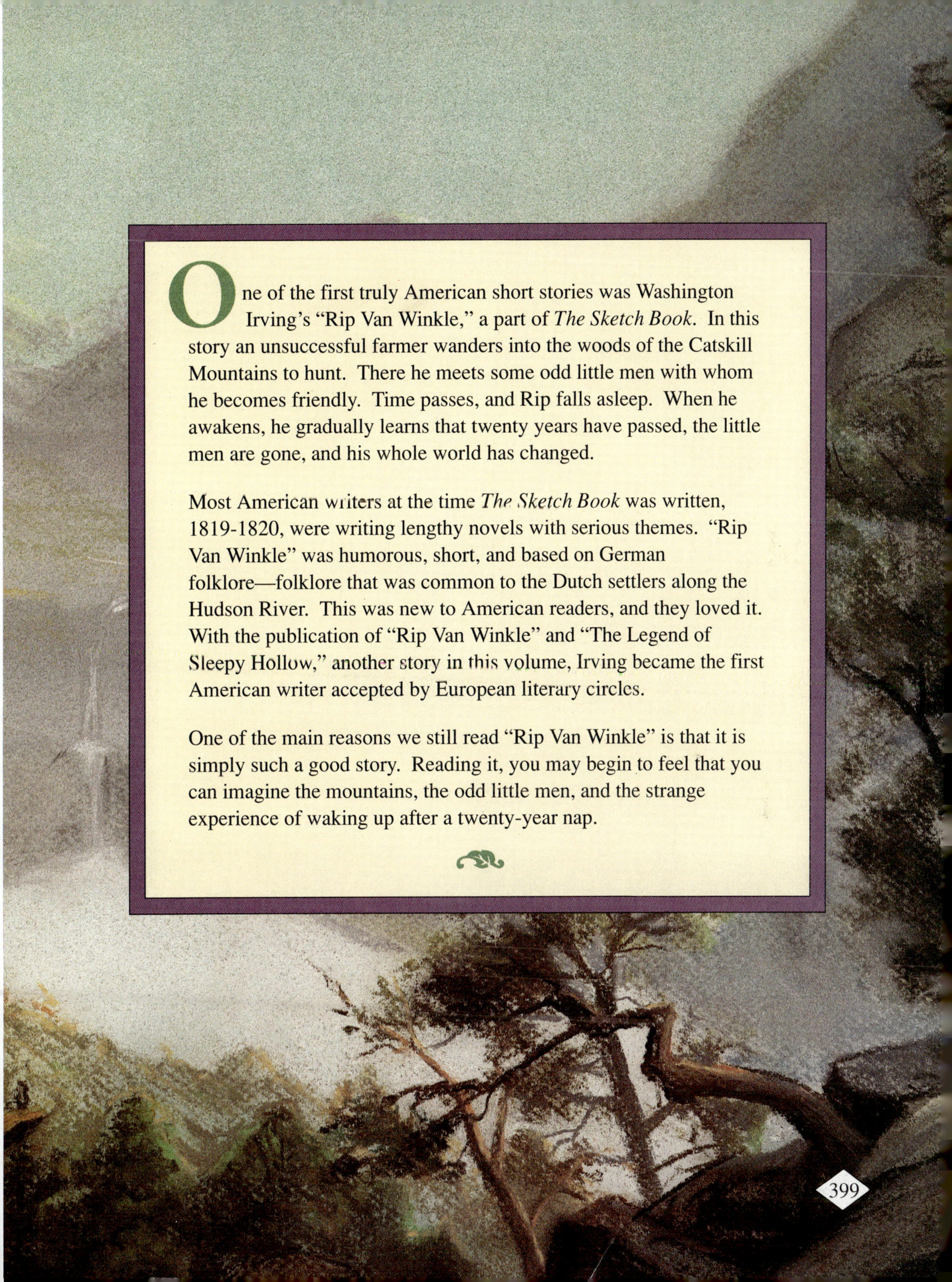

One of the first truly American short stories was Washington Irving's "Rip Van Winkle," a part of *The Sketch Book*. In this story an unsuccessful farmer wanders into the woods of the Catskill Mountains to hunt. There he meets some odd little men with whom he becomes friendly. Time passes, and Rip falls asleep. When he awakens, he gradually learns that twenty years have passed, the little men are gone, and his whole world has changed.

Most American writers at the time *The Sketch Book* was written, 1819-1820, were writing lengthy novels with serious themes. "Rip Van Winkle" was humorous, short, and based on German folklore—folklore that was common to the Dutch settlers along the Hudson River. This was new to American readers, and they loved it. With the publication of "Rip Van Winkle" and "The Legend of Sleepy Hollow," another story in this volume, Irving became the first American writer accepted by European literary circles.

One of the main reasons we still read "Rip Van Winkle" is that it is simply such a good story. Reading it, you may begin to feel that you can imagine the mountains, the odd little men, and the strange experience of waking up after a twenty-year nap.

*The Scottish lochs are a familiar sight to the people who live and work among them. It is just possible that these residents guard the secret of the Loch Ness mystery.*

Reading CORNER

# THE HORSES OF LIR

## by Roger Zelazny

The moonlight was muted and scattered by the mist above the loch. A chill breeze stirred the white tendrils to a sliding, skating motion upon the water's surface. Staring into the dark depths, Randy smoothed his jacket several times, then stepped forward. He pursed his lips to begin and discovered that his throat was dry.

Sighing, almost with relief, he turned and walked back several paces. The night was especially soundless about him. He seated himself upon a rock.

What am I doing here? he asked himself. How can I . . . ?

His gaze fell upon the heavy bronze ring with the Celtic design that he wore upon his forefinger.

It's real enough, he thought, and it had been *his*, and *he* could do it, but this . . .

He dropped his hand. He did not want to think about the body lying in a shallow depression ten or twelve paces up the hillside behind him.

His Uncle Stephen had taken care of him for almost two years after the deaths of his parents back in Philadelphia. He remembered the day he had come over—on that interminable plane flight—when the old man had met him at the airport in Glasgow. He had seemed shorter than Randy remembered, partly because he was a bit stooped, he supposed. His hair was pure white and his skin had the weathered appearance of a man's who had spent his life out-of-doors. Randy never learned his age.

Uncle Stephen had not embraced him. He had simply taken his hand, and his gray eyes had fixed upon his own for a moment as if searching for something. He had nodded then and looked away. It might have been then that Randy first noticed the ring.

"You'll have a home with me, lad," he had said. "Let's get your bags."

There was a brief splashing noise out in the loch. Randy searched its mist-ridden surface but saw nothing.

They know. Somehow they know, he decided. What now?

During the ride to his home, his uncle had quickly learned that Randy's knowledge of Gaelic[1] was limited. He had determined to remedy the situation by speaking it with him almost exclusively. At first, this had annoyed Randy, who saw no use to it in a modern world. But the rudiments were there, words and phrases returned to him, and after several months he began to see a certain beauty in the Old Tongue. Now he cherished this knowledge—another thing he owed the old man.

He toyed with a small stone, cast it out over the waters, listened to it strike. Moments later, a much greater splash echoed it. Randy shuddered.

He had worked at his uncle's boat-rental business all that summer. He had cleaned and caulked, painted and mended, spliced. . . . He had taken out charters more and more often as the old man withdrew from this end of things.

"As Mary—rest her soul—never gave me children, it will be yours one day, Randy," he said. "Learn it well, and it will keep you for life. You will need something near here."

"Why?" he had asked.

"One of us has always lived here."

"Why should that be?"

Stephen had smiled.

"You will understand," he said, "in time."

But that time was slow in coming, and there were other things to puzzle him. About once a month, his uncle rose and departed before daybreak. He never mentioned his destination or responded to questions concerning it. He never returned before sundown.

Naturally, one day Randy followed him. He had never been forbidden to do it, though he strongly suspected it would meet

[1] Gaelic (gā'lik): ancient language of Ireland and Scotland

with disapproval. So he was careful. Dressing hastily, he kept the old man in sight through the window as he headed off toward a stand of trees. He put out the CLOSED sign and moved through the chill predawn in that direction. He caught sight of him once again, briefly, and then Stephen vanished near a rocky area and Randy could find no trace of him after that. Half an hour later, he took down the sign and had breakfast.

Twice again he tried following him, and he lost him on both occasions. It irritated him that the old man could baffle him so thoroughly, and perhaps it bothered him even more that there was this piece of his life which he chose to keep closed to him—for as he worked with him and grew to know him better he felt an increasing fondness for his father's older brother.

Then one morning Stephen roused him early.

"Get dressed," he said. "I want you to come with me."

That morning his uncle hung the CLOSED sign himself and Randy followed him through the trees, down among the rocks, past a cleverly disguised baffle, and down a long tunnel. Randy heard lapping sounds of water, and even before his uncle put a light to a lantern he knew from the echoes that he was in a fair-sized cave.

His eyes did not adjust immediately when the light spread. When they did, he realized that he was regarding an underground harbor. Nevertheless, it took longer for the possibility to occur to him that the peculiar object to his left might be some sort of boat in a kind of dry dock. He moved nearer and examined it while his uncle filled and lit another lantern.

It was flat bottomed and U shaped. What he had taken to be some sort of cart beneath it, though, proved a part of the thing itself. It had a wheel on either side. Great metal rings hung loosely on both sides and on the forward end. The vehicle was tilted, resting upon its curved edge. These structural matters, however, aroused but a superficial curiosity, for all other things were overwhelmed within him by a kind of awe at its beauty.

Its gunwales, or sides—depending on exactly what the thing was—were faced with thin bronze plates of amazing design. They looped and swirled in patterns vaguely reminiscent of some of the more abstract figures in the *Book of Kells*, embossed here and there with large studs. The open areas looked to be enameled—green and red in the flickering light.

He turned as his uncle approached.

"Beautiful, isn't it?" he said, smiling.

"It—it belongs in a museum!"

"No. It belongs right here."

"What is it?"

Stephen produced a cloth and began to polish the plates.

"A chariot."

"It doesn't look exactly like any chariot I've seen pictures of. For one thing, it's awfully big."

Stephen chuckled.

"Ought to be. 'Tis the property of a god."

Randy looked at him to see whether he was joking. From the lack of expression on his face, he knew that he was not.

"Whose—is it?" he asked.

"Lir, Lord of the Great Ocean. He sleeps now with the other Old Ones—most of the time."

"What is it doing here?"

His uncle laughed again.

"Has to park it someplace now, doesn't he?"

Randy ran his hand over the cold, smooth design on the side. "I could almost believe you," he said. "But what is your connection with it?"

"I go over it once a month, to clean it, polish it, keep it serviceable."

"Why?"

"He may have need of it one day."

"I mean, why you?"

He looked at his uncle again and saw that he was smiling.

"A member of our family has always done it," he said, "since times before men wrote down history. It is a part of my duty."

Randy looked at the chariot again.

"It would take an elephant to pull something that size."

"An elephant is a land creature."

"Then what . . . ?"

His uncle held up his hand beside the lantern, displaying the ring.

"I am the Keeper of the Horses of Lir, Randy. This is my emblem of office, though they would know me without it after all these years."

Randy looked closely at the ring. Its designs were similar to those on the chariot.

"The Horses of Lir?" he asked.

His uncle nodded.

"Before he went to sleep with the other Old Ones, he put them to pasture here in the loch. It was given to an early ancestor of ours to have charge of them, to see that they do not forget."

Randy's head swam. He leaned against the chariot for support.

"Then all those stories, of—things—in the loch . . . ?"

"Are true," Stephen finished. "There's a whole family, a herd of them out there." He gestured toward the water. "I call them periodically and talk to them and sing to them in the Old Tongue, to remind them."

"Why did you bring me here, Uncle? Why tell me all these secret things?" Randy asked.

"I need help with the chariot. My hands are getting stiff," he replied. "And there's none else but you."

Randy worked that day, polishing the vehicle, oiling enormous and peculiarly contrived harnesses that hung upon the wall. And his uncle's last words bothered him more than a little.

The fog had thickened. There seemed to be shapes moving within it now—great slow shadows sliding by in the distance. He knew they were not a trick of the moonlight, for there had been another night such as this . . .

"Would you get your pullover, lad?" his uncle had said. "I'd like us to take a walk."

"All right."

He put down the book he had been reading and glanced at his watch. It was late. They were often in bed by this hour. Randy had only stayed up because his uncle had kept busy, undertaking a number of one-man jobs about the small cottage.

It was damp outside and somewhat chill. It had been raining that day. Now the fog stirred about them, rolling in off the water.

As they made their way down the footpath toward the shore, Randy knew it was no idle stroll that his uncle had in mind. He followed his light to the left past the docking area, toward a secluded rocky point where the land fell away sharply to deep water. He found himself suddenly eager, anxious to learn something more of his uncle's strange commitment to the place. He had grown steadily fonder of the old man in the time they had been together, and he found himself wanting to share more of his life.

They reached the point—darkness and mist and lapping water all about them—and Stephen placed his light upon the ground and seated himself on a stony ledge. He motioned for Randy to sit near him.

"Now, I don't want you to leave my side, no matter what happens," his uncle said.

"Okay."

"And if you must talk, speak the Old Tongue."

"I will."

"I am going to call the Horses now."

Randy stiffened. His uncle placed his hand upon his arm.

"You will be afraid, but remember that you will not be harmed so long as you stay with me and do whatever I tell you. You must be introduced. I am going to call them."

Randy nodded in the pale light.

"Go ahead."

He listened to the strange trilling noises his uncle made, and to the song that followed them. After a time, he heard a splashing, then he saw the advancing shadow . . . Big. Whatever it was, the thing was huge. Large enough to draw the chariot, he suddenly realized. If a person dare harness it . . .

The thing moved nearer. It had a long, thin neck atop its bulky form, he saw, as it suddenly raised its head high above the water, to sway there, regarding them through the shifting mist.

Randy gripped the ledge. He wanted to run but found that he could not move. It was not courage that kept him there. It was a fear so strong it paralyzed him, raising the hair on the back of his neck.

He looked at the Horse, hardly aware that his uncle was speaking softly in Erse[2] now.

The figure continued to move before them, its head occasionally dipping partway toward them. He almost laughed as a wild vision of a snake-charming act passed through his head. The creature's eyes were enormous, with glints of their small light reflected palely within them. Its head moved forward, then back. Forward . . .

[2]Erse (ers): language characteristic of the Gaelic-speaking people of Scotland

The great head descended until it was so close that it was almost touching his uncle, who reached out and stroked it, continuing to speak softly all the while.

He realized abruptly that his uncle was speaking to him. For how long he had been, he did not know.

". . . This one is Scafflech," he was saying, "and the one beside him is Finntag. . . ."

Randy had not realized until then that another of the beasts had arrived. Now, with a mighty effort, he drew his eyes from the great reptilian head which had turned toward him. Looking past it, he saw that a second of the creatures had come up and that it, also, was beginning to lean forward. And beyond it there were more splashing sounds, more gliding shadows parting the mists like the prows of Viking ships.

". . . And that one is Garwal. Talk to them, so they'll know the sound of your voice."

Randy felt he could easily begin laughing hysterically. Instead, he found himself talking, as he would to a large, strange dog.

"That's a good boy . . . . Come on now . . . . How are you? Good old fellow. . . ."

Slowly he raised his hand and touched the leathery muzzle. Stephen had not asked him to. Why he had done it he was not certain, except that it had always seemed a part of the dog talk he was using and his hand had moved almost as if by reflex when he began it.

The first creature's head moved even nearer to his own. He felt its breath upon his face.

"Randy's my name, Scafflech," he heard himself telling it. "Randy . . . ."

That night he was introduced to eight of them, of various sizes and dispositions. After his uncle had dismissed them and they had departed, he simply sat there staring out over the water. The fear had gone with them. Now he felt only a kind of numbness.

Stephen stood, stooped, retrieved the light.

"Let's go," he said.

Randy nodded, rose slowly, and stumbled after him. He was certain that he would get no sleep that night, but when he got home and threw himself into bed the world went away almost immediately. He slept later than usual. He had no dreams that he could recall.

They were out there again now, waiting. He had seen them several times since but never alone. His uncle had taught him the songs, the guide words and phrases, but he had never been called upon to use them this way. Now, on this night so like the first, he was back, alone, and the fear was back, too. He looked down at the ring that he wore. Did they actually recognize it? Did it really hold some bit of the Old Magic? Or was it only a psychological crutch for the wearer?

One of the huge forms—Scafflech, perhaps—drew nearer and then hastily retreated. They had come without being called. They were waiting for his orders, and he sat shaking.

Stephen had been ill much of the past month and had finally taken to his bed. At first, Randy had thought it to be influenza. But the old man's condition had steadily worsened. Finally he had determined to get him a doctor.

But Stephen had refused, and Randy had gone along with it until just that morning, when his uncle had taken a turn for the worse.

"No way, lad. This is it," he had finally told him. "A man sometimes has a way of knowing, and *we* always do. It is going to happen today, and it is very important that there be no doctor, that no one know for a time . . . ."

"What do you mean?" Randy had said.

"With a doctor there would be a death certificate, maybe an autopsy, a burial. I can't have that. You see, there is a special place set aside for me, for all of the Keepers . . . . I want to join my fathers, in the place were the Old Ones sleep . . . . It was promised—long ago . . . ."

"Where? Where is this place?" he had asked.

"The Isles of the Blessed, out in the open sea . . . You must take me there . . . ."

"Uncle," he said, taking his hand, "I studied geography in school. There's no such place. So how can I . . . ?"

"It troubled me once, too," he said, "but I've been there. . . . I took my own father, years ago. . . . The Horses know the way. . . ."

"The Horses! How could I—How could they—"

"The chariot . . . You must harness Scafflech and Finntag to the chariot and place my body within it. Bathe me first, and dress me in the clothes you'll find in that chest . . . ." He nodded toward an old sea chest in the corner. "Then mount to the driver's stand, take up the reins, and tell them to take you to the Isles . . . ."

Randy began to weep, a thing he had not done since his parents' deaths—how long ago?

"Uncle, I can't," he said. "I'm afraid of them. They're so big—"

"You must. I need this thing to know my rest. —And set one of the boats adrift. Later tell the people that I took it out. . . ."

He wiped his uncle's face with a towel. He listened to his deepening breathing.

"I'm scared," he said.

"I know," Stephen whispered. "But you'll do it."

"I—I'll try."

"And here . . . ." His uncle handed him the ring. "You'll need this—to show them you're the new Keeper . . . ."

Randy took the ring.

"Put it on."

He did.

Stephen had placed his hand upon his head as he had leaned forward.

"I pass this duty to you," he said, "that you be Keeper of the Horses of Lir."

Then his hand slipped away and he breathed deeply once again. He awakened twice after that, but not for long enough to converse at length. Finally, at sundown, he had died. Randy bathed him and clothed him as he had desired, weeping the while and not knowing whether it was for his sadness or his fear.

He had gone down to the cave to prepare the chariot. By lantern light he had taken down the great harnesses and affixed them to the rings in the manner his uncle had shown him. Now he had but to summon the Horses to this pool through the wide tunnel that twisted in from the loch, and there place the harnesses upon them. . . .

He tried not to think about this part of things as he worked, adjusting the long leads, pushing the surprisingly light vehicle into position beside the water. Least of all did he wish to think of aquaplaning across the waves, drawn by those beasts, heading toward some mythical isle, his uncle's body at his back.

He departed the cave and went to the docking area, where he rigged a small boat, unmoored it and towed it out some distance over the loch before releasing it. The mists were already rising by then. In the moonlight, the ring gleamed upon his finger.

He returned to the cottage for his uncle and bore him down to a cove near the water entrance to the cave. Then his nerve had failed; he had seated himself and had not stirred since.

The splashing continued. The Horses were waiting. Then he thought of his uncle, who had given him a home, who had left him this strange duty . . . .

He rose to his feet and approached the water. He held up his hand with the ring upon it.

"All right," he said. "The time has come. Scafflech! Finntag! To the cave! To the place of the chariot! Now!"

Two forms drifted near, heads raised high upon their great necks.

I should have known it would not be that easy, he thought.

They swayed, looking down at him. He began addressing them as he had that first night. Slowly, their heads lowered. He waved the ring before them. Finally, when they were near enough, he reached out and stroked their necks. Then he repeated the instruction.

They withdrew quickly, turned, and headed off toward the tunnel. He moved away, making for the land entrance to the place.

Inside, he found them waiting in the pool. He discovered then that he had to unfasten most of the harnessing from the chariot in order to fit it over them, and then secure it once again. It meant clambering up onto their backs. He removed his boots to do it. Their skin was strangely soft and slick beneath his feet, and they were docile now, as if bred to this business. He talked to them as he went about the work, rubbing their necks, humming the refrain to one of the old tunes.

He worked for the better part of an hour before everything was secure and he mounted the chariot and took up the reins.

"Out now," he said. "Carefully. Slowly. Back to the cove."

The wheels turned as the creatures moved away. He felt the reins jerk in his hands. The chariot advanced to the edge of the pool and continued on into the water. It floated. It drifted behind them toward the first bend and around it.

They moved through pitch blackness, but the beasts went carefully. The chariot never touched the rocky walls.

At length, they emerged into moonlight and mist over black water, and he guided them to the cove and halted them there.

"Wait now," he said. "Right here."

He climbed down and waded ashore. The water was cold, but he hardly noticed it. He mounted the slope to the place where his uncle lay and gathered him into his arms. Gently, he bore him down to the water's edge and out again. He took hold of the reins with a surer grip.

"Off now," he said. "You know the way! To the Isles of the Blessed! Take us there!"

They moved, slowly at first, through a long, sweeping turn that bore them out onto the misty breast of the loch. He heard splashings at either hand, and turning his head he saw that the other Horses were accompanying them.

They picked up speed. The beasts did seem to have a definite direction in mind. The mists swept by like a ghostly forest. For a moment, he almost felt as if he rode through some silent, mystical wood in times long out of mind.

The mists towered and thickened. The waters sparkled. He gave the creatures their head. Even if he had known the way, it would have done him little good, for he could not see where they were going. He had assumed that they were heading for the Caledonian Canal, to cut across to the sea. But now he wondered. If the Keepers, down through the ages, had been transported to some strange island, how had it been accomplished in earlier times? The Canal, as he recalled, had only been dug sometime in the nineteenth century.

But as the moonlit mists swirled about him and the great beasts plunged ahead, he could almost believe that there was another way—a way that perhaps only the Horses knew. Was he being borne, somehow, to a place that only impinged occasionally upon normal existence?

How long they rode across the ghostly seascape, he could not tell. Hours, possibly. The moon had long since set, but now the sky paled and a bonfire-like sunrise began somewhere to the right. The mists dispersed and the chariot coursed the waves beneath a clear blue sky with no trace of land anywhere in sight.

The unharnessed Horses played about him as Scafflech and Finntag drew him steadily ahead. His legs and shoulders began to ache and the wind came hard upon him now, but still he gripped the reins, blinking against the drenching spray.

Finally, something appeared ahead. At first he could not be certain, but as they continued on it resolved itself into a clear image. It was an island, green trees upon its hills, white rocks along its wave-swept shores.

As they drew nearer, he saw that the island was but one among many, and they were passing this one by.

Two more islands slipped past before the Horses turned and made their way toward a stone quay at the back of a long inlet at the foot of a high green slope. Giant trees dotted the hillside and there were several near the harbor. As they drew up beside the quay, he could hear birds singing within them.

As he took hold of the stone wall, he saw that there were three men standing beneath the nearest tree, dressed in green and blue and gray. They moved toward him, halting only when they had come alongside. He felt disinclined to look into their faces.

"Pass up our brother Keeper," one of them said in the Old Tongue.

Painfully, he raised his uncle's soaked form and felt them lift it from his arms.

"Now come ashore yourself, for you are weary. Your steeds will be tended."

He told the Horses to wait. He climbed out and followed the three figures along a flagged walk. One of them took him aside and led him into a small stone cottage while the others proceeded on, bearing his uncle's form.

"Your garments are wet," said the man. "Have this one," and he passed him a light green-blue robe of the sort he himself had on, of the sort in which Randy had dressed his uncle for the journey. "Eat now. There is food upon the table," the man continued, "and then there is the bed." He gestured. "Sleep."

Randy stripped and donned the garment he had been given. When he looked about again, he saw that he was alone. He went to the table, suddenly realizing that his appetite was enormous. Afterward, he slept.

It was dark when he awoke, and still. He got up and went to the door of the cottage. The moon had already risen, and the night had more stars in it than he could remember ever having seen before. A fragrant breeze came to him from off the sea.

"Good evening."

One of the men was seated upon a stone bench beneath a nearby tree. He rose.

"Good evening."

"Your Horses are harnessed. The chariot is ready to bear you back now."

"My uncle . . . ?"

"He has come home. Your duty is discharged. I will walk with you to the sea."

They moved back to the path, headed down to the quay. Randy saw the chariot, near to where he had left it, two of the Horses in harness before it. He realized with a start that he was able to tell that they were not Scafflech and Finntag. Other forms moved in the water nearby.

"It is good that two of the others travel the route in harness," the man said, as if reading his mind, "and give the older ones a rest."

Randy nodded. He did not feel it appropriate to offer to shake hands. He climbed down into the chariot and untwisted the reins from the crossbar.

"Thank you," he said, "for—everything. Take good care of him. Goodbye."

"A man who dines and sleeps in the Isles of the Blessed always returns," the other said. "Good night."

Randy shook the reins and the Horses began to move. Soon they were in open water. The new Horses were fresh and spirited. Suddenly Randy found himself singing to them.

They sped east along the path of the moon.

### ♦ LIBRARY LINK ♦

*If you enjoyed reading* The Horses of Lir *and would like to delve more deeply into the mysteries of Celtic legends, try* The Grey King *(Newbery Award) by Susan Cooper,* A String in the Harp *by Nancy Bond, and* The Road to Camlann *by Rosemary Sutcliff.*

## *Reader's Response*

How did you feel about the Horses of Lir when the author first described them and at the end of the story?

# WRITING ABOUT READING

## *Describing an Imaginery Creature*

You read about several imaginary creatures in this unit. Some, like Pegasus, were beautiful. Others, like the Horses of Lir, were mysterious giant reptiles "with skin strangely soft and slick." The writers who created these creatures used details to appeal to your senses of sight, smell, hearing, and touch. These details helped you understand how the creatures looked, smelled, sounded, and felt.

When you write descriptive prose, you should also try to appeal to the reader's senses. Now you can write about the Loch Ness monster using as many details as possible to describe the creature.

### *Prewriting*

Before you begin writing, it helps to list as many details about your subject as possible. Making a chart will help you to organize the details. The chart below lists details about the Loch Ness monster based on recorded reports in "Mystery of Loch Ness."

**Loch Ness Monster Description Chart**

| | |
|---|---|
| *What does the monster look like?* | ♦ Black and shiny<br>♦ One or more humps or fins<br>♦ Rounded head, long neck, and thick body |
| *What noises does it make?* | ♦ Unknown, but often reported splashing water |
| *How does it move?* | ♦ Very swift<br>♦ Moves serpentine fashion in the water |
| *What does it smell like?* | ♦ No reports of smell |

### *Writing*

Use the details in the chart to write a two paragraph description of the Loch Ness monster. If you want, you can reread "Mystery of Loch Ness" to find more details. Start with a sentence that states the topic, that is, the Loch Ness monster. Then support your first sentence with details that appeal to the reader's senses of sight, smell, hearing, and touch. Make the reader visualize the monster by effectively using descriptive details.

### *Revising*

Read your description to make sure you have included all of the details you want. Does your description give an accurate idea of the monster based on reports? Would it be possible for someone to make a drawing of the monster based on your description?

### *Proofreading*

Check your description for errors in spelling, punctuation, and grammar. Then make a clean copy.

### *Publishing*

Use your description and those of your classmates to make a book of Loch Ness monster descriptions. Decide what the title should be and what the front cover should look like.

# WORKING TOGETHER

## *Drawing Your Own Conclusions*

In this unit, you read about some of the imaginary creatures that have appeared in literature, movies, animated cartoons, and radio broadcasts. You also read an article about the mystery of Loch Ness. Your group will now develop your own theory about this mystery.

To help your group work well together, you should take responsibility for one or more of these tasks:

- Contributing ideas
- Recording people's ideas
- Showing appreciation for the contributions of other people
- Agreeing or disagreeing in a pleasant way

Begin by reviewing information from the article. Discuss the evidence that seems to support the theory that something unusual lives in Loch Ness. Record people's ideas on the left half of a sheet of paper. Then discuss why many people are skeptical of these ideas. Write these reasons on the right half of your paper. As a group, evaluate the information from the article. Use your common sense and your imagination to draw your own conclusions about the mystery of Loch Ness. Together, agree on a theory that you can all support. Be prepared to explain what your group decided, and why you reached your conclusion.

# BOOKS TO ENJOY

***Beauty: A Retelling of the Story of Beauty and the Beast*** by Robin McKinley *(Harper, 1978)* Embellished for older readers in this classic tale of a girl who, to save her father's life, goes to live in a monster's castle.

***Aliens in the Family*** by Margaret Mahy *(Scholastic, 1985)* Jake's family is struggling to accept and believe in one another in spite of their differences when an alien from a different dimension needs their help.

***A Swiftly Tilting Planet*** by Madeleine L'Engle *(Farrar, 1978)* Fifteen-year-old Charles Wallace undertakes a perilous journey through time with the help of a unicorn in an attempt to stop the destruction of the world.

***Watership Down*** by Richard Adams *(Macmillan, 1974)* The reality of rabbit life is maintained in this English fantasy of a band of intrepid rabbits who learn and grow as they seek a new home in a dangerous world.

***The Hobbit*** by J. R. R. Tolkien *(Houghton Mifflin, 1984)* A comfort-loving hobbit joins a throng of dwarfs on a dangerous quest through strange, dark lands. This enchanting story is full of suspense, humor, and wisdom.

UNIT FOUR

# FREE TO CHOOSE

*Being free implies the responsibility of making choices.*

*How do you decide what is the right thing to do?*

OLD BROOKLYN BRIDGE,
*painting by Joseph Stella, American, 1941*

*For five cents you could buy a whole pack of President cards . . . and some difficult decisions.*

# President Cleveland,

# *Where Are You?*

*by Robert Cormier*

That was the autumn of the cowboy cards—Buck Jones and Tom Tyler and Hoot Gibson and especially Ken Maynard. The cards were available in those five-cent packages of gum; pink sticks, three together, covered with a sweet white powder. You couldn't blow bubbles with that particular gum, but it couldn't have mattered less. The cowboy cards were important—the pictures of those rock-faced men with eyes of blue steel.

On those wind-swept, leaf-tumbling afternoons we gathered after school on the sidewalk in front of Lemire's Drugstore, across from St. Jude's Parochial School, and we swapped and bargained and matched for the cards. Because a Ken Maynard serial was playing at the Globe every Saturday afternoon, he was the most popular cowboy of all, and one of his cards was worth at least ten of any other kind. Rollie Tremaine had a treasure of thirty or so, and he guarded them jealously. He'd match you for the other cards, but he risked his Ken Maynards only when the other kids threatened to leave him out of the competition altogether.

You could almost hate Rollie Tremaine. In the first place, he was the only son of Auguste Tremaine, who operated the Uptown Dry Goods Store, and he did not live in a tenement but in a big white birthday cake of a house on Laurel Street. He was too fat to be effective in the football games between the Frenchtown Tigers and the North Side Knights, and he made us constantly aware of the jingle of coins in his pockets. He was able to stroll into Lemire's and casually select a quarter's worth of cowboy cards while the rest of us watched, aching with envy.

Once in a while I earned a nickel or dime by running errands or washing windows for blind old Mrs. Belander, or by finding pieces of copper, brass, and other valuable metals at the dump and selling them to the junkman. The coins clutched in my hand, I would race to Lemire's to buy a cowboy card or two, hoping that Ken Maynard would stare boldly out at me as I opened the pack. At one time, before a disastrous matching session with Roger Lussier (my best friend, except where the cards were involved), I owned five Ken Maynards and considered myself a millionaire, of sorts.

One week I was particularly lucky; I had spent two afternoons washing floors for Mrs. Belander and received a quarter. Because my father had worked a full week at the shop, where a rush order for fancy combs had been received, he allotted my brothers and sisters and me an extra dime along with the usual ten cents for the Saturday-afternoon movie. Setting aside the movie fare, I found myself with a bonus of thirty-five cents, and I then planned to put Rollie Tremaine to shame the following Monday afternoon.

Monday was the best day to buy the cards because the candy man stopped at Lemire's every Monday morning to deliver the new assortments. There was nothing more exciting in the world than a fresh batch of card boxes. I rushed home from school that day and hurriedly changed my clothes, eager to set off for the store. As I burst through the doorway, letting the screen door slam behind me, my brother Armand blocked my way. He was fourteen, three years older than I, and a freshman at Monument High School. He had recently become a stranger to me in many ways—indifferent to such matters as cowboy cards and the Frenchtown Tigers—and he carried himself with a mysterious dignity that was fractured now and then when his voice began shooting off in all directions like some kind of vocal fireworks.

"Wait a minute, Jerry," he said. "I want to talk to you." He motioned me out of earshot of my mother, who was busy supervising the usual after-school skirmish in the kitchen.

I sighed with impatience. In recent months Armand had become a figure of authority, siding with my father and mother occasionally. As the oldest son he sometimes took advantage of his age and experience to issue rules and regulations.

"How much money have you got?" he whispered.

"You in some kind of trouble?" I asked, excitement rising in me as I remembered the blackmail plot of a movie at the Globe a month before.

He shook his head in annoyance. "Look," he said, "it's Pa's birthday tomorrow. I think we ought to chip in and buy him something . . ."

DAIRY

I reached into my pocket and caressed the coins. "Here," I said carefully, pulling out a nickel. "If we all give a nickel we should have enough to buy him something pretty nice."

He regarded me with contempt. "Rita already gave me fifteen cents, and I'm throwing in a quarter. Albert handed over a dime—all that's left of his birthday money. Is that all you can do—a nickel?"

"Aw, come on," I protested. "I haven't got a single Ken Maynard left, and I was going to buy some cards this afternoon."

"Ken Maynard!" he snorted. "Who's more important—him or your father?"

His question was unfair because he knew that there was no possible choice—"my father" had to be the only answer. My father was a huge man who had worked at the Monument Comb Shop since the age of fourteen; his booming laugh—or grumble—greeted us each night when he returned from the factory. A steady worker when the shop had enough work, he quickened with gaiety on Friday nights and weekends, and he was fond of making long speeches about the good things in life. In the middle of the Depression, for instance, he paid cash for a piano, of all things, and insisted that my twin sisters, Yolande and Yvette, take lessons once a week.

I took a dime from my pocket and handed it to Armand.

"Thanks, Jerry," he said. "I hate to take your last cent."

"That's all right," I replied, turning away and consoling myself with the thought that twenty cents was better than nothing at all.

When I arrived at Lemire's I sensed disaster in the air. Roger Lussier was kicking disconsolately at a tin can in the gutter, and Rollie Tremaine sat sullenly on the steps in front of the store.

"Save your money," Roger said. He had known about my plans to splurge on the cards.

"What's the matter?" I asked.

"There's no more cowboy cards," Rollie Tremaine said. "The company's not making any more."

"They're going to have President cards," Roger said, his face twisting with disgust. He pointed to the store window. "Look!"

A placard in the window announced: "Attention, Boys. Watch for the New Series. Presidents of the United States. Free in Each 5-Cent Package of Caramel Chew."

"President cards?" I asked, dismayed.

I read on: "Collect a Complete Set and Receive an Official Imitation Major League Baseball Glove, Embossed with Lefty Grove's[1] autograph."

Glove or no glove, who could become excited about Presidents, of all things?

Rollie Tremaine stared at the sign. "Benjamin Harrison, for crying out loud," he said. "Why would I want Benjamin Harrison when I've got twenty-two Ken Maynards?"

I felt the warmth of guilt creep over me. I jingled the coins in my pocket, but the sound was hollow. No more Ken Maynards to buy. "I'm going to buy a candy bar," Rollie Tremaine decided.

I was without appetite, indifferent even to my favorite treat. I thought of how I had betrayed Armand and, worst of all, my father.

"I'll see you after supper," I called over my shoulder to Roger as I hurried away toward home. I took the shortcut behind the church, although it involved leaping over a tall wooden fence, and I zigzagged recklessly through Mr. Thibodeau's garden, trying to outrace my guilt. I pounded up the steps and into the house, only to learn that Armand had already taken Yolande and Yvette uptown to shop for the birthday present.

I pedaled my bike furiously through the streets, ignoring the indignant horns of automobiles as I sliced through the traffic. Finally I saw Armand and my sisters emerge from the Monument Men's Shop. My heart sank when I spied the long, slim, package that Armand was holding.

"Did you buy the present yet?" I asked, although I knew it was too late.

"Just now. A blue tie," Armand said. "What's the matter?"

"Nothing," I replied, my chest hurting.

He looked at me for a long moment. At first his eyes were hard, but then they softened. He smiled at me, almost sadly, and

[1]Lefty Grove (lef' tē grōv): American League pitcher from 1925–1941; winner of 300 games

touched my arm. I turned away from him because I felt naked and exposed.

"It's all right," he said gently. "Maybe you've learned something." The words were gentle, but they held a curious dignity, the dignity remaining even when his voice suddenly cracked on the last syllable.

I wondered what was happening to me, because I did not know whether to laugh or cry.

Sister Angela was amazed when, a week before Christmas vacation, everybody in the class submitted a history essay worthy of a high mark—in some cases as high as A-minus. (Sister Angela did not believe that anyone in the world ever deserved an A.) She never learned—or at least she never let on that she knew—we all had become experts on the Presidents because of the cards we purchased at Lemire's. Each card contained a picture of a President, and on the reverse side, a summary of his career. We looked at those cards so often that the biographies imprinted themselves on our minds without effort. Even our street-corner conversations were filled with such information as the fact that James Madison was called "The Father of the Constitution," or that John Adams had intended to become a minister.

The President cards were a roaring success and the cowboy cards were quickly forgotten. In the first place we did not receive gum with the cards, but a kind of chewy caramel. In the second place the competition for collecting the cards was fierce and frustrating—fierce because everyone was intent on being the first to send away for a baseball glove and frustrating because although there were only thirty-two Presidents, including Franklin Delano Roosevelt, the variety at Lemire's was at a minimum. When the delivery man left the boxes of cards at the store each Monday, we often discovered that one entire box was devoted to a single President—two weeks in a row the boxes contained nothing but Abraham Lincolns. One week Roger Lussier and I were the heroes of Frenchtown. We journeyed on our bicycles to the North Side, engaged three boys in a matching bout and returned with five new

Presidents, including Chester Alan Arthur, who up to that time had been missing.

Perhaps to sharpen our desire, the card company sent a sample glove to Mr. Lemire, and it dangled, orange and sleek, in the window. I was half sick with longing, thinking of my old glove at home, which I had inherited from Armand. But Rollie Tremaine's desire for the glove outdistanced my own. He even got Mr. Lemire to agree to give the glove in the window to the first person to get a complete set of cards, so that precious time wouldn't be wasted waiting for the postman.

We were delighted at Rollie Tremaine's frustration, especially since he was only a substitute player for the Tigers. Once after spending fifty cents on cards—all of which turned out to be Calvin Coolidge—he threw them to the ground, pulled some dollar bills out of his pocket and said, "The heck with it. I'm going to buy a glove!"

"Not that glove," Roger Lussier said. "Not a glove with Lefty Grove's autograph. Look what it says at the bottom of the sign."

We all looked, although we knew the words by heart: "This Glove Is Not For Sale Anywhere."

Rollie Tremaine scrambled to pick up the cards from the sidewalk, pouting more than ever. After that he was quietly obsessed with the Presidents, hugging the cards close to his chest and refusing to tell us how many more he needed to complete his set.

I too was obsessed with the cards, because they had become things of comfort in a world that had suddenly grown dismal. After Christmas a layoff at the shop had thrown my father out of work. He received no paycheck for four weeks, and the only income we had was from Armand's after-school job at the Blue and White Grocery Store—a job he lost finally when business dwindled as the layoff continued.

Although we had enough food and clothing—my father's credit had always been good, a matter of pride with him—the inactivity made my father restless and irritable. The twins fell sick and went to the hospital to have their tonsils removed. My father was confident that he would return to work eventually and pay off his debts, but he seemed to age before our eyes.

When orders again were received at the comb shop and he returned to work, another disaster occurred, although I was the only one aware of it. Armand fell in love.

I discovered his situation by accident, when I happened to pick up a piece of paper that had fallen to the floor in the bedroom he and I shared. I frowned at the paper, puzzled.

"Dear Sally, When I look into your eyes the world stands still . . ."

The letter was snatched from my hands before I finished reading it.

"What's the big idea, snooping around?" Armand asked, his face crimson. "Can't a guy have any privacy?"

He had never mentioned privacy before. "It was on the floor," I said. "I didn't know it was a letter. Who's Sally?"

He flung himself across the bed. "You tell anybody and I'll muckalize you," he threatened. "Sally Knowlton."

Nobody in Frenchtown had a name like Knowlton.

"A girl from the North Side?" I asked, incredulous.

He rolled over and faced me, anger in his eyes, and a kind of despair too.

"What's the matter with that? Think she's too good for me?" he asked. "I'm warning you, Jerry, if you tell anybody . . ."

"Don't worry," I said. Love had no particular place in my life; it seemed an unnecessary waste of time. And a girl from the North Side was so remote that for all practical purposes she did not exist. But I was curious. "What are you writing her a letter for? Did she leave town, or something?"

"She hasn't left town," he answered. "I wasn't going to send it. I just felt like writing to her."

I was glad that I had never become involved with love—love that brought desperation to your eyes, that caused you to write letters you did not plan to send. Shrugging with indifference, I began to search in the closet for the old baseball glove. I found it on the shelf, under some old sneakers. The webbing was torn and the padding gone. I thought of the sting I would feel when a sharp grounder slapped into the glove, and I winced.

"You tell anybody about me and Sally and I'll—"

"I know. You'll muckalize me."

I did not divulge his secret and often shared his agony, particularly when he sat at the supper table and left my mother's special butterscotch pie untouched. I had never realized before how terrible love could be. But my compassion was short-lived because I had other things to worry about: report cards due at Eastertime; the loss of income from old Mrs. Belander, who had gone to live with a daughter in Boston; and, of course, the Presidents.

Because a stalemate had been reached, the President cards were the dominant force in our lives—mine, Roger Lussier's and Rollie Tremaine's. For three weeks, as the baseball season approached, each of us had a complete set—complete except for one President, Grover Cleveland. Each time a box of cards arrived at the store we hurriedly bought them (as hurriedly as our funds allowed) and tore off the wrappers, only to be confronted by James Monroe or Martin Van Buren or someone else. But never Grover Cleveland, never the man who had been the twenty-second *and* the twenty-fourth President of the United States. We argued about Grover Cleveland. Should he be placed between Chester Alan Arthur and Benjamin Harrison as the twenty-second President or did he belong between Benjamin Harrison and William McKinley as the twenty-fourth President? Was the card company playing fair? Roger Lussier brought up a horrifying possibility—did we need *two* Grover Clevelands to complete the set?

Indignant, we stormed Lemire's and protested to the harassed storeowner, who had long since vowed never to stock a new series. Muttering angrily, he searched his bills and receipts for a list of rules.

"All right," he announced. "Says here you only need one Grover Cleveland to finish the set. Now get out, all of you, unless you've got money to spend."

Outside the store, Rollie Tremaine picked up an empty tin and scaled it across the street. "Boy," he said. "I'd give five dollars for a Grover Cleveland."

When I returned home I found Armand sitting on the piazza steps, his chin in his hands. His mood of dejection mirrored my own, and I sat down beside him. We did not say anything for a while.

"Want to throw the ball around?" I asked.

He sighed, not bothering to answer.

"You sick?" I asked.

He stood up and hitched up his trousers, pulled at his ear and finally told me what the matter was—there was a big dance next week at the high school, the Spring Promenade, and Sally had asked him to be her escort.

I shook my head at the folly of love. "Well, what's so bad about that?"

"How can I take Sally to a fancy dance?" he asked desperately. "I'd have to buy her a corsage . . . And my shoes are practically falling apart. Pa's got too many worries now to buy me new shoes or give me money for flowers for a girl."

I nodded in sympathy. "Yeah," I said. "Look at me. Baseball time is almost here, and all I've got is that old glove. And no Grover Cleveland card yet . . ."

"Grover Cleveland?" he asked. "They've got some of those up on the North Side. Some kid was telling me there's a store that's got them. He says they're looking for Warren G. Harding."

"Holy Smoke!" I said. "I've got an extra Warren G. Harding!" Pure joy sang in my veins. I ran to my bicycle, swung into the seat—and found that the front tire was flat.

"I'll help you fix it," Armand said.

Within half an hour I was at the North Side Drugstore, where several boys were matching cards on the sidewalk. Silently but blissfully I shouted: President Grover Cleveland, here I come!

After Armand had left for the dance, all dressed up as if it were Sunday, the small green box containing the corsage under his arm, I sat on the railing of the piazza, letting my feet dangle. The neighborhood was quiet because the Frenchtown Tigers were at Daggett's Field, practicing for the first baseball game of the season.

I thought of Armand and the ridiculous expression on his face when he'd stood before the mirror in the bedroom. I'd avoided looking at his new black shoes. "Love," I muttered.

Spring had arrived in a sudden stampede of apple blossoms and fragrant breezes. Windows had been thrown open and dust mops had banged on the sills all day long as the women busied themselves with housecleaning. I was puzzled by my lethargy. Wasn't spring supposed to make everything bright and gay?

I turned at the sound of footsteps on the stairs. Roger Lussier greeted me with a sour face.

"I thought you were practicing with the Tigers," I said.

"Rollie Tremaine," he said. "I just couldn't stand him." He slammed his fist against the railing. "Jeez, why did *he* have to be the one to get a Grover Cleveland? You should see him showing off. He won't let anybody even touch that glove. . ."

I felt like Benedict Arnold and knew that I had to confess what I had done.

"Roger," I said, "I got a Grover Cleveland card up on the North Side. I sold it to Rollie Tremaine for five dollars."

"Are you crazy?" he asked.

"I needed that five dollars. It was an—an emergency."

"Boy!" he said, looking down at the ground and shaking his head. "What did you have to do a thing like that for?"

I watched him as he turned away and began walking down the stairs.

"Hey, Roger!" I called.

He squinted up at me as if I were a stranger, someone he'd never seen before.

"What?" he asked, his voice flat.

"I had to do it," I said. "Honest."

He didn't answer. He headed toward the fence, searching for the board we had loosened to give us a secret passage.

I thought of my father and Armand and Rollie Tremaine and Grover Cleveland and wished that I could go away someplace far away. But there was no place to go.

Roger found the loose slat in the fence and slipped through. I felt betrayed: weren't you supposed to feel good when you did something fine and noble?

A moment later two hands gripped the top of the fence and Roger's face appeared. "Was it a real emergency?" he yelled.

"A real one!" I called. "Something important!"

His face dropped from sight and his voice reached me across the yard: "All right."

"See you tomorrow!" I yelled.

I swung my legs over the railing again. The gathering dusk began to soften the sharp edges of the fence, the rooftops, the distant church steeple. I sat there a long time, waiting for the good feeling to come.

## ♦ Library Link ♦

*If you liked this short story by Robert Cormier, you might enjoy reading some other stories by him in* Eight Plus One, *from which this selection was taken.*

## Reader's Response

Do you think Jerry did the right thing by selling the card of President Grover Cleveland to Rollie Tremaine? Explain.

## Thinking It Over

1. Why do you think the narrator said that "you could almost hate Rollie Tremaine"? How did you know what he meant?
2. In what decade do you think this story took place? Cite examples to support your opinion.
3. Why do you think the narrator felt he had betrayed his brother and father?
4. What is the significance of the title of the story?
5. Do you think the good feeling that Jerry refers to at the end of the story ever came to him? Explain.

## Appreciating Literature

Characters in literature develop or change just as people do in real life. Changes often occur in characters when events or people cause them to think hard about what's really important. Think about how Jerry changes in this story. What events or people cause this change?

## Writing to Learn

**THINK AND DISCOVER** Robert Cormier teaches us quite a bit about what life was like during an earlier time. Name three things you discovered about this era as you read the story. You might start with the example below, or choose your own.

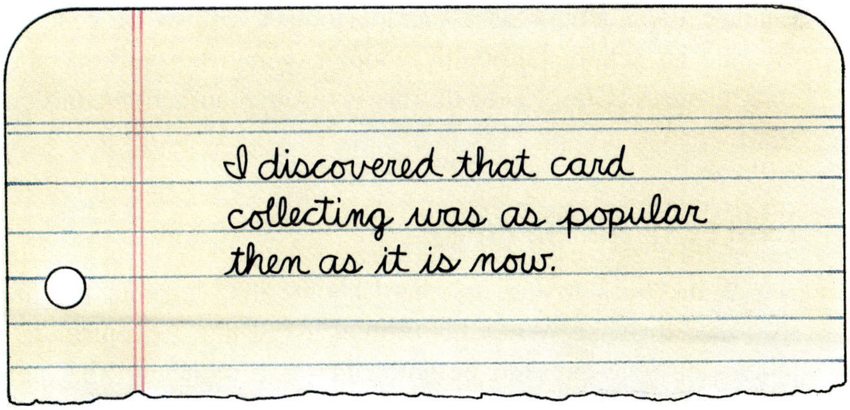


**WRITE** Use the information from your chart and fill a page in your journal. Tell why you may or may not have enjoyed living during the time period of this story.

Thinking ◆ Reading ◆ Writing

# Evaluating Actions and Consequences

In "President Cleveland, Where Are You?" the main character, Jerry, makes two important choices: he keeps some of his money instead of contributing it toward his father's present, and he sells his President Cleveland card in order to help his brother Armand. The last choice is particularly difficult, as he reflects: "I felt betrayed: weren't you supposed to feel good when you did something fine and noble?"

The actions characters take, and the consequences, or results, of those actions form the core of most stories. As a reader, you probably form many judgments about the things characters decide to do. You evaluate their actions as clever or foolish, selfish or generous. To evaluate an action thoroughly, though, you need to think about its consequences. One way to do this is through an action/consequences chart.

## *Learning the Strategy*

Think back to the first hard choice that Jerry in the previous story had to make. When his brother asked him to contribute to his father's birthday present, he withheld some money so that he could buy more cowboy cards. Almost immediately afterward he felt the pang of guilt, and you, as an active reader, made a quiet judgment about his act. An action/consequences chart can help you see your thinking in this way:

**Action:**

Withheld money

**Consequences:**

He wasn't able to buy cards.

He felt guilty and ashamed.

His father got a simple blue tie as a gift.

My judgment: Jerry shouldn't have held back his money.

## *Using the Strategy*

You can evaluate the actions of the same character in other situations, or of characters in other stories, with the same type of diagram. Draw and complete the action/consequences chart below on a separate sheet of paper. When you have finished, think about Jerry's second "hard choice," examine the consequences, and state your judgment.

**Action:**

Gives up valuable card

**Consequences:**

____________________

____________________

____________________

My judgment: ____________________

## *Applying the Strategy to the Next Selection*

As you read the next selection, "Maria Pepe, Girl of Courage," you will be asked to evaluate characters' actions. Then you will make an action/consequences chart for one action.

The writing connection can be found on page 529.

# MARIA PEPE
# GIRL OF COURAGE

by Geraldo Rivera

*Maria Pepe was perfectly happy playing baseball on one of her city's Little League teams. Then she was faced with a painful decision.*

By the bottom of the third inning, the baseball game had been turned into a rout. In the Hoboken, New Jersey, Little League contest, the home team, called the Young Democrats, was on the short end of a nine-to-one score. The old wooden bleachers of Stevens Park, though, were still packed, despite the lopsided score. As a matter of fact, thought Carmen Ronga, the coach of the trailing Young Democrats, it was one of the largest and most vocal crowds he could remember, and he didn't want to disappoint them.

"C'mon, c'mon, let's go, fellas. . . . We can still pull this one out of the fire." Clapping his hands as he walked up and down in front of his bench, the coach certainly didn't seem like a man whose team was eight runs behind. After the Young Democrats failed to score in the third inning, Mr. Ronga did some shuffling.

"Okay, listen up. We're making some changes," he said, as he pulled his lineup sheet out of his back pocket.

Crossing out some, and putting checks next to other names on his list, he benched many of his starters and brought in the reserves.

Ronga then made his big move, bringing his left fielder in to pitch. The coach was a bit apprehensive. He knew the new pitcher could throw hard, but he was afraid that the big crowd had made her nervous.

"Okay, Maria. This is it. Go out there and blast it past them."

As she walked out to the pitcher's mound, slamming the ball in and out of her glove, it was a historic moment for Little League baseball. For the first time, the organization, which oversees leagues for 2-1/4 million young boys around the world, was to have a girl playing—and pitching, no less—in one of its games.

Twelve-year-old Maria Pepe took about a half-dozen warm-up pitches, then signaled to the catcher to throw the ball around the infield. She was ready. The umpire called, "Batter up!" and while the crowd shouted its support of Maria, around came her arm, the pitch, "Ball one!"

"Ohhh!" the crowd sighed. Maria took off her baseball cap, wiped her forehead with the back of her glove arm, and flipped her ponytail back over her shoulder. In a few seconds, she was ready, and threw again. "Ball two!"

"Come on, Maria! You can do it! Blow it past him!" She smiled, recognizing her dad's voice roaring out from the bleachers. She kicked at the dirt around the pitcher's mound, taking her time. Getting the signal from her catcher, she let loose with her fast ball.

"Strike one!" The batter had taken a mighty cut at the third pitch, but Maria had indeed blown it past him. "Yeah!" The crowd was on its feet. The excitement in the slightly faded green-plywood confines of Stevens Park was like pennant fever; it was as if a World Series were at stake. She threw again.

"Strike two!"

A called strike. The batter had been so confident that Maria's first pitch into the strike zone had been a fluke, he watched her next pitch all the way, anticipating a ball. But she had fooled him, and the count was even at two balls, two strikes.

"Strike three!"

The batter had gone down swinging, and from the stands the crowd enthusiastically roared its approval. Maria had struck him out. Both sides went scoreless after that, the game ending in an anticlimactic nine-to-one victory for the opposing team.

"But wasn't Maria great?" Coach Ronga smiled. "I'm going to make her the starting pitcher in next week's game against the Hoboken Elks."

Maria pitched in that game against the Elks, and played right field in the game after that. Unfortunately, she couldn't lead her team to victory in either contest, the Young Democrats losing both games by lopsided scores. But Maria had won another victory—the respect of her teammates and coaches.

"Her fast ball is as good as or better than any of the boys'. And she's not a bad batter, either," said her coach.

Then the bombshell hit. Responding to all the publicity generated by Maria's entrance into the formerly all-boys league, the national office of Little League issued a statement. With it, they revoked the charter, and cancelled the league insurance, not only for Maria's team, but for the whole Hoboken league. Ten teams, with two hundred ballplayers, were affected by the reaction. The sponsor of Maria's Young Democrats, confronted with the choice of losing Maria or the whole league, reluctantly agreed to drop his twelve-year-old star right-hander from the lineup. He asked Coach Ronga to assume the responsibility of telling Maria and her parents about the decision.

The team's sponsor said later, "I didn't want to drop her from the team, especially after she showed us all how well she could do, once she had the chance. But the national office didn't just kick our team out of the league. They knocked the whole Hoboken city league out! And we didn't want to jeopardize the two hundred other kids who play Little League baseball in this town." He also pledged that he was not going to take the action meekly. He promised to go over the rule book carefully, to find if there were any legal grounds to challenge the decision.

Maria Pepe, the center of the great Little League controversy, grew up in Hoboken. She had been playing sandlot baseball in the city with the boys long before she joined the Little League.

"She was almost always the only girl in the games, but they always let her play. They even used to watch out for her crossing the street and all. They loved her, and she loved the game," her mother said of her.

Maria started playing baseball at about the age of five, when she would shyly ask the boys in her building if they would let her play with them. She had to ask quite a few times, but by sheer perseverance she was finally given a chance to get into a ballgame. After that, the boys never objected. Maria was a good ballplayer, and on the roughly drawn baseball diamonds of the vacant lots of the city, whether or not you were a good ballplayer was all that really counted.

It had been in the spring of 1972 that Maria came home with some papers for her parents to sign. She told them that she wanted to try out for a team in the Hoboken league, called the Young Democrats. Her father was astounded. He took his glasses off and put the newspaper down. A longshoreman who had been working the piers for the last twenty-nine years, Mr. Pepe was something of a traditionalist. "But, honey"—Mr. Pepe smiled gently as he rested one of his big burly arms on his daughter's shoulder— "the Little League is for boys. They aren't going to let a girl play." Maria was an obedient child, and though she was disappointed, she was ready to accept any reasonable decision. But she was also curious.

"But, Daddy, what if I can play better than the boys can?"

"That doesn't count, sugar. It's for boys, not for girls."

"Why?"

Mr. Pepe furrowed his brow and thought for a while. Unable to come up with a logical answer quickly enough, he turned to Mrs. Pepe. "You tell her."

"It's just always been that way." But that answer was also unsatisfactory to Maria. It didn't even sound right to her parents. Sensing an opening, Maria seized the opportunity to explain that the coach of the team, Carmen Ronga, had told her she could go to the tryouts. If she was good enough, the coach had added, he'd let her play. All she really needed now was her parents' permission.

Totally on the defensive, and under the unswerving gaze of his daughter, Mr. Pepe told Maria that they would give it some thought. As twelve-year-olds almost always do, Maria happily accepted the vague "maybe" as a definite "yes."

"Thank you, Daddy!" she squealed, as she kissed both of them on the cheek and ran out of the apartment on her way down to the lot across the street. She had left the papers on the kitchen table in front of them.

"You know something? . . . She's right." It was Mr. Pepe who spoke first. He was smiling again and shaking his head back and forth. He picked up the application forms and leafed through them.

"I don't know," said Mrs. Pepe as she walked over to the stove to pour another cup of coffee. "What if she gets hurt?"

"Oh, come on . . . she's been playing ball with the same kids since she was this high," said Mr. Pepe, holding his hand at about the level of the tabletop. "The only difference now is that she'll have a uniform."

Not wanting to disappoint Maria, Mr. and Mrs. Pepe gave their consent. "It means everything in the world to her. How could we say no?" said Mrs. Pepe.

**Should Maria's parents have decided this? What were the consequences?**

So Maria was there on the first day of the league tryouts, and, as expected, she easily made the team. From the beginning of the season, however, her spot in the Young Democrats' lineup generated tremendous controversy. Although most of the initial reaction was favorable, some was not. There were parents of children on the opposing teams who were genuinely angry at the situation. It was as if her playing somehow detracted from their own sons' accomplishments.

The controversy also fostered a great deal of local interest in Little League games. With each successive game played by the Young Democrats, there were more spectators in the stands, and more reporters and photographers on the field. Finally the word got to the national office, and that was the beginning of the end of Maria's career in organized baseball.

By the time Maria played her third game as a Young Democrat, even her parents were being subjected to abuse and scorn by a vocal minority of Little League fans. The attacks were by no means limited to strangers. One afternoon Mrs. Pepe was bringing a basket of laundry down to the machines in the basement. She got into the same elevator with two women she'd known for years, also heading down to do the wash.

"It's not right, Angie," immediately said one of them.

"What isn't?"

"Maria's playing in the Little League. What's she trying to do, wreck it for all the other kids?"

"All the neighbors are talking about it," joined in the other woman.

"Well, I'm surprised at you two!" responded Mrs. Pepe angrily, after recovering from her momentary shock. "This whole excitement is ridiculous. Imagine two grown-up women getting so worked up because one little girl wants to play baseball." The elevator door opened onto the basement. Mrs. Pepe added one footnote before storming over to an empty washing machine. "She's got just as much right to play as any other child!"

Many people, however, supported Maria's precedent-setting activities. Her father's longshoremen's local, for instance, took a poll and unanimously decided that they were behind her all the way.

Maria's abbreviated career was marked by escalating unpleasantness. Following the decision from the national Little League office, she was more than just a trend-setting girl in a formerly all-boys world. Maria was publicly made the cause for the break up of the city's entire league.

Was the Little League office correct in allowing Maria to play? What were the consequences for Maria? For other children in the Hoboken Little League?

The pressure on Maria and her parents for her to quit the team built enormously. Where once she could count her coaches and teammates on the Young Democrats as ardent supporters of her right to play, most now began to waiver, and finally became polite opponents of that right. But it was the grown-ups who really let her have it. When she was outdoors, she would be stopped by adults she scarcely knew or didn't know at all.

"Little girl, because of you, my son Johnny can't play baseball anymore. Now, how does that make you feel?"

"Maria, do you think it's right for you to spoil the summer for two hundred other children?"

"Maria, just because of your pride, all the other kids are going to have a rotten time."

At first she would face the attackers with her hands on her hips and her chin proudly raised. "I should be allowed to play. I can play as good as anyone!"

The cumulative effect of the personal attacks made her quiet and thoughtfully introverted. She was a spunky kid, and would, under ordinary circumstances, never run away from a fair fight. Maria's playing ability on the field had silenced the challenge of the skeptics, but there was no real answer for people who criticized just the fact that she was a girl, and one who had cost the entire league its right to play.

Slowly walking home the day after her third game, she reached a decision. As she walked past the school and across the street toward her building, Maria decided to throw in the towel. "It was just that I didn't want to hurt all the other kids' chances to play ball," she explained later. "And I already figured that I'd caused people enough trouble. . . . I just didn't think it was fair anymore."

With that decision made, she walked into the apartment. She was surprised to see Mr. Ronga, her coach, there talking to her parents. There was an awkward pause in their conversation when the adults saw her coming in. Maria, still standing by the door, quickly realized that they had been talking about her. "I'm going to quit," she said before they could say anything to her.

"I think it would be the best thing to do, dear," her mother consoled her.

Mr. Ronga had come over to the Pepe home to explain to Maria and her folks the reluctant decision that he and Mr. Farina, the team sponsor, had made to drop her from the team. The decision she had reached by herself spared them that embarrassment.

After announcing what she was going to do, Maria walked quickly through the living room and into the bedroom she shared with her sister, Michele. Shutting the door quietly behind her, Maria stood there for a second before throwing herself on her bed in tears.

Should Maria and Mr. Ronga have decided this? Say why you think as you do.

After her resignation, Hoboken officials began criticizing the Little League for having forced her out. As the negative publicity mounted, the national office issued its first formal statement on Maria's situation. It claimed that girls shouldn't be allowed to play because baseball was a contact sport, and girls were more prone to injury than boys the same age.

It was an old argument that had always been successfully invoked whenever any girl sought to challenge the league's "boys-only" rule. But times were changing, and in Maria's case there were plenty of people to assist in the process of change. Later in the same week that Maria had been dropped, the Essex County chapter of the National Organization for Women interceded in her behalf. The organization filed a suit against the National Little League, charging the organization with discriminatory practices. NOW alleged that the league, which uses public land to play its games, had discriminated against Maria because she was a girl.

During the following week, a field representative for the State Division on Civil Rights announced that medical opinions were being sought to determine if girls between the ages of eight and twelve were really physically inferior to boys in that same age group. Meanwhile, Maria had to content herself with sandlot baseball. The closest she got to the Little League after her ouster was rooting for her old teammates from the sidelines.

The Hoboken league managed to start up again, but it was without support, franchise, or insurance coverage from the national headquarters. Instead of folding the league, civic leaders announced that organized baseball would continue. The city government assumed the responsibility for any game-related injuries. But despite the fact that Hoboken was going it alone, Maria was still barred from playing, in the hope that the national organization would reinstate the league's charter.

While order—and baseball—resumed in Hoboken, the legal action started on Maria's behalf was causing chaos among the fifteen men on the national board of the league. A three-day hearing held before the State Division on Civil Rights was producing some very unexpected results. The weight of the evidence given by expert psychologists and doctors supported the conclusion that girls between the ages of eight and twelve could play baseball with no greater risk of injury than boys in the same age group. The major legal prop in the Little League's policy of excluding girls from play was being called out on strikes.

Sylvia B. Pressler, the division hearing officer, finally ruled that the league had been unlawfully discriminating against Maria, specifically, and against all other New Jersey girls who wanted to play Little League ball.

"The Little League," concluded Mrs. Pressler, "is as American as hot dogs and apple pie." She added that there was absolutely no reason, physical or psychological, "why that piece of Americana should be withheld from Maria or any other girl."

Hoping to send the legal fight into extra innings, the Little League appealed to the Appellate Division of the State Superior Court. Beaten on the argument that little girls were more fragile than little boys, the national office changed its game plan. Relative safety no longer the issue, the league maintained that it was a private and not a public accommodation. As such, the league contended that it was exempt from New Jersey's law against sex discrimination.

The court finally ruled in the court case, and it ruled in Maria's favor that Little League was indeed a "public accommodation, because the invitation to play baseball is open to children in the community at large, with no restriction whatever."

School was back in session by the time the issue was being resolved. When Maria walked into the apartment after school, she eagerly listened as her mother read the reports of her legal victory.

"Hurray!" she shouted, parading around the apartment living room.

Michele and brother Mark had listened with her to the good news.

"We won! We won!" they were all yelling as they marched around and over the living-room furniture and through the rest of the house.

Do you think that the court decision was correct? What were the consequences for Maria? For others?

By the time Maria's father had come home from work, about an hour later, the excitement had died down. When Mrs. Pepe told her husband the news of the victory, he knocked on the girls' bedroom door and went in to congratulate Maria.

"Not bad. Not bad. How do you feel about the whole thing now? Do you think it was worth it?" he asked her.

"Of course she does, Daddy," answered Mark, an enthusiastic and very proud younger brother. The kids were all sitting on Maria's bed, bubbling happily, as they read and reread the newspaper accounts of the court's decision.

"Well, what do you think, Maria?" Mr. Pepe asked again.

"I'm happy, Daddy," she said softly. "I'm mostly happy for all the other girls who'll get the chance to play."

"But what about you, sugar—aren't you happy for yourself?" asked her father with uncharacteristic softness.

"I guess so, Daddy, but . . ."

"But what, Maria?"

"I'm too old to play now."

The victory had come too late for Maria Pepe. At thirteen she was already over the Little League hill and no longer eligible to play.

**Evaluate one action in this story by completing an action/consequences chart. When you have finished, state your judgment.**

**How did you trace the consequences of the action you chose for your chart?**

The next spring, the first under the new ruling, 50 girls joined the 175 boys who turned out to register for the Hoboken Little League. "I never expected that many," said the town's recreational superintendent, with a wide grin.

In June 1974, defeated in New Jersey, and facing dozens of legal challenges in other states, officials of Little League, Inc., announced that they would "defer to the changing social climate" and permit girls to play on their teams.

## *Reader's Response*

How did you feel about the decision by the team's sponsor to try to drop Maria from the team? Explain your answer.

## Thinking It Over

1. Why was Maria such an unusual member of her team and league?
2. How did people react to Maria's playing on the Little League team?
3. What reason did the team's sponsor give for deciding to drop Maria from the team?
4. Were you surprised that Maria decided to quit the team? Why?
5. Do you think Little League would now be open to girls if the Maria Pepe case had not come along? Why?
6. What do you think might have happened if Maria had not voluntarily quit? What did you think about in making your prediction?

## Appreciating Literature

Nonfiction articles sometimes contain the same elements that make up fictional stories—conflict, turning point, resolution, and even an ironic twist at the end. Explain how the author uses these elements in "Maria Pepe, Girl of Courage."

## Writing to Learn

**THINK AND EVALUATE** Maria Pepe had a difficult decision to make. If you had had to face her problem, what would you have done? Look at the chart below. Copy and complete it with two additional reasons that would support her decision and two additional reasons against it.

| For | Against |
| --- | --- |
| Maria opened new opportunities in athletics for girls | Maria violated tradition. |
| | |

**WRITE** Use the information in the chart you made to help you reach a decision. Write an answer to this question: If you had been Maria Pepe, what would you have done?

Using Formulas

# Reading Mathematics

Suppose you have to find the area of a circle. A mathematical rule describes a method you use to solve this type of problem. If this rule were written in everyday language, it would be long and awkward. Therefore, mathematicians use a shorthand method for writing these rules. This shorthand is called a mathematical formula.

A mathematical formula uses symbols to express a rule in a short, quick way. Sometimes the symbols are simply letters that stand for a particular measure. For example, mathematicians often use the letter *r* as a symbol for the radius of a circle. Other symbols stand for specific numbers.

Use these steps to help you to read and interpret a formula.

1. Identify the meanings of the symbols used in the formula. Usually the meanings of some of the symbols are given in your book.
2. Think about or write the rule that the formula expresses.
3. Once you have read and interpreted the formula, you can go ahead and use your mathematical skills to solve the formula.

## *How to Read and Interpret a Formula*

To find the area of the shaded ring at the right, you could subtract the area of the smaller circle from the area of the larger circle. The formula:

$$A = \pi(r_1)^2 - \pi(r_2)^2$$

is the rule for finding the area of the shaded ring.

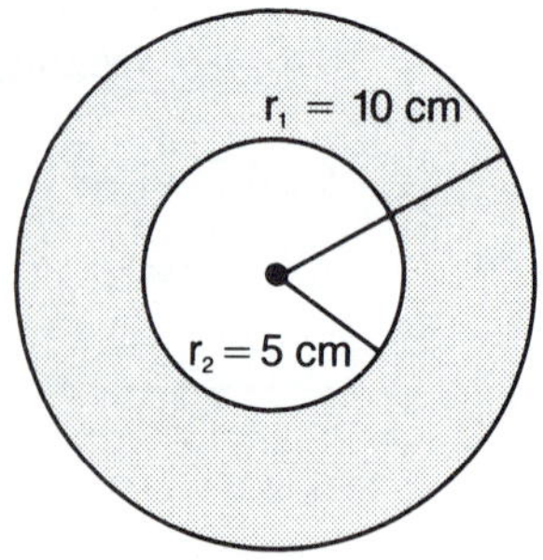

First, identify the meanings of the symbols in the formula. The letter used is often the first letter of the word that it represents. In the formula:

- A stands for the area of the shaded ring.
- $r_1$ stands for the radius of the first circle.
- $r_2$ stands for the radius of the second circle (the smaller one).
- $\pi$ is the symbol for pi, which is equal to approximately 3.14.
- $r^2$ means that the radius is squared, or multiplied by itself.

Once you have identified the meanings of the symbols, you can think about or write what the formula means. The relationship expressed by the formula $A = \pi(r_1)^2 - \pi(r_2)^2$ is:

> The area of the shaded ring is equal to the difference between the areas of the two circles.

You know from the diagram that $r_1 = 10$ cm and $r_2 = 5$ cm. You were given an approximate value for $\pi$. Now, substitute the numerical values you know into the formula.

$$A = \pi\,(r_1)^2 - \pi\,(r_2)^2$$
$$A = 3.14\,(10)^2 - 3.14\,(5)^2$$

Finally, compute the value of A. Remember to use the standard order of operations. (First, compute the exponents. Then, do all multiplication and division. Finally, do all addition and subtraction.)

$$A = 3.14\,(10)^2 - 3.14\,(5)^2$$
$$A = 3.14\,(100) - 3.14\,(25)$$
$$A = 314 - 78.5$$
$$A = 235.5\text{ cm}^2$$

So, the area of the shaded ring is 235.5 $\text{cm}^2$. Note that *$cm^2$* stands for *square centimeters*.

**As You Read** Read the following page from a mathematics textbook. Then answer the questions on page 459.

# Area—Triangles, Trapezoids

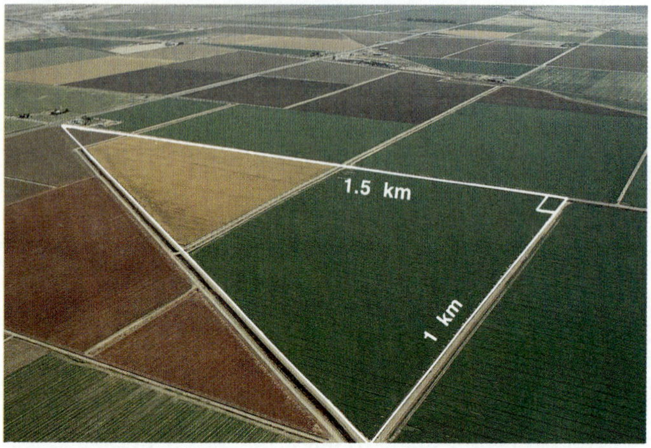


Surveyors make topographical surveys by taking aerial photographs. Mr. Diaz photographed this triangular-shaped parcel of land. What is the area of the parcel?

The area of a triangle is one half the area of a parallelogram with the same base and the same height. In the figure at the right, the diagonal of the parallelogram divides it into two congruent triangles.

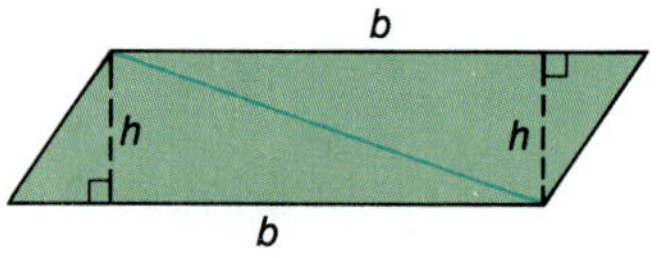


**Area = $\frac{1}{2}$ × base × height**

Another name for the height of a triangle is *altitude*.

$A = \frac{1}{2}bh$

The area of the parcel of land is $\frac{1}{2} \times (1 \text{ km}) \times (1.5 \text{ km}) = 0.75 \text{ km}^2$.

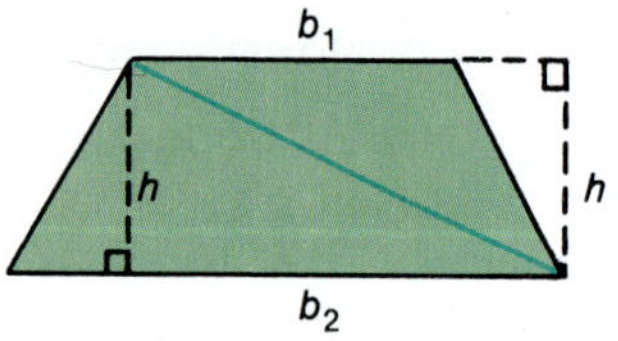


Divide a trapezoid into two triangles. The area of the trapezoid is the sum of the areas of the two triangles.

$$A = \frac{1}{2}b_1h + \frac{1}{2}b_2h = \frac{1}{2}h(b_1 + b_2)$$

For the trapezoid at the right, if $h = 5$ m, $b_1 = 8$ m, and $b_2 = 14$ m, then $A = \frac{1}{2}(5 \text{ m})(8 \text{ m} + 14 \text{ m}) = \frac{1}{2}(5 \text{ m})(22 \text{ m}) = 55 \text{ m}^2$.

## CLASSWORK

**Find the area of each figure.**

1.

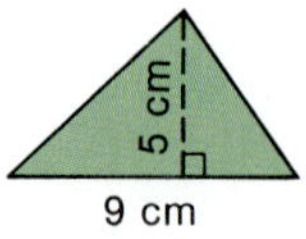


2.

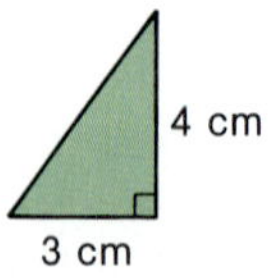


3.

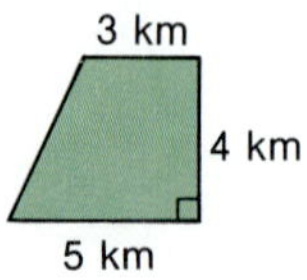


4.

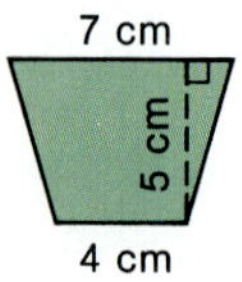


5. triangle: $b = 12.8$ cm, $h = 10.3$ cm

6. trapezoid: $h = 8.2$ m, $b_1 = 6$ m, $b_2 = 10.5$ m

## *Using What You Have Learned*

**1.** Look at the formula $A = \frac{1}{2}bh$.

a. Why is the letter A used for area?

b. What symbols are used to represent base and height?

**2.** Look at the formula for the area of a trapezoid on page 458. What do the small numbers 1 and 2 stand for?

**3.** The formula for a trapezoid is $A = \frac{1}{2}b_1h + \frac{1}{2}b_2h$. Write in your own words the relationship that this formula expresses.

**4.** Why do you think we use formulas instead of using words to express a mathematical relationship?

**5.** Look at exercise 1 on page 458. Answer the following questions.

a. What is the formula for the area of a triangle?

b. Write the relationship that the formula expresses.

c. Substitute the numerical values you know.

d. Compute the area of the triangle.

**6.** Work out the answer to exercise 6 on page 458.

Examples and excerpts are from *Silver Burdett & Ginn Mathematics,* © *1988.*

# THE CONFIDENCE GAME

## by Pat Carr

*It has been said that winning isn't everything . . . but sometimes it feels that way!*

My confidence started draining out my toes the day Angela Brady showed up at the pool for workout. I even started to chew the inside of my cheek, a nervous habit I usually reserve for fighting the fear that clutches at me just before a race. In a way, I guess I knew it was a race between Angela and me for the backstroke position on our team relay for National Championship.

I hadn't even seen her swim yet, but the whole team knew she had been swimming for a famous club in California. We were just a small city team, only two years old. But we had a coach whose middle name was motivation. He'd motivated me into swimming a grueling three miles a day, and now I was actually in

the running to compete at the Nationals. Or I was until Angela showed up.

"Okay, swim freaks, hit the water for an 800 meter free-style warm-up!" barked Coach. Then he added in a more human voice, "Angela, why don't you try lane four today?"

Lane four was the fast lane, my lane. I'd had to earn my place in that lane by swimming 400 meters in less than five minutes. Now all Angela had to do was jump in. It wasn't fair.

I didn't think I could pretend friendliness, so I started the 800 before Angela hit the water. But I didn't even have time to settle into my pace when I felt the water agitating behind me. I stroked harder, but I could still feel the churning water of someone closing in on me. I soon felt a light touch on my foot.

In swim workouts, it's one of the rules that when a teammate taps your foot, you move to the right to let that swimmer go ahead of you. I knew that, and I also knew that I was interfering with Angela's pace by not letting her pass me. My conscience told me to move over, but something stubborn kept my body in the middle of the lane.

At the end of the 800, I glanced up and saw Coach staring at me. Realizing that he had seen me refuse to let Angela pass, I took a deep breath and ducked underwater.

When the workout was over, everyone crowded around Angela, asking her if she knew any Olympic swimmers and stuff like that. Finding a quiet corner for myself, I slipped on my warm-up suit, draped a towel over my head, and hurried toward my bike.

"Hey, Tobi! Where are you going?" someone shouted.

I didn't answer, just hopped on my bike and pedalled fast.

It was like that for the next two weeks. At every workout Angela was the star of the show; I was an invisible stagehand. Even worse, during time trials she beat me in all four strokes and took my place as lane leader.

I was miserable. And I was scared, too; scared that Angela was taking away my chance at the Nationals, a chance I had earned by a lot of hard work.

I started to show up late to workouts so that I wouldn't have to talk to anyone. I even walked on the bottom of the pool and faked my stroke, a swimmer's cheating trick I'd never used before. It was easy to catch up to Angela that way. And I always managed to be underwater when she gave our lane instructions.

I'll admit I wasn't very happy with my actions. But my jealous feelings were like a current I couldn't swim against.

The day before the Riverdale Meet, Coach called me over. At that moment I would rather have tried to talk to King Kong.

"Tobi, I want to talk to you about sportsmanship," he began.

"Sportswomanship, in this case, Coach," I quipped, hoping to distract him.

"Okay, sportswomanship," he said, taking me seriously. "Or whatever you want to call it when one athlete accepts a better athlete in a spirit of friendly competition."

"Maybe the so-called better athlete is not as good as everyone thinks," I mumbled.

Coach left a big silence for my statement to fall into. I started to chew the inside of my cheek again.

"Let's stop talking about this athlete and that athlete," he said softly, "and talk instead about Tobi and Angela. She has made better time than you, Tobi. And that is an objective fact, not something everyone thinks."

He paused. I stared at my toes, which were curling under my feet as if trying to hide.

"The worst of it, Tobi, is that your attitude is hurting your performance. Do you know that your times have become worse in the last two weeks? Maybe showing up late and walking on the bottom have something to do with that," he said. My face felt as if it had been splashed with hot pink paint.

"Do you have anything you want to say?" he asked. I shook my head. "That's all then, Tobi. I'll see you tomorrow at the Riverdale Meet."

The next morning I was too nervous to eat my special breakfast of steak and eggs. This meet would decide who was going to Nationals.

The early skies were still gray when I arrived at the Riverdale pool for the warm-up session. The other swimmers were screeching greetings at each other like a flock of gulls. I jumped into the water to cut off the sound and mechanically began to stroke.

Half an hour later, I shuddered as the public address system squealed. The meet was about to start. After climbing out of the pool, I quickly searched the heat sheet for my name. Disappointed, I saw that I had just missed making it into the last, and fastest qualifying heat. Angela's name, of course, was there. She'd taken my place just as she had at the trials.

Better not to think about Angela at all, I told myself, recalling Coach's words. Better to concentrate on my own race. Carefully, I went over Coach's instructions in my mind, shutting out the milling crowd around me, swimming my race perfectly, over and over again in my head, always perfectly.

"Would you like an orange?"

Without looking, I knew whose voice it was. "It's good for quick energy," continued Angela, holding the orange out to me.

"No thanks," I said. "I've got all I need." I saw that she was about to sit down next to me, so I added, "I don't like to talk before a race."

She nodded sympathetically. "I get uptight, too. The butterflies are free," she said with a nervous laugh.

For a moment I felt a little better toward her, knowing that she had the jitters, too. Then I remembered that she didn't have to worry.

"You'll be an easy winner," I said.

"You never know," she replied uncertainly.

My heat was called. Up on the blocks, I willed my muscles into obedience, alert for the starter's commands. At the gun, I cut into the top of the water smoothly.

I swam exactly as I had been imagining it before the race, acting out the pictures in my mind. I felt the water stream past me, smooth, steady, and swift. When I finished, I was certain I had done my best in that heat.

Overwhelmed by exhaustion, I sat on the deck for several minutes, eyes closed, totally spent. I knew I was missing Angela's heat, but I was too tired to care.

The sound of the announcer's voice was like a crackling firecracker of hope bursting through my fatigue. Then I heard my name. I'd made it!

I also heard Angela's name, but it was several minutes before I realized that my name had been called last. That meant my time had been better. Figuring there must have been a mistake, I checked the official postings; but there were our times with mine four seconds faster.

Heading for the gym, where all the swimmers rest and wait for the heats to be called, I saw Angela sitting with her back against the wall alone. Her shoulders were rounded in a slump.

It could be me, I whispered to myself, remembering what it feels like to mess up a race. There's no worse anger than the kind you feel toward yourself when you've ruined something you care about. I knew how she felt, and I also knew there was no way I could make up for the way I had acted. But I just had to try.

"I don't talk before races, but I do talk after them. Sometimes it helps," I said, knowing Angela had every right to tell me to go drown myself.

"Talk if you want to," she murmured.

"Well, I will, but I was hoping you'd talk, too."

She hesitated, and I saw her trying to swallow. "I will as soon as I'm sure I'm not going to cry," she whispered.

So I babbled on for a few minutes about the meet, some of the other swimmers, the team standings, anything. I knew it didn't matter what I said as long as I kept talking.

All at once, Angela interrupted my opinion of the snack bar's hamburgers. "I do this all the time," she burst out. "I do great at workouts; then comes a meet, and something happens. I just can't do it."

"Maybe you don't know how to play the confidence game," I

said. She looked at me suspiciously, but I went on. "How do you psych yourself up for a race?"

"I don't exactly." She was twisting the ends of the towel into tiny corkscrews. "I just try to block it out, not think about it."

"What about during a race?"

"I concentrate on not making mistakes."

"Very negative methods," I commented.

"What do you mean?"

"Well, take my positive approach. First, I think about all the good things I've done in previous races. Then I plan my upcoming race carefully, going over each detail in my mind, picturing myself the perfect swimmer. Then when I'm in the water, I tell myself to do it again, only this time for real."

"And you win," Angela added with a smile. Now I really felt bad, remembering how I had acted when Angela had done better than I in workouts.

"Listen, I have an idea," I said. Maybe I *could* make it up to her. "You swim faster than I do, right?" Angela looked doubtful.

"Yes, you do, that's an objective fact," I insisted. "Now my idea is that you use me as a pacer in the backstroke final this afternoon."

At first Angela wasn't sure, but I soon had her convinced; and we were planning our strategy when Coach showed up.

"What's going on here?" He gave me an accusing look.

"We've got it all settled," Angela spoke up. "Tobi and I are going to be a team from now on."

"All right!" he said, giving us a smile usually reserved for winners.

As Angela and I sat together on the ready bench, I had conflicting thoughts about helping her. What was I doing anyway? Handing her my relay position on a silver platter, that's what.

I hadn't time to get worked up over it, though, because the whistle blew, and we stepped up to the blocks. At the sound of the gun I was into the water with barely a splash, skimming the surface like a water bug.

As I reached the wall, I pretended all my strength was in my

legs as I flipped and pushed off. Pull hard, hard, hard, I told myself, muscles aching from the effort. Then on the last lap, I concentrated on a single word. Win! I shot through the water and strained for the finish.

Immediately, I looked to Angela's lane. She was there, but it was too close to tell who had won. She gave me the thumbs up sign, and I returned it.

I stared at the electronic scoreboard. Usually it didn't take long for the times to appear, but now it remained blank for so long I was beginning to worry that a fuse had blown.

*Please, please let me be the winner*, I whispered over and over. Finally, the winning times flashed on. I blinked away the chlorine haze, or maybe tears. Angela had won. I managed to give her a congratulatory hug.

"I couldn't have done it without you, Tobi," she bubbled.

"You did it, girls!" Coach couldn't keep himself from shouting, he was so excited. "You've just raced yourself to the Nationals!"

I had never felt so left out, so disappointed in my whole life. "Well, at least Angela has," I said, struggling to smile.

Coach looked startled. "And you did, too, Tobi."

What was he talking about? "I saw that Angela won the place on our relay team."

"That's right, but you missed something. You both swam so fast that you made qualifying times for the *individual* backstroke event!"

I was stunned. I had concentrated so hard on the relay place I hadn't even thought about the individual events.

"So you'll both go to the Nationals!" Coach couldn't resist doing a couple of dance steps, and I was so ecstatic, I joined him. But a wet concrete swim deck is not an ideal dance floor.

"Look out!" yelled Angela, as we just missed falling into the water. "I don't want my partner to break a leg. We've got a long way to go before the Olympics."

"What?" I gasped.

"Just doing some positive mental rehearsing," she grinned.

"A little confidence sure goes a long way," I retorted.

Still, maybe that *is* something to think about!

## Reader's Response

Do you think Tobi did the right thing when she shared her ideas on winning with Angela? Explain.

## Thinking It Over

1. Summarize what happened on Angela's first day of swim practice.
2. Why was the Riverdale Meet so important?
3. What is the confidence game? How did you figure it out?
4. Why do you think Tobi decided to help Angela?
5. What do you think the story might be saying about human nature?

## Appreciating Literature

Pat Carr often uses figures of speech to describe her character's feelings: "My jealous feelings were like a current I couldn't swim against." Notice how this simile conveys the feeling of helplessness against the emotion as well as a sense that she tried to struggle against it. Look for other uses of figurative language and explain why you think the author uses them.

## Writing to Learn

**THINK AND COMPARE** Think about the personal characteristics of Tobi and Angela. In many ways they were alike, and in many ways they were different. Copy and complete the diagram below to list their likenesses and differences.

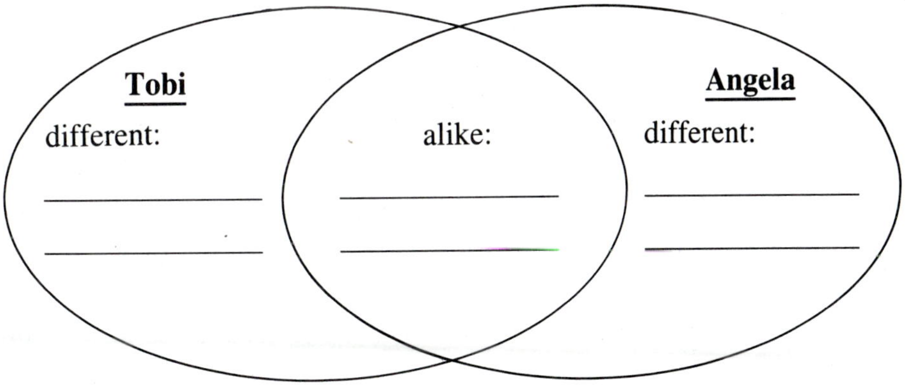


**WRITE** Make a prediction. Write a paragraph explaining which girl you think will be the most successful at the national competitions, and explain why. Use the information in your diagram to help you decide.

# Independence Hall

by Charles Kuralt

*Once upon a time a decision was made at Independence Hall, and that decision has affected all our lives from that day to this.*

"I say let us wait." John Dickinson of Pennsylvania stood in this hall, July 1st, 1776, and begged the Continental Congress to be reasonable. "The time is not yet ripe for proclaiming independence. Instead of help from foreign powers, it will bring us disaster. I say we ought to hold back any declaration and remain the masters of our fate and our fame. All of Great Britain is armed against us. The wealth of the Empire is poured into her treasury. We shall weep at our folly."

John Dickinson was not a timid or frightened man. He was a great old Quaker patriot, and he had a good argument. At the moment he spoke, British grenadiers were sweeping down from Canada, British guns were bombarding Charleston, and just ninety miles away an incredible British armada was entering New York harbor—five hundred ships carrying thirty-two thousand troops, the best army in the world. That army could march to Philadelphia and take this building and arrest this Congress any afternoon it chose to do so. So John Dickinson pleaded, "Let us not brave the storm in a paper boat."

The delegates paid him respectful attention. John Adams and his cousin, Sam, hot for independence, impatient with the delay, sat listening. Thomas Jefferson sat back in the corner. He had already written the Declaration of Independence. It spoke his thoughts. Beside him, old Benjamin Franklin, also silent, his mind made up.

But every mind was not made up. Pennsylvania and South Carolina were opposed to independence; Delaware was divided; New York undecided. All through the spring and into the summer they had sat here and wrangled, their tempers growing hot with the season. Young Edward Rutledge of South Carolina had said of John Adams and the New Englanders, "They will bring us ruin. I dread their low cunning and those leveling principles which men without character and without fortune possess." And John Adams had said of Rutledge, "Rutledge is a perfect bobolink, a swallow, a sparrow, a peacock, excessively vain, excessively weak."

Now, Rutledge and Adams and the rest listened to John Dickinson speaking gravely from the heart: "Declaring our independence at a time like this is like burning down our house before we have another."

It was John Adams who rose to his feet. He was not John Dickinson's equal as a speaker, and everything he had to say he had said before. He never said it better than on that July afternoon: "We've been duped and bubbled by the phantom of peace. What is the real choice before us? If we postpone the declaration, do we mean to submit? Do we consent to yield and become a conquered people?

No, we do not! We shall fight! We shall fight with whatever means we have—with rusty muskets and broken flints, with bows and arrows, if need be. Then why put off the declaration? For myself, I can only say this: I have crossed the Rubicon. All that I have, all that I am, all that I hope for in this life, I stake on our cause. For me, the die is cast. Sink or swim, live or die, to survive or perish with my country—that is my unalterable resolution!"

That night, John Dickinson went home, put on his militia uniform, and rode away to join his regiment. He could not vote for independence, but he could fight the British. That night, Edward Rutledge changed his mind. South Carolina would not stand in the way of unanimity. That night, Caesar Rodney, a man dying of cancer, rode through the night on horseback in a storm to Philadelphia to cast the deciding vote for Delaware. And so, when secretary Charles Thomson called the roll on July 2nd, of the twelve colonies voting, all twelve voted for independence. It was done. What remained was the declaring of it.

The next morning, July 3rd, an anonymous note was found on President Hancock's table. It said, "You have gone too far. Take care. A plot is framed for your destruction, and all of you shall be destroyed." It suddenly occurred to them that there might be a lighted powder keg under the floor; there was an uproar. There were volunteers to search the cellar. Then crusty old Joseph Hewes of North Carolina stood up to say, "Mr. President, I am against wasting any time searching cellars. I would as soon be blown to pieces as proclaim to the world that I was frightened by a note."

Without searching any cellars, the Continental Congress proceeded to a consideration of the Declaration of Independence. They're immortal words now, but of course they weren't when Charles Thomson read them for the first time: "When in the Course of human events. . ." And for two days Jefferson sat back in the corner and fumed as they all toyed with his masterpiece. "Did we really have to call the King a tyrant quite so often?" They changed some of the "tyrants" back to "King." "Did we have to bid the British people our everlasting adieu[1]?" They struck that out. And Jefferson's mightiest passage, his denunciation of slavery, that was struck

[1]adieu (ä - dyoo′): good-bye

out, too, at the insistence of Georgia and South Carolina. Jefferson wrote elsewhere, "Nothing is more certainly written in the book of fate than that these people are to be free."

But finally, all the cuts and changes were done, and what remained was a document still noble enough to inspire the tired delegates and bold enough to hang them all. It was read through one more time to the end: ". . . And for the support of this Declaration, with a firm reliance on the Protection of Divine Providence, we mutually pledge to each other our Lives, our Fortunes and our sacred Honor." There was one final vote, and President Hancock announced the result with the use of a new phrase: "The Declaration of the United States of America is unanimously agreed to." There was no cheering, no fireworks; not yet. The delegates simply walked out into the night of the Fourth of July thinking their own thoughts, some of them no doubt remembering what John Dickinson had said: "This is like burning down our house before we have another." Others hearing Tom Paine: "The birthday of a new world is at hand. We have it in our power to begin the world all over again."

John Adams walked to his boarding house to write a letter to a friend. "Well," he said, "the river is passed. The bridge is cut away."

## *Reader's Response*

Which of the people at the Continental Congress would you like to have talked to, and why?

## Thinking It Over

1. Compare John Adams and John Dickinson's arguments regarding the proclamation of independence.
2. Why do you think John Dickinson put on his militia uniform and joined his regiment?
3. What do you think was meant by the statement that the Declaration of Independence was "still noble enough to inspire the tired delegates and bold enough to hang them all"?
4. Why do you think there was no cheering after the delegates had unanimously agreed to the Declaration of Independence?
5. The final statement is, "The river is passed. The bridge is cut away." What does this mean? How do you know?

## Appreciating Literature

In this selection, Charles Kuralt reports on events that occurred over two hundred years ago in a way that makes them come alive for the reader. Think about how Kuralt achieves this dramatic effect. How is this description of the Continental Congress different from what you've read in your history books?

## Writing to Learn

**THINK AND DECIDE** The Declaration of Independence grew from strong minds and determined wills. Find three quotations from the article that favor the American Revolution, and three that oppose it.

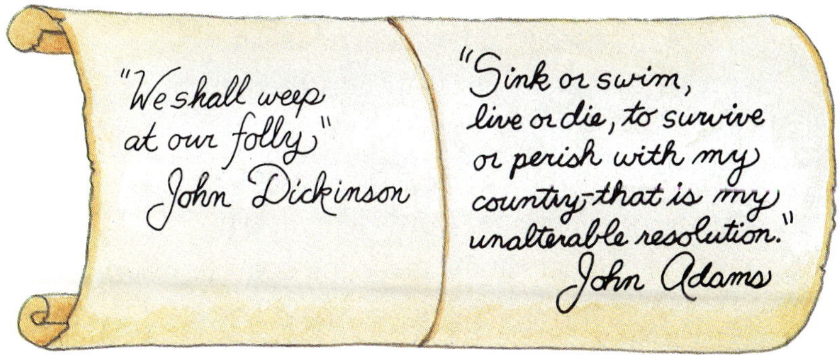


**WRITE** If you were casting a vote on July 4, 1776, what stand would you take? To explain why you chose to vote as you did, write a quotation for yourself.

A LESSON IN HISTORY—DECORATION-DAY, 1881, *lithograph by S. G. McCutcheon.*

# Refugee in America

There are words like *Freedom*
Sweet and wonderful to say.
On my heart-strings freedom sings
All day everyday.

There are words like *Liberty*
That almost make me cry.
If you had known what I knew
You would know why.

LANGSTON HUGHES

# Women

They were women then
My mama's generation
Husky of voice—Stout of
Step
With fists as well as
Hands
How they battered down
Doors
And ironed
Starched white
Shirts
How they led
Armies
Headragged Generals
Across mined
Fields
Booby-trapped
Ditches
To discover books
Desks
A place for us
How they knew what we
*Must* know
Without knowing a page
Of it
Themselves.

ALICE WALKER

*from The Rhode Island Black Heritage Society*

*In the year 1810, choosing a motto for her sampler seems to be the most pressing decision Elizabeth Douglas has to make . . . until, suddenly, her everyday routine is shattered.*

Because the Lloyds' household was a very regular one, Elizabeth sat down every afternoon at exactly the same hour to sew on her sampler. Sewing was no easy task for an active girl who liked to be doing other things. But nobody, of course, ever thought of excusing her from it or ever dreamed of her growing up without having covered at least one square of linen with neat letters and figures.

The sampler was supposed to give her practice in all the different stitches of embroidery. Below the alphabet and the figures up to ten it showed a small, carefully outlined picture of a willow tree and a tombstone. It was to be finished with her name and a motto such as *The good die young* or *Waste not, want not.*

There was so much to do in that thick-walled stone house, looking from its low hill out upon the bay, that there was no real

Award
Winning
Author

time during the day when any older person could say with reason, "Elizabeth, you should be at your sewing." But when candlelight came—when the baking and sweeping, the dressing of chickens, and the curing of hams could not go forward so quickly by the dimmer light, then it was that her mother always said, "Now, Elizabeth," and the girl knew the sampler could not be avoided. It never occurred to her to hate it; she only knew that she liked doing anything else a great deal better.

She had sat down to it this October evening, with a wild wind swinging about the house and making the waves crash upon the shore below the hill. Elizabeth was alone, or almost alone; for her father and mother had driven five miles to the nearest town for the weekly marketing and had left Elizabeth with only deaf old Nora, the cook, who, as everyone knew, would fall asleep in her rocking chair in the little room above the kitchen the moment the last of the work was finished.

Not even the wind that blew in around the deep-framed windows, setting the candles to flickering—not even the slamming of the shutters—could rouse her. But as Elizabeth paused to slip the end of a thread into the slim eye of her needle there came a sound that, it seemed, would wake any sleeper on earth. *Boom!*

The great crash sounded from out on the water, where just at twilight she had looked out to see the smooth surface of the bay with not even a fishing boat in sight. *Boom!* This time all the windows in the house rattled and the glasses clattered on the dresser. *Boom!* The sound came a third time.

Elizabeth jumped up and ran to the window. What could it be? This was a time of peace, the year of 1810. It had been thirty years since the guns of the Revolution had echoed along those shores, and it would be two more years before another war was to break out between England and America.

She wondered for a puzzled minute if it could be pirates. It was quite true that pirates had landed on this coast within the memory of people not very much older than herself. She pressed her face against the pane, trying to peer out. How black it was outside! Yet there beyond the point was the ghostly form of a ship, dark against the duller darkness of the water. It was a bigger ship than those that usually came up the bay. She saw a great flash of red flame as once again a cannon crashed, and against its light she could make out, near the shore and struggling on the top of a towering wave, the dark shape of a small boat with three men in it.

The blackness shut down again and there was nothing to be heard except the roaring of the wind. Then in a moment of brief calm there came a sound more surprising than any she had yet heard—a voice, little and distant, calling out, calling her own name.

"Elizabeth! Elizabeth Lloyd!"

She rushed to the door, lifted the latch, and immediately felt the wind snatch it from her hand and swing it wide, letting in a driving splatter of rain. Old Nora had actually been awakened by the cannon shots, which shook the house, and was thumping down the stairs. Elizabeth stood on the sill, holding back the door so that all the light that was possible would come shining out upon the darkness of the night.

The men in the boat needed a signal to guide them to the strip of beach just below the house. Her flash of light seemed to have shown them the direction; for she was almost certain that she heard, in another quiet moment, the sound of the bow on the gravel. She waited. How the wind roared!

Again there was a crash of the ship's cannon, its report followed a moment later by the splitting of wood. Voices and the tramp of feet were coming up the path. Somebody said, "They got our boat that time." And a deeper voice answered: "It's lucky we were no longer in it. Go easy there, mate; he's too tired to move another step." Three figures came out of the darkness, two of them supporting a third. The little group stumbled across the doorstep and stood blinking in the light of the warm kitchen.

Elizabeth closed the door against the rain and, as is always the duty of a hostess when guests come in out of the cold and wet, bent to put another log on the fire. One did that and then asked questions. But when she straightened up to look at the unexpected visitors, she had no need to ask. She cried out quickly, "Why, it's Cousin Nathaniel!"

"We thought this must be my uncle's house and that you at least would hear our hail."

Her cousin Nathaniel Holmes was only a year or two older than her own fourteen years; but he looked like a man indeed with his tall figure, his white, tired face, and his rough seaman's coat.

The broad-shouldered man beside him said in a big, friendly voice, "'Tis a shame to frighten you, young mistress, but men who are fleeing for their lives will take shelter anywhere."

"You did not frighten me," she answered bravely.

They were helping their comrade into the armchair in which she had been sitting. When once the tall man with graying hair had dropped back on the cushions, her cousin Nat stooped, picked something off the floor, and handed it to her.

"Your sampler, Elizabeth," he said with a broad smile. "I know how you love to sew, and I see how prettily you have made the

tombstone. I fear you are to be badly interrupted in your favorite work this night. You wonder why we are here? Have you ever heard men speak of the custom of the British Navy—that of taking seamen by force?"

She had indeed, and her cheeks colored angrily as she thought of it. All America was excited over this same matter, which was to end by leading two friendly nations into war with each other. England had need of sailors and gunners for her warships, and since the life on board was hard, cruel, and dangerous, very few men would offer themselves for it. As a result the officers were ordered by their government to take men where they could, and take them they did.

They had fallen into the way of stopping American vessels at sea, searching them, and declaring that certain able seamen were really British and must be carried on board English ships to serve

in His Majesty's Navy. It was of little use for the American captains to fight against them. The English battleships always had a row of cannon with which to back up their demands. Many a good man was rowed away and taken on board a proud, tall-sailed English vessel, each looking back to his own ship and to his comrades, who perhaps he was never to see again. But here it seemed were three, at least, who had dared to refuse and had made this bold effort to escape.

"Yes," Nat said, looking up to answer the question in Elizabeth's eyes, "they took us all three, though Bo'sun Leonard here is an old sailor, and though I am not yet a real seaman, for I sailed only six months ago. We swore to one another that we were not going to fight for the British king."

He held out his thin, cold hands to the blaze, saying no more, for he did not seem to think it was necessary to tell just what they had done. It was the broad-shouldered man, Dan Peters, who finished the account. He gave it in the most matter-of-fact way in the world. It was plain to see that all three were too weary to think of much of anything except that they were warm and safe here, at least for a few minutes.

Peters told of how they were carried away in a boat with four British sailors and a lieutenant, all armed with pistols and heavy swords. They made Peters pull an oar in the middle of the boat; but as they came near the towering side of the British vessel he saw, to his amazement, that Nat had leaped up to seize the officer around the middle, pinning his arms so that he could not draw his sword. The brief, hard struggle ended in the lieutenant's being flung overboard, while the two older Americans each fought with the sailor nearest him.

"We swung them over the side like sacks of gravel," Peters related cheerfully. "They were so taken by surprise that they had no time to fight. The last one jumped to save us the trouble, and we caught up the oars and slipped away into the twilight, for it was just beginning to get dark. All those we dropped overboard got to the ship, and before she could get her cannon aimed at us we were in among the islands. But we didn't dare land anywhere along the swampy shores."

The war vessel had followed, most of the shots from it going wide in the dark, but a few of them were good guesses that almost hit their mark. Higher and higher up the bay they had come, the men in the boat fighting so hard against the wind and tide that Leonard, the old sailor, was fainting at the oars, and even the other two could scarcely lift and dip the heavy blades.

"Then we saw your light."

Old Nora, like Elizabeth, had without a word turned herself to caring for the comfort of the guests. She brought a great bowl of stew from the cupboard, poured it into a big iron kettle, and hung the kettle on the swinging hook. Nat helped her to lift it, and she nodded thanks and greeting to him, but she asked no questions. She had been deaf so long that she was used to the idea of not having things explained to her. She trotted back and forth, casting curious looks at the weary and dripping guests, but she stirred and seasoned the soup, cut bread from the long loaf, and said nothing. Elizabeth, however, kept no such silence.

"What will you do next?" she asked, looking from one to the other.

They were all three quiet, so that the beat of the rain outside and the harsh voice of the wind were the only sounds. The storm roared, then dropped an instant, and in the stillness there came to all of them the sound that no person who lives by the sea can ever fail to recognize—the creak of oars in their oarlocks. Even Bo'sun Leonard, sitting with closed eyes in the big chair, heard it and raised his drooping head.

"It's only a matter of minutes before they'll be here." It was the first time he had spoken, but his words were quick and very clear. "They can't fail to visit the only house that's in sight. You're to go on, you two. Do you hear me? That's orders. I can't move; but you're to get away, and I will stay here."

It is the habit of every sailor to obey the commands of his superior. Nat and Peters hesitated a minute. Then Nat turned suddenly to the door of the bedroom opening from the kitchen. "Carry him in there," he said. "There's no time even to get him upstairs. And by some chance they may not search the house."

They lifted Leonard, bore him into the room, and laid him on the bed. He did not speak again or even open his eyes, but he made an impatient motion with his hand. They were to go.

"If we could get across the hill to the Mallory's house," Nat said, "we could get Ephraim Mallory and his three sons to stand by us, that I know. We could make a dash back and get Leonard away safe, even if the British had already laid hands on him. But if harm should come to you, Elizabeth—"

"No harm will come to us—two women who have done nothing," Elizabeth answered boldly, more boldly than she felt. "We will keep them back as long as we can." She put her mouth close to Nora's ear and shouted. "We are going to have still more guests. Pile up the fire and bring out the biggest ham."

Nat hesitated a moment in the doorway. Peters said, as he

went through the door, "And if they do follow us, little mistress, would you try to flash a light at the window, maybe, if you could do it without danger? Then we would know where to make a stand." The door banged, and Elizabeth was left in the kitchen, listening.

The wind, roaring over the hill, drowned the noise of their retreating steps, but in the shelter of the house another sound began to be very plain, the heavy, orderly tramp of marching feet coming up from the landing—many of them, it seemed, oh, very many. Then there were voices, a thundering knock, and a command, "Open, in the king's name."

They all came in together—a tall officer wrapped in a dripping cape, a file of men behind him, their shoes, their hair, their rough blue coats streaming with the rain.

Elizabeth made her most polite curtsy, just as she had seen her mother do when important guests arrived. "My parents are from home," she said calmly, "but we shall do our best to make you comfortable. You—you look as though you might be in need of refreshment."

The officer—it might possibly have been the same lieutenant whom Nat had thrown out of the boat—swung his rapid glance about the room. The big, spotless kitchen was bright with the leaping fire and its reflection in the polished copper pots and pans. Elizabeth was laying a white cloth on the long table. Nora had unwrapped the ham and was already cutting delicate, rosy slices. The officer looked, hesitated, and then sat down in the big chair.

"The men will march better if they have some food," he said. "That was a long row we had, searching along the shore. Dobbs, go out and see that guards are placed around the house. If there is anyone hiding here it will be impossible to get away while they are watching. We may as well give ourselves the relief of a little warmth and food and look for those runaway rascals later on. Well, young woman, let me see what your house has to offer."

It was a splendid feast that the old farmhouse gave its guests that night. The whitest linen out of the great chest in the parlor, the glass dishes and the blue plates that had come from England with Elizabeth's great grandmother, the polished silver spoons were all brought forth. The choicest preserves, the last vegetables from the garden, the ham cured by a recipe a hundred years old made a supper fit for King George III himself instead of one of his lower and lazier officers. "Have you this?" the blue-uniformed man would ask now and again. "Do you not have that?"

"In a minute, sir; in just a minute," Elizabeth would answer. She lingered over the serving as long as she dared, she ducked curtsies when she received an order, she did everything to make the meal last a little longer.

Nora went back and forth, waiting on the men who sat humbly upon the benches by the fire while their commander dined alone at the long table. It was fortunate that farmhouses of that day had generous supplies in their storerooms. A large company it was, ten men, with even larger appetites.

The minutes went by, oh, so slowly. Nat and his comrade would be across the farm, Elizabeth was thinking; they would be climbing the hill; once over the top they would be within reach of the Mallory's house. How long, how very long it took to reach shelter on this stormy night. But time was passing. Triumph colored her cheeks. They were growing safer every minute, safer . . . .

"And now," ordered the British officer, pushing his chair back suddenly, "I have even a mind to lay me down to take a little rest before I start out in the storm again. Light me a candle. I will go into the bedroom yonder and sleep a little."

*No! Oh, no!* Elizabeth had almost cried out the words in her terror, but she put her hand over her mouth and held them back. "We have better rooms above," she managed to say, her voice shaking, "if it would please you just to walk up the stairs."

"In an American farmhouse the best bed is always in the spare chamber below," he answered stubbornly. "I have been on shore often enough to learn that." He yawned widely and got up. "In our wandering life we must learn how to sleep comfortably when we can."

He walked across the kitchen. Elizabeth had lighted the candle and stood shaking, holding out her arm to bar the door. How, how could she stop him? She looked hopefully past him to old Nora beside the fire. Could not Nora think of something? But no, what did she understand?

The officer stopped, staring at her as she barred the way. His heavy brows drew together in a suspicious frown. "What is this? You have, after all, something hidden in that room? Out of my way!" He stepped forward.

Old Nora dropped a spoon with a great clatter. She took one limping step across the floor and flung the kitchen door wide open. "Don't waste time," she cried in her trembling old voice. "It was that way they went. Can't you see the marks of their feet beyond the doorstone? Go, if you have any hope of catching them."

There was a thump of heavy feet, a clash of swords drawn, a hail of orders as the men jumped up, seized their arms, and swung toward the door. The officer snatched up his cloak. "Why did you not tell me this before?" he roared at Nora.

"Eh? I'm so deaf, how was I to know your errand? Nobody tells me anything." He was over the sill, but he swung around on the doorstep to give a final order.

"Dobbs, stand here and do not let either of these women pass. Keep three men to guard the windows so that they cannot make a signal. Do not follow us until we are well away." He was gone, and the door slammed behind him.

Elizabeth stood for a second trembling, wondering what she should do next. Then she seized a lantern from its hook on the wall, lighted it at the fire, and sped up the stairs. The door as well as the windows was guarded, but the men would not be watching that little round opening, hardly a real window, just above the roof of the kitchen.

She was beside it; she had wrapped her skirt about the lantern to hide its light; and she had climbed out through the space, which was little bigger than the porthole of a ship. The shingles on the roof below were wet and slippery, but she knew how to run across them, knew that she must keep running or she would fall. She ended with a bump against the stone chimney. Steadying herself with one arm against the warm, rough stones, she made her way around the chimney and was on the peak of the kitchen roof, facing the distant hill.

Fearlessly she swung the lantern once, and again and again. A deep voice below shouted to her to stop. She took no notice, and suddenly, a humming bullet went past her and hit against the chimney. The crash of the big pistol would give warning, even if the swinging light was not enough. Nat and his companion would know that the British were coming behind them. The lantern fell

from her hand and broke on the stones below, but she had given her wild signal of danger and could do no more.

It had taken but a few seconds to run across the roof, but now it was slow minutes as she crawled back in the wind and the wet. Once inside and downstairs, she stood close to Nora by the fire. Her knees felt suddenly like water and her voice was trembling.

"Nora," she said close to the old woman's ear, "how could you tell them where Nat had gone?"

"It was better to give the old one a chance, even at the cost of a bit of danger to the young ones," answered Nora. "Yes, you told me nothing, but it did not take me long to guess what was going on. I saw the Revolution; I've been by before this when hunted men were hiding from their enemies." She drew a great breath and smoothed her apron. "Sakes, but we have a lot of dishes to wash up. Men do be great ones for messing a kitchen!"

Elizabeth was not of much help in setting the place to rights. Again and again she stood at the back door, straining to hear any sound that the wind might carry. Was that a distant shout and another? What was that? Voices that were far-off. They were nearer; they were coming this way. Had they taken her cousin? Would they in the end lay hands on poor Bo'sun Leonard, lying helpless within? Oh, Nat! Oh, Nat!

There was shouting and stumbling before the door. It swung back, and a dripping figure, sword in hand, was on the doorstep. Here was no blue coat or gold lace; here was no heavy British seaman. This thin, long figure could be only one person—her cousin Nat!

Nathaniel threw his weapon down upon the table, where there were still standing the dishes and glasses that had been used for the lieutenant's dinner.

"'Tis the wrong men who have feasted in this house tonight," he said. "Such a dinner! And we out there in the dark, hungry! May the Mallory boys come in?"

There was enough left, for the farmhouse could feed one company and still have plenty remaining for another. Nora, smiling broadly, brought them more and more food; the fire leaped on the hearth, and everyone together tried to give an account of what had happened. Nat and Peters were just coming over the hill with the Mallorys behind them when they saw Elizabeth's signal and found a favorable place to make a stand against the advancing British.

"They could not guess our numbers in the dark, and they decided, after the first attack, to retreat to their boat," Nat said. "They will have a pretty row out to their ship, for she has had to stand offshore in this wind. Here's a pleasant journey to them, and may they take profit by the lesson they have learned. It is not well to lay hands on American seamen."

"The whole British nation may learn an even better one in time," Dan Peters added; but most of his remark was lost in the hollow of the cup of cider he had raised to his lips.

It was easy to see by looking at Bo'sun Leonard that he must stay where he was for many days. Perhaps, indeed, he would never be able to go to sea again. But the other two stood up at last and said good night.

"We have to join our ship," Nathaniel said. "Our skipper will be in need of sailors, and he was to stop at Norfolk, where we can meet him." The night's adventures seemed to mean little to men whose days and hours were passed among the dangers of the sea. "No, we can spend no more time except to offer you our thanks, Elizabeth Lloyd."

Two hours later Elizabeth's father and mother came home. Their daughter was sitting by the table, quietly stitching away at the task that she had begun so much earlier. She looked up as her parents came in.

"There is a guest in the spare chamber," she remarked calmly, "and there have been others here to supper. And see, Mother, I have finished my willow tree. Instead of the verse at the bottom I am going to embroider *Liberty forever*. And then I am never going to sew another sampler. I think, now that I am fourteen, that I have other things to do besides stitching pictures of tombstones."

### ♦ LIBRARY LINK ♦

*If you enjoyed Cornelia Meigs's short story, you might want to read Paula Fox's* The Slave Dancer.

## Reader's Response

Do you think Elizabeth was unusually courageous for a person in her situation? Explain why or why not.

## Thinking It Over

1. Summarize the main events of the story. How would you explain to another student the way you worked out your summary?
2. What custom of the British Navy was described in this story?
3. What do you think was Elizabeth's bravest act?
4. What do you think was symbolized by the sampler in the story?

## Appreciating Literature

In this story, notice how the author helps the reader to experience the setting through the senses of hearing and sight. When Elizabeth hears the boom of the cannon and runs to the window, the reader feels a sense of isolation and helplessness at the fury of the elements—the wind and the waves, and the blackness of the night. How do you think the description of the setting contributes to the mood of the story?

## Writing to Learn

**THINK AND EVALUATE** Elizabeth, Nat, and Nora each made a decision that required courage, but which decision required the *most* courage? Copy the decisions below in the order you decide on—from most courageous to least courageous.

**Decision 1:** Elizabeth decides to risk her own life by flashing a lamp and giving a warning to her cousin Nat and his friends.

**Decision 2:** Nat decides to risk the lives of the Lloyds by leaving a wounded seaman with them.

**Decision 3:** Nora decides to risk the lives of the American seamen when she tells the British that the runaway seamen had been there.

**WRITE** Write a paragraph telling which decision you felt required the most courage, and give reasons to support your opinion.

# Literature Link

## *How can you remember the key points of an article?*

Look at these classified advertisements. Isn't it amazing how much information these ads can cram into such a tiny space?

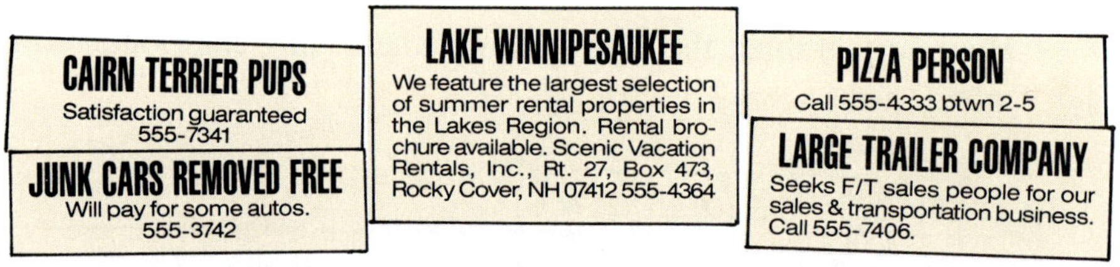


Classified advertisers choose their words carefully, including only the most important points. You can probably figure out why they use this strategy. First of all, they need to get and hold the attention of a reader who is scanning the ads for quick information about what's for sale. In addition, since the advertisers must pay for the amount of newspaper space they use, short ads save them money.

You can also put summarizing to good use when you read. Summing up information may not save you money, but it can certainly help you understand and remember the key points of an article.

### *What's the Point?*

In Unit 1, you practiced the strategy of paraphrasing. By putting ideas into your own words, you learned to check your understanding of detailed information. When you paraphrase, it is important to cover each detail, so it is not important to be brief. When you summarize you also use you own words, but you focus only on important points, using the fewest words possible.

A good way to practice summarizing is to write one sentence to sum up one paragraph. Try writing a one-sentence summary for this paragraph from "Mystery of Loch Ness." Don't get lost in the details. Keep your sentence brief and to the point.

> The sightings do not appear to fit any particular pattern, and the observers often confuse shape, size, and speed, and sometimes can't tell the head from the tail, but there is an uncanny similarity to the way the said animals are described as moving—with, for example, bursts of speed and side splashing, as might be produced by those flipper-like "appendages." And at the same time, so many of the eyewitness reports agree on color (generally black or gray) and on the location of sightings (around the mouths of rivers running into the loch).

Did you focus only on the most important points when writing your summary? If so, your sentence might read something like this:

> People disagree about details, but they tend to agree about the Monster's movements, color, and location of sightings.

Of course, your summary will be expressed in your own words. As with paraphrasing, it's *your own words* that demonstrate that *you* understand what you have read.

## *A Record of Your Understanding*

You can see that if you read a whole article, stopping from time to time to write one-sentence summaries of the main points, you would have a good grasp of the information and a record of the important ideas that you want to remember. So try these tips as you practice summarizing:

- Concentrate on one paragraph at a time to make sure you understand the point of each paragraph.
- Identify the main idea. For long paragraphs, you may want to make a list of key points.
- Use only the most important points to write a one-sentence summary. Don't include unimportant details.
- When you have completed the article, you can use your summary sentences as a summary of the article.

As you get better at using this strategy, you may find it better to write a summary sentence for a few paragraphs at a time. It depends on how an author organizes the information. At the start, it's probably a good idea to summarize just one paragraph at a time.

Here's another paragraph from the Loch Ness Monster article. When you're finished reading, practice writing a sentence summary.

> Next in the circumstantial case for the Loch Ness Monster are the pictures, which have been of all kinds, still and motion picture, color and black and white, made on and beneath the surface. Although only two dozen or so pictures have survived to fit the label "Loch Ness Monster," and although all—without exception—are controversial, they all have been taken by seemingly reputable people. Some of the photographers have been amateurs, it is true, but some, such as Harold Edgerton, the MIT (Massachusetts Institute of Technology) professor who is world-renowned for his skill at designing underwater photographic equipment, are highly skilled professionals.

Is your summary sentence brief and to the point? See if you think this sentence does the job as well as yours:

> While all photographs of the Monster are controversial, they were taken by photographers who seem reputable, including some professionals.

Notice the details that were omitted from the summary. Did you omit the same details?

The biographical article "Free at Last" is filled with the details of the life of Dr. Martin Luther King, Jr. Use the summary-sentence strategy to focus your understanding on the key points of the article.

# FREE at LAST
## by Coretta Scott King

*Martin Luther King, Jr., was a man who felt that his country would fulfill its dream of "liberty and justice for all" if there were racial equality and dignity for all Americans. He and his wife, Coretta Scott King, worked for justice in many places and many ways in the 1950s and 60s.*

My husband, Martin Luther King, Jr., was a man who had hoped to be a Baptist preacher in a large, southern, urban congregation. Instead, by the time he died in 1968, he had led millions of people into shattering forever the southern system of segregation of the races. He had fashioned a mass black electorate that eliminated overt racism from political campaigns and accumulated political power for blacks beyond any they had ever possessed in the United States. Above all, he brought a new and higher dimension of human dignity to black people's lives.

I met Martin in Boston in 1952, when he was twenty-three years old. I had grown up in rural Alabama, attended Antioch College in Ohio, and was studying music at the New England Conservatory. Martin was working toward a doctor of philosophy degree at Boston University. Before coming to Boston, Martin had earned a B.A. in sociology from Morehouse College in Atlanta and a B.D. from Crozer Theological Seminary in Pennsylvania. His father, Reverend Martin Luther King, Sr., a sharecropper's son, was pastor of the Ebenezer Baptist Church in Atlanta. His mother, Alberta Williams King, was a minister's daughter. Martin felt a deeply serious call to the ministry when he was a seventeen-year-old junior at Morehouse. At the age of eighteen he was ordained and made an assistant pastor at Ebenezer Church. I thought I did not want to marry a minister, but Martin was an unusual person. He was such a good man. If he ever did something a little wrong, or committed a selfish act, his conscience devoured him. At the same time he was so alive and so much fun to be with. He had a strength that he imparted to me and others that he met.

Martin always had a deep commitment to helping his fellow human beings. He told me that the turning point in his thinking came while he was at the seminary, when he learned about the revered Indian leader, Mahatma Gandhi. From Gandhi's philosophy of love and nonviolence, Martin discovered the method for social reform that he had been seeking for so many months.

Martin and I were married in 1953. The next year, Martin took up his first pastorate, at the Dexter Avenue Church in Montgomery, Alabama. We moved back to the South, which was still

**Martin Luther King felt a deeply serious call to the ministry.**

the totally segregated society into which we had been born. In 1954 the United States Supreme Court ruled that separate educational facilities for black and white children were unequal and unconstitutional. Further court decisions requiring school integration produced violent reactions in the South. All public facilities continued to be forcibly segregated. High taxes at the voting polling places prevented most blacks from being able to cast their ballots.

In Montgomery, the rules of the Montgomery City Bus Lines required blacks to sit and stand at the rear of the buses, even if there were empty seats in the front section, which was reserved for whites. Furthermore, blacks had to pay their fares at the front of the bus, get off and walk to the rear to reboard through the back door. Drivers often pulled off and left them after they had paid their fares. On December 1, 1955, Mrs. Rosa Parks, a woman highly respected in the black community, boarded a bus to return home after her day's work as a seamstress in a downtown department store. She sat down in the first row behind the section reserved for whites. Soon the bus driver ordered Mrs. Parks to give up her seat to a boarding white man and stand farther back in the bus. When she quietly and tiredly refused, the driver got off the bus to get a policeman, who arrested her. At the courthouse, Mrs. Parks called her friend E. D. Nixon, who came down and signed a bail bond for her. Mr. Nixon phoned Martin and me the next day to describe the incident and to urge a boycott of the buses.

Martin agreed and offered the Dexter Avenue Baptist Church as a meeting place. Over forty leaders from all segments of the black community came to the meeting. They formed the Montgomery

Improvement Association (MIA), elected Martin president, and organized a boycott starting on December 5. For over a year, the fifty thousand black people in Montgomery walked and carpooled to their jobs, schools, and churches. . . .

Arrests and acts of violence only consolidated the boycotters and raised enthusiasm for our nonviolent protest movement. We realized the movement was more than local; it was a surge toward a national, even international, assertion of the individual's right to freedom and self-respect. It led to the Supreme Court's affirmation that Alabama's laws requiring segregation on buses were unconstitutional. On December 21, 1956, Montgomery's buses were peacefully integrated.

As I wrote later in my book, *My Life with Martin Luther King, Jr.*, "Montgomery was the soil in which the seed of a new theory of social action took root. Black people had found in nonviolent direct action a militant method that avoided violence but achieved dramatic confrontation, which electrified and educated the whole nation. . . . Without hatred or abjectly bending their knees, the demand for freedom emerged in strength and dignity. Black people had been waiting for this, and instinctively they seized the new method and opened a new era of social change."

**Rosa Parks sits in the front of a bus following the bus boycott.**

Martin was now a hero to America's black people. Shortly after the boycott, *Time* magazine ran a cover story on Martin, calling him "the scholarly Negro Baptist minister who in little more than a year has risen from nowhere to become one of the nation's remarkable leaders of men."

Inspired by the Montgomery bus victory, movements sprang

up in other cities. Martin thought all these activities should be coordinated to have the broadest good effect. After a series of meetings, the first of which was held at the Ebenezer Baptist Church in Atlanta, we helped found the Southern Christian Leadership Conference (SCLC) in 1957. Martin was elected president. From the first, the SCLC was church oriented in leadership and membership and in the concept of nonviolence. Martin did not call for disobedience of all laws, only for disobedience of unjust laws. He always believed in the supremacy of a higher moral law.

Between 1957 and 1959, Martin commuted between Montgomery and SCLC headquarters in Atlanta. He was invited to preach and lecture throughout the country. In 1959 we went on a pilgrimage to India to better understand Gandhi's nonviolent philosophy. Toward the end of 1959, Martin realized he had to devote full time and effort to the civil rights struggle, and so in 1960 we left our wonderful Dexter congregation and moved to Atlanta, where Martin became co-pastor with his father of the Ebenezer Baptist Church.

Demonstrations were continuing throughout the South with some successes. There were sit-ins to desegregate lunch counters and restaurants. The first group of Freedom Riders, black and white people organized by the Congress for Racial Equality to protest segregation on interstate buses, left Washington, D.C., by Greyhound on May 4, 1961. SCLC backed the Freedom Rides, and Martin served as chairman of their coordinating committee. Despite acts of violence against the Freedom Riders and subsequent arrests, the Freedom Rides continued. . . .

SCLC decided to join the Alabama Christian Movement for Human Rights in a massive campaign against segregation in Birmingham. Protests started in April 1963, with lunch-counter sit-ins. After city officials obtained an Alabama state court injunction against the demonstrators, Martin and other leaders determined to defy the injunction. On Good Friday they set off from church, marching peacefully. Bull Connor ordered them all arrested. Martin used the time in prison to write his now-famous "Letter from Birmingham Jail," in which he explained the necessity for peaceful protest to bring about social change.

Students take part in a lunch counter sit-in.

Woman protests refusal to seat blacks at lunch counter.

Dr. and Mrs. King are cheered during the Montgomery boycott.

**Between the Washington Monument and the Lincoln Memorial, huge crowds gather to hear King's "I Have a Dream" speech.**

While Martin was in jail, President John Kennedy and Attorney General Robert Kennedy directed public attention to the Birmingham situation, which finally culminated in a real victory for the movement when white city officials and merchants sat down with black leaders to hammer out a settlement. Peaceful integration came because militant nonviolence forced negotiation and agreement.

After Birmingham, nearly a thousand cities became engulfed in protests against segregation. This encouraged us to join in organizing a march on Washington to dramatize the need for new federal legislation to integrate blacks completely into American society. On August 28, 1963, we participated in a mass rally with 250,000 people who had traveled from all over the country to Washington, D.C. Martin delivered his I Have a Dream speech from the steps of the Lincoln Memorial, and afterward President Kennedy met with the leaders of the march. . . .

**During the March on Washington, civil rights leaders meet with President Kennedy and members of his staff. Dr. King is flanked by Whitney Young (left) and John Lewis. On President Kennedy's right is A. Philip Randolph; to his left are Vice-President Johnson, Walter Reuther, and Roy Wilkins.**

**Dr. and Mrs. King hug when informed of the Nobel Peace Prize.**

In October 1964, we learned that Martin had been awarded the Nobel Peace Prize. He and I were overcome with pride and joy and a tremendous feeling of responsibility. This was not just a prize for civil rights but for contributing to world peace. Martin said in his acceptance speech in Oslo, "I feel as though this prize has been given to me for something that really has *not* yet been achieved. It is a commission to go out and work even harder for the things in which we believe." Martin divided the $54,000 prize among SCLC, Congress of Racial Equality, Student Nonviolent Coordinating Committee, NAACP, National Council of Negro Women, and the American Foundation on Nonviolence.

By the summer of 1965, President Johnson, with the support of the civil rights community and its allies, had pushed through Congress and signed into law the long-awaited Civil Rights and Voting Rights acts, which finally put the federal government behind integration. But many of the urban ghettos of the North were erupting in violence. . . .

In 1968, Martin was deeply involved in organizing a Poor People's Campaign to demonstrate in a mass way for economic as well as civil rights, which he had always considered dependent upon each other. He went to Memphis, Tennessee, to lead six thousand protestors on a march in support of striking sanitation workers. On April 4, while Martin stood talking on the second-floor balcony of his Memphis motel room, a sniper shot and killed him. He was thirty-nine years old.

During his lifetime, Martin wrote three books and saw his speeches and sermons collected in two volumes. Martin always pleaded for positive, constructive action. The triple evils of poverty, racism, and war were his concerns wherever they were found in the world. He devoted his life to the process of uprooting them.

# I Have A Dream

## Martin Luther King, Jr.

. . . I say to you today, my friends, even though we face the difficulties of today and tomorrow, I still have a dream. It is a dream deeply rooted in the American dream.

I have a dream that one day this nation will rise up and live out the true meaning of its creed: "We hold these truths to be self-evident, that all men are created equal."

I have a dream that one day on the red hills of Georgia, sons of former slaves and sons of former slaveowners will be able to sit down together at the table of brotherhood.

I have a dream that one day even the state of Mississippi, a state sweltering with the heat of injustice, sweltering with the heat of oppression, will be transformed into an oasis of freedom and justice.

I have a dream that my four little children will one day live in a nation where they will not be judged by the color of their skin but by the content of their character. I have a dream today!

I have a dream that one day, down in Alabama, . . . right there in Alabama, little black boys and black girls will be able to join hands with little white boys and white girls and walk together as sisters and brothers. I have a dream today!

I have a dream that one day "every valley shall be exalted, every hill and mountain shall be made low, the rough places will be made plain, and the crooked places will be made straight, and the glory of the Lord will be revealed, and all flesh shall see it together."

This is our hope. This is the faith that I go back to the South with.

With this faith we will be able to hew out of the mountain of despair a stone of hope. With this faith we will be able to transform the jangling discords of our nation into a beautiful symphony of brotherhood.

With this faith we will be able to work together, to pray together, to struggle together, to stand up for freedom together, knowing that we will be free one day.

And this will be the day. This will be the day when all of God's children will be able to sing with new meaning, "My country 'tis of thee, sweet land of liberty, of thee I sing. Land where my fathers died, land of the pilgrim's pride, from every mountain side, let freedom ring." And if America is to be a great nation, this must become true.

So let freedom ring from the prodigious hilltops of New Hampshire.

Let freedom ring from the mighty mountains of New York.

Let freedom ring from the heightening Alleghenies of Pennsylvania.

Let freedom ring from the snowcapped Rockies of Colorado.

Let freedom ring from the curvaceous slopes of California.

But not only that.

Let freedom ring from Stone Mountain of Georgia!

Let freedom ring from Lookout Mountain of Tennessee.

Let freedom ring from every hill and molehill of Mississippi, from every mountainside, let freedom ring.

And when this happens, and when we allow freedom to ring, when we let it ring from every village and every hamlet, from every state and every city, we will be able to speed up that day when all of God's children, black men and white men, Jews and Gentiles, Protestants and Catholics, will be able to join hands and sing in the words of that old Negro spiritual, "Free at last! Free at last! Thank God Almighty, we are free at last!"

### ♦ Library Link ♦

*During his lifetime, Martin Luther King, Jr., delivered many speeches. The selection you just read is an excerpt from the original "I Have a Dream." If you would like to read the entire speech, you can find it in* A Testament of Hope, *which is a collection of Dr. King's writings.*

## ◆ *Reader's Response*

What does Martin Luther King, Jr.'s speech mean to you?

## Thinking It Over

1. What is the main idea of the opening paragraph of the introduction by Coretta Scott King?
2. Who was probably the biggest influence on Martin Luther King, Jr.'s philosophy of nonviolent protest?
3. What single event does Coretta Scott King cite as the beginning of the nonviolent protest movement?
4. According to Mrs. King, what was the appeal to black Americans of nonviolent direct action?
5. What do you think was Martin Luther King, Jr.'s greatest contribution to civil rights?

## Appreciating Literature

"Free at Last," by Coretta Scott King, is a biographical article in which the author's purpose is to inform the reader about the life of Martin Luther King, Jr. "I Have a Dream" is a speech in which Martin Luther King, Jr.'s purpose is to inspire and to persuade people that change is possible. Compare the different styles of the two pieces. What are some of the devices Martin Luther King, Jr. uses that help to persuade and inspire?

## Writing to Learn

**THINK AND DECIDE** Martin Luther King, Jr., changed the world with his dream. What is your dream? If your dream came true, how would it change our world?

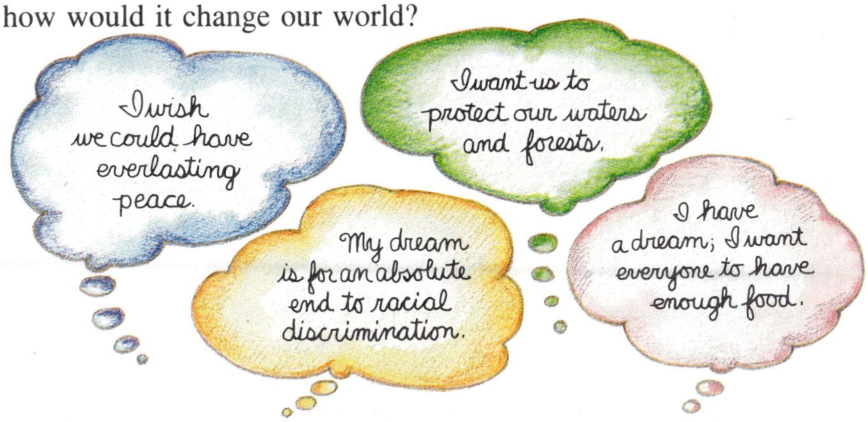


**WRITE** Explain your dream of an improvement in social conditions. Share a hope for helping to solve a world problem.

WORLD OF READING

# Magazine

News About Reading

## Books That Made History

"So this is the little woman who made the big war."

These are the words Abraham Lincoln said to Harriet Beecher Stowe when he met her for the first time. What did he mean? For many years there had been increasingly bitter disagreements between the Northern and Southern states. Then Mrs. Stowe's novel *Uncle Tom's Cabin* was published. An engrossing story that powerfully portrayed the evils of slavery, it fired people's emotions and helped ignite the Civil War.

*Common Sense* by Thomas Paine was another of the many books that have directly affected history. It inspired colonial leaders to fight for independence from Great Britain. When George Washington's troops were cold and hungry and ready to give up, he had these words of Thomas Paine's read aloud to them: "These are the times that try men's souls. The summer soldier and the sunshine patriot will, in this

The cover of an early edition of the powerful novel *Uncle Tom's Cabin*

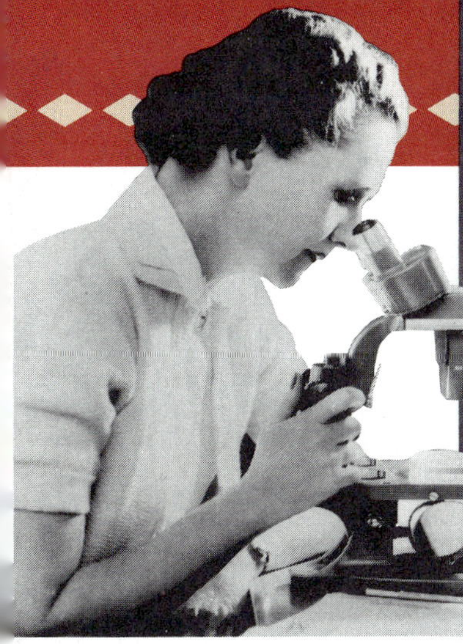

In *Silent Spring*, Rachel Carson argued against the use of pesticides.

crisis, shrink from the service of their country. . . . Tyranny . . . is not easily conquered." The newly inspired troops fought on.

In 1962, Rachel Carson's *Silent Spring* alerted the world to the danger of pesticides. She warned that they were poisoning the food supplies of animals, birds, and fish and would soon contaminate the human food supply as well. Because of her work, we now have many laws restricting the use of dangerous pesticides.

***Rachel Carson's* Silent Spring *alerted the world to the danger of pesticides.***

Henry David Thoreau was a writer in the last century who directly affected history in our time. His essay "Civil Disobedience" argued that people should refuse to obey the laws that they felt were unjust. That's exactly how the Civil Rights movement began in the 1950s. People refused to sit in the backs of buses or stay out of segregated restaurants, as the law required them to do, because they believed that those laws were unjust. As Thoreau advocated, they resisted in a nonviolent way.

It is difficult to imagine what our country would be like today if these books had not been written. They are examples of the precious freedom of expression allowed Americans, and the ideas in these books have been a positive force all over the world.

***Take a look at a magazine that made history. LIFE magazine's photographic format raised the awareness of Americans on a variety of topics of national interest. Look for back issues in your library.***

Thoreau's essay on civil disobedience influenced Martin Luther King, Jr. (right), as he developed his ideas about peaceful demonstrations and nonviolent action.

# Literature Link

## *How can fiction make historical events seem more real?*

Use your imagination and put yourself in the driver's seat. Just feel the hot, dry wind blowing in your face. Can you smell the dust that is kicked up by the horses' hooves as you urge them on through the valley? Can you feel your back aching from lurching all day on a hard bench?

### *Mixing Fact and Fiction*

Just as pictures help you visualize the past, historical fiction helps you step back in time. In fact, authors of historical fiction purposely use real events to build a story that's entertaining and compelling as well as historical. Take, for example, "It's Not the

Great Wall, but It Will Last Forever," an historical fiction story from Unit 2. While the author relates the fictional account of one man's role in the building of the railroads, she also tells about a real historical event. As a result, you have a realistic image of what happened when the Central Pacific Railroad brought workers from China to lay track and blast their way through the Sierra Nevada, the mountains that stood in the way of the railroad. The following is a conversation between two of the workers as they swing dangerously in a basket down the side of a cliff.

> "Lo Tung?" Wei's voice was lost in the emptiness. "Lo Tung, will we go home one day? And will we talk strong about what we did in America?"
>
> "Yes," Lo Tung said. "And we will tell how we built this railroad. It is not the Great Wall, but it will last forever."
>
> The basket had stopped now. Far, far above them arms waved. It was the signal. This was where they must work.

How does dialogue like this originate? You know the author could not possibly have been on the cliff to hear the conversation, so she must have created it herself. Like other authors of historical fiction, she was weaving together fact and fiction. If you wonder which parts of a historical fiction story are fact and which are fiction, you might read further in history texts to find out.

You can see how a story like this makes history come alive. Reading historical fiction can let you in on the fascinating details of what life was like for people in the past—before there were airplanes, cars, and fast food.

The next selection, "Life from the River," is historical fiction. See if you become involved in the struggle to survive as the author takes you back in time to the Northwest in the 1830s.

*Usually we base our decisions on what we believe is right, but sometimes the choices are not so clear, and their consequences are grave.*

# LIFE FROM THE RIVER

by Jan Hudson

*A smallpox epidemic has hit the Canadian Blackfoot Indian tribes. Already, Otter and Almost-Mother, Sweetgrass's brother and stepmother, have come down with the dreaded disease. Shabby Bull, Sweetgrass's father, has gone to visit the neighboring tribes. As the story opens, Sweetgrass is facing the responsibility of getting food for the sick ones.*

"Sweetgrass, wake up. Sweetgrass!"

My mind surfaced lazily from its cool numb dream. Someone wanted me to do something. Again. Probably something I couldn't do.

"What is it?"

The mists of morning filled our tipi. Those big begging eyes looked like Little Brother's. Couldn't be. They were Otter's eyes. Otter wouldn't beg. But I knew how hunger twists inside and drives you to things you think you'd never do.

Some scabs had fallen from my brother's face last night, leaving ugly pits in the skin. Who else would be pitted the next time I saw them? Inside me a deep voice answered: the lucky ones would be pitted. The others I would never see again.

"Sweetgrass? Are you awake?"

"I am now. What do you want?"

"Do you feel Mother is going to die? Am I going to die?"

I hesitated. "No, I do not feel it."

"Are you sure?"

"Pretty well. All the signs look good."

"But Mother is still burning inside."

"True, but you have both lived many days. Grandmother said that with smallpox most of our people die right away. They die and swell up like the baby." I tried to force a laugh through my tight throat. "Do you think I would stay here if you were dying?"

Otter smiled in a way I had never seen before. The softness around his eyes had nothing to do with smallpox.

"If I live, I will give you anything you want."

"Just be my good brother Otter."

He gave me his hand and I held it between mine.

"I tried to go hunting this morning," he said after a while.

"Otter!"

"You were asleep. Why not go?" he said.

"You are still too weak."

"I almost didn't get out of the tipi. I feel I must get well now, sister. Tomorrow I will try again to go hunting."

"Your spirit is rising, but it is still tender. Just rest."

Otter would not hear me. "I can hunt with the bow and arrow and you cannot."

"Just rest."

At long last he relaxed. Luckily he was still too weak to do more than talk.

"So you must not be sad," he continued. "I wanted you to hear me, not to worry, you know, if you. . . ."

If I got the smallpox.

I patted his hand and tucked him in. Otter was right. We had better be ready for the sickness coming to me, also. But he was wrong to think he could hunt tomorrow morning, or even the following morning. He must rest for many days, and most of all, if he was to care for us as I had done, he must eat well.

As I put on my mittens and prepared to go out, I couldn't help thinking. Why was the pox so slow coming to me? Most of the time I didn't think of getting it. Me die? I would make Otter ready for it, but never would I give in! I would find power to live. *Ahksi Kiwa!* My heart sang with the warriors.

I fear nothing!

There was a ghostly world lying between our tipi and my rabbit snare. The night before, Chinook, the warm mountain wind, had melted each tree's robe of snow and then blew fast away to the south. Set free for a moment, the snow-water froze again as ice. Each tree, each twig and bud, wore a shining shield that the arrows of the sun bounced off, so dazzling my eyes that there seemed to be no skeletons beneath their bright flesh. This was a world of clearest shadows, the shadows of light.

Axe in hand, I shuffled over the icy surface crust, feeling myself the only creature in this world. Where was the flashing silver of my snare? In the snow's light, it would be hard to see, but I knew exactly where I had placed it. Right beneath those bushes bordering the stream.

The snare was empty! My heart jerked in disbelief at the sight. I shut my eyes and wished it full with a fat, white mound of rabbit.

I had to sit down. For the first time since Father left, I felt sick, really sick. A dizziness had caught me and left me weaker than I had ever been before. I had no choice but to lay back on a shiny crest of ice, and let come whatever was in store.

Overhead the sun hummed down from a pale blue sky. I lost myself in the vastness of it all. The world behind me could have vanished for all I knew.

A raven's laugh brought me back. The sun had wandered on, and a light blanket of cloud overcast the sky. It was getting colder.

I took off my mitten and felt my face for spots. There were none. One small relief.

But what could I do? I couldn't go back without food.

And there were those hungry horses to feed as well. Frustrated, I took up our big axe and swung hard at the last unstripped poplar on this side of the stream. I cut its bark off in rings. As I pulled the inside bark from the rings like I had so often done before, I realized how weak I was fast becoming.

I threw down what strips I had gathered and picked up our bright axe. I might not have much time, I heard myself say.

I headed towards where Otter had hobbled the mares and stallions in the woods behind our tipi, inside the little meadow.

Stumbling through the fringing trees, I seemed to be in a dream where I knew what I had to do. I had to find the horses. We were starving. Horses. Meat. In this dream, the scattered tree stumps were helping me. All the tall ones were Father and the short ones were Little Brother. But the dark figures changed back into stumps when I looked straight at them. Visions come easy when a person is sick and hungry.

Move carefully now. I must not startle the horses. Into the bitter cold of my nose and mouth crept a faint, foul odour.[1]

Something was wrong.

From my narrow edge of the meadow there were no standing shapes to be seen. Everything wavered in front of me. Where were our horses?

There was no eating here.

My family's ill luck had now fully ripened. There was nothing here for me to do.

I turned on my heel and hauled my clean axe home.

I chopped and boiled old pemmican sacks for soup while Otter rested on his elbow watching me. Almost-Mother was enjoying a much quieter sleep for the first time. She was getting better, but when she awoke she would need good food. This sack soup tasted of meat and grease, but it was pretty thin. If Otter didn't like it, he kept his comments to himself.

"What are we going to do?" he asked after he had eaten his share.

"There are many more pemmican sacks."

"Not enough. Have you thought about the dogs?"

"They left long ago. And the wolves beat us to the horses."

Otter's flushed skin darkened further. We sat silent together awhile, listening to our mother moaning from time to time.

"I'll check my snare tomorrow morning."

On the eighth morning after Father left us, Almost-Mother's blisters had hardened to scabs. I held her graying head on my lap and spooned pemmican-sack soup into her. She swallowed the watery broth greedily.

For the first time, she turned her face so that her eyes could look into mine. She smiled weakly. Her spirit flickered brighter, like coals being blown on.

Somewhere I would find food for my family.

Out I crept again under the cold dome of the world. Winter was coming back again, full force. Summer seemed only a lying dream

[1]Some words in this selection are spelled in the British style.

to me. I couldn't shake mocking memories of food eaten for the taste of it, berries thrown on the grass in laughter. I forced my moccasined feet forward. Soon I would be too weak to move them at all. Without smallpox, I might live in this way another moon or longer, hoping for my father's return. But the others would die. Aiii, already I was so lonely.

Was Father alive? Pretty Girl? Grandmother? Eagle Sun? The thought of them alive somewhere was a small fire to warm my freezing spirit.

The world was black with shadow, blue-white with sky and snow today—nothing else. The light shimmered off the snow, making my eyes ache. I dragged my axe behind me. If my snare was still empty, there would at least be the untouched poplars on the far side of the stream. If horses ate the green inside bark, then so could we. I found it hard to control my trembling which came partly from desperation, partly from weakness.

I reached the snare, and its loop was empty. Always empty. So I took it apart.

My damp, mittenless fingers froze to the wire as I unwrapped it from the small tree. By the time I had the snare unsnarled, my hands were cut and white with numbness. Dragging axe and wire, I trudged up the river.

Under my feet the ice seemed to sway, and sometimes my eyes flooded with a gray fog. I would wait until I got some strength back before I went on. To walk blind on the ice is a good way to die.

Black Eagle did that once. It was long ago, in the year of the famine. He stepped on a rotten piece of ice, out on one of the rivers in the foothills. His family never saw Black Eagle again, not even to bury his body. Here in front of me thrust a big stone. The dark patch on its sunny side was just like the patch Black Eagle stepped through.

I bent over and stared into that dark ice. It was almost clear, showing water beneath its brittle frozen layers. Something moved in the darkness. With a start, I stepped back a bit. Did the dead seek me to join them?

The movement came again, and I saw it to be a black and narrow slash of a shadow, floating under the ice. As long as my arm at least. It moved sideways again. A river demon's fish!

If I fell through the ice that fish would eat me.

I remembered a story. Sometimes fish were eaten by people. Not by the Blackfoot, but others like the Cree. Our warriors called them fish-eaters in insult.

I hadn't heard any stories of the Cree being wiped out by river demons.

The ice was very thin here. It felt like a sign to me, the sign I had been seeking.

An evil fish waited under the ice. I would catch him and cook him. I shook with fear and power and loathing. Now.

When I hit the axe on the ice, the demon was gone like a shot. If he wanted my spirit as much as I wanted his, he'd be back.

I chipped with the blade until a bowl-shaped sheet of ice broke out. I swung the axe high and gave the ice underneath a good blow. The metal sunk in sweetly, and the water made a sucking sound when I pulled out the axe. How good to hit something!

I chipped out a big hole.

What to do now? I sat on a snowdrift to rest. How do the Cree catch fish?

I shut my eyes and tried to picture, one by one, my dizzy thoughts. Could a fish be grabbed? Not likely with them being so quick and slippery.

Could a fish be shafted upon an axe blade? Maybe. But when my mind pictured it, the fish split, then sank out of sight.

Could a fish be caught like a rabbit in a wire?

I opened my eyes.

I pulled off my mittens again and forced my stiffening fingers to wrap the loose end of the snare around the axe handle. It was hard to get it tight. I cut myself a few times.

The snare must go quietly into the water. I lay down on my belly on the ice.

Down it dipped into the dark hole. Success. The whole loop went all the way under the water. I was afraid I wouldn't have enough wire. I got my mittens back on and prepared myself for a wait.

My plan was to let the fish get his head all the way through before yanking. I had a lot of time to think about it.

I never really noticed before how noisy a quiet forest can be. There's always a bird somewhere calling out to his friends. The wind is always there, rising and falling, talking to every tree. Even the ice groaned.

The ice. At first it was just cold. Then it hurt. It sent out fingers under my blankets, up and down my spine. I got a little worried when a wash of numbness settled in, but I didn't dare move or make a sound.

Then a big pointed head glided into view right under my nose. It stopped short a hand's width from my snare. Dark, cold eyes on the sides of its head could see everywhere. I didn't move a muscle.

What now?

I held my breath, and he flicked his fins again. A shivering thought:

fish needn't follow paths like rabbits do. This creature could swim here or there or even under, and miss my trap!

I knew I had to make my move, but nothing must frighten him. Steady now. I eased the snare over the evil head so gently that it made only an arrowhead ripple where the wire parted the water.

Then the fish shot forward!

I jerked back on the axe handle. I had him!

But how well? Jumping to my feet, I hauled up on the axe handle. The demon thrashed and thumped along the bottom of the ice before I could get his head free. Then up!

A shower of drops rained down behind him as he landed splat on the ice. His eyes were fierce and he bared a mouthful of terrible tiny teeth. Another flip, a flop, and somehow the fish escaped the wire.

I felt my entire life fall with him in that moment.

The mottled green body arched this way and that. His tail gave the ice mighty slaps, skittering him back toward the hole.

He came to rest on the jagged edge of the icehole, his head only smelling distance from the open water. I jumped fast to catch him. It was life against life. I sat on top of him, holding his slippery, writhing body between my legs, and grabbed his gill.

With my other hand, I stretched for the axe, caught the wire, pulled it over. Then I cracked him smartly between the eyes.

I dared not loosen my grip until the fish was truly dead. At last it gave its final spasm.

Underneath us the river trembled. I froze. It should be a moon or more before the ice broke. Would the river demons take me?

But the air was full of nothing, nothing but a delicious smell. The ice did not crack and the river didn't move any more.

I went home in triumph.

A pemmican bag thrown into the soup cut down its fishy smell. A handful of roots rounded out the taste. Almost-Mother drank several spoonfuls that evening and smiled at me again. It was a fine thing to see.

Otter drank some too and even ate flesh from the pointed bones. He said he was going to get sick. But he didn't.

I ate also, and went again to the river to catch another fish for my family, the next day and the next. But I went with a buffalo robe to lay on, and dried seeds as bait. And I got quite good at brewing tasty broths.

No river demon took me either.

Otter's smallpox scabs fell off day by day. Almost-Mother's blisters dried, and her face filled out and lost its shadow of the death-sign. All because of the fish.

Then came the morning of our seventeenth day. While Almost-Mother and Otter were still asleep, I stretched an unfinished hide on the floor and got busy with my rubbing-stone. Now I was strong enough to work some of the unfinished hides to replace the dirty ones I'd had to throw out.

A warm chinook wind spilled down from the mountains that morning and washed across the creek to shake our home. At first I did not worry. Our tipi pegs were driven deep into the ground. Stones and ice pinned the skirts likewise. I knew we would be safe no matter how hard the wind blew.

It hit the land so fiercely the sound was almost like a creature howling. And there were other spooky noises too—scraping, thuds, and scratchings. I knew it must be dried twigs and branches kicked up against the tipi's front.

It was almost like someone dropping his packs outside, like a shadow-man fumbling at our flap to come in. Someone like a traveller . . . or a spirit.

It couldn't be. But I heard the sounds happening.

I leaped up and grabbed my friend the axe. There was one last rattle and the triangular flap of our door fell open. Wind gusted around my ankles and filled the tipi. A bending head and a craggy hand reached in. My breath hid scared in my throat. Was that the top-tied hair of a Crow warrior? Or was it. . . .

I must stand ready. *Ahksi kiwa!*

Legs, then shoulders, appeared through the tipi flap, and the man straightened himself. Braids lay across his shoulders in the Blackfoot way, not in any other. The face was a face I knew beneath its scarring and deathworn look.

Shabby Bull, alive, had come home.

Smallpox wounds were pink upon my father's skin. He stood cold-face, making no welcoming sign; his body blocked the wind and the pale dawn light. He stared at the axe in my hand, the two bundled sleepers on the floor, and at the empty place where the finished hides should be.

"Where are the others?" my father asked.

"Otter and Mother are asleep, Father, and the babies are dead." It felt strange to see him, not at all as I expected.

"The babies are dead in Crying Dog's camp as well. And so are Crying Dog and the rest of his family." Father turned and tied the door flap behind him.

I pulled the blankets from the sleeping faces so Father might see them and their healing scars. He stood before them for a moment. Then he told me it was good and I was to pull the blankets up again so no one would wake.

He turned to walk to the man's place at the back of the tipi behind the fire. That limp is bad, I thought, as he dragged his left foot across the floor cover. He stopped by the kettle. Even through the stink of unfinished hides and the smoke of the fire I could smell the telltale odour of fish. *Aiii.*

My heart froze helplessly waiting.

"Daughter, what have you done?"

"We are living, Father," I tried to explain. "Otter and Mother and me, we are living. In Crying Dog's camp the people are dead."

He glowered at the floor while silence roared between us. Black stubby lashes rimmed my father's dark, unblinking eyes. My mouth tasted salty with blood.

"May you not mourn for this, Sweetgrass."

I knew I would not mourn, ever. My fingernails were cutting into the palms of my hands. I made myself uncurl them.

"Father, I threw out your robes. They were dirty with smallpox."

He was staring at the floor still.

"I tried *hard* to feel which trail to follow," I added, promising myself not to cry. "Father, I am not a warrior!"

"Not a warrior," he repeated, shifting his weight heavily. "But you now are a woman."

Stunned, I looked into his eyes to confirm his words. They were old, much older than when he left, but they were shining clear and proud.

"Come, give an old man a hand to sit down."

I did as he said. His weight on my shoulder, his arm round my waist was sweet indeed.

"I brought you a present. Look outside."

I could hardly see for the tears, but there on the ground by the door lay a freshly-killed white rabbit.

In the sky, the sun was climbing.

### ♦ Library Link ♦

*Sweetgrass's decision to feed fish to her starving family is just one of many experiences she encounters during a year of trial and hardship. You can read more about this brave Blackfoot Indian maiden in the novel,* Sweetgrass *by Jan Hudson, from which this selection was taken.*

## *Reader's Response*

Do you think Sweetgrass was right to go against the custom of her tribe in order to try to save her family? Explain why or why not.

## Thinking It Over

1. Why did Otter think that he and his mother might die?
2. What one thing did Sweetgrass want from Otter if he lived?
3. What special "sign" did Sweetgrass feel she had been given?
4. Why do you think Sweetgrass felt "fear and power and loathing" when she thought of catching and cooking the fish?
5. What do you think would have happened if Sweetgrass had not caught a fish to feed her family?
6. Why did Sweetgrass's father tell her that she was now a woman?
7. Was Sweetgrass forgiven by her father at the end of the story? How do you know?

## Appreciating Literature

Reading about life in other places and other times can sometimes help us to look at our own way of life with new eyes. What are some things you take for granted that Sweetwater didn't have? How does this story give you a better understanding of the challenges of surviving in the wild?

## Writing to Learn

**THINK AND DECIDE** During hard times, people may violate common tradition. In "Life from the River," Sweetgrass catches a fish even though it is a forbidden food. Complete the action/consequences chart on your own paper to help you reach a judgment about her action of catching the fish.

| **Action:** | **Consequences:** |
| --- | --- |
| Sweetgrass catches a fish from the river. | ____________ |
| | ____________ |
| | ____________ |
| | ____________ |
| My judgment: | ____________ |

**WRITE** Write a paragraph that explains the consequences of Sweetgrass's action. Include your judgment.

TIME OUT FOR BOOKS

ALA Notable Book
IRA Children's Book Award

***"That's what being an adult is—making decisions for yourself."***

from *After the Dancing Days* by Margaret I. Rostkowski

Annie's father is a doctor and has been away for almost two years caring for wounded soldiers during World War I. Her Uncle Paul was killed, fighting in France. But the war is over now. Father is coming home, even if Uncle Paul will never return. Annie and her mother want to resume a way of life that will not remind them of the war.

But Father chooses to work at the local veteran's hospital with the wounded men who will take a long time to heal, if they ever do. Grandfather volunteers to visit the hospital to read to the men. Gradually Annie is drawn to the hospital, too—the patients are lonely and long for a cheerful smile. Mother avoids knowing about her family's experiences at the hospital. The war is over, for her.

One of the young men Annie befriends at the hospital is Andrew. The war may never be over for him, as his injuries have left his face horribly disfigured. The horror of Andrew's injuries intensifies for Annie when she learns that Andrew freely enlisted—as a farmer's son, he could have stayed safely at home.

If you read *After the Dancing Days*, you will explore with Annie the complex questions of war, peace, heroism, and duty as she grapples with the truth of her uncle's death and her friendship with Andrew.

# The Gift of the Magi

by O. Henry

*Sometimes love involves sacrifice. There are times, however, when that sacrifice takes a surprising turn.*

Reading CORNER

One dollar and eighty-seven cents. That was all. And sixty cents of it was in pennies. Pennies saved one and two at a time by bulldozing the grocer and the vegetable man and the butcher until one's cheeks burned with the silent imputation of parsimony that such close dealing implied. Three times Della counted it. One dollar and eighty-seven cents. And the next day would be Christmas.

There was clearly nothing to do but flop down on the shabby little couch and howl. So Della did it. Which instigates the moral reflection that life is made up of sobs, sniffles, and smiles, with sniffles predominating.

While the mistress of the home is gradually subsiding from the first stage to the second, take a look at the home. A furnished flat at $8 per week. It did not exactly beggar description, but it certainly had that word on the lookout for the mendicancy squad.

In the vestibule below was a letter-box into which no letter would go, and an electric button from which no mortal finger could coax a ring. Also appertaining thereunto was a card bearing the name "Mr. James Dillingham Young."

The "Dillingham" had been flung to the breeze during a former period of prosperity when its possessor was being paid $30 per week. Now, when the income was shrunk to $20, the letters of "Dillingham" looked blurred, as though they were thinking seriously of contracting to a modest and unassuming D. But whenever Mr. James Dillingham Young came home and reached his flat above he was called "Jim" and greatly hugged by Mrs. James Dillingham Young, already introduced to you as Della. Which is all very good.

Della finished her cry and attended to her cheeks with the powder rag. She stood by the window and looked out dully at a gray cat walking a gray fence in a gray backyard. Tomorrow would be Christmas Day and she had only $1.87 with which to buy Jim a present. She had been saving every penny she could for months, with this result. Twenty dollars a week doesn't go far. Expenses had been greater than she had calculated. They always are. Only $1.87 to buy a present for Jim. Her Jim. Many a happy hour she had spent

planning for something nice for him. Something fine and rare and sterling—something just a little bit near to being worthy of the honor of being owned by Jim.

There was a pier-glass between the windows of the room. Perhaps you have seen a pier-glass in an $8 flat. A very thin and very agile person may, by observing his reflection in a rapid sequence of longitudinal strips, obtain a fairly accurate conception of his looks. Della, being slender, had mastered the art.

Suddenly she whirled from the window and stood before the glass. Her eyes were shining brilliantly, but her face had lost its color within twenty seconds. Rapidly she pulled down her hair and let it fall to its full length.

Now, there were two possessions of the James Dillingham Youngs in which they both took a mighty pride. One was Jim's gold watch that had been his father's and his grandfather's. The other was Della's hair. Had the Queen of Sheba lived in the flat across the airshaft, Della would have let her hair hang out of the window some day to dry just to depreciate Her Majesty's jewels and gifts. Had King Solomon been the janitor, with all his treasures piled up in the basement, Jim would have pulled out his watch every time he passed, just to see him pluck at his beard from envy.

So now Della's beautiful hair fell about her rippling and shining like a cascade of brown waters. It reached below her knee and made itself almost a garment for her. And then she did it up again nervously and quickly. Once she faltered for a minute and stood still while a tear or two splashed on the worn red carpet.

On went her old brown jacket, on went her old brown hat. With a whirl of skirts and with the brilliant sparkle still in her eyes, she fluttered out the door and down the stairs to the street.

Where she stopped the sign read: "Mme. Sofronie. Hair Goods of All Kinds." One flight up Della ran, and collected herself, panting. Madame, large, too white, chilly, hardly looked the "Sofronie."

"Will you buy my hair?" asked Della.

"I buy hair," said Madame. "Take yer hat off and let's have a sight at the looks of it."

Down rippled the brown cascade.

"Twenty dollars," said Madame, lifting the mass with a practised hand.

"Give it to me quick," said Della.

Oh, and the next two hours tripped by on rosy wings. Forget the hashed metaphor. She was ransacking the stores for Jim's present.

She found it at last. It surely had been made for Jim and no one else. There was no other like it in any of the stores, and she had turned all of them inside out. It was a platinum fob chain simple and chaste in design, properly proclaiming its value by substance alone and not by meretricious ornamentation—as all good things should do. It was even worthy of The Watch. As soon as she saw it she knew that it must be Jim's. It was like him. Quietness and value—the description applied to both. Twenty-one dollars they took from her for it, and she hurried home with the 87 cents. With that chain on his watch Jim might be properly anxious about the time in any company. Grand as the watch was, he sometimes looked at it on the sly on account of the old leather strap that he used in place of a chain.

When Della reached home her intoxication gave way a little to prudence and reason. She got out her curling irons and lighted the gas and went to work repairing the ravages made by generosity added

to love. Which is always a tremendous task, dear friends—a mammoth task.

Within forty minutes her head was covered with tiny, close-lying curls that made her look wonderfully like a truant schoolboy. She looked at her reflection in the mirror long, carefully, and critically.

"If Jim doesn't kill me," she said to herself, "before he takes a second look at me, he'll say I look like a Coney Island chorus girl. But what could I do—oh! what could I do with a dollar and eighty-seven cents?"

At 7 o'clock the coffee was made and the frying-pan was on the back of the stove hot and ready to cook the chops.

Jim was never late. Della doubled the fob chain in her hand and sat on the corner of the table near the door that he always entered. Then she heard his step on the stair away down on the first flight, and she turned white for just a moment. She had a habit of saying little silent prayers about the simplest everyday things, and now she whispered: "Please God, make him think I am still pretty."

The door opened and Jim stepped in and closed it. He looked thin and very serious. Poor fellow, he was only twenty-two—and to be burdened with a family! He needed a new overcoat and he was without gloves.

Jim stepped inside the door, as immovable as a setter at the scent of quail. His eyes were fixed upon Della, and there was an expression in them that she could not read, and it terrified her. It was not anger, nor surprise, nor disapproval, nor horror, nor any of the sentiments that she had been prepared for. He simply stared at her fixedly with that peculiar expression on his face.

Della wriggled off the table and went for him.

"Jim, darling," she cried, "don't look at me that way. I had my hair cut off and sold it because I couldn't have lived through Christmas without giving you a present. It'll grow out again—you won't mind, will you? I just had to do it. My hair grows awfully fast. Say 'Merry Christmas!' Jim, and let's be happy. You don't know what a nice—what a beautiful, nice gift I've got for you."

"You've cut off your hair?" asked Jim, laboriously, as if he had not arrived at that patent fact yet even after the hardest mental labor.

"Cut it off and sold it," said Della. "Don't you like me just as well, anyhow? I'm me without my hair, aren't I?"

Jim looked about the room curiously.

"You say your hair is gone?" he said, with an air almost of idiocy.

"You needn't look for it," said Della. "It's sold, I tell you—sold and gone, too. It's Christmas Eve, boy. Be good to me, for it went for you. Maybe the hairs on my head were numbered," she went on with a sudden serious sweetness, "but nobody could ever count my love for you. Shall I put the chops on, Jim?"

Out of his trance Jim seemed quickly to wake. He enfolded his Della. For ten seconds let us regard with discreet scrutiny some inconsequential object in the other direction. Eight dollars a week or a million a year—what is the difference? A mathematician or a wit would give you the wrong answer. The magi brought valuable gifts, but that was not among them. This dark assertion will be illuminated later on.

Jim drew a package from his overcoat pocket and threw it upon the table.

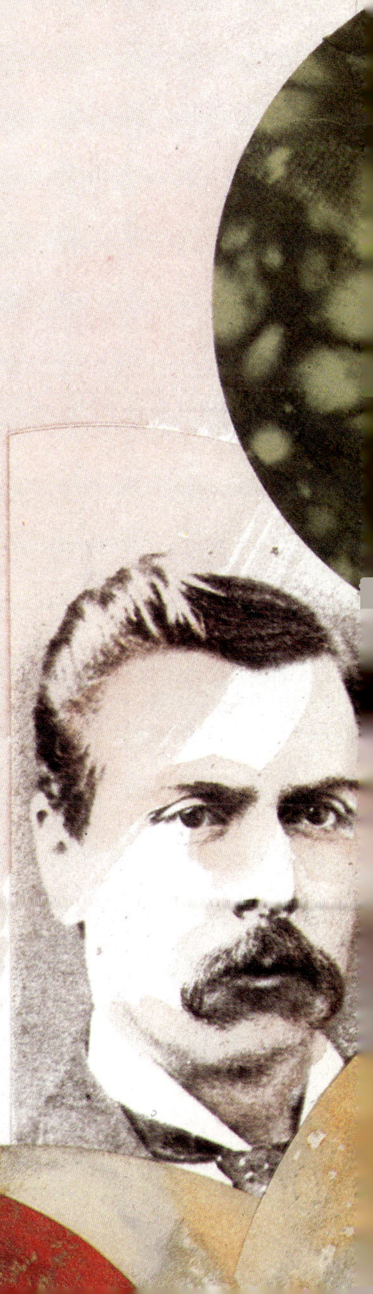

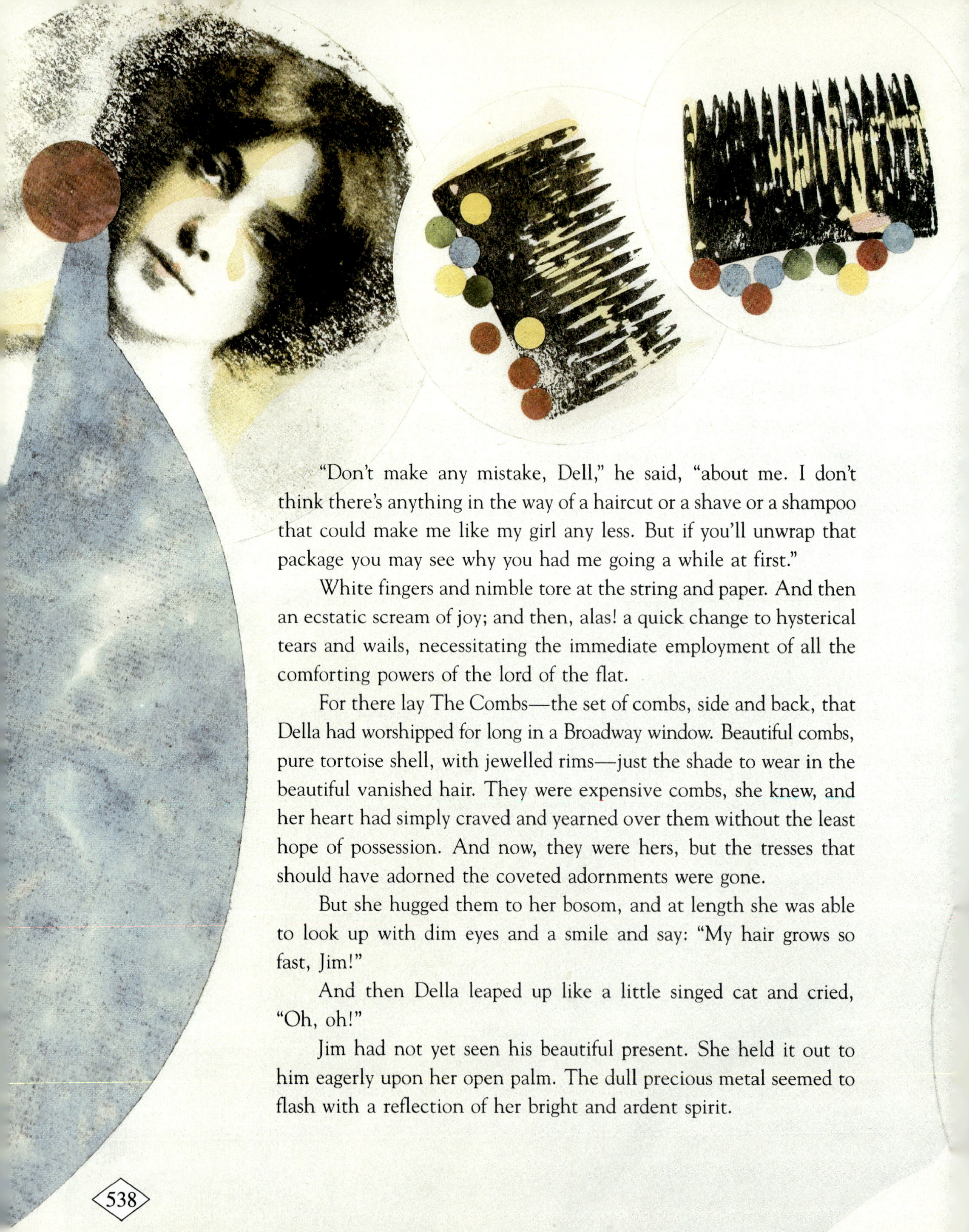

"Don't make any mistake, Dell," he said, "about me. I don't think there's anything in the way of a haircut or a shave or a shampoo that could make me like my girl any less. But if you'll unwrap that package you may see why you had me going a while at first."

White fingers and nimble tore at the string and paper. And then an ecstatic scream of joy; and then, alas! a quick change to hysterical tears and wails, necessitating the immediate employment of all the comforting powers of the lord of the flat.

For there lay The Combs—the set of combs, side and back, that Della had worshipped for long in a Broadway window. Beautiful combs, pure tortoise shell, with jewelled rims—just the shade to wear in the beautiful vanished hair. They were expensive combs, she knew, and her heart had simply craved and yearned over them without the least hope of possession. And now, they were hers, but the tresses that should have adorned the coveted adornments were gone.

But she hugged them to her bosom, and at length she was able to look up with dim eyes and a smile and say: "My hair grows so fast, Jim!"

And then Della leaped up like a little singed cat and cried, "Oh, oh!"

Jim had not yet seen his beautiful present. She held it out to him eagerly upon her open palm. The dull precious metal seemed to flash with a reflection of her bright and ardent spirit.

"Isn't it a dandy, Jim? I hunted all over town to find it. You'll have to look at the time a hundred times a day now. Give me your watch. I want to see how it looks on it."

Instead of obeying, Jim tumbled down on the couch and put his hands under the back of his head and smiled.

"Dell," said he, "let's put our Christmas presents away and keep 'em a while. They're too nice to use just at present. I sold the watch to get the money to buy your combs. And now suppose you put the chops on."

The magi, as you know, were wise men—wonderfully wise men—who brought gifts to the Babe in the manger. They invented the art of giving Christmas presents. Being wise, their gifts were no doubt wise ones, possibly bearing the privilege of exchange in case of duplication. And here I have lamely related to you the uneventful chronicle of two foolish children in a flat who most unwisely sacrificed for each other the greatest treasures of their house. But in a last word to the wise of these days let it be said that of all who give gifts these two were the wisest. Of all who give and receive gifts, such as they are wisest. Everywhere they are wisest. They are the magi.

AWARD WINNING AUTHOR

*When given a choice of gifts, how do you decide which to choose? People usually have a reason for the choices they make.*

# The Princess and THE TIN BOX

by James Thurber

Once upon a time, in a far country, there lived a king whose daughter was the prettiest princess in the world. Her eyes were like the cornflower, her hair was sweeter than the hyacinth, and her throat made the swan look dusty.

From the time she was a year old, the princess had been showered with presents. Her nursery looked like Cartier's window. Her toys were all made of gold or platinum or diamonds or emeralds. She was not permitted to have wooden blocks or china dolls or rubber dogs or linen books, because such materials were considered cheap for the daughter of a king.

When she was seven, she was allowed to attend the wedding of her brother and throw real pearls at the bride instead of rice. Only the nightingale, with his lyre of gold, was permitted to sing for the princess. The common blackbird, with his boxwood flute, was kept out of the palace grounds. She walked in silver-and-samite slippers to a sapphire-and-topaz bathroom and slept in an ivory bed inlaid with rubies.

On the day the princess was eighteen, the king sent a royal ambassador to the courts of five neighboring kingdoms to announce that he would give his daughter's hand in marriage to the prince who brought her the gift she liked most.

The first prince to arrive at the palace rode a swift white stallion and laid at the feet of the princess an enormous apple made of solid gold which he had taken from a dragon who had guarded it for a thousand years. It was placed on a long ebony table set up to hold the gifts of the princess's suitors. The second prince, who came on a gray charger, brought her a nightingale made of a thousand diamonds, and it was placed beside the golden apple. The third prince, riding on a black horse, carried a great jewel box made of platinum and sapphires, and it was placed next to the diamond nightingale. The fourth prince, astride a fiery yellow horse, gave the princess a gigantic heart made of rubies and pierced by an emerald arrow. It was placed next to the platinum-and-sapphire jewel box.

Now the fifth prince was the strongest and handsomest of all the five suitors, but he was the son of a poor king whose realm had been overrun by mice and locusts and wizards and mining engineers so that there was nothing much of value left in it. He came plodding up to the palace of the princess on a plow horse and he brought her a small tin box filled with mica and feldspar and hornblende which he had picked up on the way.

The other princes roared with disdainful laughter when they saw the tawdry gift the fifth prince had brought to the princess. But she examined it with great interest and squealed with delight, for all her life she had been glutted with precious stones and priceless metals, but she had never seen tin before or mica or feldspar or hornblende. The tin box was placed next to the ruby heart pierced with an emerald arrow.

"Now," the king said to his daughter, "you must select the gift you like best and marry the prince that brought it."

The princess smiled and walked up to the table and picked up the present she liked the most. It was the platinum-and-sapphire jewel box, the gift of the third prince.

"The way I figure it," she said, "is this. It is a very large and expensive box, and when I am married, I will meet many admirers who will give me the precious gems with which to fill it to the top. Therefore, it is the most valuable of all the gifts my suitors have brought me and I like it the best."

The princess married the third prince that very day in the midst of great merriment and high revelry. More than a hundred thousand pearls were thrown at her and she loved it.

*Moral: All those who thought the princess was going to select the tin box filled with worthless stones instead of one of the other gifts will kindly stay after class and write one hundred times on the blackboard, "I would rather have a hunk of aluminum silicate than a diamond necklace."*

Reading CORNER

# The Gift-Giving

by Joan Aiken

*The giving of gifts is a tradition that has been with us for a long time. But sometimes the gift is more than what is contained beneath the gift wrap.*

The weeks leading up to Christmas were always full of excitement, and tremendous anxiety, too, as the family waited in suspense for the Uncles, who had set off in the spring of the year, to return from their summer's traveling and trading: Uncle Emer,

Uncle Acraud, Uncle Gonfil, and Uncle Mark. They always started off together, down the steep mountainside, but then, at the bottom, they took different routes along the deep narrow valley, Uncle Mark and Uncle Acraud riding eastward, toward the great plains, while Uncle Emer and Uncle Gonfil turned west, toward the towns and rivers and the western sea.

Then, before they were clear of the mountains, they would separate once more, Uncle Acraud turning south, Uncle Emer taking his course northward, so that, the children occasionally thought, their family was scattered over the whole world, netted out like a spider's web.

Spring and summer would go by in the usual occupations, digging and sowing the steep hillside garden beds, fishing, hunting for hares, picking wild strawberries, making hay. Then, toward St. Drimma's Day, when the winds began to blow and the snow crept down, lower and lower, from the high peaks, Grandmother would begin to grow restless.

Silent and calm all summer long she sat in her rocking chair on the wide wooden porch, wrapped in a patchwork comforter, with her blind eyes turned eastward toward the lands where Mark, her dearest and firstborn, had gone. But when the winds of Michaelmas began to blow, and the wolves grew bolder, and the children dragged in sacks of logs day after day, and the cattle were brought down to the stable under the house, then Grandmother grew agitated indeed.

When Sammle, the eldest granddaughter, brought her hot milk, she would grip the girl's slender brown wrist and demand: "Tell me, child, how many days now to St. Froida's Day?" (which was the first of December).

"Eighteen, Grandmother," Sammle would answer, stooping to kiss the wrinkled cheek.

"So many, still? So many till we may hope to see them?"

"Don't worry, Granny, the Uncles are *certain* to return safely. Perhaps they will be early this year. Perhaps we may see them before the feast of St. Melin" (which was December the fourteenth).

And then, sure enough, sometime during the middle weeks of December, their great carts would come jingling and trampling along the winding valleys. Young Mark (son of Uncle Emer), from his watchpoint up a tall pine over a high cliff, would catch the flash of a baggage-mule's brass brow-medal and would come joyfully dashing back to report.

"Granny! Granny! The Uncles are almost here!"

Then the whole household, the whole village, would be filled with as much turmoil as that of a kingdom of ants when the spade breaks open their hummock. Wives would build the fires higher, and fetch out the best linen, dried meat, pickled eggs; set dough to rising, mix cakes of honey and oats, bring up stone jars of preserved strawberries from the cellars; and the children, with the servants and half the village, would go racing down the perilous zigzag track to meet the cavalcade at the bottom.

The track was far too steep for the heavy carts, which would be dismissed and the carters paid off to go about their business. Then with laughter and shouting, amid a million questions from the

children, the loads would be divided and carried up the mountainside on muleback, or on human shoulders. Sometimes the Uncles came home at night, through falling snow, by the smoky light of torches; but the children and the household always knew of their arrival beforehand, and were always there to meet them.

"Did you bring Granny's Chinese shawl, Uncle Mark? Uncle Emer, have you the enameled box that Aunt Grippa begged you to get? Uncle Acraud, did you find the glass candlesticks? Uncle Gonfil, did you bring the books?"

"Yes, yes, keep calm, don't deafen us! Poor tired travelers that we are, leave us in peace to climb this devilish hill! Everything is there, set your minds at rest—the shawl, the box, the books—besides a few other odds and ends, pins and needles and fruit, and a few trifles for the village. Now, just give us a few minutes to get our breath, will you, kindly—" as the children danced round them, helping each other with the smaller bundles, never ceasing to pour out questions: "Did you see the Grand Cham? The Akond of Swat? The Fon of Bikom? The Seljuk of Rum? Did you go to Cathay? To Muskovy? To Dalai? Did you travel by ship, by camel, by llama, by elephant?"

And, at the top of the hill, Grandmother would be waiting for them, out on her roofed porch, no matter how wild the weather or how late the time, seated in majesty with her furs and patchwork quilt around her, while the Aunts ran to and fro with hot stones to place under her feet. And the Uncles always embraced her first, very fondly and respectfully, before turning to hug their wives and sisters-in-law.

Then the goods they had brought would be distributed through the village—the scissors, tools, medicines, plants, bales of cloth, ingots of metal, and musical instruments; after that there would be a great feast.

Not until Christmas morning did Grandmother and the children receive the special gifts that had been brought for them by the Uncles; and this giving always took the same ceremonial form.

Uncle Mark stood behind Grandmother's chair, playing on a small pipe that he had acquired somewhere during his travels; it was made from hard black polished wood, with silver stops, and it had a mouthpiece made of amber. Uncle Mark invariably played the same tune on it at these times, very soft. It was a tune that he had heard for the first time, he said, when he was much younger, once when he had narrowly escaped falling into a crevasse on the hillside, and a voice had spoken to him, as it seemed, out of the mountain itself, bidding him watch where he set his feet and have a care, for the family depended on him. It was a gentle, thoughtful tune, which reminded Sandri, the middle granddaughter, of springtime sounds, warm wind, water from melted snow dripping off the gabled roofs, birds trying out their mating calls.

While Uncle Mark played on his pipe, Uncle Emer would hand each gift to Grandmother. And she—here was the strange thing—she, who was stone-blind all the year long, could not see her own hand in front of her face, she would take the object in her fingers and instantly identify it. "A mother-of-pearl comb, with silver studs, for Tassy . . . it comes from Babylon. A silk shawl, blue and rose, from Hind, for Argilla. A wooden game, with ivory pegs, for young Emer, from Damascus. A gold brooch, from Hangku, for Grippa. A book of rhymes, from Paris, for Sammle, bound in a scarlet leather cover."

By stroking each gift with her old fingers, frail as quills, Grandmother, who lived all the year round in darkness, could discover not only what the thing was and where it came from, but also the

color of it, and that in the most precise and particular manner, correct to a shade. "It is a jacket of stitched and pleated cotton, printed over with leaves and flowers; it comes from the island of Haranati, in the eastern ocean; the colors are leaf-brown and gold and a dark, dark blue, darker than mountain gentians—" for Grandmother had not always been blind; when she was a young girl she had been able to see as well as anybody else.

"And this is for you, Mother, from your son Mark," Uncle Emer would say, handing her a tissue-wrapped bundle, and she would exclaim, "Ah, how beautiful! A coat of tribute silk, of the very palest green, so that the color shows only in the folds, like shadows on snow; the buttons and the button-toggles are of worked silk, lavender-gray, like pearl, and the stiff collar is embroidered with white roses."

"Put it on, Mother!" her sons and daughters-in-law would urge her, and the children, dancing round her chair, clutching their own treasures, would chorus, "Yes, put it on, put it on! Ah, you look like a queen, Granny, in that beautiful coat! The highest queen in the world! The queen of the mountain!"

Those months after Christmas were Grandmother's happiest time. Secure, thankful, with her sons safe at home, she would sit in the warm fireside corner of the big wooden family room. The wind might shriek, the snow gather higher and higher out of doors, but that did not concern her, for her family, and all the village, were well supplied with flour, oil, firewood, meat, herbs, and roots. The children had their books and toys, they learned lessons with the old priest, or made looms and spinning wheels, carved stools and chairs and chests with the tools their uncles had brought them. The Uncles rested and told tales of their travels; Uncle Mark played his pipe for hours together, Uncle Acraud drew pictures in charcoal of the places he had seen, and Granny, laying her hand on the paper covered with lines, would expound while Uncle Mark played: "A huge range of mountains, like wrinkled brown lines across the horizon; a wide plain of sand, silvery blond in color, with patches of pale, pale blue; I think it is not water but air the color of water. Here are strange lines across the sand where men once plowed it, long, long ago; and a great patch of crystal green, with what seems like a road crossing it. Now here is a smaller region of plum-pink, bordered by an area of rusty red. I think these are the colors of the earth in these territories; it is very high up, dry from height, and the soil glittering with little particles of metal."

"You have described it better than I could myself!" Uncle Acraud would exclaim, while the children, breathless with wonder and curiosity, sat cross-legged round her chair. And she would answer, "Yes, but I cannot see it at all, Acraud, unless your eyes have seen it first, and I cannot see it without Mark's music to help me."

"How does Grandmother *do* it?" the children would demand of their mothers, and Argilla, or Grippa, or Tassy would answer, "Nobody knows. It is Grandmother's gift. She alone can do it."

The people of the village might come in, whenever they chose, and on many evenings thirty or forty would be there, silently listening, and when Grandmother retired to bed, which she did early for the seeing made her weary, the audience would turn to one another with deep sighs, and murmur, "The world is indeed a wide place."

But with the first signs of spring the Uncles would become restless again, and begin looking over their equipment, discussing maps and routes, mending saddlebags and boots, gazing up at the high peaks for signs that the snow was in retreat.

Then Granny would grow very silent. She never asked them to stay longer, she never disputed their going, but her face seemed to shrivel, she grew smaller, wizened and huddled inside her quilted patchwork.

And on St. Petrag's Day, when the Uncles set off, when the farewells were said and they clattered off down the mountain through the melting snow and the trees with pink luminous buds, Grandmother would fall into a silence that lasted, sometimes, for as much as five or six weeks; all day she would sit with her face turned to the east, wordless, motionless, and would drink her milk and go to her bed-place at night still silent and dejected; it took the warm sun and sweet wild hyacinths of May to raise her spirits.

Then, by degrees, she would grow animated, and begin to say, "Only six months, now, till they come back."

But young Mark observed to his cousin Sammle, "It takes longer, every year, for Grandmother to grow accustomed."

And Sammle said, shivering though it was warm May weather, "Perhaps one year, when they come back, she will not be here. She is becoming so tiny and thin; you can see right through her hands, as if they were leaves." And Sammle held up her own thin brown hand against the sunlight to see the blood glow under the translucent skin.

"I don't know how they would bear it," said Mark thoughtfully, "if when they came back we had to tell them that she had died."

But that was not what happened.

One December the Uncles arrived much later than usual. They did not climb the mountain until St. Misham's Day, and when they reached the house it was in silence. There was none of the usual joyful commotion.

Grandmother knew instantly that there was something wrong. "Where is my son Mark?" she demanded. "Why do I not hear him among you?" And Uncle Acraud had to tell her: "Mother, he is dead. Your son Mark will not come home, ever again."

"How do you *know*? How can you be *sure*? You were not there when he died?"

"I waited and waited at our meeting place, and a messenger came to tell me. His caravan had been attacked by wild tribesmen, riding north from the Lark Mountains. Mark was killed, and all his people. Only this one man escaped and came to bring me the story."

"But how can you be *sure*? How do you know he told the *truth*?"

"He brought Mark's ring."

Emer put it into her hand. As she turned it about in her thin fingers, a long moan went through her.

"Yes, he is dead. My son Mark is dead."

"The man gave me this little box," Acraud said, "which Mark was bringing for you."

Emer put it into her hand, opening the box for her. Inside lay an ivory fan. On it, when it was spread out, you could see a bird, with eyes made of sapphires, flying across a valley, but Grandmother held it listlessly, as if her hands were numb.

"What is it?" she said. "I do not know what it is. Help me to bed, Argilla. I do not know what it is. I do not wish to know. My son Mark is dead."

Her grief infected the whole village. It was as if the keystone of an arch had been knocked out; there was nothing to hold the people together.

That year spring came early, and the three remaining Uncles, melancholy and restless, were glad to leave on their travels. Grandmother hardly noticed their going.

Sammle said to Mark: "You are clever with your hands. Could you not make a pipe—like the one my father had?"

"*I*?" he said. "Make a pipe? Like Uncle Mark's pipe? Why? What would be the point of doing so?"

"Perhaps you might learn to play on it. As he did."

"*I*? Play on a pipe?"

"I think you could," she said. "I have heard you whistle tunes of your own."

"But where would I find the right kind of wood?"

"There is a chest, in which Uncle Gonfil once brought books and music from Leiden. I think it is the same kind of wood. I think you could make a pipe from it."

"But how can I remember the shape?"

"I will make a drawing," Sammle said, and she drew with a stick of charcoal on the whitewashed wall of the cowshed. As soon as Mark looked at her drawing he began to contradict.

"No! I remember now. It was not like that. The stops came here—and the mouthpiece was like this."

Now the other children flocked round to help and advise.

"The stops were farther apart," said Creusie. "And there were more of them and they were bigger."

"The pipe was longer than that," said Sandri. "I have held it. It was as long as my arm."

"How will you ever make the stops?" said young Emer.

"You can have my silver bracelets that Father gave me," said Sammle.

"I'll ask Finn the smith to help me," said Mark.

Once Mark had got the notion of making a pipe into his head, he was eager to begin. But it took him several weeks of difficult carving; the black wood of the chest proved hard as iron. And when the pipe was made, and the stops fitted, it would not play; try as he would, not a note could he fetch out of it.

Mark was dogged, though, once he had set himself to a task; he took another piece of black chest and began again. Only Sammle stayed to help him now; the other children had lost hope, or interest, and gone back to their summer occupations.

The second pipe was much better than the first. By September, Mark was able to play a few notes on it; by October he was playing simple tunes made up out of his head.

"But," he said, "if I am to play so that Grandmother can see with her fingers—if I am to do *that*—I must remember your father's special tune. Can *you* remember it, Sammle?"

She thought and thought. "Sometimes," she said, "it seems as if it is just beyond the edge of my hearing—as if somebody were playing it, far, far away, in the woods. Oh, if only I could stretch my hearing a little farther!"

"Oh, Sammle! Try!"

For days and days she sat silent or wandered in the woods, frowning, knotting her forehead, willing her ears to hear the tune again; and the women of the household said, "That girl is not doing her fair share of the task."

They scolded her and set her to spin, weave, milk the goats, throw grain to the hens. But all the while she continued silent, listening, listening, to a sound she could not hear. At night, in her dreams, she sometimes thought she could hear the tune, and she would wake with tears on her cheeks, wordlessly calling her father to come back and play his music to her, so that she could remember it.

In September the autumn winds blew cold and fierce; by October snow was piled around the walls and up to the windowsills. On St. Felin's Day the three Uncles returned, but sadly and silently, without the former festivities; although, as usual, they brought many bales and boxes of gifts and merchandise. The children went down, as usual, to help carry the bundles up the mountain. The joy had gone out of this tradition, though, and they toiled silently up the track with their loads.

It was a wild, windy evening; the sun set in fire, the wind moaned among the fir trees, and gusts of sleet every now and then dashed in their faces.

"Take care, children!" called Uncle Emer as they skirted along the side of a deep gully, and his words were caught by an echo and flung back and forth between the rocky walls: "Take care—care—care—care . . ."

"*Oh!*" cried Sammle, stopping precipitately and clutching the bag that she was carrying. "I have it! I can remember it! *Now* I know how it went!"

And, as they stumbled on up the snowy hillside, she hummed the melody to her cousin Mark, who was just ahead of her.

"Yes, that is it, yes!" he said. "Or, no, wait a minute, that is not *quite* right—but it is close, it is very nearly the way it went. Only the notes were a little faster, and there were more of them—they went up, not down—before the ending tied them in a knot—"

"No, no, they went down at the end, I am almost sure—"

Arguing, interrupting each other, disputing, agreeing, they dropped their bundles in the family room and ran away to the cowhouse where Mark kept his pipe hidden.

For three days they discussed and argued and tried a hundred different versions; they were so occupied that they hardly took the trouble to eat. But at last, by Christmas morning, they had reached agreement.

"I *think* it is right," said Sammle. "And if it is not, I do not believe there is anything more that we can do about it."

"Perhaps it will not work in any case," said Mark sadly. He was tired out with arguing and practicing.

Sammle was equally tired, but she said, "Oh, it *must* work. Oh, let it work! Please let it work! For otherwise I don't think I can bear the sadness. Go now, Mark, quietly and quickly, go and stand behind Granny's chair."

The family had gathered, according to Christmas habit, around Grandmother's rocking chair, but the faces of the Uncles were glum and reluctant, their wives dejected and hopeless. Only the children showed eagerness, as the cloth-wrapped bundles were brought and laid at Grandmother's feet.

She herself looked wholly dispirited and cast down. When Uncle Emer handed her a slender, soft package, she received it apathetically, almost with dislike, as if she would prefer not to be bothered by this tiresome gift ceremony.

Then Mark, who had slipped through the crowd without being noticed, began to play on his pipe just behind Grandmother's chair.

The Uncles looked angry and scandalized; Aunt Tassy cried out in horror: "Oh, Mark, wicked boy, how *dare* you?" but Grandmother lifted her head, more alertly than she had done for months past, and began to listen.

Mark played on. His mouth was quivering so badly that it was hard to grip the amber mouthpiece, but he played with all the breath that was in him. Meanwhile, Sammle, kneeling by her grandmother, held, with her own warm young hands, the old, brittle ones against the fabric of the gift. And, as she did so, she began to feel what Grandmother felt.

Grandmother said softly and distinctly: "It is a muslin shawl, embroidered in gold thread, from Lebanon. It is colored a soft brick red, with pale roses of sunset pink, and thorns of silver-green. It is for Sammle . . ."

## Reader's Response

These stories contain literary surprises. As you read, could you predict the story endings? Which conclusion most surprised you? What did you expect to happen in place of what really happened?

# Writing About Reading

## *Writing about an Important Decision*

In this unit, you read selections in which characters made important decisions. While reading each selection, you may have asked yourself, "Would I have made the same decision?" For example, if you had been Jerry in "President Cleveland, Where Are You?" would you have sold your president card to Rollie Tremaine for five dollars?

In a three-paragraph paper, you will have an opportunity to analyze the conflict that one character faced, discuss what the character did, and tell what you would have done differently. You will summarize the character's decision, state your own decision, and support your decision.

### *Prewriting*

To prepare yourself to write a paper about a decision, take notes about the following:

- the character's conflict
- the character's decision
- the decision you would have made

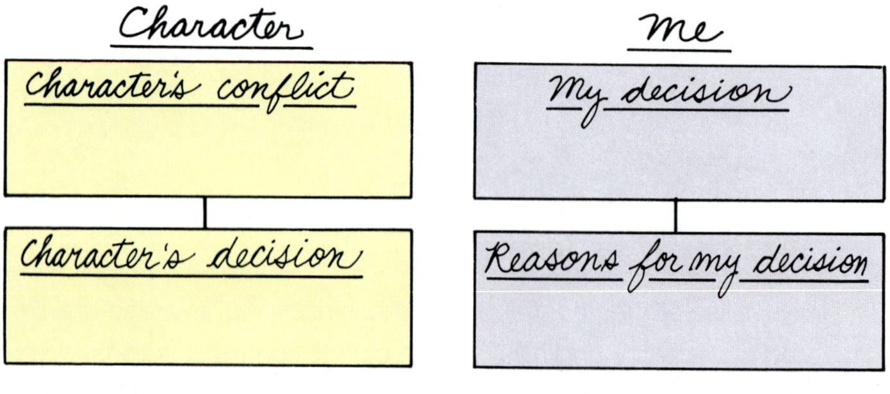

### *Writing*

Use your notes to write three explanatory paragraphs supporting your decision. Introduce the character and the conflict. Review the character's decision and any reasons the character had for that decision. Then explain how you would have handled the situation. Support your decision with facts and reasons. For good supporting reasons, think back to the episodes in the story you are writing about. Also, recall things you have learned from your own experience.

### *Revising*

Reread your explanatory paragraphs. Will your readers understand the character's conflict and decision? Have you expressed your own decision clearly and supported it with sound reasoning?

### *Proofreading*

Correct errors in spelling, punctuation, and grammar. Then make a clean copy.

### *Publishing*

Contribute your paper, if you wish, to a class publication entitled *New Decisions*. With your classmates, discuss the alternatives that have been presented for dealing with characters' conflicts.

# WORKING TOGETHER

## *Making a Name Poem*

The personal strengths and qualities of the main characters in the selections in this unit determined the decisions they made and the actions they took. For example, Maria Pepe's decision to try out for Little League baseball showed her confidence and talent; her decision to stand up to criticism showed her courage; and her decision to quit the team so that the other children could play showed concern for others.

**NAME POEM FOR MARIA**

Makes a good team player.
A
R
I
A

P
E
P
E

Your group will now write a name poem for one of the characters in this unit. Before you begin, decide who will be responsible for one or more of these tasks:

- Encouraging everyone to participate
- Recording ideas
- Checking to make sure everyone understands the work
- Giving additional ideas if someone needs help

First, recall together the story characters in this unit. Agree on one character for whom you will write a name poem. Write the character's name down the left-hand side of a sheet of paper. Then brainstorm words or phrases that describe the character's actions, special qualities, and achievements. Keep a list of people's ideas, and then take turns filling out each line of the name poem. If someone has trouble thinking of a line, others may help. The poem does not have to rhyme, but each line should begin with a letter from your character's name. When the poem is finished, choose one person in your group to read it aloud.

# BOOKS TO ENJOY

***Dust of the Earth*** by Vera and Bill Cleaver *(Lippincott, 1975)* The Drawns begin to understand the strength of their family ties as they share in the danger and hard work of homesteading in the South Dakota Badlands.

***Profiles in Courage*** by John F. Kennedy *(Harper, 1988)* A former President depicts eight famous Americans who in their own time fought for what they believed for the sake of principle, regardless of the consequences.

***Across Five Aprils*** by Irene Hunt *(Berkley, 1987)* This historical fiction novel chronicles the Civil War through the Creighton family's experiences. Jethro Creighton's older brothers join opposing armies while he remains on the family farm.

***Martin Luther King, Jr.,*** by Jacqueline L. Harris *(Watts, 1983)* This biography of the black leader who was awarded the Nobel Peace Prize tells how a caring man used his commitment to nonviolence in the struggle for civil rights.

***Mohandas Gandhi*** by Glenn A. Cheney *(Watts, 1983)* This biography briefly depicts the main events and primary influences of this man who was most responsible for leading India to independence from Great Britain.

# BROWSING FOR BOOKS

## *Reading for Pleasure*

Your social studies teacher assigns thirty pages of reading in your textbook for a test next week. For your science class, you have to find and read two books about cells, and prepare an oral report. Your English teacher tells you to choose a book from the reading list for a book report, and you must keep up with class assignments at the same time.

So what happens to that great mystery novel that you got for your birthday? It probably gets buried at the bottom of your locker, forgotten until June. That doesn't have to happen. There are ways to enjoy your novel and still keep up with your homework. In fact, having a book to read for pleasure can even *help* with your work for school. You have probably noticed that after you have been reading a history textbook for a while, you stop taking in information very effectively. When that happens, use your mystery novel to break up your history reading. Read history for a while, then switch to your novel for fifteen minutes. If you alternate back and forth, you'll be able to discover "whodunit," and still learn something about World War II!

There are other ways to combine reading for pleasure with your work. Set aside a specific amount of time to read when you get home from school, before you start your homework. Or, after an especially busy week, use part of the weekend to relax with a good book. Instead of letting your novel gather dust on your desk, or get buried in your locker, read it and enjoy it. It isn't always easy, but you can *make* time. Think of some places in your schedule where pleasure would fit particularly well. For example, ten minutes before you go to bed at night is a good time to read. You will find it easy once you get started, especially if you have an exciting or interesting book to explore.

NOVELLA

AWARD WINNING AUTHOR

# WINTER THUNDER

by Mari Sandoz

The snow began quietly this time, like an afterthought to the gray Sunday night. The moon almost broke through once, but toward daylight a little wind came up and started white curls, thin and lonesome, running over the old drifts left from the New Year storm. Gradually the snow thickened, until around eight thirty the two ruts of the winding trails were covered and undisturbed except down in the Lone Tree district, where an old yellow bus crawled heavily along, feeling out the ruts between the choppy sand hills.

As the wind rose, the snow whipped against the posts of a ranch fence across the trail, and caked against the bus windows, shutting in the young faces pressed to the glass. The storm increased until all the air was a powdery white and every hill, every trace of road, was obliterated. The bus wavered and swayed in its direction, the tracks filling in close upon the wheels as they sought out the trail lost somewhere far back, and then finally grasped at any footing, until it looked like some great snowy, bewildered bug seen momentarily through the shifting wind. But it kept moving, hesitating here, stalling there in the deepening drifts, bucking heavily into them, drawing back to try once more while the chains spun out white fans that were lost in the driving snow which seemed almost as thick, as dense. Once the bus had to back down from a steep little patch that might have led into a storm-lost valley with a ranch house and warmth and shelter. It started doggedly around, slower now, but decisive, feeling cautiously for traction on the drifted hillside. Then the wheels began to slip, catch, and then slip again, the bus tipping precariously in the push of the wind, a cry inside lost under the rising noise of the storm.

For a long time it seemed that the creeping bus could not be stopped. Even when all discernible direction or purpose was finally gone, it still moved, backing, starting again, this way and that, plowing the deepened slope, swaying, leaning until it seemed momentarily very tall and held from toppling only by the thickness of the flying snow. Once more a wheel caught and held under the thunder of the red-hot smoking exhaust. It slipped, and held again, but now the force of the wind was too great. For a moment the tilting bus seemed to lift. Then it pivoted into a slow skid and turned half around, broadside. Slowly it went over, almost as though without weight at all, settling lightly against a drift, to become a part of it at that thickening place where the white storm turned to snowbanks, lost except that there were frightening cries from inside, and a hiss of steam and smoke from the hot engine against the snow.

In a moment the door was forced outward, the wind catching a puff of smoke as dark, muffled heads pushed up and were white in an instant. They were children, mostly in snowsuits and in sheepskin coats, thrust down over the bus side, coughing and gasping as the force of the blizzard struck them, the older ones hunching their shoulders to shield themselves and some of the rest.

Once more the engine roared out and the upper back wheel spun on its side, free and foolish in its awkward caking of snow. Then the young woman who had handed the children down followed them, her sheepskin collar up about her head, her arms full of blankets and lunch boxes.

"You'll have to give it up, Chuck," she called back into the smoking interior. "Quick! Bring the rest of the lunches—"

With Chuck, sixteen and almost as tall as a man, beside her, Lecia Terry pushed the frightened huddle of children together and hurried them away downwind into the wall of storm. Once she tried to look back through the smother of snow, wishing that they might have taken the rope and shovel from the toolbox. But there was no time to dig for them on the under side now.

Back at the bus thick smoke was sliding out the door into the snow that swept along the side. Flames began to lick up under the leaning windows, the caking of ice suddenly running from them.

The glass held one moment and burst, and the flames whipped out, torn away by the storm as the whole bus was suddenly a wet, shining yellow that blistered and browned with the heat. Then there was a dull explosion above the roar of the wind, and down the slope the fleeing little group heard it and thought they saw a dark fragment flying past overhead.

"Well, I guess that was the gas tank going," Chuck shouted as he tried to peer back under his shielding cap. But there was only the blizzard closed in around them, and the instinctive fear that these swift storms brought to all living creatures, particularly the young.

There was sobbing among the children now, a small one crying out, "Teacher! Teacher!" inside the thick scarf about her face, clutching for Lecia in her sudden panic.

"Sh-h, Joanie. I'm right here," the young woman soothed, drawing the six-year-old to her, looking around for the others, already so white that she could scarcely see them in the powdery storm.

"Bill, will you help Chuck pack all the lunches in two, three boxes, tight, so nothing gets lost? Maggie's big sirup bucket'll hold a lot. Throw all the empties away. We'll have to travel light—" she said, trying to make it sound a little like an old joke.

"My father will be coming for me soon—" the eight-year-old Olive said primly. "So you need not touch my lunch."

"Nobody can find us here," Chuck said shortly, and the girl did not reply, too polite to argue. But now one of the small boys began to cry. "I want my own lunch box too, Teacher," he protested, breathless from the wind. "I—I want to go home!"

His older brother grabbed at his arm roughly with a mittened hand. "Stop it, Fritz," he commanded. "You can't go home. The bus is—" Then he stopped, looking toward the teacher, almost lost only an arm's length away, and the full realization of their plight struck him. "We can't go home," he said, so quietly that he could scarcely be heard in the wind. "The bus is burned and Chuck and Miss Lecia don't know where we are—"

"Sure we know!" Chuck shouted against him without looking up from the lunch packing, his long back stooped protectively over his task. "Don't we know, Lecia? Anyway, it won't last. Radio this morning said just light snow flurries, or Dad wouldn't have let me take the bus out 'stead of him, even sick as he was." The tall boy straightened up, the lunch boxes strung to the belt of his sheepskin to bang together in the wind until they were snow-crusted. "Baldy Stever'll be out with his plane looking for his girlfriend soon's it clears a little, won't he, Lecia?" he said. "Like he came New Year's, with skis on it."

But the bold talk did not quiet the sobbing, and the teacher's nod was lost in the storm as she tied scarves and mufflers across the faces of the younger children, leaving only little slits for the eyes, with the brows and lashes already furred with snow. Then she lined up the seven, mixing the ages from six-year-old Joanie to twelve-year-old Bill, who limped heavily as he moved in the deepening snow. One of the blankets she pinned around the thinly dressed Maggie, who had only a short outgrown coat, cotton stockings, and torn overshoes against the January storm. The other blanket she tied around herself, ready to carry Joanie on her back, Indian fashion, when the short little legs were worn out.

Awkwardly, one after another, Lecia pulled the left arm of each pupil from the sleeve, buttoned it inside the coat and then tied the empty sleeve to the right arm of the one ahead. She took the lead, with little Joanie tied to her belt, where she could be helped. Chuck was at the tail end of the clumsy little queue, just behind Bill with the steel-braced ankle.

"Never risk getting separated," Lecia remembered hearing her pioneer grandfather say when he told of burying the dead from the January blizzard of 1888 here, the one still called the school children's storm. "Never get separated and never stop moving until you find shelter—"

The teacher squinted back along the line, moving like some long snowy winter-logged animal, the segmented back bowed before the sharpening blizzard wind. Just the momentary turn into the storm took her breath and frightened her for these children hunched into themselves, half of them crying softly, hopelessly, as though already lost. They must hurry. With not a rock anywhere and not a tree within miles to show the directions, they had to seek out the landmark of the ranch country—the wire fence. So the girl started downwind again, breaking the new drifts as she searched for valley ground where fences were most likely, barbed-wire fences that might lead to a ranch, or nowhere except around some hay meadow. But it was their only chance the girl from the sand hills knew. Stumbling, floundering through the snow, she kept the awkward string moving, the eyes of the older ones straining through frozen lashes for even the top of one fence post, those of the small ones turned in upon their fear as the snow caked on the mufflers over their faces and they stumbled blindly to the pull from ahead.

Once there was a bolt of lightning, milky white in the blizzard, and a shaking of thunder, ominous winter thunder that stopped the moving feet. Almost at once the wind grew sharper, penetrating even Chuck's heavy sheepskin coat, numbing the ears and feet as panting, sobbing, the children plowed on again, the new drifts soon far above Lecia's boots, and no visibility, no way to avoid them.

With their hands so awkwardly useless, someone stumbled every few steps, but the first to fall was Bill, the others, the crying ones too, standing silent in the storm, not even able to slap one frozen hand against another while the boy was helped up. After that others went down, and soon it was all that the teacher and the boy Chuck could do to keep the children moving as they pushed through the chop hills and found themselves going up what seemed a long wind-swept, wind-frozen slope, Lecia carrying Joanie on her back most of the time now. But they kept moving somehow, barely noticing even the jack rabbit that burst out among their feet and was gone into the storm. Otherwise there was nothing.

After a long, long time they reached what seemed a high ridge of hills standing across the full blast of the north wind that bent them low and blinded. Suddenly Chuck's feet slid off sideways into a hole, a deep-cupped blowout hidden by the storm. Before he could stop, he had drawn the rest tumbling after him, with an avalanche of snow. Crying, frightened, the smaller ones were set to their feet and brushed off a little. Then they all crouched together under the bank to catch their breath out of the wind, shivering, wet from the snow that had fallen inside their clothes, which were already freezing hard as board.

"With the blowouts always from the northwest to the southeast," Chuck shouted into the teacher's covered ear, "the wind's plainly from the north, so we're being pushed about due south. That direction there can't be a house for five, six miles, even if we could find it—unless we got clear out of our home country—"

The girl shivered, empty with fear. "—So that's why we haven't found a fence," she said slowly. "We're probably in the old Bar M summer range, miles and miles across. But we can't go any other direction—"

"I could alone; I could make it out alone!" Chuck shouted suddenly, angrily.

For a moment the teacher was silent, waiting, but when he added nothing more, she said: "You can't leave these little ones now, Chuck. Even if you were sure you could find a ranch—"

There was no reply, except that the boy with the steel brace began to cry, a reddening from his ankle coming up through the snow that was packed into his overshoes around the brace. Others were sobbing too, and shaking with cold, but the younger ones were very quiet now, already drowsing, and so the young teacher had to get to her feet and help lift the children out of the blowout. Slapping the muffler-covered cheeks, shaking the smaller ones so hard that the caked snow fell from them, she got the line moving again, but very slowly. She was worn out too, from the path-breaking and with Joanie in her arms to warm the child, keep her from the sleep of freezing that came upon her on Lecia's back, with only the thin blanket against the ice of the wind.

They seemed to be going down now, through a long deep-drifted slope, plowing into buried yucca clumps, the sharp spears penetrating the snowsuits, even the boot tops. Here a few head of cattle passed them, less than three feet away and barely to be seen. They were running, snow-caked, blinded, bawling, and Lecia squinted anxiously back into the storm for others, for a herd that might be upon them, trample them as surely as stampeding buffaloes. But there were no more now, and she could see that Chuck was shouting, "Little chance of its clearing up soon, with that snow thunder and those cattle already drifting so fast—all the way from the winter range!"

Yes, drifting fast with the force and terror of the storm, even hardy, thick-haired range cattle running!

Then suddenly one of the younger boys cried out something. "Teacher!" he repeated, "I saw a post!"

But it must have been a trick of the wind, for there was only the driving snow, except that the sharp-eyed Maggie saw one too, ahead and to the right—a snowy post with only the upper foot out of the drifts, holding up a strand of gray wire taut and humming in the cold.

For a moment Lecia could not see through the blurring of her eyes. At least this was something to follow, but which way? To her signal Chuck lifted his arm and dropped it. He didn't recognize the fence either, and so the teacher took the easier direction, leftward, only sideface to the wind, although it might lead to the hills, to some final drift where the fleeing cattle would end.

Moving slowly along the fence, Lecia knew that it could not be much farther anyway. Her arms were wooden with cold and the weight of the child, her legs so weary in the deepening drifts that with each step it seemed that she could never lift a snow-caked boot again.

Then suddenly Chuck was doubling up the line. "I think I know where we are! That old split post just back there's where we made a take-down running coyotes with Dad's hounds this fall. If I'm right, this is Miller's north meadow, and there's a strip of willows down ahead there, off to the right—"

For a moment the girl set Joanie into the deep snow, panting, and even when she caught her breath, she was afraid to speak.

"How far to a house?" she finally asked, her lips frozen.

"There's no house along this fence if it's the Miller's," Chuck had to admit. "It just goes around the meadow, three, four miles along."

"You're sure—" the teacher asked slowly, "—sure there's no cross fence to the ranch? You might get through, find help in time—"

The boy could only shake his snowy head and then, thinking that the storm hid this, he shouted the words on the wind. No, no cross fence, and the ranch was five miles south. Not even a haystack left in the valley here. Miller had had his hay balers in this fall, hauled it all out for his fancy Angus herd.

Then they must take a chance on the willows, with Bill hardly able to limp along, Joanie too heavy to carry, and several others worn out. So they wallowed through the drifted fence and tried to keep parallel to its direction, but far enough in the meadow to see any willows. There must be willows now.

Suddenly Lecia went down in what must have been a deep gully, the ground gone, the girl sinking into soft powdery snow to her shoulder. Panting, choking, she managed to get Joanie and the rest back out and the frightened ones quieted a little. Then she swung off right along the barer edge of the gully, seeking a place to cross. The wind was blowing in powerful gusts now, so that she could scarcely stand up. Bent low she dragged at the line behind her, most of the children crawling in the trench she plowed for them. There was no

crying now—only the slow, slow moving. Perhaps they should dig into the snow here below the gully bank. Indians and trappers had done that and survived. But they had thick-furred buffalo robes to shut out the cold and snow, and they were grown men, tough, strong—not helpless, worn-out children, their frozen feet heavy as stone, with only an overgrown boy and a twenty-three-year old girl to lead them, keep them alive.

More and more often Lecia had to stop, her head down, her arms dropping the weight of the little girl. But there seemed to be a shallowing in the gully now, and so it was time she tried to break a path through it and turn back toward the fence if they were not to wander lost as so many did that other time, long ago, when a teacher and her nine pupils were lost, finally falling to die on the prairie. They must cling to the fence here, if it went no farther than around the meadow. At least it was proof that something existed on the earth except the thick, stinging blizzard, with a white, freezing, plodding little queue caught in the heart of it, surrounded.

Once when the girl looked up from the running snow it seemed there was something darkish off to the right, little farther than arm's reach away. She saw it again, something rounded, perhaps a willow

clump, low, snow filled, and possibly with more near by. Signaling to Chuck, Lecia turned down to it—a willow covered as in sleep, but with at least two more bushes just beyond, larger, darker, and standing closer together, their longer upper arms snow-weighted, entwined over the drifts. There, between the clumps, out of the worst of the storm, she left the children squatted close, the blankets held over them. With the belts of her coat and Chuck's, they tied the longer brushy tops of the two clumps together as solidly as they could. Then, fighting the grasping wind, they managed to fasten the blankets across the gap between the willows, to hold awhile. Behind this protection Lecia dug through the snow to the frozen ground while Chuck gathered dead wood. Inside a close little kneeling circle of children they built a fire pile with some dry inner bark and a piece of sandwich paper for the lighting. Awkwardly, with freezing hands the teacher and Chuck hurried, neither daring to think about matches, dry ones, in any pocket after this stumbling and falling through the snow.

The two smaller children were dropping into the heavy sleep of exhaustion and cold and had to be held in their places by the older ones while Chuck dug swiftly through his pockets, deeper, more awkwardly, then frantically, the circle of peering eyes like those of fearful young animals, cornered, winter-trapped.

Down to his shirt, Chuck found some in his pocket, six in a holder made of two rifle cartridges slipped together. Hurrying clumsily he struck one of the matches. It sputtered and went out, the flames sucked away. They had to try again, making a closer circle, with the coattails of the children thrown up over their heads to shut out the storm. This time the match caught on the waxed paper and the diamond willow began to snap and sizzle in the snow, throwing a dancing light up to the circle of crouching children.

But it seemed even colder now that they had stopped walking and Lecia thought of the night ahead, with the temperature down to twenty-five or thirty below zero. Beyond that she would not look now but to get through this night they must have a great pile of wood, and they must have shelter even to hold the fire.

"We can't both go out at one time," the teacher told Chuck in their planning, somehow making it seem as for a long, long time. "It's too risky for the children. We might not get back."

The boy looked around from the fire he was nursing, and upward, but there was still no thinning of the storm, the area of snowy visibility almost as small as the confines of their new meat-freeze room at the ranch. Even so he gave the girl no sign of agreement.

Lecia set willow poles into the snowbanks as she went to look for wood, none farther apart than the outstretched reach of her arms. She found more willows, each clump sitting alone in the isolation of the driving storm, so cold now that the green wood snapped off like glass. Each time it was only by the row of sticks in the drifts that she managed to stagger her blinded and panting way back against the wind with her load of wood.

The brushier portions she piled behind the blankets of the shelter to catch the snow and shut out the wind. Some, long as fish poles, she pushed through the willow clumps and across the opening between, in a sort of lattice inside the bellying blankets that Eddie and Calla tried to hold in place. They were the first of the children to separate themselves from the snowy composite, the enforced coordinate that had been the queue driven by the storm, the circle that shielded the sprouting fire. Now they were once more individuals who could move alone, hold the blankets from blowing inward, pile the dry powdery snow from the ground against and between the sticks, trying to work it like plaster, building a wall between the clumps of willows. Even Bill helped a little, as far as he could reach without moving the bad ankle. They worked slowly, clumsily, pounding their freezing hands at the fire, but returning.

By one o'clock the north wind was cut off so that the fire fattened and burned higher, softening the ice caked to the clothing until it could be knocked off, and softening the face of the drift reached by the wind-blown heat. The children packed this against the north wall too, and into the willow clumps both ways, drawing the rounded wall inward toward the top along the bend of the willows, making what looked like half of an Indian snow shelter, or the wickiup Calla had seen at the country fair, just high enough at the center for a seven-year-old to stand up, the snow walls glistening rosy in the firelight as the wind was shut off.

"That's a good job!" Chuck shouted over the roar of the storm as he tried to rub circulation into Joanie's waxen feet. The small girl

was beginning to cry out of her sleep with the first pain; others began too, their ears and hands swollen and purpling, their toes painful as their boots thawed. But it seemed that the feet of the nine-year-old Maggie must be lost, the ragged old overshoes and cotton stockings so frozen that she had to cut them away with Eddie's knife. Under them her feet were like stone, dead white stone, although the girl was working hard to rub life into them. She worked silently and alone, as had become natural long ago, her thin face pinched and anxious with the pain and the alarm.

Of them all only Olive seemed untouched. She was dry in her heavy waterproofed snowsuit with attached rubber feet inside the snow boots. And she was still certain that her father would soon come for her.

"He would not care to leave me in such an unpleasant place—"

When they had the semicircular wall of the shelter drawn in as far as the snow would hold, Lecia decided to pull the blankets away from the outside and use one over the top, with the belt-tied willows sticking through a smoke hole cut in the center. But as the blankets came down, part of the loose snow wall was blown in by the force of the blizzard, the huddle of children suddenly white again, the fire almost smothered. So the wall had to be rebuilt in discouragement, but with care, using more brush and sticks, more fire-softened snow to freeze in place as soon as it was struck by the storm. Lecia had to stop several times for her hands too, pounding them hard, holding them over the fire, the diamond sparkling. She tried to turn the ring off before the swelling became too great and then gave it up. The wall must be finished, and when it was solid, Calla came to whisper under the roar of the wind. "Bill's been eating the lunch," she said.

"Oh, Bill! That's not fair to the others, to your own little sister Joanie!" Lecia cried. Suddenly not the good teacher, she grabbed up the containers and hung them on high branches out in plain sight for watching, for reminders and derision from the other children. "Why, it may be days before we are found!" she scolded, in her exasperation saying what should have been kept hidden in silence.

Before the boy could defend himself with a plea of hunger or his usual complaint about the crippled foot, some realization of their plight had struck the others. Even little Fritz, with the security of an older sister and brother like Calla and Eddie along, began to sob. Only the round-cheeked Olive was calm, the others angered to see it, wanting to shout against her outsider's assurance, to tell her she was too stupid and green to know that her father could not come for her in such a blizzard, that he would never find her if he could get through. But they were silent under the teacher's admonitory eye. And, as in the schoolhouse and on the playground, Bill had withdrawn, except that now it could not be more than a foot or two.

As the frozen earth between the willow humps became soggy, Calla and Eddie helped move the others around so that there was room to draw the fire first one way and then another, to dry and warm the ground. Lecia watched to see that they set no one afire and then bowed her head out into the storm again. Chuck was dragging in willows for the night. They drove sticks into the hardening drifts around the front of the shelter and piled brush against them to catch the snow. It filled in as fast as they worked until there was no more than a little crawling hole left. Then Chuck laid a mat of brushy sticks on the ground and packed soft snow into them to freeze, making a handled slab big enough to close the low doorway. Now, so long as the blanket with the smoke hole stayed tied over the top they could be as warm as they wished in the little shelter that was scarcely longer than a tall man—a close cramping for the teacher, Chuck, and the seven pupils, but easily warmed with a few fingers of wood, an Indian fire. Safe and warm so long as the shelter stood against the rising ferocity of the blizzard, and the willows lasted.

By now the cold stung the nose and burned the lungs, the snow turned to sharp crystals that drew blood from the bare skin. It drove the teacher and Chuck in to the fire, shaking, unable it seemed, ever to be warmed through again. Lecia opened her sheepskin coat, hung up her frozen scarf and cap and shook out her thick brown hair that gleamed in the firelight. Even with her tawny skin red and swollen, her gold-flecked hazel eyes bloodshot, she was still a pretty girl, and the diamond on her hand flashed as she hunted for the stick of white salve to pass around for the raw, bleeding lips. It was all she could do.

Now they tried to plan for what was to come, but here they were as blind as in the flight through the storm. There would be sickness, with the noses already running, Joanie coughing deep from her chest, and worst of all, Maggie's feet that seemed to be dying. Besides, the fire must be kept going and the food spread over three, perhaps four, days.

Here Bill raised his complaining voice, "You ain't our boss outside of school! We'll do what we want to. There ain't enough to eat for everybody."

"You mean *isn't*, not *ain't,*" the teacher corrected firmly. "And talking like that—when you've barely missed one lunch time!"

"You ain't never my boss," Chuck said casually, "—only about the kids while in the bus, like you do with my dad when he's driving. I sure can do what I want to here, and I'll do it."

Slowly the girl looked around the ring of drowsy, firelit eyes upon her, some uneasy at this bold talk to their teacher, but some smaller ones aping the defiance of the big boys. Chuck, who sat almost a head taller than Lecia, grinned down at the pretty young teacher but with an arrogance that was intended to remind her he saw nothing here as his responsibility, nothing this side of the bus except saving himself.

Unable to reply in words that would not frighten the children more, the teacher looked past the fire into the boy's broad, defiant face, into his unblinking, storm-red eyes, the look commanding at first, then changing to something else in spite of herself, into a sort of public test, until it seemed she dared not turn her gaze away or at that instant the sixteen-year-old boy must assert his victory by plunging out into the storm and perhaps destroy himself, perhaps bring death to all of them.

Before this silent, incomprehensible struggle the children were uneasy and afraid, even the coughing stilled, so that the storm seemed very loud outside the smoke hole. But little Fritz was too young to be held so for long. "I'm hungry!" he shouted against the restraining hand of his sister. "I want my lunch!"

As though freed, released, Chuck sat back and grinned a little at the small boy. Matter of factly the teacher washed her raw hands with snow and held them over the fire. Then she spread her napkin on her lap and set out all there was in the eight lunches now: fourteen sandwiches, most of them large, six pieces of Sunday cake, a handful of cookies, a few pieces of candy, and six apples and two oranges, frozen hard. There were two thermos bottles of milk, and these Lecia pushed away into the snow wall.

"If somebody gets sick and can't eat solid food," she said to the owners, their eyes following her eyes in consternation. Even with the best management, there would be no food of any kind in a few days, but this the small owners could not yet understand.

The frozen fruit she handed to Chuck and, without meeting the girl's eyes, he set it around the coals for toasting, to be eaten now because it would not keep well, and might sicken leaner stomachs. In the meantime, Lecia set one lunch box filled with snow near the fire and packed away all except four of the big sandwiches into the others, the eyes of the children following her hands here too, even as she hung the containers back above her head. Then she divided the four sandwiches into halves and passed them around.

"Eat very slowly," she cautioned. "Blizzards usually last three days, so we must make what we have here last too, probably clear to Thursday, or longer."

But Bill seemed not to be listening. "Chuck's eating!" he suddenly protested. "He ain't, *isn't*, in on the lunches."

For a moment the teacher looked sternly at the boy. "After Chuck carried them all from the bus, helped you through the bad places, and helped to make the shelter and the fire!" the girl said in astonishment. "Now we'll have no more of this bickering and complaint. Here we are equal partners, and not one of us will get out of this alive unless we keep working together. Even your comic books should have taught you that much! And don't think this is play. You remember what the storm of 1888 was called in your history book—because so many school children died in it. That storm was short, not over two days most places, nothing for length like the one we had holiday time this year, and no telling about this one. Most of the children in 1888 died because somebody got panicky, didn't think, or they didn't stick together—"

There was silence all around the fire now, the storm seeming to rise, the children edging closer to each other, glancing fearfully over their shoulders as though toward night windows with terrible things stalking outside.

"Oh, we're O.K.," Chuck said optimistically. "We can last three days easy here—" the rebellion gone from him, or hidden for the moment.

Thinking of a five-day storm, the teacher looked around the frightened, sooty faces, the children coughing and sniffling, their pocket tissue gone, the few handkerchiefs hung to dry and wondered if any, even the man-tall Chuck, would be here by then.

But Olive, the newcomer, was unconcerned. "I should like another sandwich, Miss Terry. From my own lunch, please," she said with the formality of an old-fashioned boarding school for eight-year-olds. "I won't need the rest. My father will come for me when it is time."

"He won't find you—" Maggie said as she rubbed at her feet, color seeping into them now, an angry gray-splotched purple, with pain that twisted the thin face.

"My father will come," Olive repeated, plainly meaning that he was not like the fathers of the others here, particularly Maggie's, who had been unemployed since the war. Things had not been good for a long time. If Maggie lost her feet now, it was because she had no warm snowsuit and high boots like the others, only the short old coat above her skinny knees, the broken overshoes with the soles flopping.

But there was still a cheerful face at the fire. Although little Fritz's cheeks seemed swollen to bursting and his frosted ears stood away under the flaps of his cap, he could still show his gap-toothed grin in mischief.

"If we don't get home till Thursday, Teacher, Baldy'll be awful mad at you when he comes flying out Wednesday—"

The rest laughed a little, drowsily. "Maybe Baldy won't be flying around that soon," Eddie said, and was corrected by Calla's sisterly concern. "Don't say Baldy. Say Mr. Stever."

But the teacher busied herself hanging up everything loose. Then with Chuck's knife she slit the remaining blanket down the middle and fastened half around each side against the snow wall, like a tipi lining. By the time the white blizzard darkness came, the smaller children had all been taken outside for the last time and lay in fretful, uneasy sleep. Olive had been the last, waiting stubbornly for her father until she toppled forward. Calla caught her and made room for the girl still murmuring, "Papa—"

Finally the last sob for parent and home was stilled, even Joanie asleep, her feverish head in the teacher's lap, her throat raw and swelling, with nothing except hot snow water to ease the hollow cough. There were half a dozen lozenges in Lecia's pocket but these must be saved for the worst time that would surely come.

The children were packed around the fire like little pigs or puppies on a very cold night. Chuck was at the opposite side from Lecia, the boys on his side, the girls on hers, with Calla and her brothers around the back. The older ones lay nearer the wall, their arms over the younger to hold their restlessness from the fire.

But Bill was still up, drawn back under the willows, his head pulled into his sheepskin collar, his ankle bent to him. He watched the teacher doze in fatigue, met her guilty, waking gaze sullenly. But finally he reached down into his pocket and drew out something in waxed paper.

"I didn't eat the piece you gave me—" he said, holding out his half of the sandwich.

"Bill! That was fine of you," the girl said, too worn out for more as she reached up to put it away.

"No—no, you eat it. I guess you didn't take any."

A moment Lecia looked at the boy, but he avoided her as he edged himself around Chuck closer to the fire, turning his chilled back to the coals, and so she ate the buttered bread with the thick slice of strengthening cold beef, while more snow was driven in through the smoke hole and settled in sparkling dust toward the little fire. There were white flashes too, and the far rumble of winter thunder.

"Is—is there lots of willows left?" Bill asked.

The teacher knew what he meant—how many clumps, and if so far out that someone might get lost.

"I think there are quite a few," she replied, needing to reassure the boy, but unable to make it a flat lie.

A long time he sat silent. Finally he pulled his cap off and shook the long yellowish hair back from his petulant face. "I wonder what Mother's doing—" he said slowly, looking away, his hand seeking out the tortured ankle. Lecia motioned him to hold it over to her and so she did not need to reply, to ask what all the mothers of these children must be doing, with the telephone lines still down from the other storm, and surely nobody foolish enough to try bucking this one, unless it might be Olive's father, the new Eastern owner of the little Box Y ranch.

With snow water heated in the lunch tin, Lecia washed the poor stick that was the boy's ankle, gently sponging the bone laid almost bare where the frozen snow and the iron brace wore through the scarred and unhealthy skin.

"It looks pretty bad, Bill, but you probably won't have to put the brace back on for days—" Lecia started to comfort but it was too late, and she had to see fear and anger and self-pity darken the face in the firelight. Because nothing could be unsaid, the girl silently bandaged the ankle with half of the boy's handkerchief. "Now get a little sleep if you can," she said gently.

The boy crawled in next to Eddie as though Ed were the older, and for a long time the teacher felt the dark eyes staring at her out of the shadowy coat collar as though she had deliberately maneuvered this plunge into the blizzard.

Several times before midnight the girl started to doze but jerked herself awake at the frozen creak of the willow shelter, to push the out-tossed arms back and replenish the fire.

Eddie's cough began to boom deep as from a barrel. He turned and moaned, digging at his chest, Calla helpless beside him, her sleep-weighted eyes anxious on the teacher. Maggie too was finally crying now. Her feet had puffed up and purpled dark as jelly bags, with the graying spots that would surely break and slough off, perhaps spread in gangrene. Yet all Lecia could do was turn the girl's feet from the fire and push them behind the blanket against the snow to relieve the pain and itching a little. Perhaps only freeze them more. Lecia touched the girl's forehead to calm her but felt her stiffen and start to pull away from this unaccustomed kindly touch. Then Maggie relaxed a little and as the teacher stroked the hot temples, she wondered how many days it might be before help could get through. Suddenly their plight here seemed so hopeless, the strength and wisdom of her twenty-three years so weak and futile, that she had to slip out into the storm for calm. And finally Maggie slept, worn out, but still tearing at her feet.

To the weary girl watching, half asleep, at the fire, the roar of the storm rose and fell like the panting of a great live thing, sometimes a little like many great planes warming up together. If only she had married Dale Stever New Year's, they would be in the Caribbean now, these children all safe at home, with probably no other teacher available so soon. Once Lecia turned her swollen hand to the fire, watching the ring catch and break the light into life, and tried to recall the fine plans Dale had made for them. He wasn't a rancher's son like those who usually took her to parties and dances—like Joe, or Wilmo, or even Ben, of the local bank. Dale had come from outside last summer and bought up the sale pavilion in town. Since then he flew all around the surrounding ranch country in a plane the color of a wild canary rising from a plum thicket, gathering stock for the sales. Fairtime he took Lecia and her friend Sallie down to the state fair, and several times on long trips since, to Omaha to the ballet and to Denver. At first it seemed he was all jolly big-talk, with windy stories of his stock in an oil company down in Dallas and in a Chicago commission house. He had a touch of gray at his temples that he thought made him look distinguished when he had his hat on, and to their fathers he called himself the Dutch uncle of the two girls. But gradually he concentrated on Lecia, and at Christmas there was the big diamond and the plane ready to fly south. He even took her to the school board to ask for a release from her contract.

"No," the old school director told the girl. "Bill Terry was a friend of mine, brought me into the country. I can't help his granddaughter marry no man in a rush hurry."

Dale laughed confidently and put his arm about the girl's shoulder as they left, but somehow Lecia couldn't break her contract. They must wait until school was out.

Soon after midnight, Lecia was startled out of a doze by the sound of cattle bawling somewhere in the roar of the storm, like the herds that passed her home in the night of the May blizzard three years ago, when so many died in the drifts and lakes that the whole region was a stench far into the summer. Then suddenly the girl realized where she was, and hurried bareheaded out into the storm. The bawling was very close; any moment hundreds of storm-blinded cattle might be running over the little willows, over their own two clumps.

Lecia dragged burning sticks from the fire, but in an instant the storm had sucked their flame away. So, with her arms up to shield her eyes from the snow that was sharp as steel dust, she stood behind the shelter shouting the "Hi-ah! Hi-ah!" she had learned when she helped the cowboys push cattle to market. It was a futile, lost little sound against cattle compelled to run by an instinct that could not be denied, compelled to flee for survival before the descent of the arctic storm, never stopping until trapped in some drift, or boldly overtaken in some open fence corner to freeze on their feet, as Lecia had seen them stand.

Realizing her danger as a warmth crept over her, the girl stumbled back into the shelter and crouched at the fire. She barely noticed the sting of returning blood in her ears and face while she listened until the drifting herd had surely passed, made more afraid by the knowledge of this thing that drove cattle galloping through the night, the power of it, and how easily it could overcome the little circle of children here if it were not for the handful of fire, for the walls of the storm's own snow.

Toward morning the weary girl knew that she could not keep awake. She had stirred Chuck to sit up a while, but he was unable to shake off the weight of sleep so heavy on an overgrown boy. Trying to remember how the Indians carried their fire—something about moss and damp, rotted wood—Lecia pulled old dead roots from the willow butts and laid them into the coals with the ends sticking far out. Even with waxed paper handy it would be a desperate chance. Willows burned as fast as kindlings and there were only five matches, including the one from Eddie's pocket, and no telling how many spoiled by dampness.

Even so, it was sweet to let herself sink into darkness, but it seemed that she awoke at once, stiff and cold from the nightmare that reached into the waking black, even the ashes of the fire spot cold. With the waxed paper held ready, the girl blew on the ends of the unburnt roots her hands found, carefully, breathless in her fear. At last a red spark glowed deep in one, and when the fire was going again, she slipped outside for calm in the cold that was like thin, sharp glass in the nose.

There was still no earth and no sky, only the white storm of late dawn blowing hard. But the wood had lasted and now Lecia put on a few extra sticks and heated water to wash the goose mush from the inflamed eyes of the children. She started a rousing song: "Get up!

Get up, you sleepyhead!" but even before it was done, Joanie began to whimper, "I'm hungry— "

So the teacher laid out four sandwiches on sticks over the coals and then added another half for herself when she saw Bill watching. "There won't be anything more today except a pinch of cake unless the sun breaks through."

"If it does, we can stomp out a message on the snow," Calla said cheerfully.

"Yes, even if people can't travel for a whole week, Baldy'll come flying over to see about his girl friend," Bill said, boldly.

The younger boys laughed a little, but Chuck was more serious. "If the sky lightens at all and there's no blowing, I'll do the stomping before I leave."

"You'd run away now?" the teacher asked softly as she combed at Joanie's fine brown hair.

"Somebody's got to get help," he defended in loud words.

The children around the fire were suddenly quiet, turning their eyes to follow the tall boy as he pulled up his sheepskin collar and crawled out into the storm. And silent a long time afterward—all except Joanie, who sobbed softly, without understanding. Even Olive looked up once, but Maggie grated her feet hard along the snow wall and tore at their congestion as though she heard nothing.

Then suddenly there was stomping outside and Chuck came back in, snowy, thick frost all over his collar and cap, his brows and lashes in ice, the children pushing over toward him, as to one gone, lost. He brought more wood, and the teacher seemed to have forgotten that he had said anything about leaving. But the children watched him now, even when they pretended they didn't, and watched Lecia too, for suspicion had come in.

The teacher started as for a school day, except that the arithmetic was rote learning of addition and multiplication tables and a quick run through some trick problems: "If I had a fox, a goose, and some corn to get across a river in a boat— " and then, "If I had a dollar to buy a hundred eggs—no, I should take something that won't make us hungry."

"Like a hundred pencils?"

"Well, yes, let's take pencils. I want to buy a hundred for a dollar. Some are five cents each, poor ones two and a half cents, and broken ones half a cent. How many of each kind must I buy?"

In history and nature study they talked about the Indians that still roamed the sand hills when Lecia's grandfather came into the country. They lived the winter long in skin tipis something like the shelter here, and almost as crowded, but with piles of thick-furred buffalo robes for the ground and beds. The girls sat on one side, the boys on the other.

"Like we are here—" Fritz said, his eyes shining in the discovery. "We're Indians. Whoo-oo-oo!" he cried, slapping his mouth with his palm.

They talked about the food too, the piles of dried and pounded meat, the winter hunts, how the village and lodge were governed, and what the children did, their winter games, one almost like "button, button." The boys learned from the men—such things as arrow-making, and later bullet-making, hunting, fighting; and particularly the virtues of resourcefulness, courage, fortitude, and responsibility for all the people. A girl learned from the women—beading, tanning hides, and all the other things needed to live well with modesty, steadfastness, and generosity, and with courage and fortitude and responsibility too, for it was thought that the future of the people lay in the palms of the women, to be cherished or thrown away.

"What does that mean, Teacher?" Fritz asked, hitting out in mischief at his brother Eddie, despite Calla and the teacher both watching, then shouting he was hungry again.

The rest tried to laugh a little as Calla whispered to her small brother, trying to make herself heard against the storm, while Lecia taught them a poem about Indians. Even Joanie repeated a few lines for her, although the child leaned weak and feverish against Calla while Bill comforted his bound ankle and Maggie tried hard to pull herself out of the curious drowsiness that had the teacher frightened.

After a while the children played "button, button," and tried to tell each other poems. When Eddie got stuck on "Snowbound," Bill nudged Fritz and they laughed as easily at his discomfiture as at school, perhaps because Chuck was back and this was the second day of the storm, with tomorrow the third. Then it would clear up and somebody with a scoop shovel would get his horse along the barer ridges to a telephone.

"Maybe somebody'll just come running over the hills to find us," Eddie teased, looking at Olive, turning his face from the teacher.

Well, even if nobody came and Baldy couldn't find a place to land with skis on his plane, he would have sacks of food and blankets and stuff dropped like in the movies and the newspapers.

"I saw it in a movie once, I did," Joanie cried.

So they talked, pretending no one was looking up at the hanging lunch buckets, or sick and afraid. But Lecia did not hear them.

That night Joanie was delirious, and once Maggie slipped past the teacher out into the storm to relieve the fire of her feet. By midnight she couldn't stand on them, and the grayish spots were yellow under the thick skin of a barefoot summer, the swelling creeping above the girl's thin ankles, with red streaks reaching almost to the knees. Her eyes glistened, her cheeks were burning, and she talked of wild and dreadful things.

Lecia tried to remember all that she had read of frostbite, all that her grandfather had told, but she knew that the inflammation spreading past the frozen area was like the cold overtaking the fleeing cattle, and she had to make a desperate decision. She dug two holes deep into the snow wall and laid Maggie with her feet in them almost to her knees, wishing they had something waterproof for covering. The cold would probably freeze the girl more, but it would numb the nerves and perhaps slow the congestion and tissue starvation. Later, when the girl was restless again and crying, Lecia found the yellow spots spreading, painful and hard as boils. She burned the end of a safety pin and while Maggie's frightened eyes became caverns in her thin face, Lecia opened one of the spots. Holding the foot aside she wiped her hand on the snow, then slipped her ring from her shrunken finger and hung it on a twig overhead, where it swayed a little, like a morning dewdrop while she opened the rest of the festering.

While the girl's feet were bathed and bound in the sleeves torn from Lecia's white shirt blouse, she thrust them back into the snow. Then she gave Maggie half a cup of the milk, very quietly, hoping none would awaken to see, although none needed it more. Almost at

once the girl was asleep, to rest until the pus gathered again. But the first time Lecia returned with firewood she saw the thermos bottle half out. She jerked it from the hole. The milk was all gone, and across the little fire Olive stared at her teacher.

"It was mine," the girl said flatly.

So the time had come when the little food left must be hidden. Now, with all but Olive sleeping, was the time. When Lecia came back in, the girl held out something—the ring that had been left hanging on the twig and forgotten.

The next day and the next were the same, only colder, the drifts deeper and harder along the willows, the wind so sharp with snow that it froze the eyeballs. Lecia and Chuck covered their faces as they fought their way back against it, the wood dragging from their shoulders, tied by a strap of cloth cut off around the bottom of Lecia's coat. One at a time they went out and came back, a hand stretched ahead feeling for the next guide pole in the snow before the other let go of the last, the covered face turned from the storm to save the breath from being torn away by the wind.

All the third day there was watching out of the smoke hole for the sky that never appeared. When night finally came without star or stillness, even Lecia, who had tried to prepare herself for this eventuality, felt that she could not face another day of blizzard. Maggie no longer sat up now and both Joanie and Eddie were so sick—their fever high, their chests filling—that the teacher had to try something. She seemed to remember that the early settlers used willow bark to break a fever, so she steeped a handful in Maggie's tin cup until the liquid was strong and dark. She made the two children drink it, first experimentally, then more, and after a while they began to sweat. When they awoke they were wet, their hair clinging to their vulnerable young foreheads, but they seemed better all the next day, except weak. Then at night it was the same with Joanie.

The fourth day was like the rest, colder, with the same white storm outside, the children hunching silent upon themselves inside. Sometimes a small one sobbed a little in sickness and hunger, but it was no more than a soft moaning now, even when Lecia divided most of the little food that was left. The children, even Chuck, took it like animals, and then sat silent again, the deep-socketed eyes watching, some slyly gnawing at willow sticks and roots hidden in the palm.

Everybody around the fire was coughing and fevered now, it seemed to Lecia, the bickering going beyond childish things to quarrels about real or fancied animosities between their families. Once even Calla spoke angrily to Bill, defending her brothers.

"At least they aren't mama babies like you!"

"Mama babies! I wouldn't talk if everybody knew that my family got a start in cattle by stealing calves—"

"You can't say such things!" Calla cried, up and reaching for Bill, caught without his brace and unable to flee into the storm, Joanie crying: "Don't! Don't hit my brother!"

When Lecia returned, Chuck was holding the two apart, shaking them both. The teacher spoke in anger and impatience, too, now, and Bill's face flushed with embarrassment and shame, the sudden red like fever in his hunger-grayed cheeks.

Only Maggie with her poor feet was quiet, and Olive, sitting as though stunned or somewhere far away. The teacher knew that she should do something for this girl, only eight yet apparently so self-contained. Olive never spoke of her father now, as none of the boys teased Lecia about Baldy anymore. Olive was as remote about him as everything else since the night she drank the milk, and found the ring on a twig.

Too weary to think about it, and knowing she must keep awake in the night, Lecia stretched out for a nap. When she awoke, Olive was sitting exactly the same, but the places of Chuck and Eddie were empty—Eddie out in the blizzard after his night of sweating. Then the boys returned with wood, weak, dragging, almost frozen, and with something that Lecia had to be told outside. There seemed only one willow clump left.

One clump? Then they must start digging at the frozen butts, or even pull down their shelter to keep the fire alive, for now the boys too were believing that the storm would blow forever. Yet toward evening there was a thinning above the smoke hole, the sun suddenly there like a thin disk of milky ice from the bottom of a cup. It was almost a promise, even though the storm swept the sun away in a few minutes and the wind shifted around to the south, whipping in past the block the boys had in the hole of the shelter. The children shivered, restless. Once Eddie rose from his sleep and fought to get out, go home. When he finally awakened, he lay down in a chill, very close to the fire, and would not move until a stench of burning cloth helped rouse him. Then he drank the bitter willow bark tea too and finally slept.

Friday morning the sun came out again toward ten o'clock, the same cold, pale disk, with the snow still running along the earth, running higher than the shelter or Chuck, shutting out everything except the veiled sun. The boy came in, looked around the starved, listless circle at the fire, at the teacher too, with her face that had been so pretty Monday morning gaunt and sooty now.

He laid two red-tipped matches, half of all he had, in the girl's lap. "I'm getting out," he said, and without protest from anyone crawled through the hole and was gone.

The children were almost past noticing his desertion now, barely replying when spoken to. If the colds got worse or pneumonia struck, it would be over in a few hours. Maggie hadn't sat up since yesterday, lying flat, staring at the white storm blowing thin above the smoke hole. If any of them wondered how Lecia could keep the fire going alone, with nothing much except the willow butts left, none spoke of it. The teacher sat with her arms hanging between her knees, hopeless.

She finally stirred and put the matches away in waxed paper in her shirt pocket where her ring lay, buttoning the flap down carefully now. Joanie started to cough again, choking, turned red and then very white under the grime and grayness of her face, lying very still. Now Bill made the first gesture toward his small sister.

"Come here, Doll," he said gently, drawing her awkwardly from Lecia's lap, the child lifting her head slowly, holding herself away, looking up at him as a baby might at a stranger, to be weighed and considered. Then she snuggled against him and in a moment she was asleep.

After a long time there seemed a dull sound outside, and then Chuck was suddenly back, crawling in almost as though he had not left, panting in his weakness from the fight against the wind that had turned north again, and colder.

"Scared an eagle off a drift out there," he finally managed to say. "And there's a critter stuck in the snow—beyond the far willows. Small spring calf. Froze hard, but it's meat—"

Then the realization that Chuck was back struck the teacher. She was not alone with the children, and he too was safe for now. But there was something more. The boy who had resented them and his involvement in their plight—he had escaped and come back.

"Oh, Chuck!" the girl exclaimed. Then what he said reached her mind. "A calf? Maybe we could build a fire there so we can cut some off, if we can't get it all out." She reached for her boots. "But we'll have to go work at it one at a time—" looking around the firelit faces that were turned toward her as before, but the eyes alert, watching as though a morsel might be dropped, even thrown.

"I'll go with Chuck, Miss Lecia," Bill said softly. "He can show me and I'll show you. Save time hunting—"

The teacher looked at the crippled boy, already setting Joanie gently aside and reaching for his brace. She felt pride in him, and unfortunate doubt.

"He can probably make it," Chuck said, a little condescending. "It's not over an eighth of a mile, and I found more willows farther along the way, the drifts mostly frozen hard too. I blazed the willows beyond our poles—"

"You'll be careful—mark everything," the girl pleaded.

"We've got to. It's snowing again, and the sun's gone."

It seemed hours since the boys went out, and finally the teacher had to go after them, appalled that the younger ones had to be left alone, yet it must be done. She moved very carefully, feeling her way in the new storm, going sideways to it, from pole to pole. Then she came to a place where the markers were gone, probably blown down and buried by the turning wind. The boys were out there, lost, in at least fifteen, perhaps twenty, below zero. Without sticks to guide her way back, the girl dared go no farther but she crouched there, bowed before the wind, cupping her mouth with her mittens, shouting her hopeless: "Boys! Chuck! O-hoo!" the wind snatching it away. She kept calling until she was shaking and frozen to a frightening warmth.

But now she had to keep on, for it seemed that she heard something, a vague, smothered sound, and yet a little like a reply. Tears freezing on her face she called again and again until suddenly the boys were at her feet, there before she could see them, so much like the snow, like white dragging animals, one bowed, half carrying the other. For a few minutes they crouched together in desperate relief, the snow running over them as something immovable, like an old willow butt. Then, together, they pulled themselves up and started back. When they finally reached the shelter, out of breath and frozen, they said nothing of what had happened, nor spoke at all for a while. Yet all, even little Joanie, seemed to sense that the boys had almost been lost.

As soon as the teacher was warmed a little, she started out alone, not certain that she could make it against the storm, but knowing that she must try to get meat. She took Chuck's knife, some dry bark, waxed paper, the two matches in her shirt pocket, and a bundle of poles pulled from their shelter. Moving very carefully beyond the gap in the willow markers, she set new sticks deep, and tipped carefully with the new storm. She found the farther willow clumps with Chuck's blazing, and the brush pile the boys had made, and beside it the ice-covered head of the calf still reaching out of the snow. The hole they had dug around the red hindquarters was drifted in loosely but easily dug out. Lecia set a fire pile there and felt for a match with her numb fingers, fishing in the depths of her pocket—something round in the way, her ring. But she got the match and lighted the fire under her shielding sheepskin coat. For a long time she crouched protectively over the flame, the wind carrying away the stench of burning calf hair. As the skin thawed, she hacked at it the way Indians must have done here a thousand years ago, their stone knives sharper and more expertly handled.

At a sound she looked over her shoulder and saw a coyote not three feet away, gaunt-bellied too, and apparently no more afraid than a hungry dog. But suddenly he caught the human smell, even against the wind, and was gone. Lecia wondered if he might not return to watch just beyond the wall of storm. But she was too busy to look. As the heat penetrated the meat, she cut off one slice after another until she had a little smoky pile, not much for nine people who had lived five days on one lunch apiece, but enough to bring tears that were not all from the storm. In this meat, perhaps three pounds, might lie the life of her pupils.

Lecia scattered the fresh ashes over the calf to keep the coyotes away and piled brush into the fire hole. Then she headed sideways into the storm, so violent that it was a good thing she had the strength of a little cautious meat inside her, for it seemed no one could face the wounding snow. Numb and frightened, she managed to hold herself, not get hurried, panicked, never move until the next broken willow, the next marker was located. So she got back, to find Chuck out near the shelter digging wood from the old clumps, watching, uneasy.

It was hard for the children to wait while the thinner slices of meat roasted around the sticks. When the smell filled the little shelter, Lecia passed out toasted bits to be chewed very slowly and well. It tasted fine and none asked for bread or salt—not even Olive, still

silent and alone. She accepted the meat, but returned only distant gravity for the teacher's smile.

By now the white blizzard darkness was coming back, but before they slept there was a little piece of boiled veal for each and a little hot broth. It was a more cheerful sleeping time, even a confident one, although in the night they were struck by the diarrhea that Lecia had expected. But that was from the fresh meat and should not last.

By now Lecia could build a coal bed with rotten wood and ashes to hold a fire a long time, even with diamond willows, and so she dressed Maggie's feet, the girl light as a sack of bird bones, and prepared the night fire. For a while, Chuck and Eddie kept each other awake with stories of coyote hunts and with plans for another morning of storm, the sixth. The two boys met the day with so much confidence that Lecia had to let them go out into the storm. Eddie, only ten, suddenly became a little old man in his seriousness as he explained their plans carefully. They would make a big brush pile so that they could settle out of the wind and work the fire until they got a whole hindquarter of the calf hacked off. So the teacher watched them go out very full of hope, the hope of meat, one of the half blankets along to drag their prize in over the snow, like great hunters returning.

Bill had looked sadly after the disappearing boot soles, but without complaint. He helped Lecia with the smaller children, washing at the grime of their faces that would never yield except to soap, and took them out into the storm and back while the teacher soaked Maggie's great swollen feet. Once Bill looked over the teacher's shoulder and then anxiously into her face. Others had chilblains—his own feet were swollen from yesterday—but not like this.

"Will she lose—" he started to whisper, but he could not put the rest into words, not with a crippled foot himself.

The air was thick and white with new snow whipped by a northwest wind when Lecia went out for a little wood and to watch for the boys. But they were once more within touching distance before she could see them—very cold and backing awkwardly into the storm through the soft, new drifts, but dragging a whole hindquarter of the calf. It was a lot of meat, and surely the wind must finally blow itself out, the clouds be drained.

By the time Eddie and Chuck were warm they knew they had eaten too much roasted veal while they worked. Next Olive became sick, and Fritz, their deprived stomachs refusing the sudden meat, accepting only broth. During the night the nausea struck Lecia too, and left her so weak that she could scarcely lift her head all the next day. That night Chuck lost his voice for a while, and Joanie was worse again, her mind full of terrors, the cough so deep, so exhausting that Bill made a little tent over her face with the skirt of his coat to carry steam from a bucket of boiling snow water to her face. Then sometime toward morning the wind turned and cut into the southeast corner of the shelter, crumbling the whole side inward.

The boys crawled out to patch it with brush and snow softened at the fire, Lecia helping dry off the children, as much as she could. When they were done and she laid her swimming head down, she heard a coyote's thin, high howl and realized the wind was dying. Through the smoke hole she saw the running snow like pale windrows of cloud against the sky, and between them stars shining, far pale stars. As one or another awoke, she directed sleepy eyes to look up. Awed, Joanie looked a second time. "You mean they're really stars—?"

"Yes, and maybe there will be sunshine in the morning."

Dawn came early that eighth day, but it seemed that nothing could be left alive in the cold whiteness of the earth that was only frozen scarves of snow flung deep and layered over themselves. The trailing drifts stretched down from the high ridge of hills in the north, so deep that they made a long, sliding slope of it far over the meadow and up the wind-whipped hills beyond, with not a dark spot anywhere to the horizon—not a yucca or fence post or willow above the snow. In the first touch of the sun the frozen snow sparkled in the deep silence following a long, long storm. Then out of the hills a lone grouse came cackling over the empty meadow, gleaming silver underneath as she flew, her voice carrying loud in the cold stillness.

But the meadow was not completely empty, for out of a little white mound of drifted willows a curl of smoke rose and spread thin and blue along the hill. There was another sound, too, farther, steadier than the cackle of the grouse, a sound seeming to come from all around and even under the feet.

"A plane!" Chuck shouted hoarsely, bursting out into the blinding sunlight.

Several other dark figures crept out behind him into the frosty air, their breath a cloud about them as they stood looking northward. A big plane broke from the horizon over the hills, seeming high up, and then another, flying lower. Foolishly Chuck and Eddie started to shout. "Help! Hello! Help!" they cried, waving their arms as they ran toward the planes, as though to hasten their sight, their coming.

But almost at once the sky was empty, the planes circling and gone. For a long time the boys stared into the broad, cold sky, pale, with nothing in it except wind streaks that were stirring along the ground, too, setting feather curls of snow to running.

"Quick! Let's make a big smudge!" Lecia called out, her voice loud in the unaccustomed quiet, and fearful. She threw water on the fire inside, driving smoke out of the hole while the boys set the snowy woodpile to burning.

Before the smoke could climb far, there were planes up over the north hills again, coming fast. Now even Fritz got out into the stinging cold—everybody except Joanie, held back by Lecia, and Olive, who did not move from her place. Maggie was lifted up by the teacher to watch through the smoke hole as something tumbled from the higher plane, came falling down. Then it opened out like the waxy white bloom of the yucca, and settled toward the snow, with several other smaller chutes, bright as poppies, opening behind.

There was shouting and talk outside the shelter and while Lecia was hurrying to get the children into their caps and boots, a man came crawling into the shelter with a bag—a doctor. In the light of the fire and a flashlight he looked swiftly at Joanie and then at Olive, considered her unchanging face, lifted the lids of her eyes, smiled, and got no response. Then he examined the poor feet of Maggie, the girl like a skin-bound skeleton in this first sharp light, her eyes dark and fearful on the man's face.

The doctor nodded reassuringly to Lecia, and smiled down at Maggie.

"You're a tough little girl!" he said. "Tough as the barbed wire you have out in this country. But you're lucky somebody thought to try snow against the gangrene—" He filled a little syringe and fingered cotton as he looked around to divert the child.

"All nine of you alive, the boys say. Amazing! Somebody got word to a telephone during the night, but we had no hope for any of you. Small children lost eight days without food, with fifty inches of snow at thirty-eight below zero. Probably a hundred people dead through the country. The radio in the plane picked up a report that six were found frozen in a car stalled on the highway—not over five miles from town. I don't see how you managed here."

The doctor rubbed the punctured place in the child's arm a little, covered it, smiling into her fearful eyes, as men with a stretcher broke into the front of the shelter.

When they got outside, the air was loud with engine roar, several planes flying around overhead, two with skis already up toward the shelter and a helicopter, hovering like a brownish dragonfly, settling. Men in uniform were running toward the children, motioning where they should be brought.

They came along the snow trail broken by the stretcher men, but walking through it as through the storm. Lecia, suddenly trembling, shaking, her feet unsteady on the frozen snow, was still in the lead, the others behind her, and Chuck once more at the end. Bill, limping awkwardly, carried little Joanie, who clung very close to her brother. They were followed by Calla and Eddie, with Fritz between them, and then the stretcher with Maggie. Only Olive of all the children walked alone, just ahead of Chuck, and brushing aside all help.

There were men running toward the bedraggled, sooty little string now, men with cameras and others, among them some who cried, joyous as children, and who must be noticed, must be acknowledged soon—Olive's father and Dale Stever of the yellow plane—

But for now, for this little journey back from the smoke-holed shelter of snow, the awkward queue stayed together.

# GLOSSARY

**Full pronunciation key*** The pronunciation of each word is shown just after the word, in this way: **abbreviate** (ə brē′vē āt).

The letters and signs used are pronounced as in the words below.

The mark **′** is placed after a syllable with a primary or heavy accent as in the example above.

The mark ′ after a syllable shows a secondary or lighter accent, as in **abbreviation** (ə brē′vē ā′shən).

| SYMBOL | KEY WORDS | SYMBOL | KEY WORDS |
|---|---|---|---|
| a | **a**sk, f**a**t | b | **b**ed, du**b** |
| ā | **a**pe, d**a**te | d | **d**id, ha**d** |
| ä | c**a**r, f**a**ther | f | **f**all, o**ff** |
| | | g | **g**et, do**g** |
| e | **e**lf, t**e**n | h | **h**e, a**h**ead |
| er | b**err**y, c**are** | j | **j**oy, **j**ump |
| ē | **e**ven, m**ee**t | k | **k**ill, ba**k**e |
| | | l | **l**et, ba**ll** |
| i | **i**s, h**i**t | m | **m**et, tri**m** |
| ir | m**irr**or, h**ere** | n | **n**ot, to**n** |
| ī | **i**ce, f**i**re | p | **p**ut, ta**p** |
| | | r | **r**ed, dea**r** |
| o | l**o**t, p**o**nd | s | **s**ell, pa**ss** |
| ō | **o**pen, g**o** | t | **t**op, ha**t** |
| ô | l**aw**, h**o**rn | v | **v**at, ha**v**e |
| oi | **oi**l, p**oi**nt | w | **w**ill, al**w**ays |
| oo | l**oo**k, p**u**ll | y | **y**et, **y**ard |
| o͞o | **oo**ze, t**oo**l | z | **z**ebra, ha**z**e |
| yoo | **u**nite, c**u**re | | |
| yo͞o | c**u**te, f**ew** | ch | **ch**in, ar**ch** |
| ou | **ou**t, cr**ow**d | n̂g | ri**ng**, si**ng**er |
| | | sh | **sh**e, da**sh** |
| u | **u**p, c**u**t | th | **th**in, tru**th** |
| ʉr | f**ur**, f**er**n | *th* | **th**en, fa**th**er |
| | | zh | **s** in plea**s**ure |
| ə | **a** in ago | | |
| | **e** in agent | ’ | as in (ā′b’l) |
| | **e** in father | | |
| | **i** in unity | | |
| | **o** in collect | | |
| | **u** in focus | | |

*Pronunciation key and respellings adapted from *Webster's New World Dictionary, Basic School Edition,* 

# A

**ac•count** (ə kount′) *verb.* **1.** to explain. **2.** to be the motive or cause. —*noun.* **1.** a financial record. **2.** a description or narrative of a story or event: His *account* of the fire was exciting.

**ac•knowl•edg•ment** (ək nol′ij mənt) *noun.* **1.** a response showing something is real or true. **2.** something given or done to show a response to a gift or kindness: The actors showed their *acknowledgment* of the audience applause by bowing.

**a•cous•tic** (ə ko͞os′tik) *adjective.* having to do with the sense of hearing or sounds.

**ad•here** (əd hir′) *verb.* **1.** to stick or attach to something. **2.** to be faithful to or support. **adhered, adhering.**

**ad•vo•cate** (ad′və kāt) *verb.* to speak or write in favor or support of.

**af•fir•ma•tion** (af′ər mā′shən) *noun.* a declaration or position statement that something is true as represented.

**af•ter•math** (af′tər math) *noun.* the results of a disaster; the consequences of an event.

**ag•ate** (ag′ət) *noun.* **1.** a glassy stone with colored stripes or clouded coloring. **2.** a marble that looks like this stone.

**ag•i•tate** (aj′ə tāt) *verb.* **1.** to churn, stir, or shake up. **2.** to disturb or work up. **3.** to arouse public awareness; to debate or discuss. **agitated, agitating.**

**al•cove** (al′kōv) *noun.* a small room or part of a room set back from and opening out of a larger room; nook. **alcoves.**

**al•i•bi** (al′ə bī) *noun.* **1.** the plea or defense that an accused person was elsewhere during the commission of a crime. **2.** an excuse.

**an•ces•tor** (an′ses tər) *noun.* **1.** a person from whom you are descended; a forefather, such as a great-grandparent. **2.** something developed or derived from an earlier form. **ancestors.**

**an•ec•dote** (an′ik dōt) *noun.* a short or brief, interesting story of an event or person.

**an•guish** (ang′gwish) *noun.* pain, suffering, grief, or distress.

**an•i•ma•tor** (an′ə mā tər) *noun.* **1.** one who brings characters to life. **2.** an artist who draws animated cartoons. **animators.**

**an•ni•hi•late** (ə nī′ə lāt) *verb.* to destroy completely; to wipe out. **annihilated, annihilating.**

**an•ti•cli•mac•tic** (an′ti klī mak′tik) *adjective.* having to do with a comedown from the important to the unimportant: The walk home after the exciting game was *anticlimactic.*

**an•ti•dote** (an′tə dōt) *noun.* **1.** a remedy to counteract the effects of poison. **2.** something that works against anything harmful.

**ap•er•ture** (ap′ər chər) *noun.* an opening or hole.

**a•ris•to•crat•ic** (ə ris′tə krat′ik) *adjective.* **1.** belonging to the upper class because of birth, wealth, or intelligence. **2.** like an aristocrat; proud and noble.

**ar•ma•da** (är mä′də) *noun.* **1.** a fleet or group of warships. **2.** a fleet of vehicles or warplanes.

**ar•row•head** (ar′ō hed′) *noun.* the pointed tip or head end of an arrow.

**as•pire** (ə spīr′) *verb.* to have a great hope or desire for; to seek.

**as•sail** (ə sāl′) *verb.* **1.** to set upon by hitting or punching. **2.** to set upon very forcefully with arguments or questions: The reporters will *assail* the actors with questions.

**as•sort•ment** (ə sôrt′mənt) *noun.* **1.** a grouping or sorting of items. **2.** a variety of items; a collection of various things. **assortments.**

**as•ter•oid** (as′tə roid) *noun.* any of the many small planets or celestial bodies that move in orbit around the sun and that lie chiefly between Mars and Jupiter. **asteroids.**

**aug•ment** (ôg ment′) *verb.* to make or become greater; to increase. **augmenting.**

**agate**

**Armada** came into English from Spanish. In 1588, Spain sent an *armada,* or fleet of ships, with soldiers aboard to conquer England. Weather and English ships defeated the Spanish Armada and gave English a new word. The word had its origins as the Roman *armata* or "army." It, in turn, came from the Latin *armare,* "to arm" (for war).

**arrowhead**

bobolink

**Boycott** had its beginnings in Ireland. In 1879, poor harvests made famine likely. The Irish Land League demanded that Captain C. C. Boycott, who was managing the Irish lands of the Earl of Erne, lower the rents of the Earl's tenant farmers. When Boycott refused to do so, the tenants refused to harvest the Earl's crops. Thus, Captain Boycott gave his name to people's refusal to do something.

chisel

# B

**bach•e•lor** (bach′′l ər *or* bach′lər) *noun.* **1.** a man who has not married. **2.** an undergraduate degree received when graduating from a college or university.

**bask** (bask) *verb.* **1.** to lie or warm oneself in the sun: The swimmer was *basking* in the sun on the rocks by the lake. **2.** to enjoy some type of warm, pleasant feeling. **basking.**

**be•troth** (bi trōth′ *or* bi trôth′) *verb.* to promise in marriage. —**betrothed** *adjective.* engaged to be married.

**block** (blok) *noun.* **1.** a solid piece of some type of material, such as wood, metal, or stone. **2.** wooden platforms from which racers start. **3.** something that hinders or stops movement. **blocks.**

**board•ing•house** (bôrd′ing hous′) *noun.* a house where rooms and meals can be obtained for a fee.

**bob•o•link** (bob′ə lingk′) *noun.* a songbird, related to blackbirds, native to North America.

**bom•bard** (bom bärd′) *verb.* **1.** to attack with guns or bombs. **2.** to keep up a verbal attack by directing questions or comments. **bombarding.**

**bound•less** (bound′lis) *adjective.* having no limits or bounds: The worker's *boundless* energy seemed without end.

**boy•cott** (boi′kot) *noun.* the act of refusing to buy from, sell to, use, or deal with.

**breadth** (bredth) *noun.* **1.** the width of a thing; how broad. **2.** freedom from narrowness.

**brunt** (brunt) *noun.* the full force or main impact.

**bru•tal** (brōōt′′l) *adjective.* cruel; savage; unfeeling.

**bun•ga•low** (bung′gə lō) *noun.* a small one-story house; cottage.

**bu•reau** (byoor′ō) *noun.* **1.** a chest of drawers for clothes. **2.** an office. **3.** a government department. **bureaus.**

**bus•tle** (bus′′l) *verb.* to hurry; to move about busily and with much activity. **bustled, bustling.**

# C

**ca•lam•i•ty** (kə lam′ə tē) *noun.* **1.** tremendous suffering due to an event such as fire, flood, or war. **2.** great suffering and misery. **calamities.**

**cam•ou•flage** (kam′ə fläzh) *noun.* **1.** materials such as leaves or paint concealing soldiers, guns, and machines from their enemies. **2.** any natural disguise that protects or hides.

**ca•reen** (kə rēn′) *verb.* **1.** to lean, sway, or tip to one side. **2.** to roll or pitch from side to side while moving fast: The big marble hit my foot and went *careening* around the circle. **careened, careening.**

**care•worn** (ker′wôrn) *adjective.* appearing tired and worn out because of much care, worry, or troubles.

**ca•tas•tro•phe** (kə tas′trə fē) *noun.* a sudden event causing great misfortune or widespread damage; a terrible disaster.

**chap•er•one** (shap′ə rōn) *noun.* an older person who supervises young unmarried people to assure their proper behavior.

**chis•el** (chiz′′l) *noun.* a tool with a sharp edge used for cutting or shaping. —*verb.* **1.** to cut, form, or shape with a chisel. **2.** to cheat or swindle someone. **chiselled, chiselling.**

**chron•i•cler** (kron′i k′lər) *noun.* one who tells or writes a story or history.

**cir•cuit** (sur′kit) *noun.* **1.** going around a thing. **1.** a route made through a district by a certain person performing a special job.

**cir•cu•la•tion** (sur′kyə lā′shən) *noun.* **1.** the uncontrolled flow of something from place to place. **2.** the blood flow to and from the heart through veins and arteries. **3.** the passage of a book or money from one person to another. **4.** the number of copies of a publication sent or sold in a certain time.

**cir•cum•stan•tial** (sur′kəm stan′shəl) *adjective.* having to do with or based on a set of facts or events that may have occurred by chance.

**ci•ta•tion** (si tā′shən) *noun.* **1.** an order or summons to come to a law court. **2.** a public or official mention of praise.

**clad** (klad) *verb.* **1.** to have put on clothes; dressed. **2.** to have been covered.

**col•league** (kol′ēg) *noun.* a fellow worker, co-worker, or associate. **colleagues.**

**com•men•tar•y** (kom′ən ter′ē) *noun.* **1.** a series of notes explaining a book or a play. **2.** a series of comments or illustrations to explain a point.

**com•mit•ment** (kə mit′mənt) *noun.* **1.** being committed or a committing. **2.** a pledge or promise.

**com•pas•sion** (kəm pash′ən) *noun.* the feeling of love or pity for an unfortunate person; sympathy.

**com•pel** (kəm pel′) *verb.* to pressure to do something. **compelled, compelling.**

**com•pla•cen•cy** (kəm plā′sən sē) *noun.* **1.** a feeling of satisfaction or contentment without any awareness of actual dangers of deficiencies: Because they had made a profit so often, the club had a feeling of *complacency* about this year's fundraiser. **2.** a self-satisfaction; smugness.

**com•pul•sive** (kəm pul′siv) *adjective.* irresistible, irrational, driven. —**compulsively** *adverb.* performing an action as a result of inner drive.

**con•ceive** (kən sēv′) *verb.* **1.** to think of or form in the mind; to imagine. **2.** to grasp; to understand. **conceived, conceiving.**

**con•fec•tion** (kən fek′shən) *noun.* any kind of candy or similar sweet.

**con•fi•den•tial** (kon′fə den′shəl) *adjective.* **1.** done or said in confidence; secret. **2.** entrusted with the confidence of others.

**con•gen•ial** (kən jēn′yəl) *adjective.* **1.** getting along well with others. **2.** suits one's needs or nature; agreeable. **3.** pleasant or likeable.

**con•sen•sus** (kən sen′səs) *noun.* a general agreement; a collective opinion of the majority: We took a vote to get a *consensus* of the group.

**con•sol•i•date** (kən sol′ə dāt) *verb.* **1.** to merge or combine into one unit. **2.** to make solid; to strengthen. **consolidated, consolidating.**

**con•struc•tive** (kən struk′tiv) *adjective.* **1.** being helpful or creative; making good suggestions. **2.** having to do with construction.

**con•ti•nen•tal di•vide** (kont′'n en′t'l də vīd′) *noun.* a stretch of high ground from each side of which the rivers of a continent flow in opposite directions.

**con•vic•tion** (kən vik′shən) *noun.* **1.** being judged and found guilty of a crime. **2.** a strong, firm, or fixed belief or idea.

**con•vinc•ing** (kən vin′siŋ) *adjective.* causing one to believe or to agree; persuasive. —**convincingly** *adverb.* in a way that causes one to agree.

**cred•i•ble** (kred′ə b'l) *adjective.* **1.** to be believed; believable. **2.** deserving belief or confidence; reliable. —**credibility** *noun.* the quality of being believed.

**crys•tal•lize** (kris′tə līz) *verb.* **1.** to form or solidify into crystals. **2.** to become or form into a definite shape.

**cul•mi•nate** (kul′mə nāt) *verb.* to reach the highest point of development; to climax: The party *culminated* with a dinner in the evening. **culminated, culminating.**

**cy•lin•dri•cal** (sə lin′dri k'l) *adjective.* having the shape of a cylinder.

# D

**de•fy** (di fī′) *verb.* **1.** to resist boldly; to stand up against. **2.** to challenge; to dare.

**de•jec•tion** (di jek′shən) *noun.* sadness; discouragement; lowness of spirit.

**del•i•ca•cy** (del′i kə sē) *noun.* **1.** fineness in design, skill, make, or work. **2.** a choice food. **delicacies.**

**den•i•zen** (den′i z'n) *noun.* **1.** an animal, plant, or person that resides in a specific place. **2.** an animal, plant, or person at home in a location that is not native to it: Bats can become *denizens* of empty houses or barns. **denizens.**

**de•nun•ci•a•tion** (di nun′sē ā′shən) *noun.* an act of condemning or of giving information against.

| | | |
|---|---|---|
| **a** fat | **oi** oil | **ch** chin |
| **ā** ape | **oo** look | **sh** she |
| **ä** car, father | **ōō** tool | **th** thin |
| **e** ten | **ou** out | ***th*** then |
| **er** care | **u** up | **zh** leisure |
| **ē** even | **ur** fur | **ŋ** ring |
| **i** hit | | |
| **ir** here | ə = a *in* ago | |
| **ī** bite, fire | e *in* agent | |
| **o** lot | i *in* unity | |
| **ō** go | o *in* collect | |
| **ô** law, horn | u *in* focus | |

**Defy** is believed to go back to the Roman word for "distrust," *disfidare.* It combined the Latin *fidus* ("trustful") with the prefix *dis* ("not"). An old meaning for *defy* was "to give up allegiance to someone or something." From that it came to mean "to resist or to challenge." When you give up allegiance, you are resisting or challenging someone.

delicacy

deposit

**Eavesdropping** originally meant "to listen under the eaves to hear gossip." The eaves of a building or house are the edge of a roof. The word in Middle English was *evesdroppes*.

embroidery

**de•pos•it** (di poz'it) *verb.* **1.** to give for safekeeping, as money to a bank. **2.** to place; to put. *—noun.* **1.** something given over and placed for safekeeping. **2.** something laid down by natural forces. **deposits.**

**dep•ri•va•tion** (dep'rə vā'shən) *noun.* **1.** the act of taking away from. **2.** the condition of being denied or of being kept from having, getting, or enjoying.

**de•ride** (di rīd') *verb.* to make fun of; to laugh at; to ridicule.

**de•ri•sion** (di rizh'ən) *noun.* scornful laughter; ridicule.

**des•o•late** (des'ə lit) *adjective.* **1.** being alone; lonely. **2.** without people; deserted. **3.** laid waste; ruined.

**des•per•a•tion** (des'pə rā'shən) *noun.* the state of feeling great need or being reckless, because all hope is gone.

**des•tin•y** (des'tə nē) *noun.* **1.** the outcome that is bound to occur; one's lot: It was Lincoln's *destiny* to be a great president. **2.** the power that is believed to make things occur; fate.

**dev•as•tate** (dev'ə stāt) *verb.* to lay waste or ruin completely; to destroy. **devastated.** —**devastating** *adjective.* destructive.

**dex•ter•ous** (dek'strəs *or* dek'stər əs) *adjective.* skillful in use of hands, body, or mind; deft.

**dis•be•lief** (dis bə lēf') *noun.* a strong feeling that something is not true.

**dis•o•be•di•ence** (dis'ə bē'dē əns) *noun.* a refusal or failure to obey.

**dis•sen•sion** (di sen'shən) *noun.* disagreement; violent quarreling; discord caused by a difference in opinion.

**dis•tort** (dis tôrt') *verb.* **1.** to bend or twist something out of its normal shape. **2.** to change in a way in order to create a false impression. —**distorted** *adjective.* **1.** twisted; changed from its usual look. **2.** false.

**di•ver•sion** (də vur'zhən) *noun.* **1.** a turning aside. **2.** something distracting to the mind.

**drape** (drāp) *verb.* **1.** to decorate or cover with some type of clothing or cloth so that it hangs in loose folds. **2.** to hang or arrange in loose folds. **draped, draping.**

**dug•out** (dug'out) *noun.* **1.** a boat made by hollowing out a log. **2.** a shelter hollowed out in the ground or the side of a hill.

**dupe** (dōōp *or* dyōōp) *noun.* a person who is easily deceived or fooled. *—verb.* to fool; to cheat; to trick. **duped, duping.**

# E

**ear** (ir) *noun.* **1.** a part of the head through which sound is heard. **2.** the sense of hearing.

**eaves•drop** (ēvz'drop) *verb.* to listen secretly to others talking. **eavesdropped.** —**eavesdropping** *noun.* act of overhearing on purpose.

**ec•sta•sy** (ek'stə sē) *noun.* a feeling of great delight or joy.

**ef•fer•ves•cence** (ef ər ves'əns) *noun.* **1.** the act of rising up and bubbling out of liquid. **2.** liveliness; peppiness: The actress's *effervescence* demonstrated her high spirits.

**el•e•gant** (el'ə gənt) *adjective.* **1.** tasteful and attractive. **2.** graceful in manners and taste. —**elegantly** *adverb.*

**e•lu•sive** (i lōō'siv) *adjective.* **1.** escaping or hard to capture. **2.** hard to understand, recognize, or remember; puzzling.

**em•broi•der•y** (im broi'dər ē) *noun.* the art of making designs on cloth with a needle and colored thread.

**em•i•grant** (em'ə grənt) *noun.* one who leaves one place or country to settle in another. **emigrants.**

**em•phat•ic** (im fat'ik) *adjective.* **1.** done with force. **2.** definite, certain. —**emphatically** *adverb.*

**en•camp•ment** (in kamp'mənt) *noun.* **1.** the act of setting up and moving into a camp. **2.** a camp or the people in the camp.

**en•liv•en** (in lī'v'n) *verb.* to make more interesting or more spirited: *Enliven* your storytelling by using many gestures.

**en•rap•ture** (in rap'chər) *verb.* to delight greatly; to entrance or enchant: The group was *enraptured* by the musical show. **enraptured.**

**en•ter•prise** (en′tər prīz) *noun.* **1.** any project, task, or business that requires effort, talent, and daring. **2.** the desire and spirit for starting new projects or businesses. **enterprises.**

**en•vel•op•ing** (in vel′əp ing̃ *or* en vel′əp ing̃) *adjective.* surrounding; covering on all sides: We were hidden by the *enveloping* fog.

**ep•i•dem•ic** (ep′ə dem′ik) *noun.* the sudden and swift spread of a disease among many people.

**es•ca•late** (es′kə lāt) *verb.* **1.** to go up, as on an escalator. **2.** to grow, increase, or enlarge, usually by stages. **escalated.** —**escalating** *adjective.* growing, increasing.

**e•ter•nal** (i tur′n′l) *adjective.* having no beginning or end; lasting forever: The mountains seem *eternal* to most people.

**eu•re•ka** (yoo rē′kə) *interjection.* I have found it!: a cry or shout of joy, surprise, or happiness upon finding a thing one has been seeking.

**e•voc•a•tive** (i vok′ə tiv) *adjective.* tending to summon, arouse, or call forth: The scent of the lilacs in the greenhouse was *evocative* of springtime.

**ex•cerpt** (ek′surpt) *noun.* a passage or section taken or copied from a piece of writing, book, or tape. **excerpts.**

**ex•cess** (ik ses′ *or* ek′ses) *noun.* an amount or degree of something that is more than what is needed, wanted, or proper. **excesses.**

**ex•hor•ta•tion** (ig′zôr tā′shən) *noun.* **1.** an earnest plea. **2.** a speech that encourages or incites.

**ex•o•dus** (ek′sə dəs) *noun.* a going away; a departure by many people.

**ex•tra•ter•res•tri•al** (eks′trə tə res′trē əl) *adjective.* of or originating outside or beyond the earth.

**ex•u•ber•ant** (ig zo͞o′bər ənt *or* ig zyo͞o′bər ənt) *adjective.* full of joy, energy, and good humor. —**exuberance** *noun.* state of high spirits and liveliness.

**eye•wit•ness** (ī′wit′nis) *noun.* a person who sees something happen, such as a crime or accident, and can bear witness to the facts.

# F

**fac•ul•ty** (fak′′l tē) *noun.* **1.** the teaching staff of a school, college, or university. **2.** a special natural or acquired ability, skill, or talent: She has a *faculty* for understanding mathematics.

**fas•ci•nate** (fas′ə nāt) *verb.* to charm or attract by being interesting or delightful. **fascinated, fascinating.**

**fast** (fast) *verb.* to go without food or to go without certain foods.

**fat•u•ous** (fach′o͝o wəs) *adjective.* foolish but self-satisfied. —**fatuously** *adverb.* acting silly in a smug way.

**fear•less** (fir′lis) *adjective.* without fear; not at all afraid. —**fearlessly** *adverb.* acting bravely.

**fis•cal** (fis′kəl) *adjective.* having to do with money matters. —**fiscally** *adverb.* financially.

**flab•ber•gast** (flab′ər gast) *verb.* to amaze greatly; to astound. —**flabbergasted** *adjective.* astonished.

**flinch** (flinch) *verb.* to shrink or draw back, as from something dangerous or painful. **flinched.**

**folk•lor•ist** (fōk′lôr′ist) *noun.* a person who studies the beliefs, customs, and stories handed down from generation to generation.

**foot•hill** (fo͝ot′hil) *noun.* a hill near the base of a mountain. **foothills.**

**for•lorn** (fər lôrn′) *adjective.* pitiful or sad because of being neglected or alone. —**forlornly** *adverb.*

**for•mi•da•ble** (fôr′mə də b′l) *adjective.* **1.** causing fear or dread. **2.** very difficult; hard to do; hard to take care of.

**fran•chise** (fran′chīz) *noun.* **1.** a special right given by a government or a governing group. **2.** the right to vote. **3.** a right given to a person or group to sell or distribute products of a certain company.

**free•style** (frē′stīl′) *adjective.* having to do with an event where contestants, such as swimmers or skaters, may perform using any style or manner they desire.

| | | |
|---|---|---|
| **a** fat | **oi** oil | **ch** chin |
| **ā** ape | **o͝o** look | **sh** she |
| **ä** car, father | **o͞o** tool | **th** thin |
| **e** ten | **ou** out | ***th*** then |
| **er** care | **u** up | **zh** leisure |
| **ē** even | **ur** fur | **ng̃** ring |
| **i** hit | | |
| **ir** here | ə = a *in* ago | |
| **ī** bite, fire | e *in* agent | |
| **o** lot | i *in* unity | |
| **ō** go | o *in* collect | |
| **ô** law, horn | u *in* focus | |

**Exodus** comes from the Greek word *hodos*, which meant "a way or road." Combined with the prefix *ex*, for "out of," the word became *exodos*, or "a going out on a road"—in other words, a departure.

**foothills**

gorge

**Greenhorn** probably comes from a combination of *green*, in its meaning of "unripe" or "young," with *horns* of an animal. Thus, *green* ("young") *horns* would refer to an immature animal. From this, it came to mean "a young person without experience."

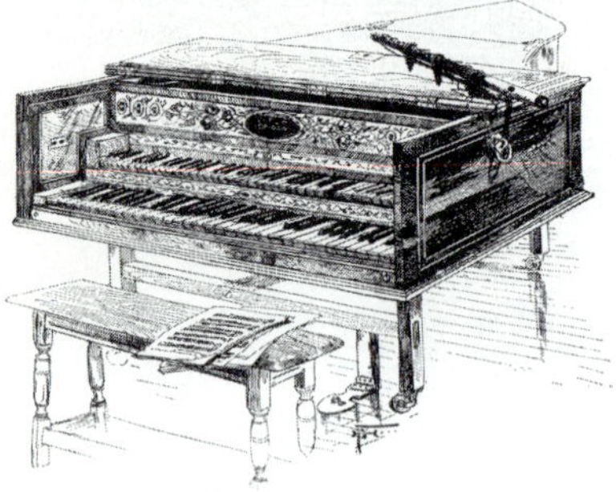

harpsichord

**fron•tier** (frun tir′) *noun.* **1.** the border area between two countries. **2.** the part of a settled area that is next to an area that is still unsettled. **3.** a new or unexplored area, as of knowledge or learning.

**fru•gal** (fro͞o′g′l) *adjective.* **1.** avoiding waste; saving. **2.** costing little money.

**fur•tive** (fur′tiv) *adjective.* **1.** done in a secret way; stealthy. **2.** sly.

# G

**gad•fly** (gad′flī) *noun.* **1.** a large fly that bothers cattle, horses, or other animals. **2.** an annoying person, especially one that wants to bring about changes.

**gal•lant** (gal′ənt) *adjective.* **1.** brave, courageous, or daring. **2.** polite, often with women.

**ga•lore** (gə lôr′) *adverb.* abundance; in great plenty; many.

**gene** (jēn) *noun.* a small part of each chromosome that influences various characteristics inherited from parents. **genes.**

**gen•er•os•i•ty** (jen′ə ros′ə tē) *noun.* **1.** the quality of being openhanded; the desire to give or share. **2.** a generous, sharing, or unselfish act.

**girth** (gurth) *noun.* **1.** the measurement around something, such as one's waist. **2.** the strap that goes around a horse to hold the saddle in place.

**gorge** (gôrj) *noun.* a narrow, deep valley or canyon separating steep walls or cliffs.

**grav•i•ta•tion•al field** (grav′ə tā′shən əl fēld) *noun.* the area around a body in space affected by its gravity; area where masses attract each other.

**grav•i•ty** (grav′ə tē) *noun.* **1.** serious, all-important, or critical behavior or condition. **2.** grave consequence, threat, or danger. **3.** the forceful pull that draws objects toward the center of the earth; gravitation. **4.** heaviness; weight.

**green•horn** (grēn′hôrn) *noun.* a novice, beginner, or person without experience doing a certain task: The *greenhorns* needed to learn to ride before they could join the roundup. **greenhorns.**

**gren•a•dier** (gren ə dir′) *noun.* **1.** in days gone by, a soldier who threw grenades. **2.** a member of a special regiment in the British army. **grenadiers.**

**gri•mace** (gri mās′ *or* grim′əs) *noun.* a twisting of the face that shows pain, disgust, or other feelings of annoyance.

**gruel•ing** (gro͞o′əl ing) *adjective.* very tiring or exhausting.

**guf•faw** (gə fô′) *noun.* loud, rough, or coarse laughter. *—verb.* to laugh in a loud, rough, or coarse way.

# H

**hail** (hāl) *verb.* **1.** to make a shouted greeting or welcome. **2.** to signal or call out to attract attention. *—noun.* **1.** the act of shouting a greeting or welcome: Our captain gave a loud *hail* as the ferryboat sailed nearby. **2.** drops of ice coming down in a storm.

**hall•mark** (hôl′märk) *noun.* **1.** a symbol or mark on something that indicates its high quality, purity, or genuineness. **2.** an outstanding feature or characteristic: The *hallmark* of this new restaurant is its excellent food and service.

**hap•pen•ing** (hap′′n ing) *noun.* something that takes place, especially by chance; an occurrence; incident; event. **happenings.**

**harp•si•chord** (härp′si kôrd) *noun.* an early piano-like instrument having its strings plucked instead of struck.

**heat** (hēt) *noun.* **1.** the condition of being hot. **2.** hot weather; high temperatures. **3.** the warming of a house or room. **4.** strong, intense emotions and feelings; excitement. **5.** one effort or trial, as in a race: Joe won the first *heat* of the qualifying races.

**hec•tic** (hek′tik) *adjective.* **1.** flushed and feverish. **2.** marked by or full of haste, excitement, or confusion.

**hid•e•ous** (hid′ē əs) *adjective.* monstrous, ugly, beastly, or disgusting.

**hi•lar•i•ty** (hi ler′ə tē) *noun.* mirth; noisy cheerfulness; gaiety.

**hoax** (hōks) *noun.* a trick, practical joke, or deception. —*verb.* to trick; to fool; to deceive.

**home•spun** (hōm′spun) *noun.* a coarse fabric woven from yarn spun at home.

**hov•er** (huv′ər *or* hov′ər) *verb.* **1.** to flap one's wings in the air or flutter or fly near one place. **2.** to be in or near one place; to stay. **3.** to be in an uncertain state; to waver. **hovered.** —**hovering** *adjective.* staying suspended in place: The *hovering* helicopter guided the rescuers to the lifeboat.

**hum•mock** (hum′ək) *noun.* a low, rounded hill, mound, ridge, or knoll.

**hunch** (hunch) *verb.* **1.** to bend one's body to form a hump; to stoop or crouch. **2.** to move, shove, or push forward by jerks. —*noun.* a feeling, guess, or suspicion based on facts not verified or known.

**hys•te•ri•a** (his tir′ē ə) *noun.* **1.** a mental condition caused by anxiety that may cause blindness, stomach ailments, or paralysis. **2.** convulsive laughter or crying.

# I

**i•de•al•ist** (ī dē′əl ist) *noun.* a person with high ideals who tries to live by them even when it may not be practical.

**ill-man•nered** (il′man′ərd) *adjective.* having bad manners; rude; impolite: The most *ill-mannered* of the gang did not treat the other workers with respect.

**im•mor•tal** (i môr′t′l) *adjective.* **1.** living or lasting forever. **2.** forever famous.

**im•pe•tus** (im′pə təs) *noun.* **1.** the momentum or force that moves a body. **2.** the driving force, incentive, or stimulus that causes action: The industrial growth was the *impetus* for urban development.

**im•print** (im print′) *verb.* **1.** to make a mark or figure by pressure or with a stamp. **2.** to fix firmly; to impress: Their hungry faces will be *imprinted* in our memories. **imprinted.**

**in•ac•ces•si•ble** (in′ək ses′ə b′l) *adjective.* difficult or hard to get to or reach.

**in•com•pre•hen•si•ble** (in′kom pri hen′sə b′l) *adjective.* cannot be understood; not clear.

**in•cred•u•lous** (in krej′o͝o ləs) *adjective.* **1.** unable, unwilling, or not ready to believe; doubting. **2.** expressing doubt or disbelief.

**in•den•ta•tion** (in′den tā′shən) *noun.* **1.** notches cut into the edge of a thing. **2.** the act of beginning a line or lines farther in from the edge of a piece of paper than the other material on the page.

**in-depth** (in′depth′) *adjective.* thorough: going into great or careful detail.

**in•di•go** (in′di gō) *noun.* **1.** a blue dye coming from a certain plant belonging to the pea family or now made artificially. **2.** deep violet-blue.

**in•dom•i•ta•ble** (in dom′it ə b′l) *adjective.* unyielding; cannot be overcome or beaten. **indomitably.**

**in•i•ti•a•tion** (i nish′ē ā′shən) *noun.* a secret or special ceremony or test that a person must go through in order to become a member of a society or club.

**in•se•cure** (in′si kyoor′) *adjective.* **1.** the feeling of not being safe; fearful. **2.** not confident; uncertain. —**insecurity** *noun.* state of being worried and afraid.

**in•te•grate** (in′tə grāt) *verb.* **1.** to fit or bring together into a whole; to unify. **2.** to make available the use of certain facilities by people of all races. —**integration** *noun.* **1.** process of uniting. **2.** doing away with segregation.

**in•tran•si•gent** (in tran′si jənt) *adjective.* uncompromising or refusing to give in.

**in•tro•vert** (in′trə vurt) *verb.* **1.** to turn or direct inward. **2.** to concentrate one's thoughts and feelings upon oneself. —**introverted** *adjective.* not outgoing; inside oneself.

| | | |
|---|---|---|
| **a** fat | **oi** oil | **ch** chin |
| **ā** ape | **o͝o** look | **sh** she |
| **ä** car, father | **o͞o** tool | **th** thin |
| **e** ten | **ou** out | ***th*** then |
| **er** care | **u** up | **zh** leisure |
| **ē** even | **ur** fur | **ng** ring |
| **i** hit | | |
| **ir** here | ə = a *in* ago | |
| **ī** bite, fire | e *in* agent | |
| **o** lot | i *in* unity | |
| **ō** go | o *in* collect | |
| **ô** law, horn | u *in* focus | |

hover

**Intransigent,** as an English word, dates from around 1882. It came into English from the French, who got the word from Spain. Spanish legislators who were members of an extreme left political party were called *los intransigentes,* meaning "the uncompromising ones."

keystone

loch

**Lunatic** comes from the Latin word for "moon," *luna.* People believed that some kinds of insanity were caused by the moon's changes.

**in•vin•ci•ble** (in vin′sə b'l) *adjective.* cannot be conquered or overcome.

**in•voke** (in vōk′) *verb.* **1.** to call upon for help or blessing. **2.** to seriously ask or appeal for. **3.** to call forth as if by magic. **invoked, invoking.**

**i•ras•ci•ble** (i ras′ə b'l) *adjective.* **1.** easily angered; quick-tempered. **2.** displaying a quick temper or feelings of anger: The *irascible* gnomes stamped their feet and yelled loudly at the giant.

**i•ron•ic** (ī ron′ik) *adjective.* **1.** expressing one meaning when its opposite meaning is intended. **2.** opposite of what may be expected: It was *ironic* to see such a sad clown.

**ir•re•sist•i•ble** (ir′i zis′tə b'l) *adjective.* cannot be withstood; overwhelming; too tempting.

# J

**jaunt** (jônt) *noun.* a short trip, especially for pleasure; excursion. **jaunts.**

**jeop•ard•ize** (jep′ər dīz) *verb.* **1.** to endanger; to risk; to expose to loss: If you continue to drive without seat belts, you *jeopardize* your safety.

**jour•nal•ism** (jûr′nəl iz'm) *noun.* the work or profession of compiling, reporting, writing, and editing the news so it can be published in newspapers or magazines or broadcast on radio or television.

# K

**key•stone** (kē′stōn) *noun.* **1.** the middle or central stone at the top of an arch which holds the other stones in place. **2.** the basic idea, the most important part, or the fundamental segment: The *keystone* to a good relationship between friends is trust.

# L

**la•bor•er** (lā′bər ər) *noun.* a worker; a person who does rough, physical, or manual work that requires more strength than skill. **laborers.**

**lame** (lām) *adjective.* **1.** crippled; limping from a foot or leg that is hurt. **2.** sore, stiff, or painful. **3.** weak or poor as in a lame excuse. —**lamely** *adverb.* acting in a lame manner.

**lank•y** (laŋ′kē) *adjective.* tall, thin, and ungraceful or awkward.

**leth•ar•gy** (leth′ər jē) *noun.* the condition of feeling or being tired, listless, or dull.

**light** (līt) *noun.* **1.** a form of energy that stimulates the eye so that a person can see. **2.** brightness. **3.** a source of light. —*verb.* **1.** to give off light. **2.** to cause or to start to burn. **3.** to get down, as from a horse. **4.** to come down after flying; to land. —*adjective.* **1.** having little weight. **2.** not heavy. **3.** not great. **4.** easily done.

**lim•it•less** (lim′it lis) *adjective.* vast; unconfined; not restricted.

**list•less** (list′lis) *adjective.* lacking energy, spirit, or interest in anything, because one is sick, tired, sad, or bored. —**listlessly** *adverb.*

**loath•ing** (lōth′iŋ) *noun.* dislike, hatred, or disgust.

**loch** (lok) *noun.* **1.** a Scottish word for lake. **2.** a Scottish word for a bay or a long, narrow arm of the sea.

**loft•y** (lôf′tē) *adjective.* **1.** very high. **2.** feeling noble, proud, or idealistic. **3.** affecting grandness; haughty.

**long** (lôŋ) *adjective.* extending quite far from end to end or from start to end; not short. —*verb.* to want greatly; to have a strong desire for; to yearn: I *long* for a sunny day.

**lu•mi•nous** (lo͞o′mə nəs) *adjective.* **1.** full of light. **2.** giving off light; bright.

**lu•na•tic** (lo͞o′nə tik) *noun.* **1.** a mentally ill person. **2.** someone who is wildly foolish.

**lure** (lo͝or) *verb.* to attract or entice by presenting something that appears to be nice or pleasant. —*noun.* a thing that attracts or entices because it offers pleasure or gain.

**lus•trous** (lus′trəs) *adjective.* having a shine or gleam; bright; glossy.

# M

**ma•es•tro** (mīs′trō *or* mä es′trō) *noun.* an Italian word for master, especially a great composer, conductor, or teacher of music.

**mag•ni•tude** (mag′nə to͞od *or* mag′nə tyo͞od) *noun.* **1.** greatness, as of size or power. **2.** importance or size.

**ma•lar•i•a** (mə ler′ē ə) *noun.* a disease, spread by a mosquito, the symptoms of which include chills, sweating, and fever.

**mal•ice** (mal′is) *noun.* a feeling or desire to hurt or to injure someone.

**man•u•script** (man′yə skript) *noun.* something, such as an article or book, written by hand or typewritten; a copy of an author's work that is sent to a publisher.

**mar** (mär) *verb.* to do harm or injury to, to damage; to spoil the looks or quality of: If you make loud noises, you *mar* the concert for others.

**mar•tial law** (mär′shəl lô) *noun.* temporary rule by the military over citizens, rather than by the usual civil authorities, in times of riots, panics, or wars.

**mass** (mas) *noun.* **1.** a body, piece, or amount with no definite size or shape. **2.** a large number or amount. **3.** the greater or main part. —*adjective.* having to do with a large number of people or things.

**me•di•a** (mē′dē ə) *noun.* channels or mass communication with the general public, such as television, radio, newspapers, motion pictures, or magazines.

**meet** (mēt) *verb.* **1.** to come upon. **2.** to be introduced or to become acquainted with. —*noun.* a meeting, as for a sports event.

**me•men•to** (mi men′tō) *noun.* an item or thing given or kept in order to remind someone of the past. **mementos** or **mementoes.**

**mem•o•ra•bil•i•a** (mem′ər ə bil′ē ə) *noun.* things that are remarkable and worth keeping or remembering.

**men•ace** (men′is) *noun.* any threat, danger, or something that may cause evil or harm. —*verb.* to threaten with evil or harm; to be the cause of danger.

**mer•chan•dise** (mur′chən dīz *or* mur′chən dīs) *noun.* things or goods that are bought and sold for profit.

**me•trop•o•lis** (mə trop′′l is) *noun.* the main, largest, or most important city in a state, country, or area.

**mi•ca** (mī′kə) *noun.* a shiny mineral that is easily split or separated into layers.

**mile•stone** (mīl′stōn) *noun.* **1.** a marker showing distance to a place. **2.** a significant or important event in history, in someone's life, etc.; a turning point.

**mime** (mīm) *noun.* a person who does mimicry or who acts by using only movements and gestures. —*verb.* to act as a mime, without speaking.

**mir•ror** (mir′ər) *noun.* **1.** a smooth surface that reflects light, especially a surface of glass which has a coating of metal. **2.** anything that truly reflects or pictures an idea, person, or object. —*verb.* to reflect in or as if a mirror were used: The looks of happiness on the students' faces after the play *mirrored* that of their proud teacher. **mirrored.**

**mo•not•o•nous** (mə not′′n əs) *adjective.* **1.** not changing in tone or pitch; spoken in the same tone. **2.** boring because of a lack of change or variety.

**mor•tise** (môr′tis) *noun.* a hole cut in a piece of wood or other material to fit another piece and form a joint. —**mortised** *adjective.* fastened by a piece of wood fitting into a hole.

**mot•tle** (mot′′l) *verb.* to mark with spots or blotches of different colors. —**mottled** *adjective.*

**mot•to** (mot′ō) *noun.* a word or brief saying that expresses a rule of conduct or how to live.

**muse** (myo͞oz) *verb.* to think about things in a quiet way for a length of time; to ponder. **mused, musing.**

| | | |
|---|---|---|
| **a** fat | **oi** oil | **ch** chin |
| **ā** ape | **oo** look | **sh** she |
| **ä** car, father | **o͞o** tool | **th** thin |
| **e** ten | **ou** out | ***th*** then |
| **er** care | **u** up | **zh** leisure |
| **ē** even | **ur** fur | **ng** ring |
| **i** hit | | |
| **ir** here | ə = a *in* ago | |
| **ī** bite, fire | e *in* agent | |
| **o** lot | i *in* unity | |
| **ō** go | o *in* collect | |
| **ô** law, horn | u *in* focus | |

**mime**

**Mortise** comes from the Arabic word *murtazz,* which means "fastened" or "fixed in." The Moors were Arabs who occupied Spain during the eighth century, and many Arabic words were adopted into Spanish. *Murtazz* became *mortaja.* In Old French, the word became *mortoise,* from which it entered Middle English as both *mortais* and *morteis.* The original Arabic meaning is preserved pretty well, since a mortise fastens two pieces of wood, one fixed in the other.

# N

**Nostalgia** comes from a combination of the Greek words *nostos* ("return home") and *algos* ("pain"). It did not mean "pain on returning home," but rather "homesickness," which is another meaning for *nostalgia*. From homesickness, the word came to mean a longing for past or faraway things.

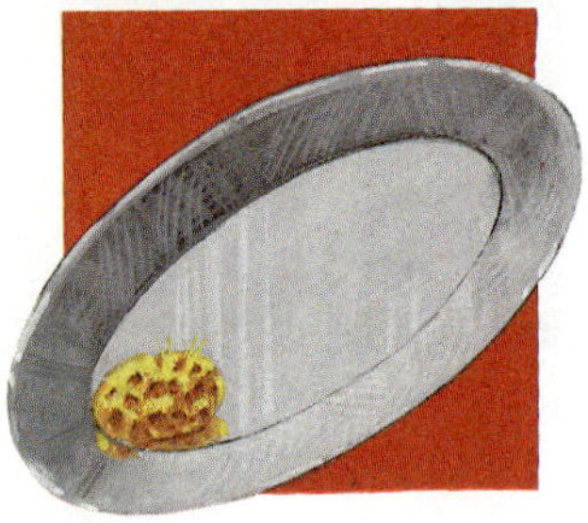

nugget

oarlocks

**na•ive** (nä ēv′) *adjective.* **1.** simple and unaffected, in a childlike or foolish way. **2.** without much experience: The *naive* tourist had never flown before.

**nar•ra•tive** (nar′ə tiv) *noun.* an account, a story, or a report of some events.

**nay-say•er** (nā′sā ər) *noun.* a person who votes "no" or feels negative about a new idea. **nay-sayers.**

**no•bil•i•ty** (nō bil′ə tē) *noun.* **1.** the condition or quality of having or showing very good character or high morals. **2.** a class or group of people who have noble titles, such as barons, dukes, duchesses, or earls.

**no•mad** (nō′mad) *noun.* a member of a people or a tribe that keeps moving because they are searching for food or pasture for their animals. —**nomadic** *adjective.* wandering.

**non•vi•o•lent** (non vī′ə lənt) *adjective.* free from violence or from acting with great force that causes injury or damage.

**nos•tal•gia** (nos tal′jə) *noun.* a longing for some place, item, or event that happened in the past.

**nov•el•ty** (nov′′l tē) *noun.* **1.** something new and different: It was such a *novelty* to think about learning to ski in the summer. **2.** any small, inexpensive article, such as a trinket or a toy.

**nug•get** (nug′it) *noun.* a rough, shapeless piece or lump, especially a lump of gold in its natural state. **nuggets.**

**numb•ness** (num′nəs) *noun.* a state of having no feeling: The *numbness* in his hand prevented his feeling the heat of the stove.

**nymph** (nimf) *noun.* in Greek and Roman myths, any of a group of lesser goddesses who lived in trees, fountains, rivers, or woods. **nymphs.**

# O

**oar•lock** (ôr′lok) *noun.* a piece or part on a rowboat that keeps an oar in place. **oarlocks.**

**ob•jec•tive** (əb jek′tiv) *adjective.* **1.** not affected or based on bias or opinion. **2.** that which is real or actual, not based on ideas or feelings. —*noun.* an end or goal.

**ob•liv•i•ous** (ə bliv′ē əs) *adjective.* **1.** not aware; unmindful; forgetful. **2.** causing forgetfulness.

**ob•sess** (əb ses′) *verb.* to fill or rule the thoughts of; to haunt the mind. —**obsessed** *adjective.* haunted; thought of nothing else.

**o•paque** (ō pāk′) *adjective.* **1.** not allowing light through; not transparent: The *opaque* material permitted no light to enter the room. **2.** dull; not reflecting light. **3.** not simple; hard to comprehend.

**op•pres•sion** (ə presh′ən) *noun.* **1.** the act of keeping down by unjust use of force; harsh rule. **2.** a feeling of being burdened by problems and worry.

**or•deal** (ôr dēl′) *noun.* **1.** an old-fashioned method to determine innocence or guilt. **2.** a difficult trial or experience.

**out•let** (out′let) *noun.* **1.** a way out; an exit; an opening to let something out. **2.** a means of using up or releasing: Doing that service project was an *outlet* for the class members who wanted to feel useful. **3.** a market or retail store where a product is sold.

**out•ra•geous** (out rā′jəs) *adjective.* **1.** causing great wrong or injury. **2.** very offensive or insulting.

**o•ver•land** (ō′vər land) *adverb.* on, over, across, by land.

# P

**pac•er** (pā'sər) *noun.* a person or animal that sets a rate of speed for other runners in a race.

**pan•to•mime** (pan'tə mīm) *noun.* **1.** a play in which the actors use gestures and movements but do not speak. **2.** gestures, without speech, that express something.

**par•o•dy** (par'ə dē) *noun.* a humorous imitation of some serious piece of writing or music or some action that mocks the original.

**pass•a•ble** (pas'ə b'l) *adjective.* **1.** capable of being traveled over, on, or through. **2.** that which is average or fairly good.

**pas•time** (pas'tīm) *noun.* way of spending spare time pleasantly; amusement. **pastimes.**

**pem•mi•can** (pem'i kən) *noun.* meat that has been dried, pounded and mixed with grease, and pressed into cakes.

**per•fo•rate** (pur'fə rāt) *verb.* **1.** to punch or make a hole or holes through. **2.** to pierce or make a row of holes, as with stamps, for easier tearing. —**perforation** *noun.* the row of holes, especially in paper, made for easier tearing.

**per•ish** (per'ish) *verb.* to be completely destroyed; to die.

**per•sist** (pər sist') *verb.* **1.** to be stubborn, not to give up. **2.** to repeat or say over and over. **3.** to endure; to continue. **persisted.**

**per•spec•tive** (pər spek'tiv) *noun.* **1.** the way things appear from a certain point according to size and shape. **2.** the ability to picture items so that they appear to look close or far, large or small. **3.** a particular viewpoint in judging and understanding events or things, especially relating one thing to another.

**pe•ruse** (pə ro͞oz') *verb.* to read carefully.

**pe•ti•tion** (pə tish'ən) *noun.* **1.** a serious request, such as a prayer. **2.** a formal written request signed by many people and sent to a person or a group in authority. **petitioner.** one who requests.

**pet•u•lant** (pech'oo lənt) *adjective.* being angry and showing anger or annoyance; peevish.

**phi•lan•thro•pist** (fi lan'thrə pist) *noun.* someone who demonstrates compassion or love for other people by donations of large sums of money to aid them.

**pi•geon•hole** (pij'ən hōl) *noun.* **1.** a hole in which a pigeon can nest. **2.** a small compartment or box in a desk often used for filing papers, usually one of a series. **pigeonholes.**

**pil•grim•age** (pil'grəm ij) *noun.* **1.** a journey to a holy place. **2.** any long or hard journey.

**plac•ard** (plak'ärd) *noun.* a poster, notice, or sign displayed in a public place: The *placard* in the park announced a race.

**pla•teau** (pla tō') *noun.* **1.** a broad stretch of level land, usually well above sea level. **2.** a period of little or no progress.

**plume** (plo͞om) *noun.* **1.** a large feather. **2.** a feather or several feathers worn on a hat as a decoration. **3.** something shaped like a plume. **plumes.**

**por•ti•co** (pôr'tə kō) *noun.* a covered walk or porch whose roof is supported by columns.

**post** (pōst) *verb.* **1.** to hang a notice on a wall or fence. **2.** to announce as if by posting signs. —**posting** *noun.* an official announcement; placard or poster. **postings.**

**prai•rie schoon•er** (prer'ē sko͞o'nər) *noun.* a large covered wagon used by pioneers heading west across the prairies.

**pre•mo•ni•tion** (prē'mə nish'ən) *noun.* a sense or feeling that something is going to happen, often something bad; a forewarning.

**pre•oc•cu•py** (prē ok'yə pī) *verb.* to interest or take up a person's attentions so that other things go unnoticed. —**preoccupied** *adjective.* absorbed in thought.

**probe** (prōb) *noun.* an instrument, usually slender, used for examining wounds or openings in the body. —*verb.* **1.** to examine with a probe. **2.** to examine or look into carefully. —**probing** *adjective.* taking a close look.

| | | |
|---|---|---|
| **a** fat | **oi** oil | **ch** chin |
| **ā** ape | **oo** look | **sh** she |
| **ä** car, father | **o͞o** tool | **th** thin |
| **e** ten | **ou** out | ***th*** then |
| **er** care | **u** up | **zh** leisure |
| **ē** even | **ur** fur | **ng** ring |
| **i** hit | | |
| **ir** here | ə = a *in* ago | |
| **ī** bite, fire | e *in* agent | |
| **o** lot | i *in* unity | |
| **ō** go | o *in* collect | |
| **ô** law, horn | u *in* focus | |

**Pemmican** comes from the Native American Cree word *pimecan*, or "fat meat," which itself came from the Cree *pime*, or "fat and greasy." Pemmican describes now, as it did then, dried, pounded meat mixed with fat.

**pigeonholes**

raceway

**Rampage,** "rushing about wildly," was originally Scottish. Beyond that, its origin is not known. It may, however, be based on a meaning of the word **ramp.** *Ramp* means "to rear" or "stand on the hind legs," as a horse might, but with the additional idea that this is threatening. Thus, *ramp* also means "to rage" or "act violently." So, it is possible that with a little change, *ramp* became *rampage.*

**Renaissance** originally meant "revival of learning" in Europe after the Middle Ages and so came to mean any rebirth or renewal. It is a French combination of the prefix *re* (in its meaning of "again") and *naissance* ("birth"). It is a word that means what it says.

**pros•pect** (pros′pekt) *noun.* **1.** the act of looking forward or ahead. **2.** a person who is a potential customer or candidate. —*verb.* to search, look for, explore for, or seek. **prospecting.**

**pul•ley** (po͝ol′ē) *noun.* a small wheel with a grooved rim over which a rope or belt can pass freely whenever the wheel is turned.

**pul•sate** (pul′sāt) *verb.* **1.** to throb or beat as would a heart or pulse. **2.** to vibrate; to quiver or shake.

**punch line** (punch′ līn) *noun.* the last line or the climax of a joke or humorous story.

**pun•gent** (pun′jənt) *adjective.* **1.** sharp, biting, or stinging in smell or taste. **2.** forceful, direct, or sharp-tongued in criticism.

## Q

**qual•i•fy•ing** (kwol′ə fī ing) *adjective.* making possible; meeting a certain standard: Paul won his *qualifying* race to enter the tournament.

**quest** (kwest) *noun.* **1.** a seeking, search, or hunt. **2.** an expedition by a knight in the Middle Ages. —*verb.* to seek or go in search.

**queue** (kyo͞o) *noun.* **1.** a single, long braid hanging down from the back of the head. **2.** a line, as of people or automobiles that are waiting for something. —*verb.* to form such a line.

## R

**race•way** (rās′wā′) *noun.* **1.** an artificial channel for conducting water. **2.** a racetrack.

**rac•ism** (rā′siz′m) *noun.* **1.** the notion that one race, usually one's own, is better than another. **2.** discrimination based on race.

**rake** (rāk) *noun.* a garden tool with a long handle having evenly spaced prongs at one end. —*verb.* **1.** to gather or scrape together as if with a rake. **2.** to search carefully. **3.** to scrape, scratch, or graze. **raked, raking.**

**ram•page** (ram pāj′) *verb.* to dash about in a violent, angry, or wild way; to rush about as in a rage. **rampaged, rampaging.**

**ra•pid•i•ty** (rə pid′ə tē) *noun.* swiftness; speed.

**re•as•sur•ance** (rē ə sho͝or′əns) *noun.* the act of restoring confidence; encouragement. **reassurances.**

**rec•i•ta•tion** (res′ə tā′shən) *noun.* **1.** an oral telling of facts, details, or events. **2.** the oral repeating of a lesson, poem, or story that has been memorized. **3.** the poem or story that is being told: Her *recitations* were always comic poems. **recitations.**

**re•com•mence** (rē kə mens′) *verb.* to begin or start again. **recommenced, recommencing.**

**rec•on•noi•ter** (rē′kə noit′ər *or* rek′ə noit′ər) *verb.* to survey, probe, or spy on or scout an area, especially to learn more about enemies in wartime.

**re•lay** (rē′lā) *noun.* **1.** a new or fresh set, as of people, workers, or horses, to replace an old or tired set. **2.** a race in which each team member performs only a certain part of the total distance.

**rem•i•nis•cence** (rem ə nis″ns) *noun.* **1.** the act of practice or thinking or speaking of the past. **2.** a memory or recollection. **reminiscences.**

**rem•nant** (rem′nənt) *noun.* **1.** the remainder or balance; what is left over, as a short piece of fabric at the end of a bolt. **2.** a remaining trace; a small, but visible sign: The man looked around his old playroom and viewed *remnants* of his childhood. **remnants.**

**ren•ais•sance** (ren′ə säns) *noun.* **1.** any rebirth or renewal, especially in the arts, literature, and learning.

**re•port** (ri pôrt′) *verb.* **1.** to tell of; to give an account of. **2.** to tell as news. **3.** to state; to announce. —*noun.* **1.** the accounting or telling of something. **2.** the statement or announcement. **3.** an explosive sound, as if made by a gun or cannon: The cannon's *report* shook the windows of houses near the fort.

**rep•u•ta•ble** (rep′yo͞o tə b′l) *adjective.* well thought of; having an honorable reputation; respected.

**re•sign** (ri zīn′) *verb.* **1.** to give up an office or position. **2.** to accept what will happen or has happened. **resigned.**

**res•ig•na•tion** (rez′ig nā′shən) *noun.* **1.** an act of giving up an office or position. The president announced Kim's *resignation* as secretary because Kim had already moved away. **2.** a written record that one intends to resign or has resigned. **3.** patient acceptance of an event, comment, or idea without any complaints.

**res•o•lute** (rez′ə lo͞ot) *adjective.* having or displaying a firm, fixed, or determined purpose.

**re•sume** (ri zo͞om′ *or* ri zyo͞om′) *verb.* **1.** to get, take, or occupy again. **2.** to begin, continue, or go on after an interruption. **resumed, resuming.**

**re•sur•gence** (ri sur′jens) *noun.* a rising again into life, activity, or prominence; a reviving.

**ret•ro•spect** (ret′rə spekt) *noun.* the act of reviewing or surveying past times or events.

**ret•ro•spec•tive** (ret′rə spek′tiv) *adjective.* looking back in the past. *—noun.* an exhibit of artwork done over some time by an artist or a group of artists.

**rev•el** (rev″l) *verb.* **1.** to make noisy fun; to make merry. **2.** to take delight in. *—noun.* noisy merrymaking.

**re•viv•al** (ri vī′v′l) *noun.* **1.** a bringing or coming back to life or into use. **2.** a re-release or reproduction of a movie, play, or certain style in fashion. **3.** a meeting or service for the purpose of arousing or reawakening religious interest.

**re•voke** (ri vōk′) *verb.* to take back, put an end to, cancel, or repeal, as a permit, license, or law. **revoked, revoking.**

**rid•i•cule** (rid′i kyo͞ol′) *noun.* **1.** words and actions, such as mocking or making fun of, that make a person seem foolish. **2.** the act of making a person seem foolish, by laughing, mocking, or making fun of. *—verb.* to laugh at or make fun of.

**rime** (rīm) *noun.* a covering or crust of frost or cooled fog. —**rimed** *adjective.* covered or coated as if with rime.

**round** (round) *adjective.* **1.** having a shape like a circle, ball, or tube. **2.** plump. **3.** full, complete. *—verb.* **1.** to make or become round. **2.** to travel, go around, or make a circuit of: The car *rounded* the curve at the end of the pond. **rounded.**

**rout** (rout) *noun.* **1.** a disorderly retreat following a defeat. **2.** an overwhelming defeat.

**roy•al•ty** (roi′əl tē) *noun.* **1.** a royal person such as a king or queen, or royal persons as a group. **2.** a share of the earnings, as from a book or an invention, paid to the writer or inventor for the right to publish, use, or make.

# S

**sa•ga** (sä′gə) *noun.* **1.** an ancient narrative recounting Scandinavian legends. **2.** any long tale of brave deeds or family history.

**salve** (sav) *noun.* **1.** any soft, greasy ointment put on burns, sores, wounds, etc. to heal them. **1.** anything that soothes.

**sam•pler** (sam′plər) *noun.* a piece of material on which designs, mottos, or words have been done in fancy stitches using a needle and embroidery thread.

**sat•u•rate** (sach′ə rāt) *verb.* **1.** to soak thoroughly or fill completely. **2.** to make something absorb so much that no more can be taken in. —**saturation** *noun.* condition of being soaked through.

**scin•til•late** (sin′t′l āt) *verb.* **1.** to give off sparks or flashes of light. **2.** to be sparkling, clever, brilliant, or witty. —**scintillation** *noun.* act of shining.

**scoop** (sko͞op) *noun.* **1.** a tool like a little shovel, used to take out portions of sugar, flour, or ice cream. **2.** the part of a dredge or steam shovel that takes up the dirt or sand. **3.** a bit of information, as a news item, heard or published before others know about it. *—verb.* to get and publish a news item before other newspapers do: The eager reporter *scooped* all of us by getting his story done and handed in early. **scooped.**

| | | |
|---|---|---|
| **a** fat | **oi** oil | **ch** chin |
| **ā** ape | **o͝o** look | **sh** she |
| **ä** car, father | **o͞o** tool | **th** thin |
| **e** ten | **ou** out | ***th*** then |
| **er** care | **u** up | **zh** leisure |
| **ē** even | **ur** fur | **ng** ring |
| **i** hit | | |
| **ir** here | **ə** = a *in* ago | |
| **ī** bite, fire | e *in* agent | |
| **o** lot | i *in* unity | |
| **ō** go | o *in* collect | |
| **ô** law, horn | u *in* focus | |

royalty

**Sampler** originally meant an "example" or "pattern." The sampler that might be framed and hung on a wall is not so different from the old meanings. It is an example of the maker's skill at needlework and shows whatever pattern the maker had in mind. Sampler comes from the Old French *essemplaire,* which means "examplar" or "something that serves as a pattern"—an example.

shingles

> **Sonar** is an acronym. An acronym is a word that is formed by combining the first letter or letters of a multi-word term. In the case of *sonar,* the term is *so*und *na*vigation *r*anging.

stampede

**scrab•ble** (skrab′'l) *verb.* **1.** to scratch, scrape, or grope with hands or paws in a disorderly or frantic way. **2.** to struggle painfully. **scrabbled, scrabbling.**

**scru•pu•lous** (skro͞o′pyə ləs) *adjective.* **1.** very careful to do what is right or proper. **2.** paying strict attention to details; exact; precise.

**scru•ti•nize** (skro͞ot′'n īz) *verb.* to look at closely; to examine carefully. **scrutinized, scrutinizing.**

**seg•re•ga•tion** (seg′rə gā′shən) *noun.* the practice of keeping people of different races separate.

**sei•zure** (sē′zhər) *noun.* **1.** act of taking in an eager, strong, or sudden way; condition of being taken. **2.** a sudden attack, as of a disease or illness.

**sen•try** (sen′trē) *noun.* a person, sometimes a soldier, who keeps watch to guard a group or to look for approaching danger. **sentries.**

**se•quel** (sē′kwəl) *noun.* **1.** something that follows something else, usually based on what occurred previously. **2.** a story, book, or movie that continues a narrative of an earlier work. **sequels.**

**ser•e•nade** (ser ə nād′) *noun.* **1.** a song, often sung outdoors in the evening by a lover. **2.** the playing or singing of such a song. —*verb.* to entertain with a song: The chorus began to *serenade* their parents with a song.

**se•rene** (sə rēn′) *adjective.* **1.** calm; fair. **2.** peaceful; unruffled.

**se•ver•i•ty** (sə ver′ə tē) *noun.* **1.** sternness; strictness. **2.** harshness; sharpness.

**sheaf** (shēf) *noun.* **1.** a bundle of stalks of cut grain, such as rye or straw, tied together. **2.** a bunch or collection of things such as papers that may be gathered or tied together.

**shin•gle** (shing′g'l) *noun.* a thin, flat piece of wood or slate laid with other pieces to form rows that overlap, as a covering for a roof. **shingles.**

**sin•cer•i•ty** (sin ser′ə tē) *noun.* the quality or condition of being honest or genuine.

**sin•ew•y** (sin′yo͝o wē) *adjective.* **1.** having tough tissues attached to muscles. **2.** firm, strong, powerful, or tough.

**skep•tic** (skep′tik) *noun.* a person who doubts, disbelieves, or questions things that most other people believe. **skeptics.**

**skep•ti•cism** (skep′ti siz′m) *noun.* attitude of doubting or not believing.

**skir•mish** (skur′mish) *noun.* a brief fight between small groups of troops, as a part of a battle. **skirmishes.**

**skit•ter** (skit′ər) *verb.* to move lightly or quickly; to skim or skip. **skittering.**

**small•pox** (smôl′poks) *noun.* a disease that causes a high fever and sores on the skin that leave permanent pitted scars.

**snare** (sner) *noun.* **1.** a trap with a noose used for catching small animals. **2.** any item that traps or catches.

**sol•i•tude** (sol′ə to͞od *or* sol′ə tyo͞od) *noun.* **1.** the condition of being alone and away from others. **2.** a lonely or secluded place. **solitudes.**

**so•nar** (sō′när) *noun.* a device or system that locates underwater objects by sending out sound waves and picking up their echoes after they strike an object and bounce back.

**sov•er•eign** (sov′rən *or* sov′ər in) *adjective.* having supreme rank; highest in power. —*noun.* a monarch; a ruler; a king or a queen: The *sovereign's* son, Prince Hal, bowed before his mother, the queen.

**spasm** (spaz′'m) *noun.* a sudden contraction of a muscle or muscles that is involuntary or that cannot be controlled.

**sphere** (sfir) *noun.* **1.** any round body, such as a globe or a ball. **2.** a star or planet. **3.** the place, range, or scope of action or being.

**splurge** (splurj) *verb.* to spend much money or time wastefully or lavishly, often just to show off: The children decided to *splurge* on gifts for their pals.

**stale•mate** (stāl′māt) *noun.* **1.** a position in chess considered a draw. **2.** a stopping place or time in a struggle because neither side can move; a deadlock; a standstill.

**stam•pede** (stam pēd′) *noun.* a sudden rushing off or flight because of panic, usually as of a herd of cattle or of a crowd of people: *Stampedes* were caused when the cattle were frightened by loud noises. **stampedes.**

**stark** (stärk) *adjective.* **1.** barren, bleak, and lonely. **2.** utter; complete. **3.** severe; unsoftened.

**strat•e•gy** (strat′ə jē) *noun.* **1.** the science of planning and waging war. **2.** a plan to gain a certain end.

**stream•bed** (strēm′bed) *noun.* **1.** the channel through which a stream of water now runs or formerly ran. **2.** the bottom of streams. **streambeds.**

**sub•ter•ra•ne•an** (sub′tə rā′nē ən) *adjective.* **1.** underground. **2.** secret; hidden.

**sul•len** (sul′ən) *adjective.* **1.** glumly quiet and keeping to oneself because one feels angry, resentful, or bitter. **2.** gloomy; dismal. —**sullenly** *adverb.* acting in a gloomy way.

**sul•try** (sul′trē) *adjective.* **1.** uncomfortably hot, humid or damp, and still. **2.** very hot.

**sum•mit** (sum′it) *noun.* the highest level or point or the top, usually of a mountain.

**sup•ple** (sup′′l) *adjective.* **1.** bending easily. **2.** able to change or adapt easily to new or different situations.

**sus•cep•ti•ble** (sə sep′tə b′l) *adjective.* easily influenced, affected, or moved. —**susceptibility** *noun.* quality of being vulnerable.

**syn•chro•nize** (siŋ′krə nīz) *verb.* **1.** to change so as to occur at the same time or speed: The dancers *synchronized* their steps perfectly. **2.** to adjust timepieces so that they agree in time. **synchronized, synchronizing.**

# T

**tal•is•man** (tal′is mən) *noun.* **1.** something, such as a ring or stone, whose carvings or engravings are supposed to bring good luck. **2.** any item that appears to have magic powers or to bring luck.

**tal•low** (tal′ō) *noun.* the hard fat from certain animals, such as cattle or sheep, melted down and used when making candles and soap.

**tap•es•try** (tap′is trē) *noun.* **1.** a heavy fabric with woven and/or embroidered designs or scenes, for hanging on walls or for coverings for furniture. **2.** a thing that is like a tapestry in difficulty or complexity: A teller of stories can weave a *tapestry* of vivid pictures for you.

**taunt** (tônt *or* tänt) *verb.* to jeer at; to make fun of; to tease. **taunted.** —*noun.* a scornful or sarcastic remark.

**tell•tale** (tel′tāl) *adjective.* revealing or showing what is meant to be hidden.

**ten•ta•cle** (ten′tə k′l) *noun.* **1.** long, thin growth from the head or mouth of an animal used for feeling, seizing, or movement. **2.** a sensitive hairlike growth on a plant. **tentacles.**

**ter•race** (ter′əs) *noun.* a raised, level platform of land, with one or more sloping sides, or a series of such platforms. —**terraced** *adjective.* formed with level platforms as on a hill: The *terraced* meadow was flat enough for the cattle to graze on easily. —*verb.* to form into or provide with a terrace or with terraces: The farmers had *terraced* the mountain so they could plant their crops.

**tes•ti•mo•ni•al** (tes′tə mō′nē əl) *noun.* **1.** a statement or letter telling about or praising a person or thing. **2.** something that is given to show thanks. **3.** a formal statement testifying to a particular fact or truth: His *testimonial* has shown us exactly how the door was unlocked.

**teth•er** (te*th*′ər) *noun.* a rope or chain for tying up an animal so that it will not roam. —*verb.* to fasten or tie to a place with a tether. **tethered.**

**thwart** (thwôrt) *verb.* to keep someone from doing an action or something from being done: —**thwarted** *adjective.* prevented; frustrated: The dog barked loudly after its *thwarted* attempts to escape over the fence.

**tol•er•ant** (tol′ər ənt) *adjective.* having or showing a willingness to let others have their beliefs.

**tor•ment** (tôr′ment) *noun.* **1.** great physical or mental suffering or pain. **2.** the cause of pain. —*verb.* **1.** to make or cause pain. **2.** to make miserable, annoy, or worry.

**tra•di•tion•al•ist** (trə dish′ən′l ist) *noun.* a person interested in handing down customs and beliefs from generation to generation.

| | | |
|---|---|---|
| **a** fat | **oi** oil | **ch** chin |
| **ā** ape | **oo** look | **sh** she |
| **ä** car, father | **ōō** tool | **th** thin |
| **e** ten | **ou** out | ***th*** then |
| **er** care | **u** up | **zh** leisure |
| **ē** even | **ur** fur | **ng** ring |
| **i** hit | | |
| **ir** here | **ə** = a *in* ago | |
| **ī** bite, fire | e *in* agent | |
| **o** lot | i *in* unity | |
| **ō** go | o *in* collect | |
| **ô** law, horn | u *in* focus | |

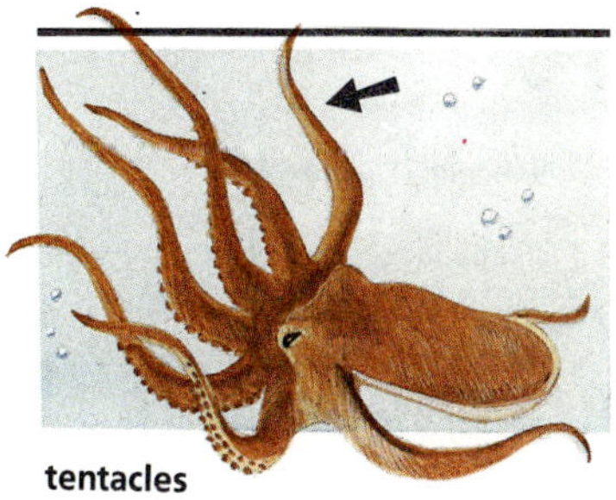

**tentacles**

**Torment** originally meant "torture with the rack or other dreadful implement." From this came the meaning of "great pain." The word comes from the Latin *tormentum,* which was an instrument for twisting or pressing and of torture. *Tormentum,* in turn, came from *torquere,* "to twist or torture." A torment of whatever kind can be real torture.

unyoked

**Vanguard** comes from the French *avant-garde*, "before guard." In this meaning it is still used to refer to the advance troops of an army. Today the word also refers to the leaders of any movement.

vessel

**trans•con•ti•nen•tal** (trans′kon tə nen′t′l) *adjective.* going from one side of a continent to the other.

**trans•pose** (trans pōz′) *verb.* **1.** to move or appear to move so as to change places or to appear to have changed places; to interchange. **2.** in music, to put into a different key. —**transposed** *adjective.* changed in order or position.

**trav•erse** (tra vurs′ *or* trav′ərs) *verb.* to pass over, move over, or pass through; to cross.

**treach•er•ous** (trech′ər əs) *adjective.* **1.** disloyal; unfaithful; betraying. **2.** not as trustworthy or reliable as it appears.

**tres•tle** (tres″l) *noun.* **1.** a frame like a sawhorse used to hold up a part of a table top or platform. **2.** a braced framework used to support a bridge, road, or railway tracks. **trestles.**

**tu•nic** (to͞o′nik *or* tyo͞o′nik) *noun.* **1.** a loose-fitting garb worn by men and women in ancient Rome and Greece. **2.** a hip-length blouse or jacket, often belted.

# U

**un•al•ter•a•ble** (un ôl′tər ə b′l) *adjective.* impossible to change.

**u•nan•i•mous** (yo͞o nan′ə məs) *adjective.* in complete agreement; sharing the same views or opinions. —**unanimously** *adverb.* acting as of one mind.

**un•a•wares** (un ə werz′) *adverb.* in an unexpected way; by surprise; without warning.

**un•der•mine** (un dər mīn′) *verb.* **1.** to tunnel or dig under. **2.** to wear away or weaken at the base or at the supports. **3.** to weaken or injure unfairly or secretively. **undermined, undermining.**

**un•der•tak•ing** (un′dər tā′king *or* un′dər tā′king) *noun.* **1.** something entered into or upon, usually a difficult or an important task. **2.** a promise or a pledge.

**un•en•ter•pris•ing** (un en′tər prī′zing) *adjective.* not full of desire, spirit, or daring.

**un•e•vap•o•rat•ed** (un i vap′ə rāt əd) *adjective.* not changed into vapor by heat; not having disappeared into the air; not vanished: The ink has stayed *unevaporated* because its bottle had a tight stopper.

**un•yoke** (un yōk′) *verb.* **1.** to free or remove from a yoke, a wooden frame that fits around a pair of oxen. **2.** to separate, disconnect, or relieve from a burden. —**unyoked** *adjective.* having had the yoke removed.

# V

**val•iant** (val′yənt) *adjective.* having or showing courage; brave. —**valiantly** *adverb.* with valor.

**van•guard** (van′gärd) *noun.* **1.** the advance troops or the front part of an army. **2.** the leaders of any movement, such as in arts or culture.

**va•por•ize** (vā′pə rīz) *verb.* to change into vapor, especially by heating. **vaporized, vaporizing.**

**vast** (vast) *adjective.* very great; huge; immense. —**vastness** *noun.* largeness of size, amount, or number.

**venge•ance** (ven′jəns) *noun.* the act of getting even in return for mistreatment. —**with a vengeance. 1.** with great force, violence, or determination. **2.** very much, too much, or more than expected.

**ven•ture** (ven′chər) *noun.* a risky or uncertain undertaking. —*verb.* **1.** to expose to danger, risk, or hazard. **2.** to dare; to take risk. **ventured, venturing.**

**ver•i•fy** (ver′ə fī) *verb.* **1.** to prove or confirm. **2.** to test, determine, or check for accuracy.

**ver•min** (vur′min) *noun.* **1.** insects and small animals that are harmful and troublesome to humans, such as flies, mice, lice, and rats. **2.** an unpleasant or harmful person.

**ves•sel** (ves″l) *noun.* **1.** a hollow container. **2.** a large boat or a ship. **3.** a tube or duct in the body's circulatory system through which blood or other bodily fluids flow. **vessels.**

**vin•di•ca•tion** (vin′də kā′shən) *noun.* **1.** the act of clearing one accused; freeing from blame. **2.** a justification; a defense; an excuse.

**vi•sion** (vizh′ən) *noun.* **1.** the ability to see; sight. **2.** the ability of seeing in the mind; a dream; a trance. **3.** the ability to imagine; insight.

**vis•u•al•ize** (vizh′oo wə līz′) *verb.* to form a mental picture or image of.

**viv•id** (viv′id) *adjective.* **1.** very bright, strong, or intense. **2.** forming or giving a clear impression in the mind. **3.** full of life or energy. —**vividly** *adverb.* in a lively or striking manner.

# W

**wage** (wāj) *verb.* to engage or take part in; to carry on. —*noun.* money paid for the services of a worker for a job done.

**wag•on train** (wag′ən trān′) *noun.* a long line of vehicles, people, and animals traveling across a part of a country.

**whim•si•cal** (hwim′zi k′l) *adjective.* full of sudden notions, desires, or fancies having no special causes; having odd notions: Tom was in a *whimsical* mood when he wore a clown costume to the Halloween party.

**wil•der•ness** (wil′dər nis) *noun.* a region that is not cultivated or lived in by any settlers; a wild area; a wasteland.

**wran•gle** (raŋ′g′l) *verb.* **1.** to argue or quarrel noisily or in an angry way. **2.** to herd or round up horses. **wrangled, wrangling.**

| | | |
|---|---|---|
| **a** fat | **oi** oil | **ch** chin |
| **ā** ape | **oo** look | **sh** she |
| **ä** car, father | **ōō** tool | **th** thin |
| **e** ten | **ou** out | ***th*** then |
| **er** care | **u** up | **zh** leisure |
| **ē** even | **ur** fur | **ŋ** ring |
| **i** hit | | |
| **ir** here | **ə** = a *in* ago | |
| **ī** bite, fire | e *in* agent | |
| **o** lot | i *in* unity | |
| **ō** go | o *in* collect | |
| **ô** law, horn | u *in* focus | |

wagon train

# About the Authors

*The authors listed below have written some of the selections that appear in this book. The content of the notes was determined by a survey of what readers wanted to know about authors.*

*Joan Aiken*

## Joan Aiken

Joan Aiken's father was the famous American poet, Conrad Aiken. She herself was born in England and is a British citizen. She says, "I still have a large notepad which I bought when I was five and filled with verse. I used to make up stories to amuse myself and had an imaginary island peopled with all the characters from my favorite fiction. My younger brother had an imaginary country too, and we used to swap details." Joan Aiken has won numerous awards, including the Mystery Writers of America Edgar Allan Poe award for best juvenile mystery and the Lewis Carroll Award. *(Born 1924)*

*Isaac Asimov*

## Isaac Asimov

Isaac Asimov has written stories, essays, fiction, and nonfiction books about dozens of different subjects. He says that he became interested in science fiction back in 1929 when he was a boy and saw an issue of *Amazing Stories*. "From then on I was hooked. I was a science-fiction fan of the most confirmed variety." Isaac Asimov says that he works at his writing every day. "I start early each day and continue typing till the number of typographical errors reaches an unacceptable concentration." From this work pattern, Isaac Asimov has become one of the most prolific writers in America. *(Born 1920)*

## STEPHEN VINCENT BENÉT

Stephen Vincent Benét, whose last name is pronounced bə nā′, was a poet, novelist, short story writer, and dramatist. He published his first book of poetry at seventeen. Several of his stories have been made into movies, including the short story "The Devil and Daniel Webster," which won the O. Henry Memorial Prize. Stephen Vincent Benét once said that he learned that poetry "was not a dead thing or an alien thing or a dry game of words. I knew there were rules and that you could break the rules but that you must never break them unintentionally." One of the greatest honors he earned was the Pulitzer Prize for poetry. *(1898–1943)*

*STEPHEN VINCENT BENÉT*

## GWENDOLYN BROOKS

The poet Gwendolyn Brooks was born in Topeka, Kansas. She says, "I loved poetry very early and began to put rhymes together at about seven, at which time my parents expressed most earnest confidence that I would one day be a writer. At the age of thirteen my poem 'Eventide' was accepted and printed by a then well-known children's magazine." When Gwendolyn Brooks was sixteen she began submitting poems to a newspaper. More than 75 of these poems were published by the newspaper. The Pulitzer Prize in poetry for "Annie Allen" is one of the many honors and awards Gwendolyn Brooks has received. She is poet laureate of Illinois. *(Born 1917)*

*GWENDOLYN BROOKS*

## Eve Bunting

*Eve Bunting*

Eve Bunting, whose full name is Anne Evelyn Bunting, was born in Maghera, Ireland, but now lives in California. Her literary achievements include an award for Best Work of Fiction from the Southern California Council on Literature for Children and Young People and the Golden Kite Award. About her writing, Eve Bunting has said, "I like to write, and I particularly like to write about Ireland. As an immigrant, although I appreciate the ever-blue skies of California, I sometimes long for the misty grays of Ireland." She also writes under the names of Evelyn Bolton and A. E. Bunting. *(Born 1928)*

## Pat Carr

Pat Carr, who has also published under the name Pat M. Esslinger, was born in Wyoming. In addition to writing, she has taught English at several universities. Pat Carr has been awarded the Mark IV Award from the Library of Congress and has received a grant from the National Endowment for the Humanities. She speaks six languages and has traveled in Europe and throughout Central and South America from Mexico to Argentina. *(Born 1932)*

## WILLA CATHER

Willa Cather was born in Virginia but grew up in Nebraska among immigrant farmers. Late in her life, she said that the most important years to her as a writer were in the 1880s during her first two years in the West. When ten years old, she moved to the Nebraska prairie land. She began work as a journalist and later became an English teacher, then a magazine editor. Several of her novels are set in the farm and prairie country of her childhood. Willa Cather, who won the Pulitzer Prize for her novel *One of Ours,* is considered to be one of our outstanding American writers. *(1876–1947)*

*WILLA CATHER*

## ELIZABETH COATSWORTH

Elizabeth Coatsworth received the Newbery Medal for *The Cat Who Went to Heaven* and the Children's Spring Book Festival Honor Award for *Under the Green Willow.* She described her life as "one of books, travel, children, household, and writing. I traveled widely for many years in the Orient, in North Africa, in Europe, and sometimes, in my books, I return to these memories. But in general I have written about New England." She began her writing career as a poet and writer of short stories and later wrote essays, novels, and books for young people. *(1893–1986)*

*ELIZABETH COATSWORTH*

## ROBERT CORMIER

According to one critic, Robert Cormier's books about teenagers "have had an impact on the field of adolescent literature well out of proportion to their number." Unlike many books for young people, Cormier's stories do not all have happy endings. The characters in his books face real-life problems. Cormier has said, "I do not write for young people but about them. I write for the intelligent reader and this intelligent reader is often 12 or 14 or 16 years old." *(Born 1925)*

*ROBERT CORMIER*

E. E. CUMMINGS

## E. E. CUMMINGS

Edward Estlin Cummings, born in Cambridge, Massachusetts, was a painter as well as a writer. He considered himself "an author of pictures, a draughtsman of words." While a student at Harvard University, he experimented with the innovative arrangement of words and lines. He began to feel that unconventional punctuation, such as signing his name without capitalization, made a strong statement of individuality. After graduation, he went to France where, during World War I, he served as a driver for an ambulance corps. After the war, he returned to the United States and settled in New York City. *(1894–1962)*

*JULIA CUNNINGHAM*

## JULIA CUNNINGHAM

Julia Cunningham, who has lived in France and Mexico, was born in Spokane, Washington. Although she has written a number of books for young people, she says that her purpose is not to write just for that audience, but rather to tell a good story. She also says, "My characters are some of the best friends I have, as real as any other. I was not aware of being a writer until age twelve when I received my first rejection letter. It's a good road to follow, full of darkness and joy." Among the joys are the literary honors Julia Cunningham has earned including the Christopher Award for her book, *Come to the Edge. (Born 1916)*

## Paul Laurence Dunbar

*Paul Laurence Dunbar*

Paul Laurence Dunbar was born in Dayton, Ohio, and eventually settled in Washington, D.C. His parents were born into slavery. They became free during the Civil War. His family struggled to make ends meet. As a young boy, Dunbar loved to listen to stories and in first grade he was jotting down the rhymes he liked best. He worked at odd jobs to help his mother, but he was always possessed with the "itch to write" and go to school. Dunbar was able to graduate from high school despite financial difficulties. Over the years Paul Laurence Dunbar's poetry, short stories, and song lyrics earned him recognition in the United States as well as in England. *(1872–1906)*

## Edward Edelson

Edward Edelson was born in New York City. In addition to being an author, Edelson has worked on several newspapers. He has been a reporter, an editor, and a science writer. His books include *Poisons in the Air, Great Monsters of the Movies,* and *Visions of Tomorrow. (Born 1932)*

## Jack Finney

Jack Finney, whose real name is Walter Braden Finney, is a freelance journalist and writer. He is perhaps best known as the author of *The Body Snatchers,* which was the basis for the science-fiction film classic *The Invasion of the Body Snatchers.* Though Jack Finney is usually considered a science-fiction writer, he has also written detective mysteries and general fiction. *(Born 1911)*

## RUSSELL FREEDMAN

*RUSSELL FREEDMAN*

Russell Freedman is a prolific writer and editor. He has written, co-authored, and edited many nonfiction books, including *Teenagers Who Made History* and *2000 Years of Space Travel.* He has also written for newspapers, television, and encyclopedias. With James Morris, he has co-authored books about animals, which include *Growing Up Wild: How Young Animals Survive, Animal Fathers,* and *How Animals Defend Their Young.* Russell Freedman won the Newbery Medal in 1987 for *Lincoln: A Photobiography,* one of the few nonfiction books ever to have won this award. *(Born 1929)*

## ROBERT FROST

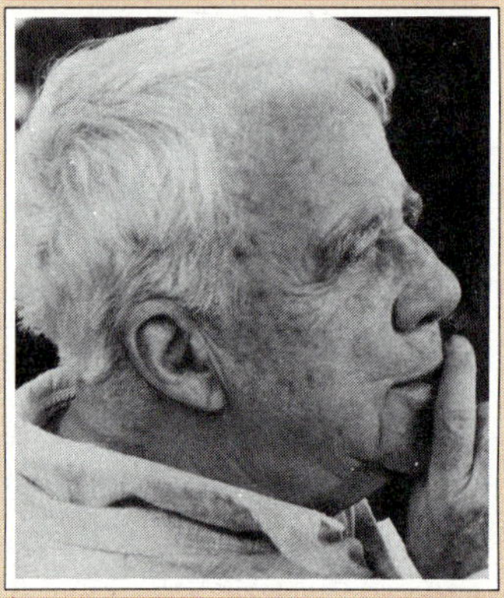

*ROBERT FROST*

Robert Frost was born in San Francisco but spent most of his adult life in New England. He wrote his first poem, in ballad form, when he was fourteen years old. Robert Frost's daughter said about their family, "Reading was most important—learning to read and being read to. Every evening of our lives we sat before the Franklin stove in the front room, under the rather dim light of the kerosene lamps, while my mother read and my father whittled, or my father read and my mother mended." In 1961, Robert Frost participated in President John F. Kennedy's inauguration ceremonies by reading two of his poems: *Dedication* and *The Gift Outright.* He received many literary awards, including the Pulitzer Prize for poetry. *(1874–1963)*

ROBERT HAYDEN

Robert Hayden grew up in Detroit, Michigan. Because his severe nearsightedness prevented him from participating in many sports activities, he turned to reading as a pastime. Of his early reading, he says, "I certainly was more devoted to poetry than to anything else. . . . I . . . was always trying to write it." His first poem, "Africa," was published after he graduated from high school. In addition to teaching at the University of Michigan and at Fisk University, Hayden published several collections of poetry. His collection *A Ballad of Remembrance* received the Grand Prize for Poetry at the First World Festival for Negro Arts in 1966. *(1913–1980)*

*ROBERT HAYDEN*

O. HENRY

O. Henry is the pen name for William Sidney Porter. Born in Greensboro, North Carolina, he moved to Texas when he was a young man and lived there for twenty years. He later moved to New York and devoted himself to writing, particularly short stories. O. Henry was a master of the short story with a surprise twist at the end. He once offered this advice, "I'll give you the whole secret of short-story writing. Here it is. Rule 1: Write stories that please yourself. There is no Rule 2. If you can't write a story that pleases yourself, you'll never please the public." *(1862–1910)*

*O. HENRY*

*Jamake Highwater*

## Jamake Highwater

Jamake Highwater, whose first name is pronounced jə mä′kə, was born in Montana. His mother was of French and Blackfoot ancestry. His father was of Eastern Cherokee heritage. He grew up, he said, "living between two cultures. The grand climax of my professional and personal life took place when Ed Calf Robe, Elder of the Blood Reserve of Blackfoot Indians conferred a new name upon me to honor my achievement in behalf of my people. It is a ceremony reserved for only the 'favored children' of the Blackfoot Nations." Jamake Highwater has written under the name of J. Marks and J. Marks-Highwater and has won numerous literary awards, including a Newbery Honor award for *Anpao: An American Indian Odyssey. (Born 1942)*

*Lee Bennett Hopkins*

## Lee Bennett Hopkins

In addition to interviewing authors and illustrators, Lee Bennett Hopkins also compiles poetry anthologies and writes poetry himself. He says that he loves writing books for young people. "Each one is a new challenge, a new day, a new spring for me. It is exciting to see each unfold, going from my typewritten copy to the joy of holding the finished book in my hand. Opening the bound copy for the first time is like seeing the big curtains being raised in a darkened theatre. It's magical, fun, scary." *(Born 1938)*

*Jan Hudson*

## Jan Hudson

Jan Hudson lived in Canada. From the time she was a young child, she was interested in writing. By learning to do extensive research when writing historical fiction, she added to her writing skills. Hiking and fossil hunting were on her list of things she enjoyed. She was the proud owner of the vertebra of a duck-billed dinosaur. Jan Hudson won second prize in Alberta Culture's first Alberta Writing-for-Young People competition. (1955–1990)

## LANGSTON HUGHES

Langston Hughes wrote award-winning poems, short stories, and novels. He said he began to write poetry because he was elected class poet when he was in grammar school. "The day I was elected, I went home and wondered what I should write. Since we had eight teachers in our school, I thought there should be one verse for each teacher, and since the teachers were to have eight verses, I felt the class should have eight, too. I said our class was the greatest class ever graduated. So at graduation, when I read the poem, naturally everybody applauded loudly. That was the way I began to write poetry." *(1902–1967)*

*LANGSTON HUGHES*

## CORETTA SCOTT KING

Coretta Scott King was born in Marion, Alabama. After her marriage to Martin Luther King, Jr., she was a voice instructor, and she gave concerts in which she sang, recited poetry, and lectured. After her husband's assassination, she honored all his previously made speaking commitments. These speeches helped earn her the respect and admiration both of people involved in civil rights causes and of those who were observers of the movement. Her book, *My Life with Martin Luther King, Jr.*, was a bestseller in the United States and in England. It has been translated into twelve languages. *(Born 1927)*

*CORETTA SCOTT KING*

## HOWARD KOCH

Howard Koch is a writer for stage, screen, and radio. He is best known for his radio script of H. G. Wells's "War of the Worlds" and for the screenplay of the movie *Casablanca*, for which he won the Academy Award for best screenplay. Following the panic and excitement caused by the radio broadcast of "The War of the Worlds," Howard Koch wrote a book called *The Panic Broadcast*. He has also written nearly thirty plays and screenplays. *(Born 1902)*

*HOWARD KOCH*

## CHARLES KURALT

CHARLES KURALT

Charles Kuralt has been a reporter, writer, and researcher of human-interest stories for the CBS-News feature "On the Road." Doing the research for this show, Charles Kuralt and his three-person crew cover about 50,000 miles a year. Although occasionally one of the stories is of a serious nature, most are on the light side. Charles Kuralt has said: "It's so important on a national news show to acknowledge that the whole world isn't in flames." He has received the Ernie Pyle Memorial Award, the Emmy Award, and, twice, the George Foster Peabody Broadcasting Award. *(Born 1934)*

## LOUIS L'AMOUR

LOUIS L'AMOUR

Louis L'Amour, who was born in North Dakota, has been a longshoreman, a lumberjack, an elephant handler, and a fruit picker. He has also written over four hundred short stories and more than fifty books. He is best known and most loved for his very popular Western novels. One of Louis L'Armour's projects was recreating an 1865 Western town. Called Shalako, the town is located near the state lines of Utah, Arizona, New Mexico, and Colorado—the only place in the U.S. where the borders of four states adjoin. Historically authentic, Shalako was planned as a live, operating town, serving not only as a tourist attraction, but also as a location for filming movies.

### Rose Wilder Lane

*Rose Wilder Lane*

Rose Wilder Lane was born in a shanty in the Dakota Territory where her parents had gone as pioneers to try to carve a new life. When they were unable to make a living there, they moved, first to the Ozark Mountains in Missouri, then to Comely, Louisiana. Rose Wilder Lane grew up with the same spirit of adventure that led her parents to try pioneering. She traveled in Turkey, Iraq, and Albania where she met tribes never before seen by foreigners. Later, she was a war correspondent in Vietnam. Like her mother, Laura Ingalls Wilder, she, too, became an author. *(1886–1968)*

### Henry Wadsworth Longfellow

*Henry Wadsworth Longfellow*

Henry Wadsworth Longfellow was a descendant of Priscilla and John Alden, about whom he wrote in one of his poems, "The Courtship of Miles Standish." He graduated from Bowdoin College, where he was a classmate of Nathaniel Hawthorne and of Franklin Pierce (fourteenth president of the United States). Longfellow was a teacher, a translator, a poet, and a writer of prose. Among the many poems he wrote, some of the best known are "The Song of Hiawatha," "Evangeline: A Tale of Arcadia," "The Village Blacksmith," and "Paul Revere's Ride." His work was so greatly admired in England, as well as in the United States, that a bust of Longfellow was placed in the Poets' Corner of Westminster Abbey in London, England, an extremely rare honor for an American. *(1807–1882)*

## ROBIN MCKINLEY

*ROBIN MCKINLEY*

When Jennifer Carolyn Robin McKinley was growing up, her father was in the Navy, and she lived in different places all around the world. One of her favorite childhood pastimes was reading books, particularly fairy tales and fantasies. The first novel she wrote, *Beauty,* is a retelling of the classic fairy tale *Beauty and the Beast.* Her novel, *The Blue Sword,* was a Newbery Honor Book, and *The Hero and the Crown* won the John Newbery Medal. Robin McKinley says that fairy tales and fantasies are still among her favorite books. *(Born 1952)*

## CORNELIA MEIGS

*CORNELIA MEIGS*

During Cornelia Meigs's long life, she wrote two plays and dozens of books and stories for young people. She wrote under her own name and under the pen name Adair Aldon. About her career, she said, "It was tolerably plain that I was meant to be a teacher; becoming a writer was not such an evident or easily accomplished process." She found "that teaching and writing went well together and that the American history that I was interested in gave me endless material for stories." One of her best-loved books is the Newbery Medal winner *Invincible Louisa,* the story of Louisa May Alcott. *(1884–1973)*

## MARGARET EVANS PRICE

Margaret Evans Price was a woman of many talents. In addition to writing books for both young people and adults, she was an artist and a book illustrator. She was also a toy designer, and in the 1930s, she and her husband founded a very successful toy company. *(1888–1973)*

## Geraldo Rivera

Geraldo Rivera began his career as a lawyer in Harlem's antipoverty neighborhood law firms. Later, he moved into news reporting for a New York City TV station. From there he became host of ABC's "Good Morning America" program. Rivera has won numerous awards for his news reporting, including the Kennedy Journalism Award which he won twice as well as seven Emmy Awards. He has also been named Broadcaster of the Year by the New York State Associated Press three times. Rivera has written several books, one of which, *A Special Kind of Courage,* portrays the lives of several young people who have triumphed over physical and mental limitations. *(Born 1943)*

*Geraldo Rivera*

## Saki

Saki, whose real name was Hector Hugh Munro, was a Scottish author. He was born in Burma, where his father was stationed. His mother died when he was a young child, and he was reared by two strict and eccentric aunts. His short stories, for which he is famous, are often about young people who are involved in a battle of wits with adults. Munro is clearly on the side of youth, and it is usually the young people who triumph. During World War I, H. H. Munro enlisted in the British army and was killed in action in France. *(1870–1916)*

*Saki*

## Carl Sandburg

*Carl Sandburg*

Carl Sandburg, the son of Swedish immigrants, is regarded as one of the major writers of the twentieth century. Few writers have received, during their own lifetimes, as many honors and as much recognition as Sandburg did. The cottage in which he was born in Galesburg, Illinois, was dedicated as a literary shrine in 1946. Even his goat farm in North Carolina was among the best known in the country. His books about Abraham Lincoln are considered one of the monumental works of this century. Carl Sandburg once wrote: "My father couldn't sign his name. He made his 'mark' on the company's payroll sheet. My mother was able to read the Scriptures in her native language, but she could not write, and I wrote about Abraham Lincoln whose own mother could not read or write! I guess that somewhere along in this you'll find a story of America." *(1878–*1967)

## Mari Sandoz

*Mari Sandoz*

Mari Sandoz (last name pronounced sən dos′) was born in the Sand Hills cattle country of northwest Nebraska. She was the second child of the fourth wife of a Swiss immigrant whom she portrayed in her first book, *Old Jules*. When she was thirteen she and her brother had to dig the family cattle out of a snowdrift. She said, "By that night I was snowblind, totally blind for around six weeks. Then I discovered I had only one eye left. But it's very useful to me, so it doesn't matter." When Mari Sandoz completed the eighth grade of the rural school she attended, she took the teachers' examination and taught school until she was old enough to enter the University of Nebraska as an adult special student. She won many literary awards, including a Newbery Honor Book, *The Horse Catcher,* and a Western Writers of America Spur Award for *The Story Catcher.* Mari Sandoz is recognized as one of our leading regional historians. *(1901–1966)*

## R. Conrad Stein

*R. Conrad Stein*

R. Conrad Stein was born in Chicago. He now lives part of the time in Mexico and part of the time in Chicago. "In Mexico," says Stein, "I enjoy reading and hiking in the mountains near my home. In Chicago I like going to Cubs games to cheer for a team that has not won a pennant since 1945." About his writing he says: "I enjoy writing fiction, but this does not always sell. So I make my living writing history and biography. History is fun to write, and it should be fun to read. History is far more than just dry dates, places, and passages of time. It is a rich and exciting study." *(Born 1937)*

## James Thurber

*James Thurber*

James Thurber wrote humorous short stories, articles, and books for young people and adults. He was also a cartoonist, and he illustrated many of his articles and stories with cartoons. As the result of a childhood accident, James Thurber lost the vision in one eye. His vision grew worse as he got older, until he was almost totally blind. Although he had to stop drawing cartoons, he could dictate his stories and articles and continued to write until his death. His book *Many Moons* won the Randolph Caldecott Medal. *(1894–1961)*

*MARK TWAIN*

## MARK TWAIN

Mark Twain was the pen name, or pseudonym, of Samuel Langhorne Clemens. As a young man, Samuel Clemens was a steamboat pilot on the Mississippi River. He took his pen name from a term used by boatmen taking soundings to find out how deep the water was. *Mark Twain* was the term for water two fathoms deep. After working as a printer, Samuel Clemens moved west working as a journalist. His humorous sketches like "The Celebrated Jumping Frog of Calaveras County" were so well-received that he decided on a literary career. Two of Mark Twain's most famous books, *The Adventures of Tom Sawyer* and *The Adventures of Huckleberry Finn,* are based on his knowledge of the lore of the Mississippi River. The author Ernest Hemingway said, "All modern literature comes from one book by Mark Twain called *Huckleberry Finn* – it's the best book we've had." Mark Twain's use of humor and his use of the local language of his characters – instead of the formal English of earlier writers – are two of his important contributions to American literature. *(1835–1910)*

*ALICE WALKER*

## ALICE WALKER

Alice Walker grew up in a large family of sharecroppers in Georgia. The youngest of eight children, she took care of cooking and cleaning the house while her mother worked. Her love of reading developed early, and was fostered by her mother and her teachers, from whom she often borrowed books. She says, "Books became my world because the world I was in was very hard." Alice Walker first began writing poetry when she was eight years old. Her first book of poetry, *Once,* published in 1968, was inspired by a trip to Africa. In addition to poetry, Alice Walker has written several novels. In 1982, she received the Pulitzer Prize for fiction. *(Born 1944)*

WILLIAM CARLOS WILLIAMS

William Carlos Williams had a double career—he was a medical doctor as well as a poet. Williams felt that his work as a doctor enhanced his poetry. He felt that a poet should "write, as a physician works, upon the things before him." He was interested in capturing the details of everyday life and he felt that poetry should reflect the lives and experiences of ordinary people. Williams worked and lived for most of his life in Rutherford, New Jersey. He received the Pulitzer Prize in 1963. *(1883–1963)*

*WILLIAM CARLOS WILLIAMS*

ROGER ZELAZNY

Roger Zelazny was born in Ohio, but now lives in New Mexico. He is primarily a science-fiction writer and has won many awards for his writing. Two of his novels, *The Dream Master* and *Lord of Light*, won the Hugo Award, which is given annually for the best science-fiction novel. "He Who Shapes" and "The Doors of His Face, the Lamps of His Mouth" won Nebula Awards for the best novellas of the year. Roger Zelazny also writes under the name of Harrison Denmark. *(Born 1937)*

*ROGER ZELAZNY*

# AUTHOR INDEX

"The Confidence Game" by Pat Carr, from *Young Miss,* September 1977 issue, copyright © 1977 Parents' Magazine Enterprises, Inc. Reprinted by permission of Gruner +Jahr USA Publishing, successor-in-interest to Parents' Magazines Enterprises, Inc.

"Conversation by Loch Ness" by Elizabeth Coatsworth. Reprinted with permission of Macmillan Publishing Company from *Down Half the World* by Elizabeth Coatsworth. Copyright © 1968 by Elizabeth Coatsworth Beston.

"The Eagle and the Oriole" from *Eyes of Darkness* by Jamake Highwater. Text copyright 1985 by Jamake Highwater. By permission of Lothrop, Lee & Shepard (A Division of William Morrow), and of the author's representatives, The Native Land Foundation.

"The Eternal Frontier" from *Frontier* by Louis L'Amour. Text copyright © 1984 by Louis L'Amour Enterprises, Inc. Slightly adapted and reprinted by permission of Bantam Books.

"Free at Last" from the introduction by Coretta Scott King to *The Words of Martin Luther King, Jr.,* selected by Coretta Scott King. Reprinted by permission of Joan Daves in care of Marian Reiner. Copyright © 1983 by Coretta Scott King.

"The Gift-Giving" adapted from *UP THE CHIMNEY DOWN and Other Stories* by Joan Aiken Enterprises Ltd. First appeared in the United States in an anthology entitled *Sixteen,* published by Delacorte for the State of Connecticut, edited by Donald Gallo. Published in Great Britain by Jonathan Cape Ltd. Reprinted by permission of Harper & Row, Publishers, Inc., and of the author's British agents, A. M. Heath & Company Limited.

"Gwendolyn Brooks, a Memoir" excerpt adapted from *Report from Part One* by Gwendolyn Brooks. Copyright © 1972 by Gwendolyn Brooks Blakeley. Reprinted by permission of Broadside Press.

"Holding On!" excerpt from *O Pioneers!* by Willa Cather. Copyright 1913, 1941 by Willa Sibert Cather. Reprinted by permission of Houghton Mifflin Company.

"Horses of Lir" from *Unicorn Variations* by Roger Zelazny. Copyright © 1984 by The Amber Corporation. Reprinted by permission of Pocket Books, a division of Simon & Schuster, Inc.

"I Have A Dream" by Martin Luther King, Jr. Copyright © 1963 by Martin Luther King, Jr. Reprinted as it appeared in *The Worlds of Martin Luther King, Jr.,* selected by Coretta Scott King. Copyright © 1983 by Coretta Scott King. Reprinted by permission of Joan Daves in care of Mirian Reiner.

"Independence Hall" reprinted by permission of The Putnam Publishing Group from *On the Road with Charles Kuralt* by Charles Kuralt. Copyright © 1985 by Charles Kuralt.

"The Inside Story" by Jeanette Leardi, © 1989 by Silver, Burdett & Ginn Inc.

"In Honor of David Anderson Brooks, My Father" by Gwendolyn Brooks, from "The Bean Eaters" in *Blacks,* copyright © 1987 The David Company, Chicago. Reprinted by permission of Gwendolyn Brooks.

"Invasion from Mars" from *The Panic Broadcast: Portrait of an Event* by Howard Koch. Copyright © 1970 by Howard Koch. Reprinted by permission of International Creative Management.

"It's Not the Great Wall, but It Will Last Forever" by Eve Bunting, © 1989 by Silver, Burdett & Ginn Inc.

"Lee Bennett Hopkins Interviews Robin McKinley," © 1989 by Silver, Burdett & Ginn Inc.

"Life from the River" excerpt adapted from *Sweetgrass,* a novel by Jan Hudson, with permission of Tree Frog Press, Edmonton. Hardback edition published by Spindlewood, Devonshire, England. Text © 1984 Jan Hudson.

"The Long Road West" from *Children of the Wild West* by Russell Freedman. Copyright © 1983 by Russell Freedman. Reprinted by permission of Clarion Books/ Ticknor & Fields, a Houghton Mifflin Company.

*The Love Letter* by Jack Finney. Reprinted by permission of Don Congdon Associates, Inc. Copyright © 1959 by Curtis Publishing Company; renewed 1987 by Jack Finney.

"maggie and milly and molly and may" is reprinted from *Complete Poems,* 1913–1962, by e. e. cummings, by permission of the American publisher, Liveright Publishing Corporation, and of the British publisher, Grafton Books, a division of the Collins Publishing Group. Copyright 1923, 1925, 1931, 1935, 1938, 1939, 1940, 1944, 1945, 1946, 1947, 1948, 1949, 1950, 1951, 1952, 1953, 1954, © 1955, 1956, 1957, 1958, 1959, 1960, 1961, 1962 by the Trustees for the E. E. Cummings Trust. Copyright © 1961, 1963, 1968 by Marion Morehouse Cummings.

"Maria Pepe, Girl of Courage" from *A Special Kind of Courage: Profiles of Young Americans* by Geraldo Rivera. Copyright © 1976 by Geraldo Rivera. Adapted and reprinted by permission of Simon & Schuster, Inc.

"Mystery of Loch Ness" from *Is There a Loch Ness Monster?* by Gerald S. Snyder. Copyright © 1977 by Gerald S. Snyder. Reprinted by permission of Julian Messner, a division of Simon & Schuster, Inc.

"The Night the Martians Landed" from *The Panic Broadcast: Portrait of an Event* by Howard Koch. Copyright © 1970 by Howard Koch. Reprinted by permission of International Creative Management.

"Nothing Gold Can Stay" by Robert Frost. Copyright 1923, © 1969 by Holt, Rinehart, and Winston, Inc. Copyright 1951 by Robert Frost. Reprinted from *The Poetry of Robert Frost,* edited by Edward Connery Lathem, by permission of the American publisher, Henry Holt and Company, Inc., and of the Estate of Robert Frost in care of the British publisher, Jonathan Cape, Ltd.

"A Peck of Gold" by Robert Frost. Copyright 1928, © 1969 by Holt, Rinehart and Winston, Inc. Copyright © 1956 by Robert Frost. Reprinted from *The Poetry of Robert Frost,* edited by Edward Connery Lathem, by permission of the American publisher, Henry Holt and Company, Inc., and of the Estate of Robert Frost in care of the British publisher, Jonathan Cape, Ltd.

"Pegasus and Bellerophon" from *Myths and Enchantment Tales* adapted from the original text by Margaret Evans Price. Copyright © 1960 by Rand McNally & Company. Reprinted by permission of Checkerboard Press, a Division of Macmillan Inc.

"Playing for Keeps" by Jack C. Haldeman II; Copyright © 1982 by Davis Publications Inc.; reprinted by permission of the author.

"President Cleveland, Where Are You?" by Robert Cormier. Copyright © 1965 by Robert Cormier. Adapted and reprinted by permission of Pantheon Books, a Division of Random House, Inc., and of the author's agents, Curtis Brown, Ltd., from *Eight Plus One* by Robert Cormier. First appeared in *Redbook* Magazine.

"The Princess and the Tin Box" by James Thurber. From *The Beast in Me and Other Animals,* published by Harcourt Brace Jovanovich, Inc. Copyright 1948 by James Thurber. Copyright © 1975 Helen Thurber. Reprinted by permission of Rosemary A. Thurber, and of the British publisher, Hamish Hamilton Ltd.

"Refugee In America" copyright 1943 by the Curtis Publishing Co. Reprinted from *Selected Poems of Langston Hughes,* by permission of Alfred A. Knopf, Inc.

"The Sampler" from *Young Americans* by Cornelia Meigs, © copyright 1936, by Ginn and Company. Reprinted by permission of Silver, Burdett & Ginn Inc.

"Saying Goodbye" from *Straight Along a Crooked Road* by Marilyn Cram Donahue. Reprinted by permission of Walker and Company.

"Someday" by Isaac Asimov. Copyright © 1956 by Royal Publications. From the book *Earth Is Room Enough.* Reprinted by permission of Doubleday, a division of Bantam, Doubleday, Dell Publishing Group, Inc.

"Standing in the Wings" by Julia Cunningham. Originally published in *The Writer* magazine, November 1976. Copyright © 1976 by Julia Cunningham. Adapted and reprinted by permission of the author.

*The Story of the Gold at Sutter's Mill* by R. Conrad Stein. Copyright © 1981 by Regensteiner Publishing Enterprises, Inc. Reprinted by permission of Children's Press, Chicago, a division of Regensteiner Publishing Enterprises, Inc.

"The Story-Teller" from *The Story-Teller: Thirteen Tales by Saki* by Saki. Selection copyright © 1982 by David R. Godine, Publisher. Reprinted by permission of David R. Godine.

"This Is Just to Say" by William Carlos Williams, from *Collected Poems, Volume I: 1909–1939.* Copyright 1938 by New Directions Publishing Corporation. Reprinted by permission of the American publisher, New Directions Publishing Corporation, and of the British publisher, Carcanet Press.

"Those Winter Sundays" from *Angle of Ascent* by Robert Hayden, copyright by Robert Hayden. Reprinted by permission of Liveright Publishing Corporation.

"Weathering the Storm" from *Let the Hurricane Roar* by Rose Wilder Lane. Copyright 1933 by Rose Wilder Lane. Copyright renewed 1961 by Rose Wilder Lane. Reprinted with the permission of Roger MacBride for the Estate of Rose Wilder Lane.

"Western Wagons" by Stephen Vincent Benét from *The Selected Works of Stephen Vincent Benét.* Published by Holt, Rinehart and Winston, Inc. Copyright 1937 by Stephen Vincent Benét. Copyright renewed © 1964 by Thomas C. Benét, Stephanie B. Mahin. Reprinted by permission of Brandt & Brandt Literary Agents, Inc.

"who know if the moon's" is reprinted from *Tulips and Chimneys* by e. e. cummings, edited by George James Firmage, by permission of the American publisher, Liveright Publishing Corporation, and of the British publisher, Grafton Books, a division of the Collins Publishing Group. Copyright 1923, 1925 and renewed 1951, 1953 by e. e. cummings. Copyright © 1973, 1976 by the Trustees for the E. E. Cummings Trust. Copyright © 1973, 1976 by George James Firmage.

*Winter Thunder* by Mari Sandoz. Copyright, MCMLI by the Curtis Publishing Company, copyright, MCMLIV by Mari Sandoz. Adapted and reprinted by permission of The Westminster Press, and of the author's agents, McIntosh and Otis, Inc.

"Women" from *Revolutionary Petunias and Other Poems* by Alice Walker, copyright © 1973 by Alice Walker. Reprinted by permission of the American publisher, Harcourt Brace Jovanovich, Inc., and of the British agents, David Higham Associates Inc.

"You, Too, Can Be a Storyteller" by David Holt. Reprinted with permission from *The Mother Earth News,* copyright © 1981. All rights reserved. Accompanying article, "The Tailor" by Nancy Schimmel from *Just Enough to Make a Story.* © 1978, 1982 by Nancy Schimmel. Used by permission of Sisters' Choice Press. All right reserved.

**BOOKS TO ENJOY**

**Page 143:** Jacket art from *The Way of the Storyteller* by Ruth Sawyer, copyright © 1976 by Viking Penguin Inc. Reprinted by permission of Viking Penguin Inc.

**Page 143:** Jacket art from *The Sword and the Circle* by Rosemary Sutcliff, copyright © 1981 by Rosemary Sutcliff. Reprinted by permission of E.P. Dutton, a division of NAL Penguin Inc.

**Page 143:** Jacket art from *The People Could Fly* by Virginia Hamilton, illustrated by Leo and Diane Dillon. Illustrations copyright © 1985 by Leo and Diane Dillon. Reprinted by permission of Alfred A. Knopf, a division of Random House, Inc.

**Page 283:** Jacket art from *On the Way Home* by Laura Ingalls Wilder reprinted by permission of Harper & Row, Publishers, Inc.

**Page 283:** Jacket art by Paul Goble from *The Horsecatcher* by Mari Sandoz, copyright 1957 by Mari Sandoz. Cover art reprinted by permission of the artist.

**Page 283:** Jacket art from *Samurai of Gold Hill* by Yoshiko Uchida, illustrated by Ati Forberg, copyright © 1972 by Yoshiko Uchida. Published by Charles Scribner's Sons, a division of Macmillan Publishing Company.

**Page 421:** Jacket art from *Beauty: A Retelling of the Story of Beauty & the Beast* by Robin McKinley, copyright © 1978 by Robin McKinley. Reprinted by permission of Harper & Row, Publishers, Inc.

**Page 421:** Jacket art from *A Swiftly Tilting Planet* by Madeleine L'Engle, copyright © 1978 by Crosswicks, Ltd. Reprinted by permission of Farrar, Straus and Giroux, Inc.

**Page 421:** Jacket art reproduced with permission of Macmillan Publishing Company from *Watership Down* by Richard Adams. Jacket illustration Copyright © 1972 by Macmillan Publishing Company.

**Page 561:** Jacket art from *Dust of the Earth* by Vera and Bill Cleaver, copyright © 1975 by Vera A. Cleaver and William J. Cleaver. Reprinted by permission of J. B. Lippincott Company, a division of Harper & Row, Publishers, Inc.

**Page 561:** Jacket art from the Commemorative Edition of *Profiles in Courage* by John F. Kennedy copyright by Harper & Row, Publishers, Inc., and reprinted with their permission.

**Page 561:** Jacket art from *Martin Luther King, Jr.* by Jacqueline L. Harris, copyright © 1983 by Jacqueline L. Harris. Reprinted by permission of Franklin Watts, Inc.

**TIME OUT FOR BOOKS**

Cover art from *Johnny Tremain* by Esther Forbes copyright © 1987 by Dell Publishing and reprinted with their permission.

**COVER:** Teresa Fasolino

**DESIGN:** Design Five, NYC and Kirchoff/Wohlberg in cooperation with Silver Burdett & Ginn

**ILLUSTRATION:** 4, Pam Levy; 5 (t) Pam Levy, (bl) Donald Cook, (br) Michelle Pelletier; 6, Gregory Dearth; 7, (t) Steve Takenaga, (b) Larry Winborg; 8, (t) David Frampton, (b) Leo & Diane Dillon; 9, Reynold Ruffins; 10–11, (l & c) Karen Watson, (r) Pat & Robin DeWitt; 14–32, Joel Spector; 47, Christa Kieffer; 48–49, Michelle Pelletier; 50–54, Michelle Pelletier; 56–62, Joan Hall; 64–65, Cathy Barancik; 66–67, Allen Davis; 68, Seymour Levy; 69, Allen Davis; 70–78, Donald Cook; 87, Heidi Stetson; 91, Sharron O'Neil; 92–93, Walter Fournier; 103, Christa Kieffer; 104–118, Pam Levy; 119, Sharron O'Neil; 120, cover art from the album, *West Side Story;* 122–123, Joe Scrofani; 124–139, Roger Boehm; 141–142, Christa Kieffer; 146–160, Joseph Mirales; 174–175, Lyle Miller; 176–188, Floyd Cooper; 190–191, Renate Seelig; 192–204, Larry Winborg; 215, Sharron O'Neil; 218, (b) Joe Van Severen; 219, (t) courtesy of the Pony Express Museum, St. Joseph, Missouri; 220–221, Laura Cornell; 222–232, Gregory Dearth; 237, Gregory Dearth; 238–246, David LaFleur; 254–258, Carol Wald; 260–261, Alex Block; 262–279, Gary Kelley; 295, Sharron O'Neil; 298–304, David Frampton; 306–307, Don Weller; 308, David Frampton; 310–322, Leo & Diane Dillon; 324, Floyd Cooper; 330–331, Andrzej Dudzinski; 332, Leo & Diane Dillon; 334–342, Scott Pollack; 355, Sharron O'Neil; 356–372, Joan Pelaez; 374, (t) Scala/Art Resource, New York, (b) Library of Congress, in *Treasures of the Library of the Congress* by Charles A. Goodrum, used with permission of the publisher, Harry N. Abrams; 375, (b) The British Library; 396–397, Reynold Ruffins; 398–399, Scott Snow; 400–417, Mercer Mayer; 418, Susan Jaekel; 420, Susan Jaekel; 424–438, Kimberly Root; 439, Sharron O'Neil; 442–454, Michael Cobb & Diane Delancy; 458, Burmar; 460–468, Cathy Diefendorf; 470–474, John Holder; 475, Christa Kieffer; 476–477, Jamie Hogan; 478–492, Beth Peck; 493, Sharron O'Neil; 494, Seymour Levy; 507–510, M. John English; 511, Susan Lexa; 512, (t) North Wind Picture Archives, (cb) Essex Institute/North Wind Picture Archives; 513, (tl) from *Silent Spring* by Rachel Carson, published in 1962 by Houghton Mifflin Company, The Riverside Press, Cambridge; 516–528, Anna Vojtech; 530–531, Peggy Tagel; 532–539, Karen Watson; 540–543, G. Brian Karas; 544–557, Pat & Robin DeWitt; 562–599, Charles Reid; 601, Susan David; 602, Claudia Sargent; 603, Susan David; 604, Claudia Sargent; 608, Meg Kelleher Aubrey; 610, Susan David; 611, Meg Kelleher Aubrey; 615, Susan David; 616, (t) Susan David; 617, Meg Kelleher Aubrey.

**PHOTOGRAPHY:** 12, Art Resource; 36–45, Will McIntyre; 48, © 1989 The Art Institute of Chicago. All Rights Reserved; 49, National Museum of American Art, Smithsonian Institution, Gift of Harmon Foundation; 56, collage photos, courtesy of Gwendolyn Brooks; 61, Harper College; 80, Will McIntyre; 82–83, Ken Lax; 84, Children's Express; 85, Ken Lax; 86, Ken Lax; 88–90, Ken Lax; 94, Rick Browne; 96, Rick Browne; 101, photo: Herb Randle, (t) from *Burnish Me Bright*, by Julia Cunningham, drawings by Don Freeman, published in 1970 by Pantheon Books, (cl) from *Come to the Edge* by Julia Cunningham, published in 1977 by Pantheon Books, (cr) from *Flight of the Sparrow* by Julia Cunningham, published in 1980 by Pantheon Books, (bl) from *The Treasure Is the Rose* by Julia Cunningham, illustrated by Judy Graese, published in 1973 by Pantheon Books, (br) from *The Silent Voice* by Julia Cunningham, published in 1981 by Dutton; 120, © 1988 Martha Swope Photography; 121, (t) Pacific Northwest Ballet's *Nutcracker,* photo: David Cooper, 1986, (b) © 1988 Martha Swope Photography; 144, *Prospecting for Cattle Range,* 1889, Frederic Remington (1861–1909), Oil on Canvas, 29 1/4" x 50 1/4," gift of Cornelius Vanderbilt Whitney, 85.60, Buffalo Bill Historical Center, Cody, Wyoming; 164, *The Oregon Trail* by Albert Bierstadt, the Butler Institute of American Art; 166–167, Denver Public Library, Western History Department; 169, The Granger Collection; 170–171, Denver Public Library, Western History Department; 175, The Thomas Gilcrease Institute of American History and Art, Tulsa, Oklahoma; 190, New York State Museum; 191, The Museum of Fine Arts, Boston © 1989. All Rights Reserved; 197, Museum of Fine Arts, Boston, MA; 206, (t) Bettmann Archive, (b) Library of Congress; 209, Bettmann Archive; 210, Wells Fargo Bank, San Francisco; 212–213, California Historical Society; 216, Tom Mangelsen/Peter Arnold, Inc.; 218, (t) © 1988 Craig Aurness/West Light; 220, Historical Picture Service, Inc.; 221, The Granger Collection; 234, "The Banjo Lesson," Henry O. Tanner, 1893, oil on canvas/Courtesy, Hampton University Museum; 248, R.R. Donnelley Cartographic Services; 284, *The Moon-Woman Cuts the Circle,* © 1943, Jackson Pollack, Oil on Canvas, Musee d'Art Moderne, Paris/The Bridgeman Art Library, London, England; 287, Wide World Photos, Disney Characters © The Walt Disney Co.; 288 © Walt Disney Productions; 289, © Warner Bros., Inc.; 290, Wide World Photos, Disney Characters © The Walt Disney Co.; 292–293, Movie Still Archives; 307, Lee Boltin Picture Library; 324, © Nancy Crampton; 327, © Nancy Crampton; 330, © Daniel J. Terra Collection, Terra Museum of American Art, Chicago; 331, The Granger Collection; 344, Wide World Photos; 347 (t) UPI/Bettmann Newsphotos, (b) Wide World Photos; 349–350, Movie Still Archives; 353, *New York Daily News;* 375, (t) © 1988 Bryan & Cherry Alexander; 376, Georg Gerster/Comstock; 380, Wide World Photos; 384, UPI/Bettmann Newsphotos; 387, Wide World Photos; 389, Peter Marlow/Sygma; 390, G. de Keerle/Gamma Liaison; 393, G. de Keerle/Gamma Liaison; 397, The Granger Collection; 422, *Old Brooklyn Bridge,* Joseph Stella (1877–1946), Oil on Canvas, 76" x 68," lent by Susan Morse Hilles, 1980; 458, photo: © Georg Gerster/Photo Researchers, Inc.; 476, North Wind Picture Archives; 477, The Rhode Island Black Heritage Society; 495, The Granger Collection; 497, Wide World Photos; 498, (t) Bob Fitch/Black Star, (b) Mat Herron/Black Star; 500, Don Uhrbrock, Robert Kelley/*Life* Magazine, Time, Inc; 501, UPI/Bettmann Newsphotos; 503, (tl & tr) Don Uhrbrock, Robert Kelley/*Life* Magazine, Time, Inc.; (b) UPI/Bettmann Newsphotos; 504, Fred Ward/Black Star; 505, Fred Ward/Black Star; 506, UPI/Bettmann Newsphotos; 513, (b) © 1965 James Karales; 514, Movie Still Archives; 514, (tc) Bettmann Archive, (tr) © 1988 Tupper Ansel Blake, (b) *Chicago Sun Times;* 601, © Frank Siteman 1988; 602, F.J. Alsop III/Bruce Coleman, Inc.; 604, Rick Smolan/Stock Boston; 605, Michael Collier/Stock Boston; 606, Tom Pantages, North Wind Archive; 607, Stephen G. Maka; 608, Leon Poindexter; 609, Owen Franken/Stock Boston; 610, © Frank Siteman 1988; 612, Tom Pantages; 613, Bettmann Archive; 614, Tom Pantages, North Wind Archive; 618, (t) Delacroix Press; 619, (t) Bettmann Archive; (b) *Los Angeles Times;* 621, (t) Bettmann Archive, (b) Leo Cardinal; 622 (t) Bettmann Archive, (b) Knopf; 623, (t) Image Specialists, Medford, Mass., Schomberg Center For Culture; 624, (t) Clarion Publishers; 625, (b) Bettmann Archive; 626, (t) Harper & Row, (b) provided by author; 627, (t) Bettmann Archive, (c) Newmarket Press; 628, (t) J. R. Baker, (b) *The Los Angeles Times;* 629, (t) Bettmann Archive; 630, (t) the National Cyclopedia of American Biography/(b) Bettmann Archive, (b) Little Brown & Co.; 631, (t) Ken Regan/Camera 5, (b) Mansell Collection, London; 632, (t) Bettmann Archive, (b) Caroline Pifer; 633, (t & b) UPI/Bettmann Newsphotos; 634, (t & b) UPI/Bettmann Newsphotos; 635, The Granger Collection, (b) Patti Perret.

D E F G H I J—VHP—97 96 95 94 93 92